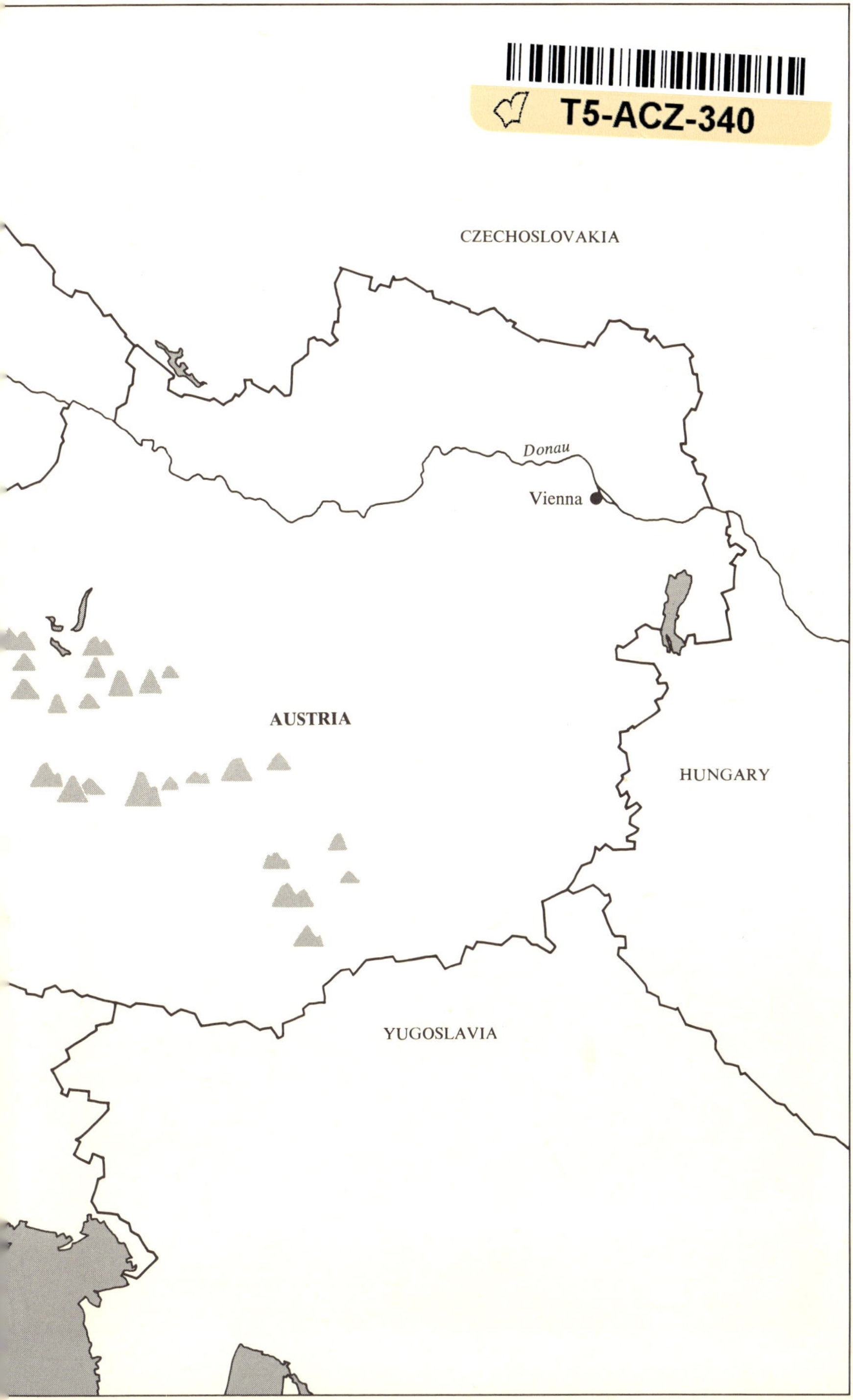
CZECHOSLOVAKIA
Donau
Vienna
AUSTRIA
HUNGARY
YUGOSLAVIA

ALL THE BEST IN
AUSTRIA
with Munich and the Bavarian Alps

Other ALL THE BEST Books

All the Best in Belgium and Luxembourg
All the Best in Bermuda, the Bahamas, Puerto Rico and the Virgin Islands
All the Best in Britain including England, Wales, Scotland and Northern Ireland
All the Best in the Caribbean including Puerto Rico and the Virgin Islands
All the Best in Central America
All the Best in Europe
All the Best in France
All the Best in Germany
All the Best in Hawaii
All the Best in Holland
All the Best in Italy
All the Best in Japan and the Orient
All the Best in the Mediterranean
All the Best in Mexico
All the Best in Scandinavia
All the Best in South America—East Coast
All the Best in South America—West Coast
All the Best in the South Pacific
All the Best in Spain and Portugal
All the Best in Switzerland

ALL THE BEST IN
AUSTRIA
with Munich and the Bavarian Alps

BY SYDNEY CLARK

With Illustrations and Maps
A SYDNEY CLARK TRAVEL BOOK

DODD, MEAD & COMPANY
NEW YORK

Copyright © 1972 by Sydney Clark
All rights reserved
No part of this book may be reproduced in any form
without permission in writing from the publisher

ISBN: 0-396-06505-8
Library of Congress Catalog Card Number: 70-184189
Printed in the United States of America
by The Haddon Craftsmen, Inc., Scranton, Penna.

Contents

Illustrations follow page 88

THE FOREGROUND OF THE PICTURE

1.	A Panoramic Look at Austria	3
2.	Basic Facts: An Index of Practicalia	16

THE BACKGROUND OF THE PICTURE

3.	A Soupçon of History	39

YOURSELF IN THE PICTURE

4.	And So to Vienna; Styrian Skyroad or Danube Riverway?	51
5.	Vienna	64
6.	The Sightseer Footloose in Vienna	79
7.	Travel in the Provinces; First Burgenland and Styria	122
8.	Carinthia, the Land of Warm Lakes	153
9.	Land Salzburg and Salzburg City	172
10.	The Salzkammergut, Halcyon Lakeland of Three Provinces	207

11.	Tyrol	224
12.	Vorarlberg, with the Principality of Liechtenstein	257
13.	Munich and Its '72 Olympics	273
14.	The Bavarian Alps, Blending with the Austrian	307
	INDEX	338

Basic Facts

The Thing about Austria	16
Air Travel to Austria	27
Austrian Foods and Drinks	67
Austrian Holidays (Dates to Enjoy or Avoid)	34
Austrian Music and Drama Festivals, Folk Pageants, Special Spectacles, Trade and Fun Fairs	31
Austrian National Tourist Offices	20
Austrian Spas for the Ill and the Well	131
Austrian Summer Study Courses	34
Austria's 400-plus Mountain Lifts	130
Austria's Winter and Its Sports	132
Climate, Clothing, Luggage	21
Customs, Austrian and United States	22
Europabus to Austria	29
Hotels, Motels, Inns and Castle Inns	66
Lakes and Lake Boats	128
Language Notes; the Valiant Score	73
Laundry and Its Problems	72
Mail, Both Ways	25
Metric Measurements and Weights	74
Money, Exchange, Tourist Costs	24
Passports and Health Certificates	19
Photography and Photographic Supplies	73
Rail Travel to Austria	29

Road Travel to Austria	30
Sea and River Travel to Austria	28
Service Charges, Taxes, Tips	70
Shopping, Shop Hours	72
Thermometers: Celsius into Fahrenheit	75
Things to Remember When Packing	23
Travel Agents	20
Travel within Austria: by Air, by Rail, by Road	122

The Foreground of the Picture

1 / A Panoramic Look at Austria

Who is Austria? what is she,
That travelers all commend her?

I ask the question only so that I may answer it, trusting that Thurio, who sang to Silvia, will pardon the paraphrase; but first let me ask some corollary questions of my own. Why did 550,000 U.S. residents visit distant Vienna and the rest of Austria last year, and why will 600,000 come this year? Why does Austria have the largest tourism count, in proportion to its population, of any country in Europe? Answers are due.

Austria is a perfect unit of travel, not so large as to be discouraging, yet not so small as to lack wide appeal. Consider, at the start, a basic fact that makes Austria unique in the world of travel. Where else will you find a small country the size of Maine, with a population of only 7,000,000, that is largely Alpine in character, providing spectacular scenery to rival that of Switzerland or Norway, yet with a capital of world stature like *Vienna,* a 1,750,000-inhabitant metropolis that in earlier times was a bulwark of western civilization, twice turning back the marauding Turkish hordes (1529 and 1683) while all Europe looked on, trembling with fear. No European city, save Rome alone, has had so long and illustrious a "career" as Vienna, yet the thing we all associate with it is primarily *music,* which has been begotten, conceived and born

/ 3

in this city for at least two and a half centuries. Gestation still continues and the musical tradition is as viable today as in the time of "Papa Haydn," Mozart, Schubert and Beethoven, not to mention the Strauss dynasty and other waltzmasters.

Salzburg, a festival city par excellence, which, to many music lovers, is almost a synonym for Mozart, adds its magic luster; and there's another festival city, Bregenz, which is much less central and therefore less widely known, that deserves an accolade to challenge Salzburg's fame. It is located at the tip end of the tail of the Austrian kite, meaning that superlative 200-mile corridor (to change my figure) stretching through Tyrol, with Innsbruck, its Alp-shadowed capital, and mountain-mad Vorarlberg clear to Switzerland, the Principality of Leichtenstein and trinational Lake Constance. Bergenz dips its toes into Lake Constance, and indeed many of its festival features are staged on a great stage in the lake.

In case sport looms larger and lustier in your view of Austria than music, you well know that both Tyrol and Vorarlberg are on the top level of world fame as centers of winter sports.

Since we've touched on the odd shape of Austria let's take a closer look at the country's geography of welcome. The variety that makes for spice in travel is nowhere more stimulating than in Austria. For hundreds of miles one rolls through Alpine splendors, for the mountains are everywhere. Maps show thirty separate ranges of them by name. In six of the nine provinces, or Länder, as they are called, namely Vorarlberg, Tyrol, with East Tyrol, Salzburg, Carinthia, Styria and Upper Austria, they are predominant. The other three, Lower Austria, Vienna and Burgenland, are less mountainous.

One should not assume that even the Alpine regions of Austria are merely an endless sea of snow peaks, for mountains imply valleys and valleys imply rivers. The valleys of Austria are of varied form but they are all alike in two respects. Each is made brilliant by verdure and each is made cheerful by roaring or chattering or whispering water.

Mountain scenery hints also of lakes, and the lakes of Austria, though less publicized than their neighbors of Switzerland and Italy, are unsurpassed for romantic charm and for exhilarating sport. There are at least twenty of them in that composite region known as the Salzkammergut. There are a round dozen in Carinthia—warm lakes these, where you can swim in May or October. Others are scattered throughout the length and breadth of the country, from the international Bodensee (Lake of Constance) to the placid Neusiedlersee, which dips furtively across the frontier of Hungary. All are lovely, some fantastically beautiful, with snow peaks soaring from their very shores. Their blues, from indigo to "washtub," a fine opaque color whose beauty is too seldom sung by poets, are of every hue the spectrum knows, and even their greens cover quite a range.

In type, these lakes vary as much as in color. The whole region of the Hallstättersee and the Gosau Lakes, guarded by the majestic Dachstein and the pinnacled Donnerkögel, matches in wild melodrama anything in the Dolomites, yet the Wörthersee, backed by the Karawanken Range, a pastel-tinted curtain of peaks shutting off Yugoslavia, is a highly civilized and gracious body of water, the queen of Carinthia's warm lakes.

Many specialties add quixotic touches to Austria's scenery. There are mountains of rock salt, where weird saline corridors and chambers may be explored. There are enormous caves of everlasting ice, Wagnerian, frosty on an August day, weirdly illumined by concealed electric lights. There are castles of every type, from Hohensalzburg, fortress-home of the aristocratic prince-bishops who made Salzburg the baroque wonder that it is, to the striking hilltop *Schloss* called Hoch-Osterwitz, once occupied by Margareta Maultasch, the "Ugly Duchess" of Tyrol and Carinthia.

One finds, tucked obscurely into remote valleys, or clambering steep hillsides, or clinging to lake edges, all sorts of special villages: Maria-Wörth, a venerable Marian community on a peninsula in the Wörthersee; Absam, where Jakob Stainer tapped the trees for violin wood; Obergurgl, the loftiest parish village in all Europe; Hallstatt, a lake village where rude Celts made their homes in the prehistoric Hallstatt Age and where now long boats, propelled like gondolas, are a standard means of transportation. One finds monkish communities like Admont, whose glory is the library of its Benedictine abbey; cultural towns like St. Wolfgang, with priceless art treasures in wood carving; pilgrim towns like Heiligenblut and Mariazell; picture-book towns like Kitzbühel and St. Johann-in-Tirol; castles like Schloss Sighartstein, near Salzburg, or Schloss Rabenstein, in Styria, that have been transformed into holiday inns for you and me; outright play villages like Zell am See and Velden. Any of these places would be interesting if discovered in average settings. They are tenfold more so when found in the settings of Austria's thirty-range Alps.

THE NINE LÄNDER OF THE CRAZY QUILT

Each *Land,* for that is the singular of Länder, has its own character and makes its own individual contribution to the improbable pattern of Austria, a fascinating design that could be generously called a tapestry, but is really a bit crazy. I'll tabulate them in a clockwise sequence, starting with Salzburg Province, which is the first one that most land travelers see.

Salzburg Province looks, on the map, as if its outlines had been drawn at random by some cartographer who had been enjoying too many *Schnäpse,* but a close study of it reveals that it is based on *valleys.* Leaving to Tyrol the Inn Valley from Landeck to Kufstein, Salzburg's most notable valley is that of the River Salzach, whose remotest headwaters are included within the provincial lines. This river flows in a great arc, passing Zell am See, the northern terminus of the Grossglockner Road (see below, under East Tyrol), and continuing through Salzburg City, the provincial capital, and then proceeds to form the Austro-Bavarian border until it unites with the Inn just short of Braunau, where one Adolf Hitler was born. Salzburg Province also includes the valley of the Gasteiner Ache clear up to Bad Gastein, where the Ache (stream) bursts from the Tauern Mountains with a deafening roar to plunge straight through that famous spa. It does *not* include more than a few outposts of the Salzkammergut, with its lovely lakes and salt mountains, the greater part of that region being in Upper Austria.

Upper Austria (Ober-Österreich) includes all of the relatively level north central part of the republic to and a little beyond Linz-on-the-Danube, which is its capital, *and* it includes, as I've just said, the heart of the Salzkammergut, with most of its lakes and with such glamorous tourist goals as St. Wolfgang, Bad Ischl and Hallstatt.

Lower Austria (Nieder-Österreich), which surrounds Vienna, is the northeastern province, whose administrative center is *in* Vienna. It includes all of the Austrian portion of the Danube from the point where the Enns flows into it, just below Linz, clear to the Czech border at Bratislava (Pressburg). The most scenic and legendary portion of the Austrian Danube is the 20-mile stretch called the Wachau, from Melk, with its grand Benedictine abbey, to Krems.

Vienna is a *separate* province, completely surrounded by Lower Austria.

Burgenland is the province nobody knows, that is, no tourist. It was a part of Hungary until World War I but went to Austria in 1920 by the Treaty of the Trianon. In 1921, after some international bickering and dickering, its capital, Sopron, was allotted to Hungary and a new capital, Eisenstadt, took over, this being the historic city of Josef Haydn and his patron, Prince Esterházy. Burgenland is a flat region of rich agriculture and vineyards and includes within its borders all but a small Hungarian tip of big, shallow, reedy Neusiedlersee (130 square miles), which looks impressive on our map but is of little holiday interest. It even dries up at rare intervals and disappears altogether, as it did in 1865 so completely that farmers grew crops in its bed for several years.

Styria (Steiermark) is the trickiest of all the Länder to grasp in geographical outlines. Its big capital, *Graz,* the second city in Austria, lies far to the southeast, on the River Mur, yet Styria includes a small but choice section of the Salzkammergut (Altaussee), not far from Salzburg, and the pilgrim town of Mariazell, which is almost in Vienna's orbit and is reached by rail only from the north, though a road toils up to it from Bruck an der Mur, some 40 miles south. The province includes, also, the superb Enns Valley, with Admont and with the celebrated rapids called *Die Gesäuse,* or The Brawling, where the River Enns rushes for 10 miles through a narrow defile between towering limestone cliffs.

Carinthia (Kärnten), adjoining East Tyrol, is the soft, southern province, the playground of Vienna, and of us, with warm-water lakes fringed by holiday resorts, the best-known being Velden. Klagenfurt is its capital, and near this city is the dramatic castle of Hoch-Osterwitz. Yugoslavia borders Carinthia on the south, and just within its frontier lies that country's most famous lake resort, much-photographed Bled.

East Tyrol (Ost Tirol) is an integral part of the Province of Tyrol (see below), but until the building of the wonderful Grossglockner Road, opened in 1935, it was little visited by foreign tourists. That skyscraping road, one of the greatest engineering feats in Europe, opened up this very lovely portion of Tyrol and it has come increasingly into its own ever since then. Lienz is its little-publicized but fascinating capital, the terminus of The Road, and the pilgrim village of Heiligenblut is among its loveliest ornaments. On East Tyrol's southern border loom the dramatic Lienzer Dolomiten, cut by the valley of the River Gail.

Tyrol (Tirol) fills out the eastern portion of Austria's western corridor, from the Arlberg through Innsbruck to and including Kitzbühel. From Innsbruck important rail lines and highways run south over the Brenner Pass to Italy and north, either by way of Kufstein or of Mittenwald, to Munich.

Vorarlberg, as we've seen, is Austria's "far west," bordered by Switzerland, the pocket principality of Liechtenstein, the tip of Lake Constance and Alpine Bavaria. Its capital is *Bregenz,* Austria's one international lake port. The whole province is carved up into lovely valleys between towering mountains, and the remoter parts of them are still *costume valleys,* where the charming *Trachten* of tradition are worn by many of the older women, especially on Sundays. The Vorarlberg-Tyrol line cuts squarely across the corridor at the Arlberg Mountain, which is pierced by the Arlberg Tunnel of a main rail line from Paris to Vienna and beyond (Arlberg Express).

SEVEN GATES TO AUSTRIA

To avoid confusion in presenting the more important gates to Austria, by road and rail, I will follow the same general clockwise sequence used for the Länder, starting with the gates that open from Munich to Innsbruck and Salzburg. (The air gate to Vienna will be omitted here, since it is so obvious. The capital's airport, at Schwechat, lies about 11 miles to the southeast.)

The *Alpine Gate from Munich to Innsbruck,* whether by road or rail, provides a spectacular approach through the Bavarian Alps, the rail line and one of two highways passing through Garmisch-Partenkirchen, the double village of winter sports, and then Mittenwald, the violin village, and Scharnitz, the lofty frontier village of Austria, which is but 30 miles from the Tyrolean capital. The descent from Scharnitz to the Inn Valley gives eloquent testimony to Austria's conquest of her scenery. Down, down, down, for 2000 feet, your car zigzags, or your train rolls along its roadbed, which is but a slender scratch in the huge rock wall. Seen from the valley the creeping train looks like a nursery toy for the youngest baby of the Mountain God. The valley, seen from the roadside or a train window, is a ribbon of purest green, knotted at one point by a darker colored ornament which is Innsbruck. There is a longer road route by way of Garmisch-Partenkirchen and the border village of Grainau, and there is likewise a longer Munich-Innsbruck rail express route, by way of Rosenheim (Bavaria) and Kufstein (Tyrol), that avoids the high mountain pass, and with it much of the monumental scenery. The motor route via Kufstein is for those who rate comfort for themselves and their car above the thrills of superscenery. The Bavarian part of it is an *Autobahn* all the way, 41 miles of it on the main Munich-Salzburg route and 26 on a southgoing branch.

The *Salzburg Gate from Bavaria* has a peculiarly easy and inviting swing, since this Mozart city is just within the Austrian frontier, and the visitor has instant initiation into Austrian civic glamour at its superlative best. The autobahn between the cities is 88 miles of smooth motoring, with mild scenery, but always lovely, and with many views of the Alpine range to the south. If you go by train you will find that Salzburg's railway station is a double one, with platforms for German trains, arriving and departing, and others for Austrian trains. Salzburg works out with special convenience as a starting point for the whole tour of Austria. You may enter the country with no preliminary plans, secure full information *within Austria,* while enjoying as much time as possible soaking up Salzburg, and then set about completing the organization of your tour. Just one caution, however, is emphatically needed. Austria's hotels, especially those of Salzburg, Vienna and Innsbruck, as well as the leading resorts, are jammed to the bursting point in the summer tourist season, from June to mid-September, and it is hardly practical to improvise one's touring during this peak period. In midwinter, too, the resort towns that promote winter sports are usually filled to the gunwales. But Salzburg is a wonderful place in which to cope with travel problems, and you'll love the city so much that you'll probably hate to leave it for anywhere else.

The *Danube Gate* opens at Passau, just within Bavaria, from which port good-sized steamers of Austrian ownership, with fairly comfortable cabins, make their way downstream in 13 hours to Vienna, a distance of 190 miles. (The *up*stream journey requires an overnight halt at Linz.) Those who enter Austria by this gate may prefer to make a stopover at some point, say Linz or Melk—*one* stopover is permitted—or to go by car or train from Passau to one or both of these points, continuing by steamer to Vienna. The steamer time from Linz is 8½ hours, from Melk only 4½ hours. Melk, as mentioned above, is noted for its Benedictine abbey, a baroque masterpiece. In 1809 the conquering Napoleon made it his headquarters for a time and generously allowed his soldiers to steal 6000 gallons of wine a day from its cellars. The scenic Wachau stretch, from Melk to Krems, is rich in castles and is peopled with figures of history and legend, including Richard Coeur-de-Lion and Blondel the Troubadour; but below Krems the river's banks flatten out and there is nothing especially notable to see except Klosterneuburg, with its Augustinian abbey, and this is so near Vienna that city throngs flock to it on St. Leopold's Day to have fun sliding down a 12,000-gallon wine cask in the abbey's cooperage.

The *Brenner Gate from Italy* provides the main entrance, whether by road or rail, for those who approach Austria from the south, though there is a minor gateway from the Italian Dolomites to Lienz. The Brenner pathway leads also through Dolomite country from Bolzano up and over the Brenner Pass and then down to Innsbruck.

The yearning of the Tyrolese capital for its lost southern province is dramatically presented to those who "read as they walk"—from Innsbruck's railway station to the center of the city. The square upon which the station stands is Südtiroler Platz. To the right and left one notes Sterzingerstrasse and Bruneckerstrasse. Sterzing and Bruneck are now Italian towns. In the latter Michael Pacher, greatest artist of the Tyrol, was born. Walking straight on from the station one traverses Brixnerstrasse, Bozner Platz and Meranerstrasse. Brixen, Bozen and Meran are now Italian cities and they give their names as Bressanone, Bolzano and Merano. St. Leonhard, birthplace and home of Andreas Hofer, supreme hero of the Tyrol, is also an Italian village, as is most of Brenner (Brennero) itself at the top of the pass. The ruin of Castle Teriolis, spiritual nucleus and name-giver to modern Tyrol, is 20 miles within the Italian border.

To the credit of Austria, be it said, this situation is not flung at the tourist in any morbid or pathetic plea for sympathy. The story of the street signs is a mute and dignified one and few tourists concern themselves with it or give more than a passing thought to the St. Germain Treaty which sheared South Tyrol from its sister province. The Brenner Gate is a very beautiful portal to vacation land under any affiliation or any name. From Brennero the train glides northward down the slope, not very precipitous here, to reach Innsbruck in 51 miles.

The *Engadine Gate from Switzerland to Landeck,* in the province of Tyrol, is a direct motor route of surpassing interest. It leads beside the roaring young River Inn from Schuls-Tarasp to the frontier town of Martinsbruck and so to Pfunds and Landeck, where one meets the Austrian railway system. The international Inn is worth knowing in every mile of its system. It rises high in the Engadine. The lake on whose upper bank St. Moritz has developed is but a widening of the Inn. From here it gallops briskly on the long and beautiful run to Austria where the mad Rosanna and Trisanna swell its volume. It rolls through Innsbruck (which means Inn Bridge) swiftly but with growing dignity, for it is now a wide and powerful stream. At Kufstein it dips into Bavaria, but cannot quite forget Austria, so it returns to form the Austro-German frontier, as we have seen, clear to Passau, where it merges with the Danube. It more than doubles the Danube's volume but generously drops its name and identity. Had early cartographers elected to call the united waters of these two rivers the Inn it would have been an entirely sensible decision but the one-syllable name would have spoiled the mighty euphony inherent in the word Danube, and more than incidentally it would have ruined the title, yet unthought of, of the world's most popular waltz, yet unwritten. A match tossed into the lake of St. Moritz would presumably find its way to the Black Sea but our own Innside journey is somewhat shorter than that. It is a run of 36 miles from Schuls-Tarasp (about 25 above the Austrian frontier) to Landeck.

The *Liechtenstein Gate,* entered by road or rail, has a touch of romance all its own. Those who make this approach by train, perhaps on the Arlberg Express, pass through a foreign country, the Principality of Liechtenstein, from border to border, under the aegis of Austria and they make the crossing in—fifteen minutes! At Buchs, on the Swiss side of the very young Rhine, the Swiss railway system ties in with the Austrian Federal Railways, and from that point one crosses the principality in an Austrian train to Austrian soil at Feldkirch. Liechtenstein's chief station, Schaan (for Vaduz the capital, 2 miles distant by bus or taxi) captures the attention of even the fast trains, only the Arlberg Express ignoring it. Good motor roads pass through Liechtenstein from Swiss Buchs to Austrian Feldkirch.

Liechtenstein, with its 65 square miles and 11,000 inhabitants, is one of the four remaining pocket states of Europe, a strange and charming relic of feudalism (Andorra, Monaco and San Marino are the other three). Since World War I it has adhered to the Swiss customs union and postal union. But the tiny state has a historic attachment to Austria. Its prince, scion of the great house of Liechtenstein, is Austrian to the core, though very loyal to his principality and honestly devoted to the welfare of his subjects. He has, among his vast possessions, a world-famous art gallery that was formerly housed in the Liechtenstein Palace in Vienna but is now in its own new building in Vaduz. Liechtenstein is a priceless heirloom of a lost era, a choice nugget of travel for those who like such geopolitical curiosities. The prince's castle, on a cliff just above Vaduz, is not only a sumptuous abode of a Graustarkian monarch but an important museum of medievalism. Schloss Gutenberg, in the extreme south of the tiny country, is still more venerable, and in this ancient (11th-century) castle, on its own hill, my family and I once spent the summer as boarders. Later, however, it was sold and the glamorous castle ceased to be a public inn.

Wrenching myself from the temptation to dally within the borders of this romantic little country (the word is right), I will cross to Feldkirch, which happens to have been the gate used on my very first entrance into Austria. It is a mellow, old-world town, its streets heavily arcaded, its market square whispering of the past. High above it rises the Shadow Castle (Schattenburg), which is anything but shadowy at night, with four lively restaurants, and through it rushes the icy River Ill, tumbling toward the Rhine.

The *Steamer Gate from Lake Constance* opens at *Bregenz,* Vorarlberg's capital, which one may reach by an Austrian or a German steamer from Constance, via Lindau, or by a Swiss steamer from Romanshorn to Lindau and a connecting steamer, or lakeside road or train, from that nearby Bavarian port town. A motor road and a good railway line run up the valley of the Rhine from Bregenz to Feldkirch, where they join the main turnpike and trunk rail line through Vorarlberg Privince to Innsbruck and all Austria.

Norman Douglas stated in *Together* that Blaufelchen, a lake fish often served in Bregenz restaurants, was the city's chief lure for him, but with no effort I can think of three other things that would have more pulling power for most of us, namely the glorious location of Bregenz, its dramatic hill, the Pfänder, reached by aerial cableway, and the ancient upper town, on the site of old Brigantium of Roman times. Another thing, which makes four, is the little narrow-gauge train that struggles up the Bregenzerachthal to Egg and Bezau. Eggs are to be found in every part of Austria (Wildegg, Rosenegg, Blumenegg, and so on). There are two in this valley, besides plain Egg, which is itself but one of three, equally plain, in different parts of Austria. The word is a corruption of the word *Ecke,* which means corner, or edge, so these names, odd to Anglo-Saxon eyes, take on beauty if one thinks of them as Wild Edge, Rose Corner, and so on. The Egg of this Vorarlberg Valley is among the loveliest "corners" in the land. It lies in the midst of a green bowl filled to the brim with wild flowers. Common buttercups, white daisies and Queen Anne's lace predominate, but there are also a few million forget-me-nots and many rarer flowers of the Alps.

On one visit I jotted down some interesting, if severely worded, notices warning the upland wanderer against indiscriminate picking of these blooms. Edelweiss, for instance, was not to be picked at all. Feuerlilie (fire lily), Alpenveilchen (Alp violet), Alpenaster and Frauenschuh (lady slipper) could be picked to the number of ten flowers only per person, ten more being allowable when, and not before, the first ten had wilted. A fine of 30 schillings was imposed for the first offense against these legal restrictions, 60 schillings for the second. I found it hard to develop much apprehension concerning such a law, obviously unenforceable without an army of flower wardens hiding behind trees and barns, nor did it seem that legal enforcement was necessary. In all regions and all periods those persons who love wild flowers will not connive in exterminating them. Those, if any, who do not love them will scarcely bother to pick them. The law of Austria is upheld by human instincts and the gorgeous flower carpets of Vorarlberg seem quite safe from depredation.

PLUS TWO STRANGE SPECIALS: PEDESTRIAN TUNNEL AND ALPINE CUL-DE-SAC

The Pedestrian Tunnel by which you may enter Austria from Germany, or vice-versa, seems as strange a means to enter a foreign country as by submarine, and the more so when you reflect that this tunnel is at the 9000-foot level, nearly two miles above the sea. It cuts through the frontier mountain called the Zugspitze, whose summit is the highest point, 9732 feet, in Germany. Without going into further detail of the ways of ascending the mountain from both countries, I may just mention here that the tunnel, which is almost half a mile long, descends sharply from the Austrian side to the German, the difference in altitude being 860 feet, so if you don't like climbing at an altitude that makes you feel as though you had shoes of lead, give thought to crossing the line downhill, from the Austrian side, bringing you to the very civilized and well-warmed German Schneefernerhaus, a mountain inn with a fine dining room and a view to make you forget your meal. Cableways lift their loads of excited tourists on both sides of the line to the very summit (Gipfel) of the two-country peak.

The Alpine cul-de-sac called Kleinwalsertal is almost as odd a means of entry from one country into another as is the lofty pedestrian tunnel, for although the Kleinwalsertal is a firm political part of the Austrian province of Vorarlberg you can reach it only from Germany, that is, unless you are an eagle, a chamois, or an extremely rugged mountaineer. It has an interesting past, for it was first inhabited, in any extensive way, by Swiss refugees in the 13th century. It is full of weirdly charming contradictions, an example being that if the Austrian police capture a misdoer they cannot take him out through Germany but must fly him over the Alps by helicopter to Bregenz, the capital of Vorarlberg, to await trial. The Kleinwalsertal is one of those engaging strayed sheep, like Llivia, a Spanish town solidly embedded in the French Cerdagne, or Baarle-Hertog, a Belgian village well within Holland, and as such it has a built-in appeal, but the sheer Alpine beauty of it, gracing both banks of the hurrying Breitach stream and climbing all the little side valleys, is what chiefly entrances the visitor who uses this, well, this what? I guess we must call it this lovely nongate to Austria.

2 / Basic Facts: An Index of Practicalia

The Thing About Austria

Austria—to be nonpractical for a moment—has an inherent likability that no one save the confirmed grouch can resist. The country has shrunk from its position as the senior partner in the vast and powerful Austro-Hungarian Empire to a modest-sized federal republic. It suffered political and geographical indignities at the hands of the treatymakers, and the further indignity of ten years of occupation by foreign troops after World War II; but the spirit of its people survived. The Austrian charm, a social axiom of Europe, is intact, as is the Austrian's warm nature. We have a saying in my family when traveling in that country that if, rarely, we encounter an official or servitor who is curt or ungracious, "He (or she) cannot be an Austrian."

There are plenty of specific things, too, that the traveler likes about Austria. It is an Alpine land whose mountain-and-lake scenery can match, glamour for glamour, that of neighboring Switzerland, and yet it has a metropolitan, cosmopolitan capital, Vienna, which is one of the grandest and most alluring large cities on earth. It has small cities of such special character that they are landmarks of tourism, Salzburg and Innsbruck being the most famous of them.

Austria's heritage of musical genius is one element of her magnetism. Salzburg owes its musical fame chiefly to one man, Mozart, and to the immense vogue of the Summer Festivals in recent years, but Vienna, one may almost say, is the very mother of music. She nursed it from its period of infancy, over 800 years ago, when Walther von der Vogelweide, to use his own words, "learnt to sing and to say" at the court of the Babenbergs. The popular minnesingers originated not in Germany but in Austria. The minne-court was in Vienna. In much later times Josef Haydn's sustained genius established the ascendancy of Austrian elements in instrumental music, but it was reserved for Mozart to clinch the victory and leave Italian rivalry far behind. Then came Beethoven to visit the Danube metropolis. He loved it and could not leave it. With him came the Golden Age of Music. Vienna was the mecca of every composer, every singer and instrumentalist. One was not established until one had received the musical accolade of this city.

Franz Schubert was born here and his genius flourished contemporaneously with that of the tempestuous Beethoven—which reminds me of a pithy remark that an Austrian friend made to me. Said he, "While Beethoven scowled and thundered over his writing, little Mozartl did it so easily." I loved that affectionate double diminutive, for little Mozartl did indeed compose as if the muse were doing it for him. Though he died, miserably and hardly noticed, at 35, he left well over 600 compositions, many of them hours long, as listed by the indefatigable Ludwig von Köchel.

Vienna's procession of the musically great marched through the decades in a more imposing column than any other city has ever mustered. Gluck, Haydn, Mozart (whose life was divided between Salzburg and the capital), Beethoven, Schubert, Brahms, Bruckner, Goldmark, Gustav Mahler, Richard Strauss (temporarily), Schönberg. The procession still marches on. I have not intended to slight the dynasty of Johann Strauss by omitting that celebrated name, but these waltz-making Strausses, with their musical rivals and followers, belong in a later section of this book where our feet begin to tap.

The universality of Austria's musical endowment is one of its wonders. The oratorio is quite as much at home in this land as the operetta, the symphony quite as much as the Wiener Lied. The opera of Vienna, often fighting against titanic odds, has held its own as one of the half-dozen greatest in the world, and a parallel statement can be made concerning the Vienna Philharmonic Orchestra. Sacred music and chamber music flourish perennially. A special genre of incidental film music, focusing on Vienna's traditional gaiety, has grown up to take its important place in the cinema industry. It has a numerous and devoted following in many lands. Choral music of all sorts, including that of the widely loved Boy Singers, is a specialty in Vienna and has carried Austrian song to a worldwide public.

Austria's heritage has become the world's heritage. "Its music is gone out through all the earth and its song to the end of the world."

I like the familiar *Dirndl* costume of Austrian girls and women. It is worn as the standard dress of tens of thousands. It gives even a rather plain girl that certain something. It makes pretty girls— and there are lots of them in Austria—downright beauties. In many valley villages the *Dirndlkleid* is almost universal and even in the towns it often predominates. It is simple, bright, genuinely lovely and submits to countless varieties of detail and color. So patently does it flatter feminine appearance that young and less young tourists often adopt it in Austria. To its credit, be it said, the costume adapts itself even to this strange use. It *still* looks natural. Dirndl shops flourish all over Austria.

I promised myself that I would not use the word *Gemütlichkeit* in this book, but a foolish vow is well broken, as Solomon must have said. Most words and phrases become trite because they are true, and such is the case with this word, as applied to Austrian character. *Gemütlich,* the adjective from which the noun is formed, means cheerful, easygoing, insouciant, joyous, companionable. A German-English dictionary, struggling for adequate interpretation, even takes a long shot at "cozy" and perhaps, after all, that is the best definition. The coziness of Austria is as undeniable as it is delightful. It is as patent to the superficial tourist as to the student of the country. Therefore every book, brochure and travel leaflet makes mention of it, and the word grows threadbare and shiny like an old suit. But old suits and old words are comfortable, as is this quality.

Passports and Health Certificates

Your passport, valid for five years, is blue gold (formerly green gold). It is one of the world's most eagerly desired treasures of printing. I've weighed mine on letter scales and find it would be worth, as gold, about $56, whereas it cost me only $10. Had it been my first it would have cost $12. If it were legal to sell it, instead of a serious criminal offense, I still wouldn't let it go for many times its gold-weight value. Even an honestly lost passport is difficult to replace, for our State Department, ever watchful for fraud, is *very* reluctant to issue a new one in such a case, so *hang onto it* as your dearest possession of travel.

To secure your passport—a husband and wife, or even a family, may have a joint one if traveling together—apply to the nearest passport office in some large city (New York has a passport agency at 630 Fifth Avenue), or to the head office in the State Department in Washington or to any local U.S. District Court. To get your *first* passport you are supposed to bring proof of citizenship, such as a birth certificate, and first or *n*th, you must bring two passport photographs (2½ by 3 inches). If your birth certificate is not available you may still secure your passport, but there will be more delay and red tape. Your second and subsequent passports are *easy* to obtain. Just present your expired one, with two new photos, fill in the application form—and pay. The usual waiting period to secure a first or later passport is about a week.

A *health certificate* (smallpox vaccination certificate) will be found in the envelope with your passport when you receive it from the State Department. In 1971 the requirement for smallpox vaccination for travelers visiting *Europe only* was dropped UNLESS "there has been an outbreak of smallpox within the last 14 days in the country or countries you have been visiting." That word "unless" is the key word, for "you never know." By all means I urge you to have your vaccination, and then have your certificate validated by the Department of Health or your local Board of Health. Your peace of mind will far outweigh the minor trouble of securing the certificate.

No visa is required for entry into Austria or Germany. Indeed, the visa requirements for holders of American and Canadian passports visiting Western Europe have virtually vanished. You can dismiss this gremlin from any cell in your mind which it may have occupied.

Travel Agents

Your travel agent is your best bet to help you win the highest rewards from your journey with the least wear and tear. At his best, and it must be admitted that some fall far below this standard, he is your expert, your doctor of pleasure. He knows what he's talking about. He knows how much you can do enjoyably in the time you have. He knows what it will cost. He knows the best and simplest ways and means. He knows hotels of different grades. He knows good restaurants, special foods, good wines. He knows half-hidden places of unusual charm that you would never find by yourself.

I am speaking of the modern, imaginative agent who takes pride in each trip he fashions, not the outmoded stereotype who can only trace a few long-trodden paths from one main center to another. My own favorite agency, to put this in personal terms, is Metropolitan Travel Service of Boston, my home city, whose owner-president, Swiss-born, multilingual Ernest W. Ruegg, is as modern as they come. Germany and Austria, incidentally, are among his very special "strongholds." Before each major trip I like to brief myself by asking him what's new in the lands to which I am going, and if, now and then, I discover something abroad that I believe will be new even to him I write in triumphant haste to tell him about it.

The *American Society of Travel Agents,* ASTA for short, has almost 500 active members and over 4000 allied members. Competition is keen and only the better ones can long survive. So pick your own expert and when you feel sure of him stick to him. Let him edit your plans and ease the bumps of travel.

The Austrian National Tourist Offices

Austria handles its program of tourist promotion very successfully, keeping the country, small though it is in area and population, steadily in fourth place, touristwise, in the "range of nations," through a vigorous Austrian National Tourist Association which maintains information offices in all leading countries. In New York the address is 545 Fifth Avenue, in Montreal, 630 Dorchester Boulevard, and in London, 16 Conduit Street, off Regent Street. The home office in Vienna, whose longwinded German name I will spare you, is at Hohenstaufengasse 3 (tel. 69–96–71), but it should be remembered that these offices exist to promote tourist traffic on a broad front to and within Austria. They are *not* travel agencies, selling tickets, booking accommodations and so forth. They steer you, offering counsels and providing tourist literature, but they do not take over your travel arrangements. An *Austria Information Office* for all the Länder will be found in the Palais Pálffy at Josefsplatz 6, behind the Hofburg.

As regards Vienna itself, the office of paramount importance is the *Vienna Tourist Office (Fremdenverkehrsverband für Wien)* at Stadiongasse 6–8, adjacent to the great Parliament Building. This efficient and friendly organization, working closely with another called the *Wiener Verkehrsverein,* maintains information offices (English spoken) in the big West Station, the South Station and at the main motorway entrances to the city, west and south, and most convenient of all after you are settled in your hotel, in the underground *Opernpassage,* a cheerful, circular shopping and café "circus" [British meaning] beneath the area where the Ring and Kärntnerstrasse meet. Information on accommodations is furnished if needed, and you may acquire a wealth of maps, folders and what-to-see-and-do literature.

Climate, Clothing, Luggage

One cannot say of Austria that the climate is *thus,* so you should take the following clothing. In my experience much of the country, including Vienna and Salzburg, has a climate about as unpredictable as that of Boston, Massachusetts, or Washington, D.C. In a sample month of July I have experienced raw, cold, rainy or drizzly days, sometimes several in a row, alternating with hot spells. Sometimes a prolonged unseasonably warm spell will fill the month of May, followed by a cold, rainy June. You just can't tell. It is fair, however, to say that the southern parts of Styria and most of Carinthia are considerably warmer and sunnier than the northern portions of Austria, and also than Tyrol and Vorarlberg to the west, where altitudes may play a part. Almost all travelers, this one included, take more things abroad than they (we) need or ever use. It is an immense advantage at every move if one can limit one's total luggage to a couple of suitcases, and this is especially important if one is to travel substantially by train or bus. When a train arrives at the station of a large city there will often be no more than three or four porters—the word is *Träger* in German, pronounced "trayger"—to meet the needs of several hundred travelers. If you can carry your own luggage you may frequently save yourself delay and annoyance. *Boarding* a train may be still more of a problem if you have heavy luggage. I have sometimes been absolutely unable to locate even *one* Träger.

Going light is easy nowadays in summer travel, or at any season in balmy lands. The drip-drys and synthetic self-ironing fabrics have multiplied and they have also mated with wool and cotton to spawn an amazing and very useful progeny. These fabrics weigh far less than older, traditional, ones did, and the fact that very many travelers of both sexes, including well-heeled tourists, now do their own nightly washing of shirts or blouses, underwear and hose makes it unnecessary to carry anything like the bulk of clothing that used to be considered essential. And few men who travel by air now take evening clothes, though these are still essential for first-class passengers on large ocean liners.

Of course the light-but-tough luggage of this Air Age can be a basic feature of your strategy to "keep your weight down."

Customs, Austrian and United States

Passing through Austria's border formalities is so simple and quick as hardly to be noticed at all. At Vienna's airport, as now in most airports all over Europe, the arriving traveler sees two passages, one for those with something to declare, the other for those with nothing to declare. Needless to say, traffic through the latter passage is heavy, that through the former sparse. Train crossings between Germany and Austria seem about as casual. On a recent crossing, passport and customs officers strolled through the corridor of my car, chatting and laughing among themselves without even a glance into the compartment I shared with others.

The racks were full of luggage. Perhaps there is some sort of agreement between the two countries, as there is between member countries of the Common Market. Austria's cigarette allowance is 400 for passengers from overseas who have not been in Europe more than 48 hours, or you are allowed 100 cigars or 1 pound of tobacco. Visitors coming from European countries are allowed half these amounts. Up to one quart of liquor may be brought in free.

Upon returning to America, one finds that customs regulations have tightened up a lot since the "good old days" when the free allowance was $500, wholesale valuation. Now it is $100 retail valuation, and only those goods actually accompanying the traveler may be included. If your goods are valued under $100 you may make an oral declaration and usually sail right through. If more than $100, every item must be written down, and you lose the $100 exemption. If you have $130 worth the duty to be paid is based on $130, not on $30, which obviously puts pressure on the traveler's conscience, but the customs men are well aware of this and I think they tend to offset this inequity a bit by blending their interpretations of the law with "the quality of mercy [that] droppeth as the gentle rain from heaven." The free liquor allowance is now one quart, available only to persons 21 and over. On goods in general, "members of a family, including minors [this means even infants a month or a day old!], may combine all their exemptions, provided that: 1. they live in one household, and 2. they are traveling together on their return to the United States." This makes a happy ending to a somewhat dreary story.

Things to Remember When Packing

Soap is a thing to remember. Almost all the better hotels provide soap, but sometimes it is a miniature that can get lost between your fingers. If you like the feel of a good-sized cake of it, and especially if you plan on nightly washings of easy things, you will bring your own.

Coat Hangers—don't laugh—may be among the mightiest of minutiae in travel. By no means do all European hotels, even of first-class rating, provide enough of them, of convenient type, especially those on which trousers may be hung, in their bedroom closets or wardrobes. If you have had the experience of draping your clothes over chair backs or suitcases—and what traveler abroad has not?—you'll know that coat hangers are absolute necessities of travel, so by all means take along a few. Plastic ones weigh nearly nothing. In case you haven't brought any, or need more, be advised that the word in German is *Kleiderbügel.*

An *alarm clock,* speaking paradoxically, can give you a fine night's rest on the night before an early-dawn departure. Hotel porters will wake you, of course, but on rare instances, even in top hotels—I could name names but won't—they fail, and that's where your alarm clock comes to your rescue. It doesn't forget.

An *adapter,* to enable you to plug your electric shaver into the wall socket, is a supermust of your packing. In case you are a first-timer you just may not know that the prongs of European shavers are round, and a little differently spaced than those of U.S. shavers. Deluxe hotels that cater to Americans usually have sockets available for both types, but many good hotels do not. Frustration mounts, and if you're on a weekend it may be 48 hours or more before you can get an adapter. In America, they should be available in any electrical supplies shop. Voltages vary wildly in Europe, even within any given country, and your shaver must be of the type that can be shifted back and forth, say between 110 and 220 volts. That will handle all except the most far-out voltages. My own solver of this problem is a Norelco.

Money, Exchange, Tourist Costs

In the spring of 1971, the far-from almighty dollar bumped the bumps and it is too early, as of this writing, to determine "if it has a future." More seriously speaking, the decline of the dollar has not, at this time, had any significant effect on tourist costs in Austria. Whereas the schilling used to be worth a trifle under 4 cents it is now worth a trifle over 4 cents. The first appreciation of the schilling, in June 1971, was only 5 per cent, but in August it was released to "float", and where it will touch terra firma no one yet knows. In Germany the dollar's slide was serious, complicated by the prolonged period of the "floating exchange," which got a head start in that country. The mark had already been officially hoisted in 1970 from its original 25-cent value to 26½ cents, but in April 1971 it began floating and quickly rose to 29 cents and at hotel cashiers' desks to a horrible 33 1/3 cents, being just three to the dollar. The end of the floating *of the mark* may be expected soon, or perhaps that's wishful, but wherever the *Deutsche Mark* finds anchorage it is sure to be a more expensive unit of currency than ever it was before. To sum this up, dollarwise, Austria is still, and very definitely, one of the less expensive countries of Europe, whereas, I must honestly say, Germany is one of the more expensive. I will implement this summary with later details.

It is advisable to buy some schillings and marks at an exchange office before your departure. A company that I have used with special satisfaction is *Perera Fifth Avenue,* at 636 Fifth Avenue, adjacent to the main entrance to the International Building, numbered 630. This firm, like others, offers for the convenience of travelers on arriving abroad *prepacks* for $10, containing, in small denominations, ten dollars' worth of whatever foreign money is desired, in this case Austrian schillings *(Schillinge)* and German DMs. Prepacks for $20 and $50 are also to be had. The firm offers a little booklet entitled *"Are You Planning a Trip to a Foreign Country?"* that is a compact compendium, no larger than a small letter, giving currency conversion tables for 20 European countries, of course including Austria and Germany. It also has pages of Tipping Suggestions, Foreign Money Regulations, and Tobacco Allowances. The firm has several offices in the J. F. Kennedy Airport and one in the Miami Airport. Another reliable exchange house that I have used is *Manfra, Tordella and Brookes,* in the north corridor, street floor, of the RCA Building, 30 Rockefeller Plaza, with an entrance also at 48 West 50th Street.

Mail, Both Ways

Of course you are going abroad to get away from it all, including the telephone and the postman, but you will be surprised, I think, by the towering importance of letters, both ways, once you *are* a few thousand miles from home.

Receiving letters in Europe is a thornier matter than sending them. Many travelers use the American Express or Cook offices in the larger cities as their foreign addresses and some use banks, but in either case this involves your knowing when such offices are open and taking time out to visit them in order to claim your mail; or else it involves delay in having letters forwarded to your local hotel in each place. I have found that for my own convenience the best solution is to pick two or three key hotels in key cities and use these, in turn, for receipt of mail. The mail clerk, who is often the head porter in the hotel, will almost always take pride in handling your correspondence efficiently and since this is a special service he should be specially and well rewarded. When you leave he will take due care in forwarding late-coming mail. The head porters of German and Austrian hotels, with golden crossed keys decorating the lapels of their uniforms, are a superior breed of human servitors.

The *postage for letters from America to Europe* by airmail, which is the only thing to use, is at present 21 cents per half ounce, postcards and postal airletters 15 cents.

Posting letters from Europe to America or elsewhere is easiest done through your hotel porters and the charges can accumulate and be billed to you at the end of your stay. In Germany and Austria I have found this a fairly safe procedure, as it would certainly not be in all lands, but there lingers in one's mind that slight residuum of doubt. He will be honest, but will he be sure to remember to put on airmail postage? I always make it a practice, upon arriving in any foreign land, to find out, right off, what the postal tariffs are for letters and postcards by surface and airmail. Then I stock up on a lot of stamps and become my own postal clerk, with no one but myself to blame if anything goes wrong.

Germany and Austria, like most other European countries, base their overseas letter rates on a 5-gram weight, a little over one-sixth of an ounce, meaning one *thin* sheet and envelope, and there is an added surcharge for each added 5 grams. This mounts up drastically if you use heavy paper or put in enclosures. Within Europe 20 grams is the basic unit of weight, and on long distances everything is supposed to go by air. To be specific about postage costs for your airmail to the folks back home, the 5-gram rate from Austria is 5½ schillings (22 cents), plus 1½ schillings (6 cents), for each extra 5 grams. Postcard airmail postage is 4 schillings (16 cents). An airmail letter weighing a half ounce would thus cost 34 cents westbound, as against 21 cents eastbound. In Germany, the rates are still higher, the 5-gram rate being 80 pfennings (24 cents), with each additional 5 grams 6 cents. The moral is plain: Watch your weight!

Picture postcards, the sending of which is a major tourist sport everywhere, can be dispatched by surface mail at a very low rate, as of printed matter, *if* their message contains only five words of conventional greeting. You must expect passage to take two or three weeks or more, as against three to five days for airmail.

Air Travel to Austria

Because of Vienna's location at the far southeastern tip end of noncommunist Europe it is important, in case you're flying to that city, to give due thought to the means of doing so. Austrian Airlines discontinued overseas flights in the spring of 1971, so that is out. Any one of the major airlines can get you to Vienna, but so far as I know Pan American is the only one that can get you there without a change of planes. What's more, it provides a daily service during a long summer season and it uses its Boeing 747 Jumbo jets. Pan Am was the pioneer buyer and flyer of the giant Jumbos and now operates by far the largest fleet of them. I have made this flight both ways, eastward from New York, westward back to Boston, and have admired the smooth performance of this "flying city" and of those who fly it. On the return trip the plane was crowded with 350 passengers, yet to my view it settled to the runway with easier grace, I thought, than did any of its smaller ancestors, way back to the DC 3. And the fleet of trim stewardesses, shedding their jaunty, derbylike hats and donning their smocks, each bearing the full name of its wearer, served the 350 passengers with as much ease, superbly organized and unflustered, and with as much speed, as if the passenger count had been a third of what it was. The company distributes a pithy, humorous little booklet, comically illustrated, called *Pan Am Cares,* with practical counsels on 11 cogent topics, and it did seem so, especially on this westbound overocean transfer of some 50,000 pounds of persons. Caring begets caring and I was full of contentment as I enjoyed my meal, then disregarded the movie and fell sound asleep. My sense of security was heightened by the knowledge that since jets came in Pan Am has not had even one fatality in more than 200,000 Atlantic crossings. (Next to Pan Am I would say that Swissair and Lufthansa, perhaps also SABENA, would be the best choices, though with change from Jumbos to lesser planes in Zurich or Frankfurt or Brussels respectively.) It should be emphasized that Pan Am has been a pioneer "all its life," and in many ways, including the "taming of the Atlantic," which its planes have flown "the firstest and the mostest," almost like intercity bus runs. It has pioneered low-cost air travel for more than a quarter of a century at various points of time when the subject was under debate in the industry. To sound a personal note, I have pioneered with it ever since 1940, when I used to soar aloft in small planes of the company for Latin-American destinations from Florida's little Dinner Key airport.

Sea and River Travel to Austria

Sea travel on *regular* transatlantic sailings is becoming little more than a memory as company after company converts to the more lucrative cruise trade. In winter you would be hard put to it to find a single ship in service to northern European ports. In summer you will do a little better, but not much. The Cunard Line and the French Line have kept up, between them, a once-weekly service, and Hapag-Lloyd, the big merger of the Hamburg-American Line and North German Lloyd, *may* ferry you to Bremerhaven; but the United States of America has not a single passenger liner in service and both Canadian Pacific and Holland-America have dropped transatlantic routes. If you are ship eager perhaps a Mediterranean port is your best bet, for the Italian Line does maintain a year-round service from New York to Genoa. The *Cristoforo Colombo* sails once a month and midway between its sailings one of the Big Two, either the *Raffaello* or the *Leonardo da Vinci,* fills in, thus providing fortnightly sailings. From Genoa to Milan to Innsbruck is no long journey, and there you are in the country that is your goal.

As for river routes, there are two, and having tried them both I can say that each is treasurable. One is operated by the Cologne-Düsseldorf Line, with its fleet of superb river liners plying the Rhine in five exciting days from Rotterdam to Basel, which is only a short distance from Constance, and so by train or lake boat to Bregenz. The other river route, and this a direct one, is operated by the Danube Steamship Company, whose big steamers, some of them paddlewheelers, provide regular summer service from Passau, at the far southeastern corner of Bavaria, to Vienna. This trip will be covered in some detail in Chapter 4.

Rail Travel to Austria

Name trains have a special charm not only for the railroad buff but for any traveler who uses rail travel, and the name trains that give access to Austria are a nobly named company. I will name just a few that stand out either for their appealing names or for their outstanding importance, or both. All are fast and rather special.

The *Mozart:* Paris—Munich—Salzburg—Vienna, an all-day train.

The *Orient Express:* famous in fact and fiction, traveling the same route but leaving Paris at night.

The *Arlberg Express,* a night train, and then daylight, Paris—Zurich—Innsbruck—Salzburg.

The *Johann Strauss:* Frankfurt—Vienna, by day.

The *Rosenkavalier:* a Munich—Salzburg—Vienna all-morning flyer.

The *Blauer Enzian* (Blue Gentian): a TEE train (Trans-Europ-Express) from Hamburg to Klagenfurt, Carinthia, via Munich and Salzburg.

The *Akropolis:* Athens—Salzburg or Athens-Vienna 32-hour journey to Salzburg, 33 hours to Vienna, Zagreb being the point of separation.

The *Wiener Walzer* (Vienna Waltz): a night train from Zurich to Vienna.

The *Mediolanum:* another TEE train, Munich to Innsbruck and by the Brenner to Milan.

The *Romulus,* Rome—Vienna, a long-day train.

Europabus to Austria

The wide-ranging luxury coaches of the Europabus network provide interesting journeys from Frankfurt to Innsbruck, Salzburg and Vienna, the tourist big three of Austria. Among other prominent routes are those from Hamburg to Innsbruck and from Venice to Salzburg and Vienna. Coach travel, which sounds slightly more elegant than bus travel, gets you much closer to the land, the villages and the people than does train travel and it can be a really pleasant mode of touring, as offered by Europabus and other high-grade companies, many of which are tied in with it. The company's services within Austria, especially its week-long, all-inclusive "Red-White-Red" circular tours will be further mentioned in the YOURSELF portion of this book, in Chapter 7. Europabus maintains a New York office at 630 Fifth Avenue.

Road Travel to Austria

The commonest approach to Austria by those who drive their own or hired cars is by the well-traveled autobahn from Munich to Salzburg to Vienna, an autobahn all the way. This is not the most scenic route but it is the most practical for the motorist who is itching to get to his goal of vibrant Vienna. Another route, exuberantly called Traumstrasse (Dream Street), that will soon be an autobahn all the way, runs from Munich by way of Rosenheim and Kufstein to Innsbruck, continuing by way of the much-photographed Europabrücke (bridge) to and over the Brenner Pass to Italy. Less comfortable but wonderfully scenic are the Alpine routes from Munich to Innsbruck, one by way of Tegernsee and the Achen Pass, the other by way of Garmisch and Mittenwald, mentioned in Chapter 1 as Gate 6, and the long Arlberg route for those who enter from Switzerland or Liechtenstein or Lake Constance. Still another route, a new motorway of major importance, though not an autobahn, that "brings the south nearer," is called the *Felbertauernstrasse,* running from Munich via Kufstein through Kitzbühel, Mittersill and the Tauern Tunnel to Lienz, the capital of East Tyrol.

Motoring is enormously popular, but for some its drawbacks offset its advantages. It is often *very* difficult to find parking or garaging space in the cities and the traffic in some cities and resorts, certainly including Salzburg, can be horrendous. Of course this can be avoided by sticking to motels and inns on the cities' fringes and using taxis or public transportation to reach their centers. If you contemplate driving in Europe you should, of course, consult your travel agent and/or your American Automobile Association (AAA) office on the matter of license requirements and so forth. Car rental companies, including the omnipresent Hertz and Avis, are available all over Germany and Austria.

Austrian Music and Drama Festivals, Folk Pageants, Special Spectacles, Trade and Fun Fairs

To view the rich fare of entertainment offered by Austria, let's do some sorting of the calendar. The country's three great festival cities, Vienna, Salzburg and Bregenz, will be considered in turn, each with its own calendar. Folk pageants will follow, and finally the lively trade fairs.

Vienna

Pre-Lent Carnival Season, featured all over Austria, comes to its grandest moment in the Vienna Opera Ball, one of Europe's most glittering social events.

May-June (four weeks): *Vienna International Music and Drama Festival:* State opera; ballet; State theater; two great orchestras, the Vienna Philharmonic and the Vienna Symphony; the Vienna Choir Boys and other choirs; *Musikvereinsquartett* in chamber music; *Lieder;* light opera. Internationally famous conductors and soloists.

All year except in July, August and half of September: *Vienna Choir Boys' Performances* on Sundays and holidays at 9:30 in the *Hofkapelle* (Court Chapel) of the Hofburg.

March-June and October 15 to December 15: Performances of the famous white Lippizaner horses in the Spanish Riding School.

Salzburg

Last week in January: Mozart Festival

April through September: Marionette Theater of Professor Hermann Aicher, for *adult* entertainment. Don't think of this as any sort of Punch-and-Judy show. It is a marvel of the first importance now with its own elegant new theater. The marionettes can perform such things as Johann Strauss's *Die Fledermaus* and Mozart's

Magic Flute, complete with a small Mozart, perhaps half life-sized, seated at the piano. I have also marveled at *The Barber of Seville,* with the shrill antics of "Figaro, Figaro, FEE-garo." The troupe has toured many countries, including the United States. Music to which the marionettes perform is on tape, but the coordination is wonderful.

Easter Music Festival: Opera and a variety of concerts.

Late July through August: *Salzburg International Music and Drama Festival,* world-known and often called Europe's ranking summer festival. Opera; ballet; symphonic concerts; significant plays such as *Jedermann* (Everyman). One feature is unique, the *Felsenreitschule* (Cliff Riding School), a theater, with boxes that were used in former times, hewn from the solid cliff. Now the rock boxes are part of the stage setting. Figures, as in *Orpheus and Eurydice,* appear *in* these boxes. There's nothing else in the world remotely like this.

Bregenz

Late July to late August: *Bregenz International Music and Drama Festival,* less known than its two rivals but produced on a level of artistry to match either of them. It is to be hoped that you can visit Bregenz at the time of its increasingly popular midsummer Festival (see Chapter 12) and it is to be hoped that *if* you plan to do so you will plan also to secure accommodations well in advance. It has sometimes been said that the Bregenz Festival is to operetta what Salzburg is to opera, though this is a loose generality. It is, at any rate, a dream of a festival centering on a vast stage set on piles in the harbor in Lake Constance.

Folk Pageantry

January 6, Epiphany: *St. Johann in Pongau—Perchtenlaufen,* a curious peasant procession and festival, starts the folk year.

First Sunday in May: *Zell am Ziller, the Gauderfest.*

First Sunday in June: *Mariazell—Narcissus Festival.*

June 21: *Summer Solstice Festivals,* with bonfires, celebrated in hundreds of Alpine villages.

Weekly in July: *Innsbruck* and many valley villages—costume festivals.

Last Sunday in July: *Mayrhofen.*

Midweekly in August: *Friesach*—open-air period plays.

First Saturday-Sunday in August: *Villach*—important *Kirtag Festival,* street parades, fireworks, dancing.

August 15: *Feast of Maria Himmelfahrt* (Assumption), celebrated in a big way throughout Austria, a feature being the *Hochbergfeuer,* or Mountain Peak Fires, when great bonfires glow in luminous chains from the mountain peaks, as, for example, above *Seefeld,* north of Innsbruck.

First Sunday in September: *Hoch-Osterwitz Castle,* in Carinthia —costume festival, with soldiers in medieval armor.

October: *Vintage Festivals,* in various places.

November 1–2: *All Saints' Festivals.*

December 6: *Feast of St. Nicholas,* with colorful glorification of popular "Saint Nick."

December 20: *Christkindl Einzug* at Innsbruck, as the Christ Child "enters."

December 24: Celebrations for *Stille Nacht, Heilige Nacht (Silent Night, Holy Night),* an *Austrian* Christmas carol beloved by all the world, composed by an organist named Franz Gruber. *Hallein,* a bit south of Salzburg, and *Oberndorf,* a bit north, celebrate with special fervor.

Trade and Fun Fairs

Twice a year, March and September: *Vienna International Trade Fairs.*

April-May; September-October: *Graz Spring and Autumn Trade Fairs.* Graz synchronizes a *Styrian Autumn Festival* with its Autumn Trade Fair in October.

Approximately first week in August: *Dornbirn International Trade and Sample Fair,* a lively event in Vorarlberg's largest town, near Bregenz, synchronized with the Bregenz Festival.

Second week in August: *Klagenfurt Lumber Fair.*

August: Innsbruck Export and Sample Fair, with special features in promotion of tourism.

Austrian Holidays (Dates to Enjoy or Avoid)

Austrian holidays can be a delightful extra ingredient of your tour, but they can also be a threat, for several of them are Catholic religious holidays unfamiliar in America, when *everything* is closed, banks, shops, post office, official tourist offices, travel agencies. On a month's spring visit I once encountered no less than three such closings, two of them *3-day shutdowns,* Saturday, Sunday, Monday, for Ascension Day, Whitsuntide and Corpus Christi. Well, here's the full list: New Year's Day; Epiphany (January 6); Easter Monday; Labor Day (May 1); Ascension Day (Thursday, 40 days after Easter); Whitmonday (7 weeks after Easter Monday) —confirmation coaches, decked with artificial flowers and drawn by two white horses, are seen in all the cities; Corpus Christi (Thursday following the 8th Sunday after Easter)—colorful processions, notably flower floats, on Hallstatt Lake and on the Traunsee, off Gmunden; Assumption Day (August 15); All Saints' Day (November 1); Christmas and the following day.

Austrian Summer Study Courses

Austria is a magnet for foreign students, fourteen years of age and up, from many countries, and not least from the United States. Summer courses are given in at least 14 cities and resorts. I will list a few of them.

For inquiry about the *Vienna International University Courses* address: Sekretariat der Wiener Hochschulkurse, Universität, Vienna I. The University's summer courses in the Social Sciences and International Relations, in the Liberal Arts, and in German language and German literature are given at the lakeside village of Strobl on the Wolfgangsee in the Salzkammergut, the period being some six weeks from about July 10. Address A-5350 Strobl, St. Wolfgang Campus, Austria.

Salzburg is rich in summer courses. International courses under sponsorship of the University of Salzburg are devoted to the German language and philology. Address the University at Faberstrasse 6. The *International Summer Academy for Fine Arts* operates within the Castle of Hohensalzburg. Address the Academy at Post Office Box 18. Salzburg's well-loved Mozarteum offers courses of three to five weeks in a wide variety of musical instruction. Address Schwarzstrasse 26. The widely known *Salzburg Seminar for American Studies,* a sort of "reverse American," occupies stately Schloss Leopoldskron, located on a small lake within Salzburg's city limits.

Innsbruck offers International Vacation Courses in German Language and Literature for Foreigners, with "sporting activities and social get-togethers, music club, excursions," which sounds like sugar-coated learning—and very good too.

Mayrhofen (Tyrol), a very lovely Zillertal village amid towering mountains, gives International Vacation Courses of the University of Innsbruck on the German language "and with Austrian literature, history, art and music, and [get this] to introduce students to the wonders of Austrian scenery." Students need only "lift up their eyes unto the hills," for Mayrhofen's setting is spectacularly lovely. Sport is not forgotten, for tennis, riding, mountain climbing and "summer skiing instruction" are offered. One of Mayrhofen's students in the summer of 1971 was Caroline Kennedy. A general committee of which one may inquire about any of these university courses is called OKISTA, with the address 1090 Vienna IX, Türkenstrasse 4/III, and if you'll grip your chair I'll reveal what the word stands for. It is *Österreichische Komittee für Internationalen Studienaustausch.* The last word means study exchange, which gives a key to the whole thing.

One more place needs mention, namely the Tyrolean village of *Alpbach,* where the *European Forum* of the Austrian College Society meets for about three weeks from mid-August for a seminar attended by university graduates from many lands to discuss world problems in a peaceful setting.

The Background of the Picture

3 / A SOUPÇON OF HISTORY

A PARAGRAPH OF THE PAST

Austria's great capital, first established by the Romans as Vindobona and later reestablished by Charlemagne as Wien, was the swirling vortex of European history for some eight centuries, from the time of the Crusades to and through the Napoleonic Interlude, until modern German power began to overshadow the dual monarchy of venerable Austria-Hungary. In the checkered story of Europe, only Rome, as stated in the opening chapter, can claim a longer and more varied past than Vienna, and as a bulwark of protection for western civilization, the city on the Danube was unique. After Otto the Great set up the Holy Roman Empire, it became a bastion, small and tentative at first, then increasingly potent, against all Eastern and Islamic marauders. Barbarossa made the East Mark (hence *Aust*ria) a hereditary duchy of the Babenbergs and it later became the East Realm. Ottokar of Bohemia built the city wall, which was destined to turn back the Turks twice, in 1529 and 1683. The wall ultimately became the celebrated Ring of Vienna, its "Girdle of Splendor," as J. A. Mahan called it. The Habsburgs, succeeding the Babenberg and Bohemian rulers as early as 1282 held on until World War I knocked them out, reducing Austria-Hungary, with its 261,000 square miles and 51,000,000 inhabitants, to a republic about one-tenth as large in area and with only about 7,000,000 inhabitants, a figure which has happily remained static to the present day. Hitler's war and the four-power occupation, lasting ten long years because of Russian obduracy, wrought further havoc, but Austria and its capital did not succumb to those hard blows and indignities. The culture, art, music and verve which have seeped from that land throughout the world continued to sustain the people's spirit, as they always had. Finally, in 1955, the occupation came to an end and in October of that year, the last of the foreign forces quit Austria. There was great jubilation as the nation regained her full freedom and sovereignty. The gala reopening of the famous Opera House in Vienna, on November 5, a social as well as musical event of world significance, seemed a symbol of a new day.

PERSONAGES OF THE PAST

The following pages, which stress Austria's celebrities in cultural fields, will include very little mention of royal personages, generals or political leaders, but for the sake of clarity a few such notes may precede the general roster.

The royal and imperial *House of Habsburg* reigned over the so-called but misnamed Holy Roman Empire from 1483 to 1806, and from that date over Austria, and after 1867 over the dual monarchy of Austria-Hungary until its collapse in 1918, when the last ruler of the line was forced to abdicate. The tragic "sunset years" of the Habsburg line bring only two emperors into view, both having lived within the memory of many persons of today. They were: durable and much-whiskered Franz Joseph, whose reign of 68 years (1848–1916) was one of the longest in history, and his great-grandnephew Charles I (1916–18), who rode out World War I and then went into exile, first in Switzerland, afterward in Madeira, where he died four years later. Other relatively recent members of the venerable house were *Crown Prince Rudolf,* only son of Franz Joseph, who died mysteriously (in 1889) in a hunting lodge at Mayerling, along with his inamorata, Baroness Maria Vetsera; *Empress Elisabeth,* cousin and wife of Emperor Franz Joseph, who was assassinated in Geneva in 1898 by an Italian anarchist; *Archduke Francis Ferdinand,* grandnephew of Franz

Joseph and heir apparent to the throne, whose assassination at Sarajevo in 1914 led directly to World War I; and *Otto,* the son of Charles I and his wife, Empress Zita. Goaded by his ambitious mother, Otto asserted his claim to the dual throne and tried by every means to make it good, but without success.

Four royal and/or military figures prominent in the Austrian background during the Habsburg era are worth noting, partly because their names are woven into the fabric of the sightseer's Vienna. I will list these four more or less chronologically, though dates overlap.

Count Ernst Rüdiger von Starhemberg (1638–1701) was a general who distinguished himself so notably in the wars against the Turks, especially during their great siege of Vienna in 1683, that he was made a field marshal and minister of state.

Prince Eugene of Savoy (1661–1736) was a French general who was refused a French army commission by Louis XIV and thereupon promptly offered his services to the Austrian imperial house, serving it with almost unparalleled brilliance in the various wars against the Turks and other foes. Two of Prince Eugene's palaces are sights of Vienna, the Belvedere Palace being an architectural masterpiece.

The Princes zu Schwarzenberg, Karl Philipp (1771–1820) and his nephew Felix (1800–52), were the two chief luminaries of a princely family serving Austria in various capacities for two or three centuries, their family palace on the Schwarzenbergplatz, with its lofty fountain, being conspicuous features of Vienna. It was Prince Karl Philipp who, with Metternich, negotiated the marriage of Princess Marie Louise to Napoleon. A portion of Palais Schwarzenberg is now a first-class hotel of special charm and significance.

Prince Metternich (1773–1859) was one of the wiliest statesmen in the history of Europe. He was instrumental in forming the Quadruple Alliance against France that brought down Napoleon, and he was the leading figure at the Congress of Vienna. For several decades after Napoleon's exile to St. Helena, Metternich's skillful and sometimes tortuous diplomacy quite dominated Europe. This period has, in fact, been labeled "the Age of Metternich."

Oh, yes, there was a post-Habsburg Austrian named *Adolf Hit-*

ler, who was born in the pleasant frontier village of Braunau am Inn. Said Virginia Creed in her guide *All About Austria,* "There seems nothing in its charming streets to account for Hitler."

It may be noticed that in the above rundown of royalty the name of Empress Maria Theresa is not mentioned, but that is not due to forgetfulness. Rather, I have such a deep-down admiration for that wonderful woman that I was reluctant to "tuck her in" here. She will have her turn, less hurriedly, in Chapter 5 as we view the great sights of Vienna.

And now for our nonroyal, nonmilitary Personages of the Past, listed by alphabet.

Anton BRUCKNER (1824–96)–*composer and organist*—was born in Upper Austria but first won musical fame as organist in the Abbey Church of St. Florian, a suburb of Linz. Here a Bruckner Festival now takes place annually in July. Bruckner's nine symphonies are his chief claim to fame, the Ninth being a deliberate challenge, in its whole composition, to Beethoven's Ninth. Critics find plenty of faults in Bruckner but admit his remarkable powers of invention. His place in the musical firmament is solidly established.

Franz von DEFREGGER (1835–1921)—*painter*—was a native of Iselsberg in East Tyrol. He painted genre and historical scenes, the former being often quaintly humorous in their revelations of country life. His work is best seen in Innsbruck's Ferdinandeum Museum.

Albin EGGER-LIENZ (1868–1926)—*painter*—a pupil of Defregger, developed talents considerably superior to those of his teacher. His work, too, is in Innsbruck's Ferdinandeum, but much more of it, some 50 paintings, are in Schloss Bruck, on a hill above his native Lienz, capital of East Tyrol.

Johann Bernhard FISCHER VON ERLACH (ca. 1656–1723)—*architect*—designed many of Austria's most famous public buildings, palaces and churches, especially in Vienna. His masterpiece is the striking baroque Karlskirche, flanked by towering "Trajan's columns" on either side of a six-columned portico. He had a hand in enlarging the Hofburg, he designed vast Schönbrunn Palace, as well as many private Vienna palaces, and he did the monumental fountain in the Hohe Markt, setting his personal stamp on a great capital as few architects have ever done. In Salzburg he designed the splendid baroque Collegiate Church.

Sigmund FREUD (1859–1939)—*psychiatrist*—was the founder of psychoanalysis, as everyone knows. He early abandoned the use of hypnotism in favor of "free association," which became the basis for his theory of curative psychiatry. He wrote a book on the interpretation of dreams that charted new paths and his work on the theory of sex enhanced his fame. His absorption in this latter field of study roused sharp attacks from many quarters, yet in his personal life he was a devoted husband and the proud father of six children. Among Freud's pupils who won fame in their own right were *Alfred Adler,* who propounded the theory of the Inferiority Complex, now a familiar phrase everywhere, and *Wilhelm Stekel,* who became an eminent international lecturer on the interpretation of dreams. Freud's daughter, Dr. Anna Freud, widely known herself as a psychiatrist, has lived for a long time in England, resentful that the Nazis (when they occupied the country) caused her father's exile because of his Jewish nationality. She has recently gone to Vienna to receive some honors but will continue to live, I understand, in England.

Franz GRILLPARZER (1791–1872)—*dramatist*—wrote a number of powerful plays, some excellent verse and just one novel, *The Poor Musician (Der Arme Spielmann)* that some critics consider the best of all his works. Grillparzer had a strong influence on later dramatists but is too little known to readers outside the German-speaking world.

Franz Josef HAYDN (1732–1809)—*composer*—could almost be called the "founder" of symphony music but he was a master also of many other types. The patronage of the Princes Esterházy and the friendship that he built up with Mozart were two of the most important spurs to Haydn's genius. His life, mostly centering in Vienna, lasted 75 years but his output of compositions would seem prodigious for a life three times that length. Several years before his death he had written, by his own tally, 118 symphonies, 83 string quartets, 66 piano sonatas, 20 piano concertos, 19 operas, some of which were for marionette theaters, 15 masses, 5 oratorios, one of them the still-popular *Creation,* a *Stabat Mater,* a long set of interludes for *The Seven Last Words of Jesus,* in additional to much other church music, 175 pieces for an instrument called the baryton, this to please Prince Nicholas, who favored that instrument. There were also numerous *divertimenti* and small compositions which he did not bother to count, and somewhere, in an odd moment, he found time to write the Austrian National Hymn, *"Gott erhalte Franz den Kaiser."* All this made a pretty good start, but "Pape Haydn" was by no means finished. He wrote a lot more compositions in his last years.

Hugo VON HOFMANNSTHAL (1874–1929)—*dramatist and poet*—is widely known to festival goers for his writing of *Das Spiel von Jedermann ("Everyman"),* popular mystery play of the Salzburg Festival. He also wrote *Der Rosenkavalier* and an adaptation of Sophocles' *Elektra,* both set to music by his intimate friend, Richard Strauss.

Franz LEHÁR (1870–1948), *composer* of *The Merry Widow, The Count of Luxemburg* and other worldwide successes, was a Hungarian, but he seems to have been "adopted" by all Austrians, and in Bad Ischl his home, now a museum, is one of that resort's major sights.

Adolf LORENZ (1854–1946)—orthopedic surgeon—became famous the world over for his development of "bloodless surgery," treating diseases of the feet by external manipulation and the use of appliances and following this with use of casts. From 1923 to 1936, Professor Lorenz made annual visits to the United States, where he was literally *besieged* by pleading patients. At 79 he underwent the Steinach rejuvenation treatment and attained the ripe age of 92, a living advertisement of the treatment's efficacy.

Gustav MAHLER (1860–1911)—*conductor and composer*—was in demand in many cities. In Vienna, Budapest, Prague, Hamburg, London and elsewhere in Europe he conducted the leading orchestras and he also did stretches with the "Met" in New York and with the New York Philharmonic. He was a stern perfectionist and raised the standards of the Vienna opera to their highest levels. As a composer he wrote two operas and a number of symphonies but these were monumental works scored for very large orchestras and for some time even the symphonies were not very much played except in Holland, under Willem Mengelberg's leadership. Gradually, however, more and more orchestras under more and more leaders have recognized their compelling power and now Mahler's works are frequently programmed.

Wolfgang Amadeus MOZART (1756–91)—*composer*—is of the very fabric of Austria and this book shall have more to say of him, especially in connection with his native city, Salzburg. He lived only 35 years but began composing at the age of 4, wrote his first opera at 11, his first oratorio at 13, so his output was tremendous in spite of his tragically early death. Mozart's sparkling grace seems a musical reflection of the Austrian spirit and no composer in any land is more universally loved and enjoyed.

Michael PACHER (ca. 1435–98)—*painter and woodcarver*—was a naturally gifted Tyrolean who achieved religious masterpieces, especially for the altars of village churches, which have continued to win the highest admiration. His greatest work is considered to be the winged high altar in the church at St. Wolfgang, a lake village in the Salzkammergut, but there is another magnificent one in the church of Heiligenblut, a popular pilgrim village of Carinthia on the Grossglockner Road. In Salzburg he is represented by a lovely Madonna on a Fischer von Erlach high altar in the Franciscan Church.

PARACELSUS (ca. 1493–1541)—*chemist and alchemist*—was a strange character, Swiss-born but living much of his life in Austria, especially Salzburg, where he is entombed in a chapel of St. Sebastian's Church. His baptismal name was Theophrastus Bombastus von Hohenheim, but he adopted the equally flowery name of Philippus Aureolus Paracelsus. He was a living paradox, often regarded as a sorcerer or charlatan because of his absorption in searching for the elixir of life and the philosopher's stone, but more often regarded as a pioneer physician who flouted the faulty practices of his day, such as indiscriminate bleeding, and laid the foundations of modern pharmaceutics. This still controversial personage was immortalized by Browning in a poem called *Paracelsus,* which is at the same time a psychological study.

Max REINHARDT (1873–1943)—*theatrical producer*—began his

career in Salzburg, and although much of his greatest work was done in Berlin he saved plenty of time for directing the Salzburg Festival for many years. During that period he owned the handsome Schloss Leopoldskron, now the seat of the Salzburg Seminar for American Studies, on a lakelet south of the city. He also took charge, for a time, of Vienna's Theater in der Josefstadt. In New York his production of *The Miracle* in 1924 was a major event of the theatrical history of that city.

Franz SCHUBERT (1797–1828)—*composer*—was, like Mozart, a boy prodigy and like him he died young, at 31. He had a gift for melody rarely matched in musical history and many of his 600 or more songs have a lyrical quality that has touched the hearts of all generations since his time. In addition to his many songs he wrote piano sonatas, masses, chamber music and eight symphonies, the most celebrated and well-loved of them being the one in B Minor commonly called the *Unfinished Symphony*. His lifelong poverty now seems incredible, but poverty was often the grim reward of genius in his day. It has been stated that Schubert received the equivalent of less than a quarter of a dollar for many of his finest songs and certainly he died a pauper. His estate was appraised at ten dollars but he left to posterity a millionaire's legacy of song.

Eugen STEINACH (1862–1944)—*physiologist*—was one of that group of brilliant Viennese professors who spread the medical fame of Vienna to every corner of the civilized world. He was the "gland man," who experimented with the transfer of sex glands from monkeys to men, in the hope of prolonging human life.

The STRAUSS DYNASTY—*"waltz kings"*—consisted of a father and three sons: Johann Strauss, father (1804–49); Johann Strauss, son (1825–99); Josef Strauss (1827–70); and Eduard Strauss (1835–1916). They were all prolific composers of waltzes and other light music, chiefly for dancing, and the rivalry among them was amazing and amusing. The younger Johann, with his *Blue Danube Waltz* and others, won more fame than his father and much more than either of his brothers. Even today, his popularity is so enormous that Vienna's leading orchestras, under famous conductors, are happy to give Strauss evenings in big concert halls, always to full audiences.

Walther VON DER VOGELWEIDE (ca. 1170–ca. 1230)—*minnesinger*—is considered to have been the Middle Ages' finest lyric poet. He wandered from court to court in Austria and Germany singing love songs and topical songs, troubadour style. He was also a famous maker of maxims. "Walter of the Birdmeadow," for such is the meaning of his name, wrote both the words and music of his songs and in Vienna, at the Babenberg court, he was a constant favorite with the Crusaders who so frequently passed to and fro through that city.

Julius WAGNER-JAUREGG (1857–1940)—*psychiatrist and neurologist*—was a Nobel Prize winner in 1926 for his malarial inoculation treatment of paresis.

Hugo WOLF (1860–1903)—*songwriter*—has been compared with Schubert for the beauty of his Lieder, of which he wrote some 500. His name and fame have spread widely in America through records and through the recitals of such gifted singers as the Viennese artist Elizabeth Schwarzkopf.

Yourself in the Picture

4 / And so to Vienna; Styrian Skyroad or Danube Riverway?

THE STYRIAN SKYROAD

Travelers heading for Vienna from Salzburg and the Salzkammergut generally use the humdrum autobahn, as I've said, but they certainly need not, for there is a wonderful mountain route from the Styrian Salzkammergut, whose capital is Bad Aussee, through the Styrian Alps to Mariazell, the most-sought pilgrim town in all central Europe, and from there, by one of several routes, to Vienna. Those who come from Germany may likewise avoid the long miles of the Salzburg-Vienna autobahn by taking the highly interesting Castle Road, so called for tourists, that strikes southeast from Frankfurt through Würzburg, the "Franconian Switzerland," Nürnberg and Regensburg to Passau, takeoff river port for the 13-hour daylight Danube ship trip to Vienna. Both approaches are *cordon bleu* feasts of scenery, historic interest and romance. We'll start with the Styrian High Way.

Bad Aussee is at the extreme northwestern tip of widely sprawling Styria, as Mariazell is at the extreme northeastern tip, so we are Styria's guests all the way except for the final run to Vienna. Bad Aussee is an important spa, known especially for its success in the treatment of liver and gall bladder ailments, and it is, as well,

/ 51

a bustling holiday resort both summer and winter. It has its important salt mountain, its chairlift to the Tressensattel (3600 feet) and a lively program of holiday sports and entertainments. Also, the provincial costumes of Styrian men and women, seen with great frequency, especially on Sundays, add their charming touches. In fact, the *men* of Styria, including high dignitaries in the cities, sometimes wear this costume, with its agreeable gray and green hues, even at dress receptions, just as ardent Scots wear their kilts in Edinburgh. Styrian women are equally eager to wear the dirndl of Steiermark, one of whose most charming variants is the Ausseer dirndl of this Alpine region. It consists of pink skirt, green bodice and lilac apron.

Altaussee, 3 miles from Bad Aussee, is a personal favorite of mine, partly because of its charming lakeside *Hotel am See,* a garden inn on the very edge of the Altausseer See (Old Outlake Lake), which sounds, and is, redundant, for the lake must distinguish itself from the town bordering it by repeating the word See. A gourmet's specialty of the hotel is *saibling,* a troutlike lake fish of delicate pink meat, and so proud is the management of this fish that it has named its bar the Saibling Bar. While I am on the subject of food I should mention that in this hotel, as in many another of good standing in Styria, hot goulash may be had *at any hour* of the day or evening. This little community has long had a more social and international tang than most places in the Salzkammergut, being a frequent goal of American and English travelers, but nature, unimpressed and unconcerned, once gave a mighty display of its power here. Back in 1920, on September 12, the Hoher Sandling, a mountain rising a little to the northwest of the lake, shook its head slightly and hurled six million cubic meters of rock and rubble into the valley below.

The "Three Lakelets" that are usually considered the southern culmination of the Salzkammergut form a chain of mountain sapphires, diminishing in size, that are visited by boats and a connecting bus in a popular *Drei-Seen-Tour.* They are the small *Grundlsee,* civilized and soft, submitting to a tourist launch and made gay by sailboats; the smaller and much wilder *Toplitzsee,* with a few human habitations clinging to its steep banks; and the minuscule

Kammersee, a mere dot of blue loveliness at the base of the Dead Mountains *(Totes Gebirge).* It was on the remote Toplitzsee, about 150 years ago, that Archduke Johann, the 13th child of Emperor Leopold II, first saw Anna Plochl, the beautiful daughter of the Aussee postmaster, and promptly fell in love with her. He eventually married her secretly in his hunting lodge, called Brandhof, south of Mariazell, and thereby so incensed the court in Vienna that he was forever barred from living at the Hofburg. Perhaps the romantic loveliness of this small lake caused the archduke to see Anna through rosy spectacles, but we are all for him anyway. He would be a dull prince who could meet a postmaster's pretty daughter in such a setting and not fall in love with her. This marriage deeply endeared the "Prince of Styria" to all his people and the warmth of it still glows. There is a statue of him in the Kurpark of Bad Aussee and his name graces various streets, bridges and inns. He remains very much in the Picture of Styria.

The motorist who pushes his Salzkammergut explorations as far as the Aussee area would do himself an unforgettable favor by continuing eastward toward Vienna by the Styrian mountain route. This is beyond a doubt one of the finest scenic treats to be had even in Austria and yet it has had strangely little exploitation and comparatively few American tourists seem ever to have heard of it at all. I will outline seriatim some highlights of this route, though selection from such a multitude is difficult.

1. *Mitterndorf* is a summer and winter resort at the 2600-foot level with an idyllic little lake, the Staussee. The place is known to ski enthusiasts as the proud possessor of one of the world's four most gigantic ski-jump platforms, the others being at Oberstdorf in Bavaria, Planica in Yugoslavia and Vikesund in Norway. Jumps of 400 to 500 feet have been made here. The longest ski jumps take up to *seven seconds* in the air and the longest ever made, 541 feet by Dieter Wolf, an East German, at Planica, must have pushed eight seconds. German skiers distinguish between *Skiflug* (ski flying), which is jumping for distance, and *Skispringen,* which is jumping for perfection of form. South of Mitterndorf, by way of contrast to winter sport, or perhaps complementing it, there is an ultramodern spa opened in 1970, called *Kurhotel Bad Heilbrunn,*

whose earthborn waters have a temperature of 82 degrees Fahrenheit. The building has 8 stories and 100 rooms, and the thermal establishment, with a pool open to all, has every conceivable up-to-date facility.

2. *Tauplitz* is a parish village at the top of the pass leading from the Salzkammergut to the Enns Valley of Styria. From this village the longest chairlift in Austria is ready to hoist you to the Tauplitzalm. The altitude of the village is 3000 feet, that of the Alm 5700 feet, and it takes 35 minutes to make the ascent, the length of the chairlift being 2½ miles. This lift operates the year round and for a good half of the year the Alm is a skiers' paradise, the sport being practiced here till the middle of May.

3. *Pürgg,* which is medieval for Burg (stronghold), is the most historically significant place on this route, for it was the early seat of the Dukes of Styria, even as far back as the 11th century. It is like a swallow's nest on a ledge of rock high above the broad Enns Valley, which we first encounter here, and was selected by the court because of its impregnability to attack. Some remains of the castle may still be seen. A 13th-century chapel, the Johanneskapelle, of heaviest Romanesque style, with some primitive frescoes perfectly preserved that date from the same early period, is still intact and near it a larger Romanesque church with some Gothic alterations, while below there is an ossuary containing 5000 skulls. If these give you a creepy feeling just look out over the broad valley and feel the stimulus of its beauty. The interesting mountain inn of Adolf Adam, by the way, seems almost as old as the "first man" and indeed the present Adam claims it was built in 950, thus antedating the church and the chapel. An enhancement of this area is the wealth of snow-white snow roses, somewhat like big narcissi, but gifted with their own delicious fragrance. They flourish only in the woods.

4. *Frauenberg* is worthy of a pause for its dramatic hilltop church, long a revered goal of pilgrims. It looms up on the left bank of the Enns.

5. *Admont and "The Brawling"* are among the highest of highlights in the Ennstal. Admont is a lovely old town situated amid Styrian immensities in a broad portion of the valley. It owes its

special distinction to a venerable Benedictine abbey, which, in turn, owes its fame largely to its library. This is of exuberant baroque design and of amazing richness for a place so remote from populous cities. It contains more than a thousand old manuscripts, among them a sort of "Rosetta Stone," being a translation of a pious homily from the Merovingian to the Carlovingian language, and there are almost a hundred thousand old books, many of them bound in vellum.

Just east of Admont the road and the railway both enter a Stygian defile called *Die Gesäuse,* which is The Roaring, or The Brawling, of the Enns River as it tumbles madly through the narrow gorge it has spent aeons in carving from the limestone hills. The engineering problems involved in building this stretch of roadway and rail line were staggering, but Austria long ago learned to take such problems in stride. Even now, however, nature will not be denied, for damaging floods and avalanches occasionally block traffic.

6. *Gstatterboden* is the perfect place to stop *in* the defile for a meal or a night or a week. It faces a tremendous wall of rock called the *Planspitze,* a super-Gibraltar cliff of the Hochtor Mountain Group. Gstatterboden is, as a matter of fact, a major center of mountaineering, but perhaps you will be deterred from rock climbing by a look at the *Bergsteigerfriedhof* in the neighboring hamlet of Johnsbach. It is very lovely to the eye but tragic to the thought, for this Friedhof ("cemetery") contains the bodies *only* of those who died in mountaineering ventures.

7. *Hieflau,* at the exit of the Gesäuse gorge, is the turntable of northern Styrian travel, where decisions must be made. If you turn south to Leoben you will pass through *Eisenerz,* an iron-mining town of great importance to Austrian economy, for its mountain of iron ore, the Erzberg, boasts the very largest open-mine workings in all Europe, or so at least it is claimed in Styria. Whether or not Kiruna, in Sweden, would contend the claim I do not know. If you set your course from Hieflau to the north, continuing straight to Amstetten, you will be within easy range of Linz to the west or Vienna to the east, but if you take the good, though wriggling, scenic road from Hieflau (by Lainbach and Gams) to the

Salza River you may follow the stream to Mariazell and be well rewarded.

8. *Mariazell,* in the extreme northeastern corner of Styria, is the most-sought town of pilgrimage in the whole of Central Europe, receiving upwards of 100,000 pilgrims a year, not to mention many thousands of pleasure-bent visitors, for this is a health resort and a winter sports center as well as a goal of pious supplicants. No pilgrim town I know, including France's Lourdes, Spain's Montserrat and Switzerland's Einsiedeln, all mountain towns, can surpass in splendor of scenery Styria's Mariazell. Its abounding beauty makes Emperor Leopold I's devotion to it more understandable. When the Black Plague ravaged Vienna in 1679 the emperor retired in haste to this mountain retreat and prayed with great zeal for his people while the stricken city labored to bury its dead. When the pest finally abated, in answer, as the monarch thought, to his prayers *in absentia,* he erected in Vienna a Trinity Column, the conspicuous *Pestsäule,* in the street called Graben, that is still one of the capital's chief sights. The *Gnadenkirche* of Mariazell, a Gothic basilica that is the largest church in Styria, contains a miraculous limewood statue of the Virgin, about two feet high, which is the reason for Mariazell's pilgrim fame. It rests on a silver altar designed by Fischer von Erlach. The image was brought here in 1157 by a Benedictine missionary-monk to whom, according to legend, the mountains opened a passage so that he might reach this upland valley safely.

THE DANUBE RIVERWAY

A day on the Danube, meaning the downstream trip on a river steamer from Passau to Vienna, can be a sheer delight, subject to the one proviso that you prove to be a "wise virgin" by engaging a cabin *weeks ahead.* The entire trip takes 13 hours by express ship (7 A.M. to 7:50 P.M.) and is fascinating all the way, but it can be exceedingly wearying if you have to battle for possession of a campstool or for a minimum of space on one of the deck benches. I know this all too well, because on one of my two trips, the first of course, I was *not* a wise virgin. I could not, for love or money, secure a cabin, and only by alertness (and perhaps selfishness) did I finally secure one of the too few campstools, which I dared not leave out of my sight for fear of having to stand up the rest of the day. The ships of the *First Danube Steamship Company* are impressively large, the older ones being paddlewheelers. The flagship of the fleet is the splendid motorship *Theodor Körner,* named for a former president of Austria, but this is used largely for 8-day excursion trips downstream from Vienna to Hungary and Rumania and 14-day trips that continue even to the Black Sea. Lesser but good steamers that are used on the express service from Passau to Vienna are the *Stadt Passau;* the *Stadt Wien;* the *Johann Strauss;* and the *Schönbrunn;* they are of modern design, but they are of one class only and the fares are so *very* low that even schoolchildren can afford the trip, as many do every summer day. You will find it advisable to spend many hours of the day in the dining rooms, from whose big windows the view is excellent, loitering over three meals and between-times tea or coffee and drinks.

What *are* the fares? You will hardly believe it when I report that, *by current exchange rates,* the whole long trip, 190 miles, costs only $7.00, and still more incredibly, a deck cabin for two IF you are able to secure one, costs only $17.00 and an "underdeck" cabin, which is frankly dismal, $7.00. Furthermore—be sure to note this —you can board the ship the night before your departure from Passau (after 8 P.M.) and use your cabin as a sleeping room *without any extra charge.* Full meals, and good ones, are to be had in the ship's two dining rooms (one generally better furnished than the other) for about $3.50, and excellent Austrian wines from Danube vineyards at similarly low prices.

Passengers boarding the ships at Linz may sleep aboard the night before a generously late 10 A.M. departure, just as at Passau prior to the earlier departure.

If the whole 13-hour trip seems forbiddingly long, you may go by car or train from Passau to Linz, cutting down the length of the steamer trip to 8½ hours, or you may continue even to Melk, at the upper end of the Wachau stretch, and thus cut the steamer trip to less than 4 hours, this latter plan being especially desirable if you have secured no cabin. Local ships supplement the expresses. In any such planning you should know that there are two portions of the long journey that are excitingly scenic, namely the first four morning hours from Passau to Linz, where the river winds between steep wooded banks, and the two afternoon hours of the lovely, Rhine-like Wachau, from Melk to Krems.

I should conclude this report on the DDSG (initials for the company's long-winded name in German) by stating that it has a hydrofoil called the *Delphin* (Dolphin) that provides excellent excursion services between Vienna and Linz, or vice versa, with halts at Krems, Dürnstein and Melk; and finally, there is a trio of *Donaubus* ships interestingly named *Maria, Kriemhild* and *Juliane,* for more localized excursions. An address for general information is: DDSG Direktion; Hintere Zollamtsstrasse 1, 1031 Vienna.

Interpolation: For Those Who Halt or Board at Linz

Linz, the animated capital of Upper Austria, is the third city in the republic, following Graz, with almost 200,000 inhabitants, yet it attracts little tourist attention, chiefly, I suppose, because it is on the direct route, both from north and west, to the country's greatest of all attractions, Vienna. It shares the fate of Amiens on the way to Paris, or even Zurich on the way to Lucerne. (The Tourist Information Bureau, Fremdenverkehrsamt, for those who wish maps and folders, is conspicuous on the Hauptplatz.)

I suppose that three out of four foreign visitors who stop at this city are music lovers concerned to visit the superb *Abbey of St. Florian,* six miles from the center, where Anton Bruckner, a native son of Upper Austria, was long organist of the abbey church (later of the Court Chapel in Vienna) and where he now lies buried in the church crypt. In early July, a Danube Festival Week is an event of Linz and St. Florian, and needless to say, Austria's great 19th-century composer is its chief inspiration, one or more of his works being played at virtually every concert during the big week.

The abbey is a notable sight in itself, one of the outstanding treasures of Christian architecture. It was founded in the year 555 to honor a Roman legionary named Florian who was drowned in the River Enns about the year 300 because he, as a convinced

Christian, refused to sacrifice to the Roman gods. Later, this martyr was canonized. The original abbey was built over St. Florian's tomb and was rebuilt in its present baroque style in the 17th and 18th centuries. The Stairway Hall, the Marble Hall and the smaller Kaiser-Zimmer are among its chief features. There is also a Bruckner-Zimmer, containing Bruckner's grand piano, brought here from Vienna.

Linz is, of course, the main port of call of the Danube steamers and for that reason it is of special importance to the tour planner. By river, this city is 130 miles from Vienna, miles that include, as we've seen, the best of the Danube scenery. By present summer schedules the steamers, mostly big sidewheelers, leave Linz at 11:20 A.M. daily and reach Vienna at 7:50 P.M., this despite almost a dozen halts, which, after all, add their little excitements to the pleasures of the day. Can there be any better way to arrive in the well-loved national capital than to "sail into it" on the great stream with which it is so closely identified in song?

The Danube Day, a Syllabus of High Points

A personally drawn syllabus of high points, set down in order and by number, may guide your sightseeing eyes, and a detailed Danube map, purchasable on the ship, will lend substance to these notes. Here, I think, are things for you to watch for with special care.

MORNING

1. *Burg Viechtenstein* (right).
2. *Schloss Marsbach* (left).
3. *Schloss Neuhaus* (left).
4. *The Jochenstein* (in midstream), a small, dramatic, shrine-crowned rock that Austrian romantics call "the little sister of the Lorelei."
5. *Schloss Ottensheim* (left), seen just before the steamer reaches Linz.

AFTERNOON

6. *Melk* (right), dominated by its huge Benedictine abbey on a wooded height. The town, quite hidden from the river, was founded in Roman times and became the seat of the Babenberg dynasty from its coming to power in 976 until the beginning of the 12th century.
7. *Schönbühel* (right), a spectacular castle looming up on a cliff close to the river, supplemented by another striking building, the *Servitenkloster,* rising from a ledge about a hundred yards downstream.
8. *Schloss Aggstein* (right), an extremely dramatic castle situated on a lofty bluff. Below it is the photogenic village of Aggsbach.
9. *Spitz* (left), a village in the vineyard-covered heart of the Wachau. For miles and miles all up and down this side of the Wachau, the banks become a glory of apricot and peach blossoms in spring, temporarily eclipsing the soberer green of the vineyards.
10. *Dürnstein* (left), the village where Richard Coeur-de-Lion, King of England, having been captured upon his return from a Crusade to the Holy Land, was held prisoner (in 1193) by Duke Leopold VI, and where Blondel, his faithful minstrel, found him. One of Dürnstein's leading hotels today (directly on the Danube) is named in the crusader's honor *Gasthof Richard Löwenherz.* If I were to pick one Danube village for my holidays it would be, I think, Dürnstein, for quite aside from its historical significance it is thoroughly appealing to the eye. So steeply do the cliffs soar up from the river's edge that a new Danube Highway has had to bore *under* the town, through a 500-yard tunnel. The vineyards of Dürnstein, and even more those of the next village, *Loiben,* produce some of Austria's best wines.
11. *Stein-Und-Krems* (left), a triune town of some size at the lower end of the Wachau. Stein, with a huge Federal jail, is ingloriously known as the Austrian Sing Sing. Und (And) is undoubtedly the only town in the world so named. One

feels that it should dress itself up by assuming the name Ampersand! Und is a *separate* town, separately governed. Krems, once a residence of Margareta Maultasch, is now a prime goal of Danube tourism, with a score of hotels.
12. *Vienna* lies 45 miles, or three hours' sail, downstream from Krems. The steamer ties up at the Reichsbrücke, which was dismally known as *Die Brücke der Roten Armee* (The Bridge of the Red Army) during the long Russian occupation, but jubilantly took its "right name" again upon the Reds' departure. From the Reichsbrücke it is but a few minutes' taxi ride to the heart of the capital.

ROUNDUP, CHAPTER 4: LODGING, EATING, SHOPPING

This chapter covers only small communities, with the one exception of Linz and a smidgen of Bavaria's Passau, for the Danube trip, but even so, a listing of some essentials may be needed.

Hotels on the Styrian Mountainway

Bad Aussee: Hotel Erzherzog Johann has just the name one would expect in this area, honoring the beloved Archduke who married the postmaster's daughter. *Hotel Paradies,* new, is about as good, but in this case perhaps romance should outfavor Paradise.

Altaussee: Hotel am See (Hotel at-the-Lake) is the one my text above reported as a special personal favorite of mine, so close to the lake as to be almost *on* it. It is now enhanced by a new indoor swimming pool.

Mitterndorf boasts two deluxe hotels, the newish *Grimmingblick,* with pool; and *Kurhotel Bad Heilbrunn,* at the like-named spa on the town's southern outskirts. In this Kurhotel, "looming" 8 stories high, a couple spend $18 for a double room and bath, which is a lot for rural Austria, but again, this *is* a spa, and it is one of the most up-to-date in Austria, beautifully equipped.

Admont has no really first-class hotel, but I have found the *Sulzer* and the *Post* quite acceptable. This interesting village, with its great abbey library deserves a new hotel, or better, a lovely Gasthof, supplementing the present presentable inn called *Gasthof Traube* (Bunch of Grapes).

Gstatterboden, which aroused my enthusiasm as a stopover place on the Styrian Mountain Route, has no hotel to write home about, but I have stayed pleasurably in the modest *Hotel Gesäuse,* named for the "brawling" of the River Enns.

Mariazell has about a dozen hotels and Gasthöfe, the leaders being the *Feichtegger* and *Drei Hasen* (Three Hares), but few Americans seem yet to have discovered it as a health center. Perhaps the pilgrim atmosphere makes them hesitate.

Separate restaurants worth listing on this mountainway scarcely exist, but one note should creep in here, namely the restaurant, or Stube, within the Benedictine abbey at Admont.

Hotels on the Danube Route

Passau, in case you spend a night in that Bavarian riverport prior to sailing for Vienna (but you may sleep on the ship) has the *Schloss Ort, if* it is in operation when you get there, at the exciting point where three rivers unite, the Inn, the Ilz and the Danube. Failing this, you should find the *Weisser Hase* (White Rabbit) acceptable. I, at any rate, have gladly made do there. Passau is Europe's forgotten city, and *should not* suffer that fate, for it has a lot to offer.

A modest but well-placed *restaurant* of Passau is the *Ratskeller,* whose large Danube-side terrace is within sight of the steamer you will board. A more central restaurant is the *Heilig-Geist* (Holy Ghost) *Stiftskeller,* with a *Weinstube* that dates back to 1358.

Linz

This large and lively city has a dozen or more hotels, headed by the centrally placed *Park,* and now aided and abetted by a good *Esso Motor Hotel,* a link of the Europe-wide chain. I have stayed in several of these links, or units, and have found them thoroughly satisfactory and even with considerable charm as an extra ingredient. This one, also with its quota of charm, is on the city's outskirts some 2 miles from the center. The main restaurant, café and shopping street is Landstrasse, with the huge and rambling *Klosterhof Restaurant,* once the library of an abbey, at Number 30. A pastry specialty of the city is a nutty, many-caloried tempter called *Linzertorte.* To sample it just stroll on Landstrasse and locate either the *Goethe Café* or the *Konditorei Wagner.* Another conspicuous tempter is *Café Traxlmayr,* which is on the Promenade, a square adjacent to Landstrasse. Shopping on this "Main Street" of Linz can be a foretaste of Vienna, but the shops do not seem to display many things distinctive of Linz, unless, perhaps, in the field of leather goods, including nice gift items.

Melk

This important tourist goal and steamer halt should have a first-class hotel, but up to now it contents itself with several small Gasthöfe, led by the *Goldener Stern* and the *Weisses Rössel* (so spelled). At Ybbs an der Donau, a river village a bit upstream from Melk, there is a very much liked *Royal Hotel Weisses Rössel* (so spelled) which makes two white horses that have an extra *e* in their names as against one, the famous lakeside inn at St. Wolfgang, that gets along fine without it. Perhaps it's like Smith and Smythe, or Clark and Clarke.

5 / VIENNA

    Wien, Wien, Nur Du Allein

"Vienna, thou alone" has been sung with spontaneity and enthusiasm by thousands, yes millions, of Vienna addicts. The song has personified that impalpable something which this city has and other cities wish they had. There is an unflagging freshness about its gay life that is inimitable, defying the centuries to stamp it out, and I do not adhere to the gloomy theory that "the old gaiety departed forever with the Empire." Of course there is a glitter about imperial courts. There is pomp and circumstance. There are brilliant uniforms and medals, but to me Vienna's innate spirit transcends all these things and is not killed by their demise.

> *"Dort wo die alten Häuser steh'n,*
> *Dort wo die lieblichen Mädchen geh'n."*

How inevitable is the mention of the "lovely girls," yet there is nothing of the satyr's wink in this line. Quite the contrary. Lovely girls were made to fill the picture. They are a part of Vienna and a most important part. Rejoice in their presence, says the song. Take them to a café in the Prater or to Grinzing's wine gardens. Take them to the romantic Wienerwald. Dance with them in the Stadtpark. Invite them to hillside restaurants like Cobenzl or Kahlenberg.

    Dancing unintroduced, by the way, is done in Austria, as in

Germany and Scandinavia, though perhaps in a humbler class of establishments such as the popular "lower-middlebrow" dance-cafés, where casual comradeship of the dance floor burgeons with ease and naturalness. This is the direct antithesis of the Latin-American idea that a "nice" girl will never, throughout her whole life, dance with anyone except the man to whom she is betrothed or married. I have experienced that amazing inhibition in the small cities of Central and South America, and even in pre-Castro Cuba, and I have experienced its opposite in Central Europe and the North. My unqualified vote is for the European idea.

> *Wien, Wien, nur du allein*
> *Sollst stets die Stadt meiner Träume sein,*
> *Dort wo ich glücklich und selig bin*
> *Ist Wien, ist Wien, mein Wien.*

Die Stadt meiner Träume (the city of my dreams) is a city of reality to increasing thousands of overseas visitors each summer and most of them, like the writer of this song, find themselves *glücklich und selig* (lucky and happy) here. Vienna has a scattering of nightclubs, some of them with lavish and excellent shows, but they seem to me somewhat alien to the city's spirit, a concession to internationalism, a rather un-Viennese snatching at artificial and presumably lucrative gaieties.

In summer, Vienna is an *outdoor city,* even in the evening. You may, with luck, have the chance to enjoy a starlight operetta in the courtyard of Schönbrunn Castle (usually in connection with the June Festival), perhaps Schubert's *Das Dreimäderlhaus* or Johann Strauss's *Der Zigeunerbaron,* or you may attend a gay concert (any Tuesday or Friday evening by present arrangements) in the huge *Arkadenhof,* a courtyard of the Rathaus where 3000 people may be seated, or you may experience an evening at Cobenzl, overlooking the city. If you are in a very folksy mood and in the company of friends you may have fun in the lowbrow but cheerful "Buffoon Prater" (Wurstelprater), or you may indulge in good talk in a Ring café, though these, I have sadly to report, are diminishing in number as "progress" finds more lucrative uses for Ring space. By daylight you may try out one of the sumptuous outdoor thermal baths in Baden, a bit south of the capital, or enjoy a canoe ride on the Old Danube or a few hours loitering in the forest.

I am by no means trying to be "wholesome." Nightclubs, movies and other indoor attractions have their definite place in the world's pattern, even in summer, but one likes, when in Vienna, to "go Viennese." Given reasonably clement weather the city lends itself to all that spells outdoors.

NINE PRACTICAL MATTERS—ON ENTERING VIENNA

Hotels, Motels, Inns and Castle Inns
Be it understood that this comment on Austria's tourist accommodations is not intended to cover any specific hotels in Vienna or elsewhere, for these will be covered at the ends of the successive chapters as each city or rural area comes up, along with specific restaurants and places of night entertainment. This is merely an explanation of the various types of lodging available to the tourist, and here they are: *Hotels* are as in any other country. *Motels* have not made great inroads into Austria but their number and spread will certainly increase. The Esso chain has come into the picture, with its first unit in Linz, and Pan American Airways, in conjunction with Gulf Oil, has announced that it will enter the European motel field, placing comfort and charm on equal levels, a move that should encourage other large companies to seek their share of tourist favor. A *Gasthof* is usually a good-sized inn, not too pretentious as a rule, but often very comfortable and with colorful design and decor. A *Gasthaus,* or *Gästehaus,* to pluralize the word for guest, is usually smaller, folksier, more personal, more family oriented. *Castle Hotels* are a big and alluring subject, for no less than 32 of them rate official listing in the pamphlet *Your Castle in Austria.* A truly wonderful and glamorous element is provided by them for our enjoyment, and I must say that many of them cater forthrightly to romance-hungary Americans. Some are genuine castles dating from way-back centuries, when they were also strongholds, and retaining their essential character while conced-

ing that plumbing is better in this century than in, say, the 13th, and acting accordingly. Others are less old, and more in the category of splendid mansions or hunting lodges converted into hotels, while a few, but very few, might fit into the picture more as luxury hotels than as honest-to-goodness castles, which does not at all mean that they are fakes. Not one of them could be thus ticketed. And that's enough for this preview of accommodations, except that I might add the *spas,* where some establishments provide a combination of health cure and first-rate accommodations and dining rooms. Such places often bear the title *Kurhaus,* meaning literally Cure House.

Austrian Foods and Drinks

Any comment on the culinary specialties of Austria, and they are special indeed, real tastebud-tinglers, should be preceded by a general listing of food names in the German language. A basic food vocabulary is essential to any visitor's study of German or Austrian menu cards and therefore, inviting those who know the whole story to skip it here, I will erect a few simple guideposts. (Spelling note: All nouns in German are spelled with an initial capital letter.)

Fertige Speisen means ready-cooked dishes.
Vorspeisen—"Fore" dishes.
Nachspeisen or *Mehlspeisen*—desserts.
Eis—ice cream.
Tagesspeise—the day's special.
Tagessuppe—the day's soup.
Kraftbrühe—consommé.
Eier—eggs.
Braten und Geflügel—roasts and poultry.
Beilagen or *Gemüse*—vegetables.
Obst—fruit.

Schweinebraten—roast pork. Any word which contains *Schwein* means that it comes from the versatile pig and you can probably guess the rest.

Kalbsbraten—roast veal. Kalb means calf and this tag will throw a light on many dishes.

Rinderbraten—roast beef. Anything with *Rind* means beef in some form.

Nierenbraten—roast loin (of veal).
Schlegelbraten—roast fillet (of veal).
Huhn (in various combinations)—fowl or chicken.
Schinken (and its combinations)—ham: (bacon is *Speck*).
Ochsenzunge—oxtongue.
Hummer—lobster.
Forelle—trout.

Among vegetables, the following names quickly become familiar:

Kartoffel—potato.
Erbsen—green peas.
Rotkohl—red cabbage.

Grüner Salat)
or *Kopf Salat*)—lettuce.
Bohnen—beans.
Spargel—asparagus.

Among fruits are the following:

Äpfel—apples.
Kirschen—cherries.
Ananas—pineapple.
Aprikosen—apricots. (Also *Marillen*)

Apfelsinen—oranges.
Birnen—pears.
Pfirsiche—peaches.
Pflaumen—plums.

Perhaps the vegetables and fruits could take care of themselves, even for those who have little or no German, but there is no doubt that the meats listed on the average German menu are a puzzle to many tourists. If one merely learns and remembers to which animals the combinations of *Schwein, Kalb, Rind* and *Schinken* belong, and that *Huhn* is a bird and *Hummer* a crustacean, that meager information alone will be the key to most menu problems.

Beer can be had everywhere in amounts varying from six-twentieths of a liter to half a liter (about a pint), or even more, both in *helles* (light) and *dunkles* (dark) types. Most tourists prefer *helles*. *Krug* (Jug) is a word for the thirsty man to know. Its lesser brother is *Krügl. Bier vom Fass* is beer on tap. The wines of Austria will be discussed below.

Finally, on the subject of eating and drinking, here are a few powerful words and phrases to know. *Frühstuck* is breakfast; *Mittagessen* is noon meal; *Abendessen* is evening meal. *Die Speisekarte* is the menu card. *Die Rechnung* is the bill (or one may say "*Be-*

zahlen, bitte," I wish to pay, please). To call the waiter one says *"Herr Ober"* (never, nowadays, the humbler word *Kellner);* or if it is a waitress one says simply *"Fräulein,"* even if she is the mother of ten children.

Typical Austrian fare is best known, of course, for its *Wiener Schnitzel,* the delicious breaded veal cutlet that has carried the city's name to all the civilized tables of the world. Excellent *Gemischter* (Mixed) *Salat* often accompanies the Schnitzel. Other delights are *Tiroler Knödeln* (Tyrolean dumplings), *Wiener Backhuhn,* much like our Southern fried chicken, *Gulasch* (so spelled in German) and various noodle *(Nudeln)* concoctions; and for rolls, the good *Wiener Semmeln.* These often come spiced with *Kümmel,* which is caraway seed, and if you don't like caraway, as I desperately don't, just say to the waiter, "Semmeln ohne Kümmel, bitte."

For dessert, Vienna is a traveler's dream, partly because of its delicate pastries. Give special thought to *Sachertorte,* a rich chocolate cake taking its name from the famous Sacher Hotel in Vienna. A standard dessert that never loses its popularity is *Apfelstrudel,* a German and Austrian version of apple pie. More specifically Austrian, a favorite too little known to tourists is *Kaiserschmarrn,* a sweet pancakelike affair full of raisins; but the emperor of all desserts is *Salzburger Nockerl,* which is a real production, a light and superlatively delicate soufflé made of egg yolks, sugar and flour. It should be eaten immediately upon its reaching your table, for it would otherwise soon collapse. Actually, your meal should be timed to meet this wondrous delicacy as its climax. And with the dessert, *coffee,* in the city that *invented the public café,* if not coffee itself. Served with *Schlagobers,* meaning gobs of thick whipped cream, Viennese coffee is the very sign and symbol of the city. If, however, you wish a demitasse of black coffee instead of the big white-capped cup, order a "Mokka." A variation of the small cup, served with whipped cream piled high over the brim, is locally (in Vienna) called an *Einspänner* (a one-horse carriage).

As for taller beverages to accompany your meals, the two in most universal demand are, of course, Austrian beers and wines. There are many good beers, favorites of my own palate being

Schwechater and Styria's good *Gösser*. A very popular soft drink is *Apfelsaft* (apple juice).

Austrian wines are good and varied, though it should be known that four-fifths of them are white. Some of the well-loved names—and don't let their polysyllables throw you—are *Klosterneuburger,* red or white types; *Vöslauer,* red; *Gumpoldskirchner, Nussberger, Hohenwarther,* white. Other white types, all from vineyards on the Danube's banks and all with splendid jawbreaking names, are *Kremser Sandgrube, Dürnsteriner Katzensprung* and *Loibner Kaiserwein*. From Burgenland vineyards bordering the Neusiedlersee come *Oggauer* (red), a personal favorite of mine, and *Ruster* (both red and white). And above all, know about the *Heuriger* wines of Grinzing, served in the cheerful little wine taverns and gardens of the Vienna suburb of that name. Heuriger wines are *new* wines, from last autumn's grapes. They may seem maidenly mild but they presently make you merry, and then—watch out. Go easy at Grinzing.

Service Charges, Taxes, Tips

Austria, like all Western European countries, imposes a service charge *(Bedienungsgeld)* on all hotel, restaurant and bar bills, the hotel charge being 10 or 15 per cent, depending on the category of the hotel and the length (or shortness) of your stay. Restaurant and bar charges are usually 10 per cent, but there is also a drink tax of 10 percent, and if hard liquor is taken there is an extra 10 per cent alcohol tax. The word for tax is *Steuer*. Fortunately for the guests' composure, hotel and restaurant service charges and taxes are almost always included in the bill, at least in Vienna and in most of the places where Americans are likely to visit. Many Americans leave small extra tips after meals, and I mean really *small*. It is unfortunate when big spenders advertize their wealth by leaving as much extra as the charge itself. This makes it awkward for Austrians and for tourists of middle means who do not like to seem stingy by comparison. Upon leaving a hotel it is expected that the guest will leave a small extra for the maid, say 5 schillings minimum for one night and 20 or 25 for a week's stay. The hotel's hall porter should certainly be remembered, too, for he

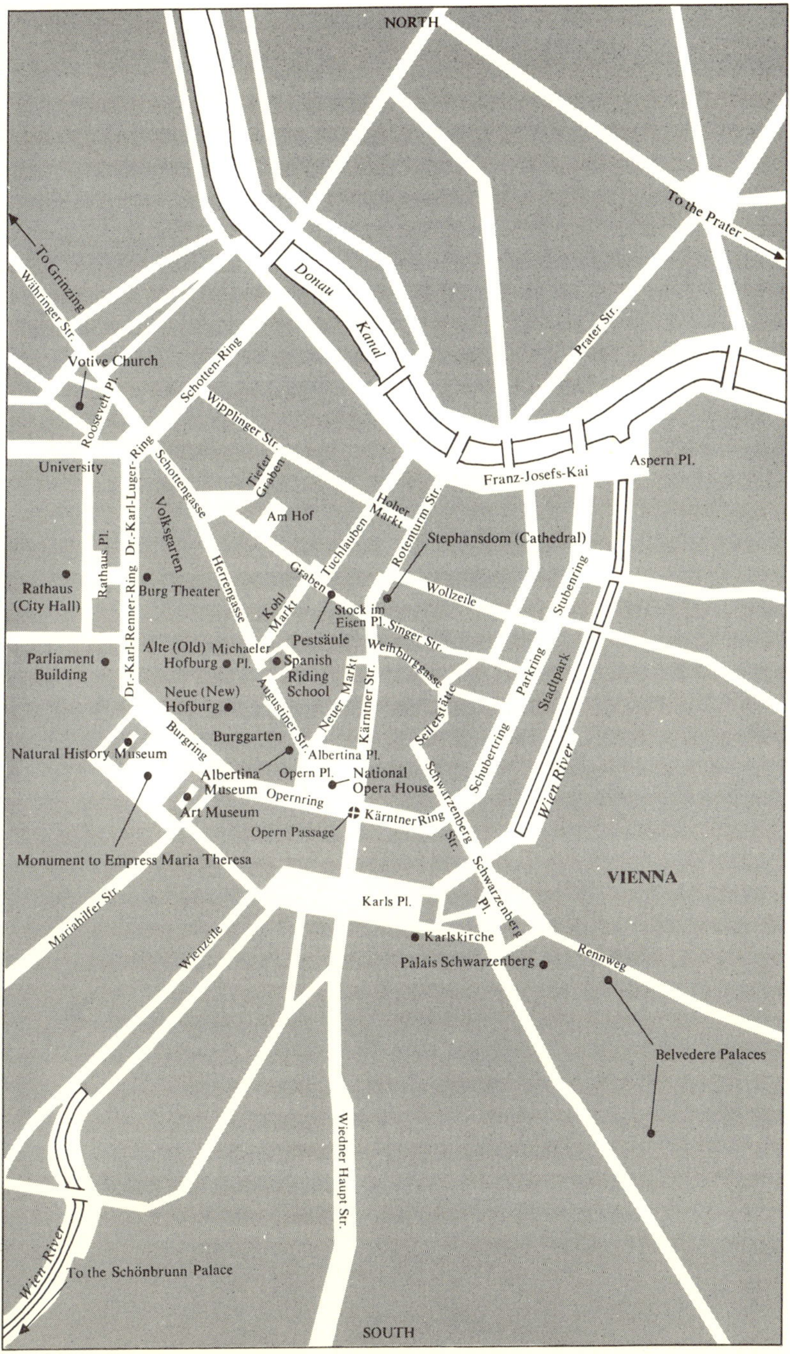
NORTH
To the Prater
To Grinzing
Währinger Str.
Donau Kanal
Prater Str.
Votive Church
Roosevelt Pl.
Schotten-Ring
Wipplinger Str.
University
Dr.-Karl-Luger-Ring
Schottengasse
Tiefer Graben
Franz-Josefs-Kai
Aspern Pl.
Hoher Markt
Rotenturm Str.
Am Hof
Volksgarten
Tuchlauben
Stephansdom (Cathedral)
Rathaus Pl.
Dr.-Karl-Renner-Ring
Herrengasse
Graben
Stubenring
Wollzeile
Rathaus (City Hall)
Burg Theater
Kohl Markt
Stock im Eisen Pl.
Singer Str.
Pestsäule
Parliament Building
Alte (Old) Hofburg
Michaeler Pl.
Spanish Riding School
Weihburggasse
Parkring
Stadtpark
Neue (New) Hofburg
Augustiner Str.
Neuer Markt
Kärntner Str.
Seilerstätte
Burggarten
Burgring
Natural History Museum
Albertina Pl.
Schubertring
Albertina Museum
Opern Pl.
National Opera House
Opernring
Art Museum
Kärntner Ring
Opern Passage
Schwarzenberg Str.
Wien River
Monument to Empress Maria Theresa
VIENNA
Schwarzenberg Pl.
Mariahilfer Str.
Karls Pl.
Wienzeile
Karlskirche
Palais Schwarzenberg
Rennweg
Belvedere Palaces
Wiedner Haupt Str.
To the Schönbrunn Palace
Wien River
SOUTH

is an important functionary of any good hotel, and can frequently make the difference between the success and failure of your stay.

Laundry and Its Problems

Good hotels seem to vary greatly in the way they handle guests' laundry. Some have laundry bags and printed charge lists at the ready, while others, equally good, may have nothing at all in the room to tell you how the matter is handled, in which case you must call up the bell captain or the housekeeper, or, better yet in my experience, find your chambermaid (call *"Zimmermädchen"*) and just give her the laundry. By signs and struggles, if you know no German, you can always get across to her the time when you must have it back. Most hotels charge extra, say 25 per cent, for 24-hour service, but in some the standard practice is to get the things back to you in the late afternoon of the same day, if you deliver them by 9 or 9:30 o'clock. In some cases the chambermaid, or porter or housekeeper, writes down on the list the date that return is desired, and here is one of those strange confusions that persist, it seems, forever. Europeans, when putting dates in figures, put the day first, the month second, whereas we put the month first and the day second. If the day is the 12th of the month or lower this can muddle things badly. For example, June 7 in America is 6.7.Year, whereas in Europe it is 7.6.Year. Why the two sides of the Atlantic cannot resolve this confusion is beyond my understanding.

Shopping, Shop Hours

Shopping in Austria, enhanced by price levels that are, at present exchange rates, the lowest in Central Europe, is a major feminine sport, and those women who practice it often find it an addictive drug. Men, too, are known to succumb when they gaze into shop windows, say on Vienna's Kärntnerstrasse, or Salzburg's Getreidegasse or Innsbruck's Maria-Theresien Strasse. The things in the capital that tempt most dangerously, and the shops wherein they lurk, will be discussed at the end of the Vienna coverage, but I may name here some specialties, pointing out first that *handicrafts* of many types are Austria's pride. Petit point articles, especially handbags and purses in great variety, are typical of the infinite care and flawless taste revealed by so many handmade articles. (We'll take a closer look at petit point in our Vienna shopping roundup.) Others are embroidered blouses, leathercraft, especially fine bags and wallets, superb articles in glassware, works of art in Augarten porcelain (including lovely figurines), knitwear, skisportwear and everything else connected with skiing, and finally, *Trachten* (peasant costumes), including dirndlwear and lodencloth. Lodencloth is lamb's wool material made rough and strong and incredibly durable.

I'll escape from the snare of naming more products of Austrian skills by stating that shopping hours in Vienna are theoretically from 8 A.M. (early birds take note) to 12:30; and from 2:30 to 6 o'clock. Actually, most of the shops in the city's center stay open continuously from 8 to 6, at least during the high tourist season.

Photography and Photographic Supplies

Our note on this subject can be short and sweet, since Austria poses no special problems for the shutterbug and cooperates by offering ample supplies of black and white and color film at shops all over the country. The only real threat is Austria's scenery, which challenges the cameraman, and woman, with ruthless persistence.

Language Notes; the Valiant Score

A menace to dabblers in a foreign language can be a too-ambitious list of several hundred words and phrases that are proposed as musts, whereas, for the average traveler, especially in Germany and Austria, where "tourist American" is known to some extent in nearly every hotel of standing and in most shops and offices, far fewer would suffice. I would propose a single valiant score, meaning *twenty*, which can be learned quickly, almost effortlessly and enduringly. Here, then, are my own personally chosen twenty (with a bonus of one), starting with the "courtesy six" and followed by words of greeting:

Thank you .... *Danke sehr, Danke Schön* or *Vielen Dank*

I beg your pardon	*Verzeihen Sie,* or simply the French *Pardon,* which is as universally understood, as is O.K.
I'm (very) sorry	*Es tut mir (sehr) Leid*
Please	*Bitte*
Don't mention it	*Bitte sehr,* or merely *Bitte*
Very good	*Sehr gut*
Good morning	*Guten Morgen*
Good day	*Guten Tag,* or, very frequently in Austria and Bavaria, *Grüss Gott* (God greet you)
Good evening	*Guten Abend*
Good night	*Gute Nacht*
What time is it?	*Wieviel Uhr ist es?*
Today; Tomorrow	*Heute; Morgen*
Where is	*Wo ist* (which should be preceded by the polite *"Bitte"*)
— a garage	*eine Garage*
— a bank	*eine Bank*
— the post office	*die Post*
— the breakfast room	*das Frühstückzimmer* (a goal that is sometimes surprisingly hard to locate)
— the toilet	*die Toilette*
Right; Left; Straight ahead	*Rechts; Links; Geradeaus*
What does that (this) cost?	*Wieviel kostet das (dieses)?*
Till we meet again (Au revoir)	*Auf Wiedersehen,* or, frequently in Austria, *Auf Wiederschauen*

Metric Measurements and Weights

Britain has definite plans to abandon its clumsy, centuries-old system of weights and measures, which the United States unfortunately inherited. I think even a date has been set for this fearfully difficult and costly changeover, namely 1975. Obviously, our country must and will come to it, however horrendous the job. Meanwhile, let us understand how to reconcile the two systems so that weights and measures may be understood.

Most international air travelers are well aware that the metric kilogram (kilo) or weight is considered to be 2.2 pounds, though it is actually a trifle more than that (2.2046). And motorists in Europe are aware that a kilometer is reckoned at 0.62 of a mile, though it is actually 0.62137. Many measurements of things that concern the traveler, including altitudes of resorts and mountain summits, are given in meters, the rough equivalent of one meter being 39 inches, and the more exact equivalent 39.37 inches. An approximation that may help the American or British tourist to change meters into yards is to consider that one meter equals one yard and one-tenth. The meter is divided into centimeters (hundredths) and millimeters (thousandths). The sightseer encounters meters and centimeters very frequently and should be able mentally to "translate" them into our clumsy forms. In weights, to revert to that part of the metric system, all bathroom scales (and others) in Europe give your weight in kilos and it is really important to be able to do some swift transposing of the figures. Just multiply by two and add 10 per cent, plus a trifle more.

Thermometers: Celsius into Fahrenheit

In the early 1700s Anders Celsius, a Swedish astronomer, devised the temperature scale that now bears his name—it used to be called Centigrade, and often still is—placing the freezing point at zero degrees and the boiling point of water under normal atmospheric conditions at seaboard at 100 degrees, surely a good and logical system. At about the same time Gabriel Daneil Fahrenheit, a German physicist, native of Danzig in what was formerly East Prussia, devised another system, placing the freezing point at 32 degrees and the boiling point at 212. Needless to say, Britain, and then the United States, adopted the clumsier Fahrenheit system. Well, to make the best of a bad deal, you may quite easily change Celsius into Fahrenheit simply by doubling the Celsius figure, subtracting 10 per cent and then adding 32. Let us take 21 degrees Celsius for an example and see how it works out: $21 \times 2 = 42$; minus 10 per cent = 37.8, plus 32 = 69.8, a good American room temperature. It is easier to change C. into F. than the other way around, and fortunately the former is exactly what most tourists in Europe wish to do. But in case mathematical curiosity stirs you, be advised that of several formulae for changing F. to C. the easiest, for me at least, is this: Subtract 32 from the F. figure, then divide the result by 9 and multiply by 5. Maybe the "new math" has some simpler method, but I must content myself with the old math.

FINDING YOUR WAY AROUND IN VIENNA

Vienna is a vast metropolis of nearly two million inhabitants and an area of 134 square miles divided into 23 districts (Bezirke). Firsttime visitors often expect to find the Danube (Donau in German) flowing directly through the city, as the Seine flows through Paris or the Thames through London, but this is not the case. A relatively narrow canalized part of it called the *Donaukanal* does flow through it, flanking the Inner City, but the main stream skirts the northeastern edge of the city and is, in turn, divided into two parts, the so-called Old Danube (Alte Donau) making an arc farther to the northeast. The insignificant River Wien, name-giver to the city, flows harmlessly from the west past Schönbrunn Palace, disappearing under pavements and parks as it nears the center, and reappearing in the Stadtpark to trickle finally into the Danube Canal. (Occasionally this tiny river floods, causing damage.)

Orientation is not difficult in Vienna, though I have found it less easy than in Paris. To sense the topography of the Inner City (District I) and the Ring around it, which constitute three quarters of all that matters to tourism, you may think of the base of a tea caddy, since that is its general shape, as any map will reveal. Its base is the Danube Canal and the remainder of it is the Ring, under eight successive names, all of which include the word Ring. Within this canal and Ring are the Opera House and the gleaming Burgtheater, the huge sprawling Hofburg (former Imperial Palace), the Volksgarten and the Burggarten, and in the very nucleus of the Inner City, the Stephansdom, Vienna's beloved archiepiscopal cathedral. Straight to this nucleus, from the Ring, runs the Kärntnerstrasse, main street of shoppers, strollers and city life, though undergoing convulsions at the moment because of the city's belated labors in the construction of a central subway system. On the outer rim of the Ring lie many great buildings, including the Museum of Fine Arts, the Natural History Museum, the Palace of Justice, the Parliament Building, the Rathaus and the University. The Stadtpark and the Rathauspark are also on this outer rim and the Karlskirche and the Votivkirche are but one lift farther out. The Ring is majestic, grand and grandiose. Nothing comparable to it, on such a scale, exists in any other European city.

Far outside the Ring, Vienna wears an outside Girdle (Gürtel) that runs for many miles in a rough parallel to the Ring. The important West Station (for Linz, Salzburg, Innsbruck, etc.) and also the South Station (for the Semmering, Graz, Carinthia, etc.) are on the Gürtel.

I do not believe it is important for the average visitor to attempt any mastery of Vienna's complex system of transportation but a few things *are* of great help to those who don't wish to be bound solely to taxis and footwork, and to those who simply *cannot get taxis* when they need them. As in any great city, taxis are often too few at rush hours, and you would save yourself from weariness and exasperation by learning, through your hall porter, where taxi stands and other "likely corners" are located. If you add to this a knowledge of where the chief hotels (whose doormen can help you) are to be found, your forethought should rival that of the Wise Virgins.

Inside the Ring there are no streetcars. There are a few busses but the distances are so negligible that most visitors disregard them and stick to footwork. On and outside the Ring there are many streetcar lines but the only ones frequently used by tourists are A and B, which follow the turnings of the Ring and the Danube Canal quay (combining to surround the whole Inner City) in a clockwise direction; and AK and BK, which do the same in a counterclockwise direction. A free use of these cars, which fairly "flow" in a continuous stream, can save a lot of tiring steps on the 3-mile Ring.

Orientation and sightseeing tours, with polyglot guides, are offered by *Austrobus,* with office at Dr. Karl Lueger-Ring 18, the usual starting point of the day tours (morning and afternoon) being in front of the Burgtheater (with free bus *to* this point from the Opera) and that of the night-life tours being on the Ring opposite the Rathaus. Since some tours cover Schönbrunn, and also such choice scenic spots as Cobenzl and Kahlenberg, most short-staying visitors learn the more outlying portions of Vienna the easy way —by rubberneck bus. The *Cosmos Reisebüro,* with office at Kärntnerring 15, offers competitive tours at similar prices.

6 / THE SIGHTSEER FOOTLOOSE IN VIENNA

"BE PREPARED"

The well-tempered tourist with experience behind him has learned how to make sightseeing as relaxed as it is stimulating. He knows he cannot see everything in the time he has, so he goes boy scout and prepares himself to see what he can and what he most desires to see. And so does *she,* his wife, and by no means always do their desires lightly meet. There is plenty, however, that both sides of any well-tempered traveling pair will surely wish to see in Vienna to fill several days. Then let them cut the ties that bind, pro tempore of course, he going his way and she hers. That way joy lies, and triumph. No one has pressed the panic button and the manifold wonders of this very great city are sifted through the sieve of sense.

An obvious way to be prepared is first of all to visit some information office, perhaps most easily the so-labeled *Information Opernpassage* in the underground "circus" I have mentioned at that nucleus of the city where the Ring and Kärntnerstrasse meet, in the lee of the Opera House. This is a branch of the Vienna City Tourist Association *(Fremdenverkehrsverband der Stadt Wien),* so it is official, dependable, with nothing to sell but help, and that its people don't *sell.* They give it to you in the form of many printed

/ 79

helps, and if needed, some spoken ones. The printed part is headed by their own pamphlet called simply VIENNA, packed with all the specific information anyone could desire, plus a 5-page, center-spread map of all the parts of the city that matter to tourists. Detailed maps of the entire city are, of course, available in the bookstores and kiosks, one good bookstore for guides and maps being in this very mart, underground.

Well informed and well mapped, you are ready to see much of Vienna in a short space of time. If you are tough fibered and don't mind frankly rushing about to see all you possibly can of the limitless cultural wealth offered by an unfamiliar metropolis, let no one laugh you out of it. People who are blessed with leisure enjoy heaping scorn on the rushers. They quite forget that these rushers may have only two or three days for Vienna in two or three decades and that they have come thousands of miles to see it. On the other hand, if you wish to view none of the great sights of Vienna but merely to live its life, relaxing in cafés and pleasure parks, let no one talk you out of *that.* Both ideas are sound, I believe, in a city so many-sided as this.

VIENNA'S GIFTS TO US

Vienna has given to mankind a wealth of gaiety, good cheer, stimulus for that very jolly occupation—living. We have noted already that it was the early home of Walther von der Vogelweide, greatest of the minnesingers, and of a less respectable but equally popular minstrel, *lieber Augustin.*

It seems that Augustin, who was the prince of vagabonds, owned nothing in the world except a dudelsack, a happy disposition and a big thirst. He lived during the reign of Leopold I at the time of the Great Plague, wandering about the city playing his dudelsack, and whenever he picked up a little money he got gloriously drunk. On one occasion he was shoveled from a gutter in which he was lying into an open grave with scores of corpses, for people were dying faster than they could be buried. The grave proved more comfortable than the gutter and Augustin had a fine long sleep. At length he awoke, refreshed and very happy, climbed out of the grave and strolled into a nearby eating place playing his dudelsack as usual. The people were amazed, for the news had circulated that poor Augustin was no more. He became a great hero, for it was obvious that the saints had intervened to raise him from the dead. But he did not let adulation go to his head. He remained a ragged minstrel, a charming, tipsy vagrant, who made people laugh in spite of the raging plague. He became to later generations a symbol of happiness in adversity. Few tourists visiting Vienna have any knowledge of Leopold I, but many know lieber Augustin, the emperor's lowliest subject, and they can sing his song, or at least hum the tune.

> *Oh, du lieber Augustin,*
> *'s Geld ist hin, 's Mench ist hin.*
> *Oh, du lieber Augustin,*
> *Alles ist hin.*

The city of Vienna has erected a beautiful fountain to her cheery son—it is two blocks west of the Palace of Justice on the corner of Neustiftgasse and Kellermanngasse—though oddly enough it pours forth a fluid with which lieber Augustin had little acquaintance—pure water.

During the minstrel's lifetime a spy of uncertain nationality, perhaps Polish, serving on behalf of Austria against the Turks, made a curious discovery. The plague had abated. The Turks had been driven away. This spy found some sacks of brown beans left behind by the Turks in their flight. He had performed valiant services for Austria, so he asked for these beans as his reward. He experimented in his headquarters outside the walls and soon succeeded in brewing from the beans a delicious drink. It occurred to him that he could make money out of the discovery. So he opened, on the little Domgasse, the first café. The new drink made a prodigious hit. And so Vienna gave to the world coffee, and more important still, the public café. One shudders to think what Europe would be like today without this institution.

I once hunted up, at Kolschitzkygasse 64, the very establishment (though others, such as the *Blaue Gans,* contest this) where the man Kolschitzky is claimed to have *brewed* the first experimental drink. There, in a café named for the man and displaying a big bronze statue of him in the act of pouring out his first cup, I sampled the beverage and pronounced it good, as I had a few thousand times before. I was amused to see that all the spoons were stamped *Kolschitzky Café—Gestohlen.* It seems that souvenir hunting in this establishment is not considered a permissible sport.

Close to the site of the first public café in the Domgasse a building still exists where, at the same time as coffee, the bread crescent was given to the world. This was first made by Peter and Eva Wendler, a baker and his wife, in mockery of the hated Turks. It was considered a good joke to eat the Turkish crescent while drinking the Turkish drink.

Good music, light perhaps, to set the feet tapping, but of high quality, complements good eating and drinking. It should have rhythm, grace, exquisite elegance. Vienna has produced such music in wholesale quantities. She has produced as well a great deal of the finest classical and church music. It is extraordinary how music of every sort that is good has flourished in this city. It can only be because virtually everyone, from Habsburg to common drudge, has always loved it. As regards this range we may recall that three of the Habsburg emperors, Maximilian, Leopold I and Josef I, were themselves musicians of some repute, and Franz Joseph, though not himself especially fond of music, patronized it effectively. He built the Opera. At the other end of the social scale, Vienna's humblest wage earners are often able to play, and criticize with discrimination, the classics of Austrian and German composers.

It is logical that such widespread musical appreciation has drawn to Vienna, over the centuries, a great many famous composers. I have entertained myself, at various times, by running down the exact locations where many of these men lived or died. Some of the houses are shown on the regular Austrobus and Cosmos city tours. (Their present uses may, in some cases, have changed since my checkups.)

Gluck, who conducted the Vienna opera for ten years and here wrote *Orpheus and Eurydice,* died at 32 Wiedner Hauptstrasse, now a business thoroughfare.

Haydn, who composed the national anthem *"Gott erhalte Franz den Kaiser,"* dear to Imperial Austria, and the *Creation Oratorio,* dear to all music lovers, died at Number 19 on the street named for him Haydngasse. It is now a Haydn Museum.

In the house at 8 Schulerstrasse, the same building running through to Domgasse 5 close to the Stephansdom, Mozart wrote *The Marriage of Figaro.* This is now the commemorative Mozart House. In other houses the composer wrote *The Magic Flute* and the *Requiem,* which is still performed every year in the chapel of the Hofburg. Mozart died in Vienna and was buried in the St. Marxer Friedhof, but the city, rich in living musicians, actually forgot his grave. One is shown today a stone which "probably" marks the spot where he lies.

Beethoven lived almost everywhere in Vienna and always in wonderful confusion and disorder. He was continually being chased out by irate landladies or sought, for some offense, by the magistrates of the law. Two of his Vienna homes, Mölkerbastei 8 and a house in Pfarrplatz, in the city's far-northern Heiligenstadt section, are memorials to the composer, but in a third home, at 5 Ungargasse, a street leading southeast from the Stadtpark, he completed his longest and perhaps most celebrated work, the *Ninth (Choral) Symphony,* most of which he had written in Baden bei Wien. I found a cobbler, a barber and a small hardware dealer at this address; also a furniture mover named Dworschak, who had in his window a chromo not of Beethoven but of the Port of Montreal!

At 9 Spiegelgasse, just off the Graben, Franz Schubert, a native Viennese, wrote the *Unfinished Symphony.* Today humble persons visit the house to toss off a glass of undistinguished wine at a small bar. Schubert was born at 54 Nussdorferstrasse, in a northern quarter, and this is now a Schubert Museum.

On the site of the house where Brahms died, in Karlsgasse, one now finds the annex of a Technical Academy.

And so one could go on, with so many names of Vienna's serious composers that it would read like a *Who's Who in Music,* yet it is with lighter music that many persons associate the Austrian capital. On two occasions, once in the Festsaal of the New Hofburg and once in the hall of the Gesellschaft für Musikfreunde, I have attended concerts entitled "Waltzes of the Dynasty-Strauss" given by the leading orchestras of Vienna. The entire program consisted of Strauss waltzes, some by Johann Strauss, *Vater,* some by Johann Strauss, *Sohn,* some by Eduard Strauss, *Enkel* (grandson). On the first occasion, which was many years ago, between wars, Grandson Strauss conducted the orchestra and even played the violin himself at times, as he led, a rather unconventional proceeding considering the dignity of the orchestra. This *Enkel* was the son of Eduard Strauss, who was a brother of Johann Strauss, *Sohn.* I have found entire evenings of Vienna waltzes a bit cloying, but the enthusiasm of the packed house was immense both times. It was the second of the dynasty, "the uncle of the Enkel," who wrote the most famous waltzes and who also brought the Viennese operetta to its pinnacle of popularity. At 54 Praterstrasse, where one may now buy sausages and hams, a tablet records the fact that in that house the second Strauss composed *The Beautiful Blue Danube.* The title of that famous composition is a charming piece of nonsense and one wonders that the sensitive Viennese let it pass. The Danube is, in general, majestic rather than beautiful and its blue is of a shade produced by silt of various shades, mostly brown or gray.

Many other composers have supplemented the efforts of the Strauss Dynasty in Vienna. There were Josef Lanner, Franz von Suppé (creator of the accordion's darling, *Poet and Peasant*), Franz Lehár *(Merry Widow)* and Leo Fall. I once attended a performance of one of Fall's operettas in a Vienna theater and thought it a very sprightly and melodic piece. It dealt with one of Europe's formerly favorite themes—an American millionaire portrayed as the perfect Philistine. (Europe's thought of us has gradually changed, at least to some extent, and in our favor.)

It is a striking tribute to the gay music of the Viennese operetta that it is still fighting a fairly successful battle with American rock all over the world. The masses, from New York to Tokyo, still like it, for it is aglow with romance and carefree gaiety.

In art, Vienna has contributed less than in other fields but in architecture its contribution is great, especially in the field of baroque, which is the outstanding feature of Viennese architecture.

At first I tried too earnestly to absorb its spirit and sometimes felt that I should be found in the gutter one day murmuring weakly that baroque did it, but I learned to love it, though not to the point of displacing my earlier love of Gothic. The vast enthusiasm which Vienna's style does evoke from some commentators proves that it can be downright intoxicating. One writer, who obviously knows what he is talking about, is drawn back in almost every paragraph to the city's *"liebliche Barock."* He cannot leave it and even finds baroque qualities in the bus conductor's method of collecting fares!

Baroque in Austria has been called the Counter-Reformation gesture of victory over the heretic, the effervescent reaction of the Triumphant Catholic Church from heretical austerity. Anyone must admire the daring grandeur of Fischer von Erlach's Karlskirche, with the two flanking Trajan columns which should, but do not, ruin the church. Anyone must admire the marvelous ensemble of the Belvedere Palaces. But when it comes to billowing stucco clouds, to gorgeous ornamentation laid on as thick as Viennese whipped cream, some viewers feel themselves sinking in the rich *Schlagobers.* The Pestsäule in the Graben has been called by G. E. R. Gedye the acid test for lovers of baroque. On first seeing it I felt myself a defeated man, but this monument too I finally came to like. Sort of.

In painting and sculpture Vienna shines more as a collector than as a producer. Few artists of great note have been natives of the city but the wonderful *Kunsthistorisches* (Fine Arts) *Museum* on the Ring is rivaled by few in Europe. Hundreds of famous paintings from many schools are to be seen here. Rubens, for instance, is at his best and a trifle less fleshy than in most of Europe's galleries. To be sure, the "Festival of Venus" is a voluptuous masterpiece and in another room the Flemish aritst's second wife, baby-faced, brown-eyed Helena Fourment, displays her corpulent nakedness little concealed by a fur cloak—very popular this painting—but Karl der Kühne (Charles the Bold of Burgundy) is the embodiment of virile, armor-clad manhood. A remarkable rufous light reflects from the lining of the warrior's cape upon his rugged face.

Rembrandt is superb, with two ruthless self-portraits, another pitiless picture of his poor, wrinkled, red-lidded old mother, and a wonderful old Jew with an open Hebrew Talmud on his kneees. The Breughel collection is the finest in the world and nearly all the other great painters of the Low Lands are here. And we find, of course, the Italians, including Raphael and Titian; the Germans, including Dürer, both the Holbeins and Lucas Cranach; the Spaniards, including, *very notably,* Velázquez; and even the English portraitists, though not at their best.

I very much like good portraits and this gallery is full of them. They need by no means be masterpieces to please my untutored gaze. If they depict a face which *must have been like that* it is almost enough for me. I noticed an odd, pale-colored portrait by one Christoph Plaudiss of an ancient man with white beard and wearing a deplorable slouch hat. He *must* have looked that way, for Plaudiss could not have invented him. Three portraits by the younger Hans Holbein left their images on my mental retina, one of a most unimportant little snub-nosed *Frau* in white cap and neckpiece, another of a very grim wife awaiting her husband's late return from "the club," the third of Königin Jane Seymour, Henry VIII's third wife, with lips most tightly pursed. Her jaunty Lord's amours may have been particularly trying that day. Other portraits that I cannot forget are: a Dürer of Johannes Kleeberger, with eyes that seem about to pop like two big kernels of corn; a Jakob Seisenegger of Archduke Ferdinand of Tyrol, most timid and apologetic of mien; a Quentin Metsys (or Quinten Massys) of a weary old man in a red garment with a skull beside him; a Bernhard Strigel of Maximilian I, with a nose like that of a macaw; a Bruyn the Elder of Cardinal Bernardus Clesius. The fat, red-robed prelate is in a dour mood and seems also to have just smelled something disagreeable. A Thin Man, marked merely "Niederländisch" and not in the museum catalogue, wore a hatchet face not to be forgotten.

These people are all as real as those of the worried, grim, exuberant, bitter, tired, facetious, overbearing, jolly persons who once possessed them. (It should be noted that even the vast acreage of this museum is far from sufficient for the display of all its treasures, so there are occasional reshufflings, but always the works exhibited are varied and interesting.)

Many other features than paintings (e.g. Egyptian, Greek, Roman antiquities, plastic and industrial arts, weapons, coins, jewels) make this museum a veritable Austrian Louvre, and in a large twin building across a grassy park from it there is another huge and important museum, this one of natural history. One could spend weeks in these two museums, but those who have no weeks to spend may forgo nine-tenths of the vast collections, saving time for a look at the bronze statue of Maria Theresa in the grassy park. She is seated amid her generals, firmly clutching in her hand the document of the Pragmatic Sanction.

One of the most amazing characters of history was this woman, and we may pause to consider her story. Maria Theresa (1717–1780) inherited the most desirable throne in Europe. In order to secure it for her, Charles VI, her father, who had no sons, proclaimed a new law permitting the daughter of a king to inherit the throne. This was the famous Pragmatic Sanction of history and Charles VI spent the last 20 years of his life securing the solemn acceptance of it, under oath, by every monarch in Europe. He died, and before he was cold those monarchs who had so solemnly sworn broke their oaths. They made a rush to seize the young queen's throne. Then she showed her mettle. With a strength, courage, native wit and knowledge of dramatic values that dazzled everyone, she faced the pack of wolves. Austria rallied to her to a man. Shs appeared before the Hungarian nobles at Pressburg, by some accounts with her infant Josef in her arms, and made a dramatic appeal. The Hungarians, with wild enthusiasm, pledged the last drop of their blood for their young queen. She fought off the pack of robber kings, outwitted them in diplomacy, humiliated them with stinging defeats, consolidated her vast, rambling empire and eventually passed it on to her son Josef in far better condition than it had ever been before.

One would suppose that all this excitement would have left to the empress little time for domestic affairs, but she bore to her consort, Francis of Lorraine, *sixteen* children, eleven girls and five boys. During much of the time when she was matching wits with the most powerful monarchs in Europe she was a nursing mother. Like most Austrian ladies of her time she became expert in embroidery and some of her finely executed work will be discussed in Chapter 7 in connection with a visit to Schloss Rabenstein.

From this digression about the empress we may return to Vienna's Gifts to Us and conclude the list of them with a salute to this city's wonderful work in lessening human affliction. I refer, of course, to the pioneering achievements of the medical faculty of Vienna's university. The most famous of these pioneers, such as Sigmund Freud, Alfred Adler, Adolf Lorenz, Julius Wagner-Jauregg and Eugen Steinach, have already been presented in the section "Personages of the Past," in Chapter 3, so their work need not be further considered here. We surely ought to love Vienna. She has done a great deal to save, prolong and benefit human life, perhaps because she herself has found life such an entertaining affair. There is no great use in hanging on to it unless it can be enjoyed, but if it is filled with graciousness, gaiety and generous friendliness, with Mozart's delicacy, with Schubert's tenderness, with Beethoven's splendor and with Strauss's infectious rhythms, then it becomes something to clutch with both hands. It has always been so with the Viennese, even in their darkest days.

THE SIGHTSEER LOOKS AT THE PAST

From the time of the Crusades, occurring between the 11th and 14th centuries, clear on until 1918, or at least until 1866, when Berlin captured the leadership of the Germanic peoples, this city on the Danube was in the very forefront of every important happening, and the heart of it has always been right where it is today. If we take our stand in the shadow of the cathedral we find ourselves within walking distance of nearly everything that is historically important in the city. No other large capital in the world is so concentrated in that respect, and what a glamorous, thrilling, outrageous, glorious past this great gray city has. There has never been anything of the Laodicean about Vienna. It has loved and hated well and been loved and hated in return. Hardly a page of its history is free from blots, yet courage, brilliance, majesty, even virtue are always cropping up. Our ensuing look at the past may repeat a few events already touched upon in the background chap-

The pre-Lenten opera ball in the restored Vienna Opera House is one of the most glittering social events on the Calendar of Europe.
VIENNA TOURIST ASSOCIATION

In Vienna's Spanish Riding School visitors thrill to the superb shows given by riders of the celebrated white Lippizaner horses.
VIENNA TOURIST ASSOCIATION

The well-loved Stephansdom (St. Stephen's Cathedral) of Vienna towers above the bustling metropolis. Viennese call it fondly "Der alte Steffl," translatable as Old Stevie.
AUSTRIAN NATIONAL TOURIST OFFICE

Right: *In the province of Styria several small rail lines delight engine buffs. This train manages 28 miles, from Gleisdorf to Birkfeld, in 2½ hours. Another, starting at Murau, is maintained solely for tourists, who operate the train on a 7-mile stretch, becoming instant engineers.* FOTO MARKO

Above: *The Bergkirche of Eisenstadt, capital of Burgenland Province, shelters the bones of Josef Haydn, whose patron, Prince Esterházy, lived in a castle nearby, now used as the seat of government.*
AUSTRIAN NATIONAL TOURIST OFFICE

The Castle of Hoch-Osterwitz, near Klagenfurt, capital of Carinthia, climbs a hill and then takes it over. There is a popular restaurant up aloft in the courtyard.

CARINTHIAN TOURIST OFFICE, KLAGENFURT

The 27-foot Dragon Fountain of Klagenfurt, carved out of stone in 1590 to commemorate a local legend, serves as a convenient perch for local pigeons. TECHNISCHE FOTOGRAFIE KLAGENFURT

The lovely and historic city of Salzburg is bisected by the hurrying River Salzach. Guests relax in a garden café at the edge of the cliff on which stands the former fortress of Hohensalzburg.

SALZBURG CITY TOURIST OFFICE

Salzburg's Marionette Theater of Professor Aicher has long since won world fame. In this theater piece the five-year-old Mozart plays at Schönbrunn Palace for Empress Maria Theresa.

AUSTRIAN NATIONAL TOURIST OFFICE

Right: *Hallstatt is a lake village of the Salzkammergut which demands the adjective picturesque, enhanced as it is by gondola-like boats on the Lake of Hallstatt. It is famous as the locale of "the Hallstatt Age," whose Celtic culture was a feature of the Iron Age.*

UPPER AUSTRIA TOURIST OFFICE

Above: *St. Wolfgang*, on the like-named lake, is one of the best-known resort villages in that four-province holiday area known as the Salzkammergut. A part of its fame is due to the Hotel Weisses Rössl (White Horse Inn), the scene of a perennially popular operetta now in its 76th year of success.

UPPER AUSTRIA TOURIST OFFICE

Schloss Ort, a hexagonal castle in the Traunsee, a lake of the Salzkammergut, is one of Austria's most photogenic structures, whether in summer or snow-shrouded winter.

UPPER AUSTRIA TOURIST OFFICE

Kitzbühel, one of Tyrol's leading winter sports centers, seems, in this picture, to have gone to bed, but it must be late, since Kitzbühel is known for its après-ski parties and other winter-evening gaieties.
TYROL TOURIST ASSOCIATION

Lermoos, in its peaceful green basin amid towering Alps, is of the essence of Tyrol, a village whose charm could be matched in a dozen other valleys. TYROL TOURIST ASSOCIATION

This Star Inn, to translate its name, presents a frescoed façade that is typical of Tyrol and Vorarlberg, as also of villages in the contiguous Bavarian Alps.

TYROL TOURIST
ASSOCIATION

The Landturm, or Feuerturn, rising from Innsbruck's Old Town, looms above a maze of narrow streets centered by the famous Golden Roof of a former ducal palace.

TYROL TOURIST
ASSOCIATION

The mile-high village of Lech, in Vorarlberg Province, has been called, along with the nearby village of Zürs, "the Skiers' Holy Land." AUSTRIAN NATIONAL TOURIST OFFICE

Bavarian types rest between liftings of vast mugs of beer. Such a mug, holding one liter, just over a quart, is known as a Mass.
GERMAN NATIONAL TOURIST OFFICE

*The famous Hofbräuhaus of Munich was called by **H. L. Mencken** "the Parthenon of beer drinking." Founded in 1589 to sell the beer of the court (Hof) brewery, it is now an immense sub-earthy beer hall, uproarious, incredibly lowbrow, and a prime tourist attraction.*
GERMAN NATIONAL TOURIST OFFICE

A night view from Marienplatz, the heart of Munich, showing (right) a portion of the new city hall and (left background) the turban-topped twin towers of the famous Frauenkirche (cathedral), with a 17th-century marble column to the Virgin centering the scene.

MUNICH TOURIST OFFICE

Neuschwanstein, the most bizarre of the three castles built by King Ludwig II of Bavaria. Because his castle-building frenzy threatened to bankrupt the country the king was deposed, but since his day, the revenue from tourist admission fees has mounted to far more than the original cost of the castles.

GERMAN NATIONAL
TOURIST OFFICE

This "avant-ski" scene is typical of many in the Austrian and Bavarian Alps. AUSTRIAN NATIONAL TOURIST OFFICE

ter (3), but this time we are *seeing* history and walking through it.

In the very center of the old city is a clearing called the *Hoher Markt.* This is actually the site of the *Praetorium* of Vindobona, Roman outpost against the barbarians. Trajan made mention of this town on his famous column in Rome. The good Marcus Aurelius lived for years and finally died in Vindobona, in the year 180, in a house on the present Marc Aurel-Strasse, leading from the Hoher Markt to the Danube Canal. The Romans held the town till about the year 400, when it sank into a coma and disappeared from the pages of history. Four centuries later, the city came to life again, perhaps through the patronage of Charlemagne. The Peterskirche and the Rupprechtskirche, a few paces west and east respectively of the Hoher Markt, claim him as their founder.

As little Wien grew in importance great names began to flash on its firmament. Emperor Otto defeated Huns and Magyars and gave to the House of Babenberg the margravate of the "East Marches." Then Barbarossa made the East Marches a hereditary duchy and the fifth Babenberg set up his little court in Wien. He was called officially Heinrich Jasomirgott from his pious habit of exclaiming *"Ja, so mir Gott helfe!"* In the Schottenkirche, a few paces northwest of the Hoher Markt, Henry Yes-So-Help-Me-God lies buried.

The Babenbergs died out and Ottokar of Bohemia seized the growing capital of what had come to be called the East Realm— Österreich—Austria. He completed the famous walls of Vienna, destined to be the bulwark of Europe against the Turk. We may thank Ottokar for Vienna's peerless Ring, which traces the line of Ottokar's wall.

But the Bohemian claimant could hardly crouch behind his wall before a Swiss count, Rudolf of Habsburg, was upon him. Rudolf was a giant, seven feet in height, it is commonly said, perhaps with "historical exaggeration." He had just secured by devious means his election as Holy Roman Emperor and could not brook the opposition of this Bohemian. So he "married his way to Vienna," turning hostile Bavaria, which sought to bar his way, into an ally by marrying his daughter to the Bavarian heir. He camped before Vienna's walls and soon starved out Ottokar and secured his surrender. Thus, in 1276, this Swiss Goliath set up as a great force the

House of Habsburg. Until 1918 it wielded a mighty influence, sometimes a baneful one, on Europe, but World War I made of this dynasty a drifting swirl of desuetude.

Between the World Wars, Vienna, governed by a Socialist regime, made valiant headway, especially in the building of comfortable flats for workers, one or two of the buildings being more than half a mile long! But in 1938 Hitler came, and Vienna went, as a national capital. From then on it was the capital of the Province of Ostmark. I visited Vienna early in 1939 and was utterly shocked by the sad and subjugated look of it. Fear and distrust were in the air and the few who dared to speak their minds in opposition to the Nazis glanced nervously about to see if they were being overheard. Jewish-run shops on Kärntnerstrasse and elsewhere were partially destroyed and boarded up. Harsh anti-Semitic signs were everywhere and portraits of Hitler were conspicuous in the windows of almost every shop that "knew what was good for it."

The Hitler Nightmare came to its logical climax in World War II and Vienna suffered severe but not fatal wounds. The city was hit by air raids 53 timees and lost one-fifth of its dwellings. Many public buildings were struck, the worst sufferers being the opera house and the cathedral, but it was artillery fire from the retreating Nazi troops near the very end of the war that did the most frightful damage to St. Stephen's and its whole vicinity. For several days a useless and destructive cross-fire was maintained. On April 12, 1945, artillery shells set fire to the church and it burned for the better part of a week. The central part of the roof fell in, the lovely Gothic choir, modeled after that of the Regensburg Cathedral, was burned out, the fine organ was transformed into twisted wreckage and the *Pummerin,* a 20-ton bell cast centuries ago from 180 captured Turkish cannon, fell from its belfry with a ghastly jangle, but the 448-foot south tower, completed in 1433, stood firm.

Soon after this tragic holocaust the war was over and Vienna set about to heal its wounds. All Austria joined in the campaign, every province contributing handsomely. In 1952 a new Pummerin was cast in St. Florian, near Linz, and escorted in jubilation to Vienna. The choir was fully restored at about the same time and new stained glass was set in the windows. Green and white tiles just like the former ones were placed on the rebuilt roof. So the Stephansdom came back to life and no part of this was due to Marshall Plan aid. Rather, it was a triumph of Austrian determination, every bit of the money for it coming from popular subscriptions and even small coin collections. The drama of this reopening almost matched that of the Opera reopening except that it was more gradual and even when the church was virtually completed the military occupiers had not yet left the city.

THE INNER CITY AND THE RING

The stroller in the Inner City would do well to establish himself in the shadow of the cathedral tower and plan his explorations from that point.

Linking the cathedral square and the Graben is a little square called Stock-im-Eisen-Platz, or Stump-in-Iron Square. On one corner of it is the Stump-in-Iron itself, one of the quaintest bits of Vienna's heritage. I have read half a dozen accounts of this curiosity and no two are quite the same. They do not even agree as to the nature of the wood. This is hardly surprising, as the gnarled old veteran, clamped onto a building by a padlocked iron bar, is completly covered with nails so that not one glimpse of the wood is to be had. Many of these nails are engraved with the initials of the persons who drove them in. Fanciful and extrordinary legends, frequently involving the devil, cluster around the stump, but no one knows for sure its significance. This industrious nail driving *may* have been a mark of initiation for smiths' apprentices. All we know for certain is that the Stump stood on this corner four centuries ago, that it was long lost to the world, that an American insurance company (Equitable) unearthed it while laying the foundation for a new building in 1891, and that all tourist agencies having to do with Vienna make a good thing out of it. It certainly does stimulate the imagination. Do you suppose, if we studied those nailhead initials long and earnestly, we could find, for instance, J. A. and dare to assume that these letters stood for Johann Aichamer, the bellfounder who built Old Steve's first Pummerin from Turkish cannons?

At this famous corner the stroller through history must decide whether to turn south through Kärntnerstrasse or west through the Graben, but the choice will not be too hard, for the latter surely offers richer rewards.

The Graben is a most unconventional street. It means "Moat" and was, in fact, the southwest boundary of Babenberg Vienna, though it was the very heart of Ottokar's Vienna. In the center of it is that extraordinary monument (several times mentioned above), the *Pestsäule,* to the Holy Trinity, erected by Leopold I in token of appreciation for the staying of the dreadful plague brought to Vienna by the Turks. This amazing column shows Father, Son and Holy Ghost atop a billowing mass of clouds inhabited by angel choirs. Leopold is sculptured too, kneeling humbly while an angel, acting as page, holds his crown.

By Bognerstrasse (Bowyer Street) or Naglerstrasse (Nailmaker Street) we push on to that huge, irregular square called *Am Hof.* The name is a reference to Jasomirgott's castle, which stood here. If we enter from the end of Naglerstrasse we cross in imagination an old drawbridge that was crossed in reality by many a great personage. Am Hof was the last stopping place of the Crusader on his way to do battle with the Infidel, his first place of refuge on his way home. Barbarossa marshaled his troops in this square, as did many another great Crusader. A contemporary of Barbarossa was Walther von der Vogelweide, whose service to the Crusaders was inestimable. He lived in the same *Hof* and stirred the warriors to valor by his minstrelsy.

Almost everything has happened in this square. The Holy Roman Empire finally expired here in 1806. Here, too, students staged the revolution of 1848 which overthrew the reactionary Metternich, and here, in that same year, a mob hanged Count Latour, the Minister of War.

The Am Hof church in this square, built by the early Habsburgs, has always provided a quiet retreat from the excitements of the square. It is dedicated to the Nine Choirs of Angels and on my first entrance I rather hoped to hear them all in action, but the church seemed uncannily still after the racket outside. It was from a balcony of this church, to repeat from above, that the Imperial Commissioner made the historic announcement, on August 6, 1806, that the Holy Roman Empire had ceased to exist.

Emerging from the far corner of Am Hof one enters the *Freyung*, another peculiarly shaped square. This owes its name to the right of sanctuary which the Scotch Church and Monastery here once afforded. Everything on the northern side of the Freyung and in the area immediately beyond it recalls the Scotch—Schottenkirche, Schottenhof, Schottengasse, Schottenbastei, even Schottenring. But these Scots were actually Irishmen. They were Benedictines and because of their piety had been invited by Jasomirgott to settle in Vienna. His successors regretted this invitation, for the Hibernians proved greedy, parsimonious and very pugnacious. Their abbot once threatened to strangle any monks of other nationalities who tried to enter the monastery. After three centuries they were ejected unceremoniously by one of the Habsburgs and replaced by German Benedictines, but the old name, or rather misnomer, lingers on today in this whole quarter of Vienna.

The eastern, southern and western sides of the Freyung are lined almost solidly by baroque palaces and in its center is the Austria Fountain. Ludwig Schwanthaler of Bavaria was commissioned to build this fountain in the middle of the last century, and thereby hangs a tale. He liked Bavarian cigars but it was difficult to get them across the border into Austria, so Ludwig made the casting of his Austria Fountain in Munich, filled it with thousands of Bavarian cigars and shipped it to Vienna. Alas, the sculptor fell ill as the casting arrived. It was set up in the Freyung and Ludwig could not rescue the cigars. It is said that they are still there, a lesson to smugglers!

We may double back on our trail from the Scotch-Irish-German quarter by the Herrengasse, or Street of the Lords. On this street is the *Landhaus* where the historic Austrian Estates met. Arriving at the *Michaeler Platz* we face that gigantic, interminable, rambling 2000-room palace, the *Hofburg*, with a newer part called the Neue Hofburg extending from it to the edge of the Ring. This will utterly discourage you if you try to "do" it with conscientious thoroughness. Do not try. Perhaps more by chance than design you will happen across many things in it, about it, that interest you. There is the famous wrought-iron Michaeler Gate, leading from the Michaeler Platz into the Michaeler Rotunda; there are the State Apartments (seen in guided tours), with many intimate relics of Franz Joseph and Elizabeth; and there is the Spanish Riding School, a great white quadrangle where marvelous performances are given (except during high summer and "high winter") on Sunday mornings at 10:45 by riding masters on spirited Lippizaner stallions. These horses, of noble Spanish or Neapolitan pedigree, used to be bred at Lippiza, near Trieste, but are now bred at Piber in one of the Styrian valleys (see Chapter 7). During the war, and for almost a decade after it, they were quartered near Wels, in Upper Austria, in the former U.S. Zone, for it was feared that if they were returned to Vienna they would be claimed by the Russians as reparations. Now, happily, the treaty has saved them and they are back where they belong in the Spanish Riding School, and glorious sleek creatures they are. They are born black or brown, even as a white swan's cygnets are born gray, but gradually turn white. On first seeing the show I could hardly accept what my eyes told me *they* saw. The beautiful animals did the English slow waltz, the minuet, a type of polka, several marches, and two horses, by name Siglavi Graina and Siglavi Beja I, did a graceful *pas de deux* to Mozart's Symphony Number 40. The climax was an impressive quadrille by eight horses, done to music of Chopin and Bizet. The riders, wearing black tail coats, white breeches, shiny riding boots and jaunty cocked hats, guided their mounts with such an extreme economy of motion and spoken command that the combinations of men and horses made the nearest approach I have ever seen to so many centaurs.

Another feature of the Hofburg, quite different, that will be sure to interest you, is the Treasury, Sacred and Secular. The sacred part contains gorgeous pontifical vestments, costly jeweled reliquaries and monstrances, the napkin of St. Veronica (*one* of them), relics of Charlemagne and various souvenirs of pious Habsburgs.

The Secular Treasury is one of the most brilliant and varied in Europe. It dazzles the eye and the imagination and brings many a figure of history squarely before us. We see the sword of Charlemagne and the Bible on which he took his coronation oath. We see the crown of King Stephen Bocskay of Hungary, fashioned by Turkish artisans; the baptismal vestments of Maria Theresa, adorned with pearls sewed on with gold thread; and the similar baptismal robe of Franz Joseph, leading us to believe that that much-whiskered monarch must once have been a baby! We see, also, a group of relics brought from the Holy Land. Odd bits these relics are—a tooth of John the Baptist, a splinter from the Sacred Manger, a fragment and a nail from the True Cross and even the Lance that pierced Christ's side. These relics may not impress us, but the romance of the Crusaders does, enhanced as it is by their gorgeous robes and mantles, purple and red silks, gloves adorned with precious stones, jeweled crucifixes, scepters, orbs and chains of gold. The Crown of the Holy Roman Emperor is here, though Italy tried to get it after World War I. It is heavy with emeralds, rubies, pearls and even some ornamental enamel work. The Imperial Crown of Austria is here, though Czechoslovakia once tried to get it. A huge ruby is on the front of the crown, surrounded by diamonds and pearls, and a giant sapphire is on the top. The Jewels of the Order of the Golden Fleece are here, though Belgium tried to get them.

Among items of sheer ornament in the Secular Treasury are two that have especially caught my eye: a rose, with stem and leaves, all of pure gold, made in 1819 by an Italian jeweler named Giuseppe Spagna; and an 18th-century bouquet of scintillating jewels 14 inches high.

One section of the Secular Treasury is devoted to Napoleonic relics. I gazed long at the solid silver cradle of l'Aiglon, Napoleon's only son, by his Austrian princess Marie-Louise. It is covered with bees, Napoleon's emblem. A silver eagle at the foot of it guarded the infant's slumber. His mother's jewel case, a small trunk of silver and green plush, is close by, and on the wall are miniatures of Napoleon, Marie Louise and their son, cumbered with the title King of Rome. The child looks happy here, a blond boy who has a moving likeness to his mother. But seldom has a short life held more misery than did his. His body now lies beside that of his father in the Invalides Church in Paris, sent there from Vienna in 1940 by Adolf Hitler, but Marie Louise lies in the vault of Vienna's Capuchin Church, near the Neuer Markt, where most of the Habsburgs lie.

A soft-voiced, brown-robed Capuchin friar guided me one day through that imperial vault, and it is a sight to see, featured always by the city bus tours, for no less than 140 Habsburgs are here elaborately entombed. There are 14 "full emperors," and 13 empresses. Old Leopold I is here, as are Maria Theresa and her consort, with 13 of their 16 children, as are Franz Joseph and Elizabeth. The Habsburg hearts lie in urns in the Augustinerkirche, adjacent to the Hofburg.

We may permit ourselves to escape from vaults and churches to one of the most inspiring sights in Europe, Vienna's famous Ring. To repeat its design, this magnificent street, 60 yards wide, forms six sides of a heptagon, the swift Danube Canal, with its quays, forming the seventh. On this Ring, itself a sort of garden the whole way, are half a dozen city parks, and a concentrated array of huge public buildings unmatched in Europe. Franz Joseph achieved this and it is his greatest monument. The old wall of Ottokar had become utterly useless and the emperor converted it into a boulevard. The glacis beyond was equally useless. State, city and army wrangled endlessly over the disposition of it, so the emperor cut the Gordian knot by appointing a special bureau to dispose of the land for the benefit of all concerned. About half the glacis was sold for $50 million, a tremendous sum a hundred years ago, and from this money came the spectacular array of buildings that make the Ring world famous. Some features of this array are the *Rathaus,* in Gothic style, the 5-acre *University Building,* which is Italian Renaissance, and the *Parliament Building,* which is surprisingly, of Greek classical design suggesting Athens in every detail, from its pillared portico and peristyle to the colossal statue of Pallas Athena before it.

The list is a long one and styles are varied. The great opera house, the Burgtheater and the two imperial museums are Renaissance, with different influences, French or Italian, apparent. The new Hofburg is sumptuous baroque. The *Votivkirche,* a structure of rare beauty, is Gothic of the Gothic, but modern. This church is the only great structure on the Ring that did not get at least a fine start from the glacis money. The people of Vienna built it with money from their own pockets. In 1853, four years before the bastion was leveled, young Franz Joseph, aged 23, was walking upon it when suddenly a Hungarian assassin sprang at him and stabbed him in the neck, inflicting, however, only flesh wounds, from which the emperor soon recovered. Vienna was deeply grateful to God for the sovereign's escape and built this superb church, which proves that a church can be both modern and beautiful. The 3 miles by 60 yards which comprise the Ring were once the most useful acres in all Christendom, since they foiled the Turk. Today they are among the most beautiful and imposing in all Christendom.

Just outside this supercircle rises the Karlskirche, the earlier mentioned baroque masterpiece of Fischer von Erlach, completed by his son. Its façade is dramatized by a portico of six Corinthian columns and the church is flanked by two 108-foot columns in imitation of Trajan's Column in the Roman forum. If this sounds like "a little of everything" you are invited to withhold judgment until you see it. It is an example, and perhaps the best example, of the jubilant baroque era which flourished in Vienna during a 60-year period of peace following the final defeat of the Turks in 1683.

NAPOLEON IN THE ARCHIVES

A special delight of some travelers, including myself, is specially available in Vienna and I must mention it here. I refer to the habit of browsing in meadows of print and correspondence that reveal dramas and melodramas of the past. The Leigh Library of Edinburgh, the Huntington Library of Pasadena and even the Record Office of London seem hardly so rich in great documents and letters as is the *Austrian State Archives Office,* to be found at 1 Minoritenplatz, in the Inner City.

Famous items are so very numerous that they seem almost to reach the saturation point. One sees the original Golden Bull, the original Pragmatic Sanction, the manuscript of Maria Theresa's speech to her Hungarian nobles, the same lady's letters to her daughter Marie Antoinette. These are all important, but the Napoleon items are so very personal, so full of mute tragedy, that often they attract major attention. I studied every paper I could see in the glass cases, trying to get some glimpses of the tremendous story of the emperor's later career and downfall. Its main chapters, as read in the Archives Office, run something like this.

1. Some harsh Napoleon-made treaties which Talleyrand signed for France and Prince Liechtenstein (an ancestor of the present prince) for Austria.

2. A letter of Napoleon (1810) addressed *"À Monsier Mon Frère l'Empereur de l'Autriche"* suing in pious phrase for the hand of his daughter Marie Louise.

3. A letter to the same emperor, Francis II, from his daugher, now a bride. Dispatched from Compiègne, it commences *Lieber Papa,* goes on to praise the bridegroom's noble qualities and then soothes the anxious parent with the words *Ich bin wirklich recht glücklich und zufrieden* (I am really very happy and contented).

4. A letter from Napoleon to Francis II dispatched some months later and addressed this time *À Monsieur Mon Frère et Beau-Père.* His wife, he reports proudly, is with child.

5. After a considerable hiatus the story goes on in a violent dispatch of 1815 sent from the panic-stricken Congress of Vienna to the Tuileries. Napoleon has escaped from Elba and the assembled diplomats bellow—"May God hurl into the abyss this latest attempt of a criminal and a powerless madman." Talleyrand has turned his coat thoroughly, for his name is among the others on this vitriolic paper.

6. A letter in Napoleon's own hand, written during the Hundred Days, to his wife who had retreated to Schönbrunn. "Join me at once in Strasbourg," he says. "I will meet you there." He closes with a strange conservatism for such a masterful man at such a time of crisis: *"Adieu mon amie. Tout à toi. Napoléon."* His penmanship is remarkably legible for him and even his signature is penned as if with anxious respect, not slapdash as on his treaties. (Marie Louise did not come. The Hundred Days concluded at Waterloo.)

7. A letter from Prince Metternich to the Austrian emperor fairly burbles with glee, reporting that Napoleon is interned on the *Bellerophon,* bound for St. Helena. (Six years elapse.)

8. The bitter ending of the story. A letter from Marie Louise, dated Parma, July 20, 1821, to her father. I managed to make out the words: "I have just read of Napoleon's death for the first time in the Piedmont journals. I could hardly have believed it had not the details been so definite."

It is as if the widow were exclaiming, "Dear dear. So he's dead." She could have said more about the passing of a pet canary. But after all, why should she care? She was having a good time in Parma. She was, moreover, expecting another baby, this time by her chamberlain.

PALACES IN CRESCENDO

There are perhaps half a hundred palaces in Vienna, not counting the mammoth Hofburg. Among them are the *Czernin Palace,* the *Harrach Palace* and that of *Prince Liechtenstein,* sovereign of the pocket principality already mentioned. Others of special historic interest are the *Schwarzenberg Palace* of a famous Austrian diplomatic dynasty, a portion of which is now a first-class hotel, and the former *Metternich Palace* of the wily prince-politician who played with kings, queens, bishops and castles as if they were chess figures. But of these lesser palaces, though there is nothing mediocre about any of them, the one of most absorbing interest, to me at least, is the *Belvedere Palace of Prince Eugene of Savoy,* which is actually two palaces, an upper one and a lower one.

The Belvedere is of prime importance on at least three counts. First, the Upper Palace is a masterpeice of secular baroque comparable to the Karlskirche in ecclesiastical baroque and it was begun by the same architect, Fischer von Erlach, though it owes its brilliance chiefly to a succeeding architect of almost equal fame, Lukas Hildebrandt. It is admirable not only for its construction and lavish decoration but for its garden setting, which is unmatched in artistic effect, I think, even by Schönbrunn. The entrance hall and banqueting hall of the Upper Palace are famous and its many rooms house an interesting *Gallery of Modern Austrian Art* of the 19th and 20th centuries. (Note "The Girl with the Yellow Straw Hat"—I hope she'll still be there—by Friedrich von Amerling, a hauntingly lovely painting.)

Second, the Belvedere is interesting because of the man for whom it was built. Prince Eugene of Savoy (1663–1736) was a French military genius who could have rendered great service to his native land but Louis XIV stupidly alienated him and even refused him an army commission. Eugene thereupon offered his services to Leopold I of Austria and for 30 years fought with masterful ability for his adopted country. He started his career in the Great Repulse of the Turks in 1683, and two more of his successful campaigns were against the Turks. Later, he added new laurels to his reputation by joining Marlborough to win the famous Battle of Blenheim (1704) against the French and Bavarians. Louis XIV tried by every blandishment and pecuniary offer to lure the prince back but he never succeeded. Eugene was a born soldier, with a consuming passion for war and glory. He was extremely brave but personally cold, severe and so sternly misogynous that he was nicknamed "a Mars without a Venus." He lived in the relatively simple and unimportant Lower Belvedere, using the Upper Belevedere for receptions and other public functions.

Third, the Upper Belvedere was the scene of the signing of the Austrian State Treaty on May 15, 1955, restoring full independence to the Federal Republic. Here Messrs. Dulles, Macmillan, Pinay and Molotov signed the treaty and then emerged to the Great Balcony to wave to the cheering Austrians gathered below. Austria was freed at the Belvedere Palace of Prince Eugene.

A current evening feature of the Upper Palace is a "Sound and Light Show." I missed it because of persistent rains, but am sure you will have better luck. I'm told the show is fascinating.

The climax of Vienna's palaces, possibly not even excepting the Hofburg, is, of course, SCHÖNBRUNN.

Schönbrunn, whose name is from a spring *(schöner Brunnen)* discovered here by an early Habsburg, was begun by Leopold I, but it was essentially the creation of Maria Theresa and the empress loved it, for this was her summer retreat. Here she was first a mother, a devoted and efficient one, to her vast brood, relegating "stateswomanship" to second place. This palace is associated with her just as the Hofburg is associated with Franz Joseph, though he was born in Schönbrunn and died there. From the time of Maria Theresa, history was made in this summer palace and one bit of musical history may be mentioned first of all, for here, in the Hall of Mirrors, a five-year-old boy from Salzburg named Wolfgang Amadeus Mozart played the harpsichord before the empress and astonished all listeners by his virtuosity.

At the palace gates are two obelisks, each surmounted by a golden eagle, and the odd thing about them is that they are not Austrian birds but French, placed there by Napoleon to humiliate his beaten foe. Such tolerance is rare in the world, but the birds are handsome and for a century and a half Austria has been content to let them stay there. Twice, in 1805 and 1809, after the victories of Austerlitz and Wagram, Napoleon lodged at Schönbrunn as conqueror and those were bitter days for Austria. Then the upstart from Corsica completed Austria's humiliation by demanding and winning the hand of the Habsburg princess, Marie Louise. Her father, Francis II, head of the proudest reigning house on the Continent, dared not refuse him.

In 1810 Napoleon married the princess and the next year their son was born and promptly named King of Rome. Four years later the King of Rome was brought to Schönbrunn when his father made an involuntary stay on the Island of Elba. Then the Congress of Vienna settled down for the longest, gayest conference that ever men (and women) held. For two or three hours each day the conferees quarreled in public debate. The rest of the time they ate and drank, flirted, danced. *"Le Congrès danse, mais il ne marche pas"* was the comment of a witty guest.

Prince Metternich gave a costly ball one evening in his own palace near the Hofburg and while things were in full swing a breathless messenger arrived to say that Napoleon had escaped from Elba. An exploding bomb in the ballroom could hardly have caused a greater panic. The stately waltz became a Rabbit Scuttle. The conference stopped dancing. The long house party was spoiled. But the Hundred Days passed and with them the shadow of Napoleon. The King of Rome, now cut down to size as the Duke of Reichstadt, lived on unhappily at Schönbrunn. His mother went off to Parma, of which she had been made Duchess. One is shown the duke's sumptuous paint box in one of Vienna's museums. Perhaps it whiled away a few hours for this resident of Schönbrunn. Finally death by tuberculosis released him. He died in the same room, the same bed, which his father had occupied in 1805 and 1809.

Only 44 of the palace's 1440 rooms are shown to visitors, in a 45-minute guided tour, but they are magnificent in the rococo style, which is, of course, baroque of acid-test exuberance. The most lavish room of them all is the "Millionenzimmer," or Million Room, so named because it cost a million florins to decorate it. Many miniatures painted on parchment adorn the walls and ceiling and they are outlined with rims of Chinese rosewood, thickly gilded. It is said that *twenty pounds* of pure melted gold were used to gild the walls, ceilings and furniture of this room, and whether this means avoirdupois or troy it is a lot of gold.

Other rooms shown (not in this sequence) include the Franz Joseph Apartments, with the simple iron bed in which the monarch died on November 21, 1916; the Empress Elizabeth Apartments; the Gobelin Salon, with enormous tapestries; the Maria-Theresien-Saal, with a large and interesting portrait of the empress; the Chinese Round Cabinet, which was Maria Theresa's private council chamber; the Blue Room, where the last of the Habsburgs, Charles I, abdicated in 1918; and the splendid white and gold Great Gallery, 140 feet in length.

An old picture in one of the rooms shows a gala procession of —it is said—911 carriages of the court and the aristocracy and this reminds us that one feature of Schönbrunn, reached by passing through an arch in the west wing, is the Wagenburg, a museum of state carriages and sleighs of the period from 1700 to 1918 scarcely equaled in Europe, unless by the National Museum of Coaches at Belem, outside Lisbon. Among them one may see the sumptuous berlin in which Marie Louise journeyed to France in 1810 and various other coaches, sleighs and sedan chairs used by her at different times. One also sees the "coach," a perambulator, in which the King of Rome was trundled about the Tuileries Gardens in Paris.

The 500-acre palace park is one of the greatest glories of Schönbrunn. Of course it is all of baroque design, including artificial ruins, but whatever your reaction to this style in general you are bound to love the magnificent pomp of these great gardens, decorated with fountains, symmetrical pools, beautifully clipped hedges, so planted as to provide grand vistas, and brilliant flower gardens, which are changed monthly by the corps of palace gardeners, all of this backed by the striking colonnade of the Gloriette on a hilltop at the southern end. The huge gardens have plenty of room on the western side for a zoo, a botanical garden with a vast palm house, a Tyrolean garden, a pheasant garden and much else, but the main avenue and Neptune Fountain, splendidly climaxed by the Gloriette, are always the center of attraction. The roof of the Gloriette, 60 feet high, may be visited, by climbing to it (no elevator) for a superb view of the Schönbrunn ensemble, with the city and the surrounding Vienna Woods as backdrop.

The war did not by an means spare Schönbrunn. It is said that 269 bombs, by an exact tally, fell on the park and palace, but a marvelous postwar job of repairing and reconditioning was rapidly done and the royal treasures and furnishings had been saved by storage in places of safety, so today's visitor can scarcely realize that a single bomb fell hereabouts. When the Austrian State Treaty was signed, the foreign ministers of America, Britain, France and Russia were treated to a state banquet in this palace and the entire imperial state dinner service of the Hofburg was brought here for use on that glittering occasion. This was the most recent historic event, and perhaps the happiest, in the long and checkered career of Schönbrunn. Peace has returned with freedom and the palace grounds are now used for certain events in connection with Vienna's annual Festival Weeks in June.

FOUR-PART ROUNDUP: HOTELS, RESTAURANTS, NIGHT FUN, SHOPS

Hotels of Vienna, a Personal Report

Hotels of Vienna, and I shall repeat this comment when we reach other Austrian cities and then Munich, are of two types, those of

European inspiration, long on personality and often long on charm, though by no means forgetting comfort, and those of American inspriation, larger, higher-rise hotels, long on comforts and usually with many varied dining rooms, yet aiming, too, at the eye-appeal of today's tastes, and often coming through with clever ideas of modern decor. Vienna hasn't yet gone in for Americanesque hotels as much, say, as Munich but a start has been made. We will look first at the top places of European stamp.

Hotel Imperial, directly on the Kärntner Ring, has long been, in my view, a "hotel apart," a special of specials. I would call it not only the leading Europe-inspired hotel of Vienna, and of Austria, but close to the top in all Europe, since it adds to a distinguished historical background just about every conceivable refinement of modern comfort and quick, unobtrusive service. The building was first erected over a hundred years ago as a palace for the Duke of Württemberg and in it many royal and noble personages, as well as nonroyal notables, have lived or visited during its palace and hotel periods. One of the nonroyal celebrities was Richard Wagner, who spent two months here in 1875 making preparations for the opening of his *Tannhäuser* and *Lohengrin* in the nearby opera house. The Imperial has six royal suites today and every guest senses the hotel's nature, suited to its name, by noting, at the head of the grand stairway, a large oil painting of Emperor Franz Joseph. This pervading atmosphere is enhanced by coats of arms, by massive marble pillars and by touches of imperial purple in the public rooms.

When Hitler took over Austria in 1938 he made his pseudoimperial speech to the Viennese crowds from a balcony of this hotel, but after the war it had a grim decade of occupancy by the Russian forces. The Russians were rough tenants in all the Austrian buildings that they occupied and after they finally pulled out, in 1955, two years and many millions of Austrian schillings were needed to restore the Imperial to its pristine glory. Today, however, one wouldn't guess that foreign forces had ever occupied it. Its creature comforts in many of the bedrooms and baths are the very best. in the bathrooms, for instance, the temperature of the water from the tub faucet and from the overhead shower is controlled by separate thermostat wheels and another such wheel controls, in cold weather, the temperature of the bathroom floor, such refinements of gadgetry making the guest feel like the original sybarite. The luxurious outsized lounge, opening from the reception lobby, invites relaxation, and to mention just one of its thoughtul features, it has nooks with writing desks at various points, each one of which is *always* supplied with its full quota of stationery. And as for the hotel's cuisine, it goes without saying that the Imperial produces delicacies of the first order, some of them original and highly imaginative.

Hotel Bristol, under the same ownership as the Imperial, is Vienna's "nuclear" hotel, by which I mean that it is in the very center of the center of the city, gracing the corner of the Kärntner Ring and Kärntnerstrasse, directly opposite the Opera and within a dozen steps of two of the escalators that lead down to the Opernpassage. Its elegance and glitter rival those aspects of its Imperial cousin and many of its bedrooms are the ultimate in gracious *luxe,* backed by modern comfort. Its central dining room displays the same assured elegance.

Hotel Sacher, located directly back of the Opera, is the glamour house of all Austrian hotels, formerly famous for its social elegance and famous to this day for much the same quality. Its public rooms, hallways, corridors and bedrooms are decorated with no less than *two thousand* works of art and it has many special features, one of them being its delightful chain of miniature hideaway dining alcoves collectively called Sacher-Stöckl. Other features are wall photographs and mementos of famous guests and a tablecloth with the signatures of scores of celebrated persons embroidered upon it, that of Emperor Franz Joseph being in the center. In one of the corridors is a cabinet, with glass doors, containing a history of the *Sachertorte,* that luscious and world-imitated chocolate cake that was devised by a proprietor-chef of the hotel's early days, Eduard Sacher, rightly taking and maintaining the name of the hotel, a name now protected by law. Virtually every one of the Sacher's 100-plus rooms enjoys its own individual decor and its public rooms are as individual as its bedrooms. The hotel has received its accolade, as it were, by having a ballet named for it, and to conclude this rather lyrical commentary, I would say that if a hotel can have charisma the Sacher has it.

Hotel Ambassador is marvelously located on the Neuer Markt, a square graced by a famous fountain of Raphael Donner, and running clear through to Kärntnerstrasse. This has been a haunt of celebrities quite as much as has the Imperial, but perhaps more for those in search of quietness, removed from excitements, as evidenced by its small, gemlike dining room, *for guests of the hotel only,* seen from the reception area through a glass wall. A feature that has been a sort of hallmark for many decades is the hotel's addiction, both in its public rooms and in its bedrooms, to silk brocade walls of a distinctive red, which my diffident eyes estimate as half way between mulberry and raspberry. The hotel itself sees the color as Schönbrunn red. Anyway, the brocades seem to add their restful touch to an already tranquil atmosphere. On the walls of the small lounge we see certain pages from the scores of Franz Lehár's works in the composer's own hand and we learn that Lehár was a close friend of the present proprietor of the hotel, a member of the Senft family, which has owned the hotel since its beginnings. For years he made it a practice to come to the Ambassador every Friday evening to be with Herr Senft. The line of celebrities who have favored the Ambassador dates back to Theodore Roosevelt and before him to Mark Twain, but these were only two of many.

Two luxury hotels on the outskirts of the city are *Parkhotel Schönbrunn,* flanking the Schönbrunn Gardens, and *Schloss Laudon,* an ancient (1130) fortress rebuilt into a residential castle in the late 17th century and expensively remade into a castle-hotel in the 1960s by its then and now owner, a wealthy coffee king. Schloss Laudon, with its 60 rooms and 100 beds is a castler's castle, located in Vienna's 14th Bezirk, which carries well into the Vienna Woods. Its public rooms, especially its lovely dining room, have instant appeal, as do its bedrooms, each one individually decorated and furnished with genuine antiques. The Schloss is surrounded on all sides by its own "trout moat," where guests may fish, and it offers a considerable array of seasonal recreations: in summer swimming, fishing, tennis and riding on saddle horses, in winter skiing, skating and horse-drawn sleighing. Bowling, on the hotel's lanes, is a year-round sport, not too common in Austria. Special features of the Laudon are its separate grill, in an old mill, its Tudor Bar, and for glamorized breakfasts, its Hunting Room. Americans flock to the Laudon, providing 80 per cent of its guests, and so forehanded are they that all rooms every year are solidly booked in advance from April to October. So, if Laudon's atmosphere tempts you be spry about applying for accommodations.

I have purposely left Pan Am's *Hotel Vienna Inter-Continental* for the last of the luxury hotels, since it is the only one of American inspiration and ownership. With 500 rooms and 1000 beds, it is by far the largest hotel in Vienna and in all Austria and it has an excellent location, many of its rooms overlooking the Stadtpark. Its deluxe nature and amenities are *selbstverständlich,* to use a good German word that can be translated as self-understood. This hotel is a favorite of American business travelers, and for good reason. Its comforts are the kind they know and rightly like, as are its eating and drinking places. Its main restaurant is called not Vier Jahreszeiten but its French equivalent, Les Quatre Saisons, with a sort of corollary called Rhapsodie. There is a brightly decorated quick-lunching Brasserie, with its own corollary called the Capriccio Bar; and there's another bar called Intermezzo, so the Italian language has its turn, but one sees no German-language "Stüberl." About half the guests of the Inter-Continental are Americans, the other half Europeans, so it seems that many people of Europe fall for American supercomforts and are willing to forgo their own traditional charms. Conventioneers, both American and European, love this hotel, for if they book well in advance they can count on as many rooms as needed, and they find every facility for conferences.

Among less-than-deluxe but very good first-class hotels the one I know best from having experienced and enjoyed its lodgings and dining rooms is the *Europa,* which, like the Ambassador, is Janus-faced, one face surveying the Neuer Markt while the other looks out on the busy doings of Kärntnerstrasse. This 9-story hotel, designed by Professor Boltenstern, the same famous architect who rebuilt the Opera, is "compact-modern," and all of its rooms have bath and radio. The Europa's rates include Continental breakfast.

The one-flight-up restaurant and the ground-floor café, with a small sidewalk terrace on the Neuer Markt, have a special appeal for me, since I can watch through its outsized windows the activities of the Neuer Markt *or* of Kärntnerstrasse, depending upon which table I select.

Of first-class hotels where I have not lodged but which I know in some detail, I would comment on three that have individual powers of attraction, namely *Hotel im Palais Schwarzenberg, Hotel am Stephansplatz,* and *Hotel am Parkring.* The first-named, already mentioned as a part of the palace of Prince Schwarzenberg (Countess Khuen is the manager) makes its main appeal as a Place of Peace, though within close reach of the Ring. Couple this with an old-world princely air—period furniture in every room—with spaciousness, and with all needed comforts, and you have something quite out of the ordinary. Americans of good breeding love this palace-hotel, and are among the Countess's most devoted guests. The hotel is of the *garni* type, meaning that it serves breakfast only.

Hotel am Stephansplatz I like for its spectacular location directly opposite the magnificent façade of the Stephansdom, the view being shared by many of the bedrooms, especially on the upper floors, and by the breakfast room, which provides this hotel's only meal. A dozen good restaurants are to be found all around the hotel and the cathedral. The hotel's entrance is around the corner but the address is Am Stephansplatz 9.

Hotel am Parkring, on that portion of the Ring whose name it takes, opposite the Stadtpark, is an up-aloft hotel, on the 3 top floors of a 13-story office building, with a view to breakfast by, lunch by or dine by—or sleep by. Built in the 60s, and perhaps with thought of getting as many rooms as possible in the space available, the Parkring offers small but modern rooms all with bath and radio. To advance still further the hotel's view potential most rooms have small but adequate balconies. Friends of mine who have stayed here loved the hotel and thought the thrill of the outlook far outweighed the slight inconvenience of their small room and bath.

A hotel built in the early 60s is the *Royal,* only one block from the Stephansdom. Its 8 floors are climaxed by the two top ones, with balconied rooms of special attractiveness and even an air of luxury.

Among the many moderate-priced hotels of recommendable quality but no great pretensions, three in which my watchful pocketbook and I have stayed with reasonable contentment are the *Kaiserin Elisabeth*—the lovely but ill-starred empress gazes at us feelingly as we enter the hotel—on Weihburggasse just off Kärntnerstrasse; the elderly but well-maintained *Kummer,* a bit out from the center on Mariahilferstrasse; and the *Erzherzog* (Archduke) *Rainer,* on the Wiedner Hauptstrasse, a long suburban thoroughfare that is a southwestern continuation of Kärtnerstrasse.

Among pensions I would give top personal rating to the *Neuer Markt,* not only for its good quality but for its stimulating outlook on the lovely square for which it is named. Another good place, and I once spent several days there with satisfaction, is the *Schneider,* on Lehárgasse, not far from the center. Still another pension, and one of the best, is the spacious *Opernring* on the "Ring of the same name" hence as central as any hostelry could be.

Restaurants of Vienna, a Personal Report

It seems almost as hard to be selective about the multitude of eating and drinking places in Vienna as it would be in Paris or London, but I will try to do some severe and careful pruning.

Zu Den 3 Husaren (To the Three Hussars; they were Hungarian Light Cavalry in Imperial days), on Weihburggasse, just off Kärntnerstrasse, doesn't "read" very personal since everybody, it seems, who comments on Vienna tends to put this at the top of the restaurant roster, or at the least sharing the top. And so do I. It has elegance, charm, superlative cuisine and equally superlative service. On the most recent of several feasts that I've enjoyed amid the candlelit old-world graciousness of this temple of gourmetry it seemed to me to have reached new heights, as my meal started with Lady Curzon turtle soup, with curry, made its way onward with a melt-in-the-mouth *Rahmbraten* (cream roast) and concluded with a famous specialty of the house, pancakes *(Pfannkuchen)* covered on one half with wild strawberries and strawberry sauce and on the other half with chocolate sauce and Schlagobers (whipped cream). Does that sound just too-too-too? If so, please withhold judgment till you try it. The Three Hussars is open only in the evening, from 6 till 1 A.M.

Zur Spanischen Hofreitschule, in the Palais Pálffy within a few steps of the Spanish Riding School for which it is named, is another place of special character, the proximity of splendid horses and their riders providing a sort of equine background. It is open for lunch and dinner, and when there is an evening show in the Reitschule you may double your pleasure by dining (early, from 6) at the restaurant, just across Josefsplatz, before attending the performance.

Zum Weissen Rauchfangkehrer (To the White Chimneysweep), on Weihburggasse adjacent to the three Hussars, is a rambling place of several small rooms of Austrian peasant style oddly lighted but interesting, and with piano music for background. It is a relaxy, take-your-time sort of place with wonderful food. A specialty, but various other dishes rival it, is *Esterházy Rostbraten,* but save room for the dessert. A chocolate cream puff—and *what* a puff—is the *pièce de résistance* and if the thought of so many calories frightens you, try a simpler but luscious *Apfelstrudel.* Or perhaps you'll see on the menu *Apfel im Schlafrock.* It means Apple-in-Its-Nightshirt and turns out to be a delicious apple dumpling. The White Chimneysweep is primarily an evening restaurant but lunch is served, too.

The *Rathauskeller* is a place of enormous proportions in (of course) the Rathaus, just outside the Dr. Karl-Lueger-Ring opposite the Burgtheater. Its *Rittersaal,* designed in imitation of the glittering Knights' Hall of old, can accommodate 2000 guests at once, and its bright newer Gothic Hall can take care of 350 more. In addition to these you'll find in the restaurant complex of the Rathauskeller several more halls, including the *Grinzingerkeller,* dominated by a giant tun that can hold up to 70,000 liters of wine. Let's settle on the biggest of all, the *Ratskeller,* where an excellent meal at surprisingly moderate cost may be had. Granting that the menu features the standard Wiener Schnitzel, the variety of dishes available is nevertheless extensive, and in this popular shrine of mass nourishment, *well* operated by the city government, I have had one of the best heaped-high Salzburger Nockerln (plural of Nockerl) that I've ever enjoyed. Wine of the Danube, maybe a Dürnsteiner, should accompany your meal, and to provide you with this your waiter (whom you will remember to address as Herr Ober) will attach an empty bottle to a long *Weinheber* (wine siphon), which then draws up the wine from the barrel so that he can serve it to you "barrel fresh." This system of siphoning wine from barrels is employed also in some of the Heuriger taverns of Grinzing, which we'll visit later, and guests always find that it adds zest to the meal.

For spooky atmosphere, obviously synthetic but interesting anyway, you may wish to try the *Alter Hofkeller,* in a cellar of the Amalien Wing of the Hofburg, entered from Schauflergasse. Here, if he isn't yet quite forgotten, they'll probably tell you that "The Third Man" used to hang out, and there's a zither to prove it. Other *Keller* and cafés claim The Third Man and actually, it seems that *Café Mozart*, on Albertinaplatz near Hotel Sacher, puts out the best claim.

The *Donauturm* (Danube Tower) *Restaurant,* actually a doubleton with an expensive international restaurant above a cheaper café-restaurnat, is Vienna's answer to the lofty revolving restaurants now found high up on radio-TV masts in so many German cities, notably including Munich (this to be viewed, and viewed from, in Chapter 13). It rises from the Donaupark, which fills a crescent of land between the Danube and the Old Danube, neither of which should be confused with the central city Danube Canal. The main restaurant of the Donauturm at the 165-meter level (541 feet), revolves at any of three different speeds in 26 minutes, 37 minutes or 52 minutes, as the management may decide, so you may have your lunch or dinner in two, three or four revolutions. The view directly below reveals a well-ordered suburban community, complete with a small lake and a sports area, plus a couple of restaurants, one, the *Au,* of excellent repute, enlivened by gypsy music. Raise your sights and you will be treated to a commanding panorama that extends from the Vienna Woods to faraway parts of Lower Austria north of the Danube. The Donauturm has its own special apéritif, fancifully called *Bel' Rosé,* composed of whisky, gin, dry Vermouth, white wine, Angostura bitters, grenadine syrup and four kinds of fruit juice, but my throat found the idea far too explosive, so I shied away from it and settled for a Scotch as lubricator. The favored main item of the meal that I recently enjoyed was a so-called *Girardirostbraten mit Nockerl* and contrary to some criticism of the cooking that I had heard I found this dish very good. The dessert was *Marillen Eisknödel,* a tasty dish that could be translated as "apricot ice cream dumpling."

Quite a number of other first-class restaurants deserve your attention and I will list a few of them. The *Altes Kerzenstüberl,* on Habsburgergasse off the Graben, is an underground candlelit place of intimate atmosphere and dependably good fare. The centrally located *Franziskaner,* on the like-named Platz, is fashionably fine, with loads of atmosphere and a wide-ranging menu. The *Kupferdachl* (Copper Rooflet)—descend to the *lower* level—is central, on Schottengasse, as is the *Landtmann,* with café terrace on the Lueger-Ring, but the *Wegenstein-Weisser Schwann* (White Swan), famous for its game dishes, is farther out, on Nussdorferstrasse.

Two small places of Vienna Stuben type are the *Hans Figlmüller Weinhaus* on Wollzeile almost in the shadow of the Stephansdom, and the *Griechenbeisl,* on the Fleischmarkt near the Danube Canal. The former is proud of its *Leberwurst,* a soft and very *different* liver sausage that my taste finds quite wonderful. The *Griechenbeisl* fairly reeks—there's no other word—with antique atmosphere, for it claims to be over 500 years old. If you grant that this place is a darling of tourists, who crowd upon it in season, you will find the place full of interest, especially for the scrawled signatures on the walls and ceiling of one of its rooms. You'll have no trouble in finding Beethoven, Wolfgang Amadeus Mozart and Richard Wagner and among many of more recent vintage Gustav Mahler, Stefan Zweig and Jan Kiepura. If you don't enjoy such crowded and comercialized shrines of the past you may at least wish "to have seen it." I felt, after once eating there, that I had been served atmosphere in lieu of good food, but perhaps the cook had an off day. The restaurant consists of seven rooms at different levels and in one or several of them Lieber Augustin is said to have first tried out his gift for minstrelsy on his Dudelsack. (Right next door to the Griechenbeisl is another atmospheric place, this in a 400-year-old house, the *Marhold,* whose food is as certainly good as that of its neighbor is dubious. Game is featured.)

Balkan eating places of good standing include *Pataky's Hungarian Restaurant* (Spiegelgasse 10); the *Czardasfürstin* (Schwarzenbergstrasse 2), another Hungarian place; and the *Balkan Grill* (Brunnengasse 13). Pataky's fairly sparkles with Magyar atmosphere and music and the food is first rate. Try its salami, then *Kalbspörkelt* and finally an Apfel Strudel (Strudel means literally "whirlpool"!) and be sure to order a bottle of sweet Hungarian Tokay wine.

A very good *Italian* restaurant, in case you go for pasta dishes, is the *Grotta Azzurra* (Blue Grotto, with decor to fit its name) on Babenbergerstrasse just outside the Burgring.

Garden restaurants, mostly outside the Ring, are found in nearly all the parks and gardens of the city, three outstanding places being the interesting *Lusthaus Café,* in the Prater, the very pleasant *Stadtpark Meierei* (Farmhouse), and also in the Stadtpark, the *Kursalon,* the latter with concerts, dancing, and for fair days, a broad café terrace and also a garden café. The *Volksgarten Café-Restaurant* is another indoor-and-outdoor place of great appeal. Still other good ones are the *Hauswirth,* at Otto Bauer-Gasse 20, in the 6th district, and the *Café Meierei Schönbrunn,* in the Schönbrunn Palace Park. Two woodsy places on high ground overlooking the city, both with triple-star views, have been mentioned above in the orientation section, namely the smart *Cobenzl* and the *Kahlenberg.* Don't miss them.

Viennese coffee houses are "of the essence." At least a dozen of them deserve honorable mention, but I shall cut them down to three: *Café Mozart,* mentioned above on Albertinaplatz near the Sacher; *Café Schwarzenberg,* on the Kärntnerring; and *Café Landtmann,* on Dr. Karl-Lueger-Ring.

Konditoreien, meaning pastry shops, are the prime places in which to forget the word diet. Every pastry you order in these places shamelessly defies all dietary rulings, for they are rich, creamy, fattening and—wonderful. Sachertorte is but one, Malakofftorte is another and Indianer Krapfen, chocolate puffs bursting with whipped cream, a third. Vienna's most celebrated Konditorei is *Demel,* at 18 Kohlmarkt, a street leading from the Graben. Others almost as good are *Lehmann,* on the Graben itself, (Number 22), and *Heiner,* with a main establishment at Wollzeile 9 and a branch at Kärntnerstrasse 21.

Snackshops (Imbissstuben) are often neglected in lists such as this, but they may be of utmost importance to the tourist short of time. Several of them are to be found on Schwarzenbergplatz and on Schottengasse, and others are more or less conspicuous all over the center, but the most convenient one for most tourists is probably the round-as-a-dollar *Imbiss-Opernpassage* in the central underground "circus" mentioned several times on earlier pages.

Finally, leaving Heuriger wine taverns and nightclub-restaurants for after-dark discussion, let me call your attention to the *Espresso* bars of Vienna, which though of Italian origin have gained extraordinary popularity with Viennese coffee lovers. It seems, perhaps, another case of Rome-north-of-the-Alps.

Night Life in Vienna, a Personal Report

I have mentioned in the opening part of this chapter the delights of witnessing starlight operetta, if luck provides it, and I can only reemphasize here that there is no more Viennese way to spend a summer evening. Johann Strauss is almost a patron saint of such occasions and his gay works (*Die Fledermaus, Wiener Blut, The Gypsy Baron,* etc.) are perennial favorites, but Schubert is, of course, also revered by the garden crowds and Jacques Offenbach is welcomed for such treats as *La Belle Hélène* and *The Tales of Hoffmann.* A long intermissin always permits the slaking of one's thirst at some nearby café or bar.

The *Volksprater,* or *Wurstelprater,* named for Hans Wurst, a famous buffoon of a former time, has been mentioned earlier, but needs further attention here. This park of popular fun fell into the doldrums during the period of occupation, for it was in a Russian occupied part of the city and fun didn't flourish with Red "comrades" all about, but it gradually came back to its former ebullience.

In a sense this is the *doyen* of all the amusement parks of the world. Copenhagen's Tivoli would be but a patch on its hem for size. New York's Coney Island is but a noisy upstart in years. The Wurstelprater was first open in 1603 and except for a few intervals has been roaring with life ever since. In normal periods it is a gigantic maelstrom of circus concessions, dance gardens, glass palaces, movies and other attractions far too numerous to mention. One notes on every hand such wonders as Mitzi, the 650-Pound Sylph, Harry the Living Aquarium, the Fairyland of the Lilliputians and a game called Arizona-Spiele, with a synthetic cowboy earnestly drumming up trade. The Great Wheel, a fixed attraction on the Vienna-by-night Austrobus tours, towers above this seething world of pleasure and lifts its endless crowds of patrons to the height of a 24-story building for a fine close-up view of the city, this deliberate circling of the air taking a quarter of an hour. The Wurstelprater is not for the fastidious pleasure-seeker but rather for the person of whatever "brow" who is not above mixing with common or garden crowds for a hilarious evening.

The *Heuriger Taverns* are as distinctive of Vienna-after-dark as the starlight operettas. They provide the feasts of new wine and old song traditional to the quaint suburb named Grinzing, but common also in Nussdorf and other suburban areas. *Heuriger Wein*, to repeat this explanation, means "this year's wine," from last autumn's grapes, and the institution of Heuriger parties dates from the era of Josef II, son of Maria Theresa, who remitted the taxes on new wine in order to give his people so jolly a time that they would pay no attention to what their monarch was doing in the political field.

Grinzing, like the Prater, is a regular goal of the night tours purveyed by the Cosmos and Austrobus organizations. But it may also be reached by tram #38 (from the Schottenring), or, more comfortably, by taxi from your hotel door. From the Grinzing tram terminus dozens of *Heurigenschenken* may be reached on foot. The establishments are indicated, in each case, by an evergreen bush hung over the door. In the livelier ones *Stimmung* (atmosphere) breaks out like a jumping rash from 8 o'clock until after midnight. On my first visit, many years ago, the wine waiter started the evening for me by placing a carafe of Heuriger on my table and then retiring without a word or a look. It was farthest from his thoughts to ask what I would have. Of course I would have Heuriger, else why was I there at all? I called him back and protested that I wished only a glass of it, not a carafe, but he would hear of no such thing. "Everybody drinks plenty here," he said firmly. "You can't enjoy the evening on less than that," and again he was gone. I was so awed by his salesmanship that I let it go at that—and I did enjoy the evening. The wine was blond, potent, faintly suggestive of vinegar.

Several Heurigenschenken cry for specific mention here, among them *Bach-Hengl* (Sandgasse 9); *Reinprecht* (Cobenzlgasse 40); *Weingut Rode* (Himmelstrasse 4); and *Das Alte Haus* (Himmelstrasse 35). I must have tried at least a dozen places, including one not named above called *Setzger's Backhendl Station,* specializing in fried chicken, for these Heuriger taverns do not hesitate nowadays to serve hot dishes with the wine. I did, in fact, have a sizzling Backhendl dish at Das Alte Haus on my latest visit and excellent it was, accompanied by French fries and a large carafe of wine. The occasional guest who likes nothing even mildly alcoholic can indulge in *Apfelsaft* (apple juice), *Heidelbeersaft* (blueberry juice), or *Johannesbeersaft (roter* or *schwarzer),* which is red or black currant juice. The first-named beverage, Apfelsaft, is much used by American lady tourists at Vienna's restaurants.

If you haven't time to go to Grinzing you may see a city edition of a Heurigenschenke at the *Paulusstube,* in the Inner City at 7 Walfischgasse, but of course this is a somewhat touristic and synthetic edition of the real thing, which is humble, hilarious, loud, bibulous—and Grinzing. If you wish merely to sample the unmellowed beverage you may do so in almost any part of the city. Two good wine parlors, of the *many* in the Inner City, are the *Augustinerkeller* (with zither music), on Augustinerstrasse behind the Opera, and the *Urbani-Keller,* at 12 Am Hof. This latter is a precise replica of an old Vieneese tavern and it is enlivened by lilting Viennese music.

Vienna's year-round evening-into-night recovered gradually but completely from its war-born, occupation-nourished slump. It is bright and gay today, by which I mean tonight. Grand opera, long since back in its proper home, is in full and scintillating swing. So is drama in the Burgtheater. So are the elegant "salon operas" (in summer only) in the little theater of Schönbrunn Castle, and so are all types of performances in all types of theaters. Comic operas, operettas and ballet are offered in the Volksoper (People's Opera) on Währingerstrasse, a theater enjoying government subvention. Here I once saw *The Bartered Bride* for the third time in my life, one of those times having been prewar, in Smetana's own Prague. I thought this one of Vienna the gayest performance of the three, if not quite the most expert.

In *symphonic music* the city of Beethoven and Schubert is, I should say, on the top level in Europe. It supports not one but two orchestras of world caliber and I have delighted in hearing them both, the *Vienna Philharmonic* and the *Vienna Symphony*. The former is the more wonderful of the two, but this should not be taken as any disparagement of the other. Their concerts are given in the *Grosse Konzerthaussaal,* on Lothringerstrasse, and the hall of the *Gesellschaft der Musikfreunde,* on Dumbastrasse.

Nightclubs are rather numerous in Vienna and a few are very good of their varying types. *Chez Nous* (Kärntnerstrasse 10) is currently popular, as is *Fledermaus (Spiegelgasse 2). The Eve,* originally called the Monseigneur, at Führichgasse 2, offers typically bold striptease revues, and the *Eden-Bar* (Liliengasse 2) is a dance temple of superior quality. All of the foregoing are very central, and there's another, the *Renz,* at Zirkusgasse 50, not within the Ring, that seems to be going strong. These places and others not named are, of course, international in type and therefore less typical of Vienna than are the delightful music cafés and the Grinzing fun taverns, where down-to-earthy high jinx prevail every evening.

Shops of Vienna, a Personal Report

Shopping in Vienna is a major occupation, or preoccupation, of many tourists, especially on the distaff side, who come to this city from overseas (or elsewhere), and it is at least a minor occupation of almost everybody, the men included. Kärntnerstrasse and the

Graben, with the streets that lead from them—Kohlmarkt *must* be named—form the center of this eager search, but of course the prices always soar on streets that are easy to reach. Outlying streets such as Mariahilferstrasse have countless small shops and a good number of department stores and there the prices are cheaper. One pays for elegance as well as for convenience.

I have roamed through the central area by the hour, or the half day, sometimes with my daughter and a Viennese friend, who is not a shopper's guide but knows her shops, and I have entered many of the leading shops to inquire for the manager and discuss with him what he has to offer. Antique shops abound on and just off Kärntnerstrasse, for this is one of the greatest centers in Europe for such eagerly sought treasures. In other goods, Vienna is world known for Augarten porcelains; beautifully embroidered blouses; *Trachten,* meaning folk dress, centering, for feminine shoppers, in the simple but lovely dirndl, which becomes young and old, excepting only the too-too corpulent; and for myself, the climax, Vienna's masterpieces of petit point, which is needlepoint done with a fine stitch as against gros point, done with a coarse stitch. Each point, it should be known, calls for two stitches. To be statistical, needlepoint with up to 103 points per square inch is called gros point, whereas petit point has up to 3122 points per square inch, meaning 6244 stitches! And on one embroidery as many as 500 colors may be required. It is vicariously exhausting just to think of it, and sensitive persons sometimes feel guilty to buy petit point at the very moderate prices charged in Vienna. I have managed to keep such worries under control and have bought something in this material on virtually every visit to Austria. And now, since I have literally drifted into this subject let me "start with the climax."

"My petit point man" (or shop)—I think of him (it) as I would of *my* doctor or *my* lawyer—is *Jolles Studios,* established for many years at Andreasgasse 7, a street that leads from Mariahilferstrasse only four blocks from the big West Station. In the salesroom of Jolles (but of course Jolles products have many outlets) you may see a wealth of wonders: bags, purses, cosmetic boxes, brooches and so on; and if the workshops upstairs are not too busy you *may* be taken through them to see some of the work, such as painting of designs, being done, though the needlework itself is done in the homes of the embroideresses. Their earnings must be pitifully small considering the painstaking work, the finest of which has to be done with the aid of a magnifying glass. Jolles offers to visitors a small English-language booklet that gives in detail the story of petit point, as it developed from the time of Maria Theresa and is manu[hand] factured [made] today.

Now to go to the center of things, on Kärntnerstrasse, I will report, almost in the form of a syllabus, some of the shops I have explored.

Müller, Number 53 (all shops are on Kärntnerstrasse unless otherwise stated), has a good array of handicrafts.

W. F. Adlmüller, Inc. (I shall use Inc. instead of the multisyllabic German equivalent), Number 47, is a widely known shop selling high-grade clothing for women and, in a lesser way, for men. It is a three-center company, with fine shops also in Badgastein and Munich. This Vienna shop is in the Palais Esterházy. It was burned down in 1969 but has been rebuilt, though the company does not have as much space in it as formerly. A private gambling club operates on an upper floor. Adlmüller goes in for haute couture as well as ready-made clothes, and is well known in that field.

J. Mayr and A. Fessler, Number 37, has everything that concerns writing materials, plus a line of small gifts and Wiener souvenirs.

J. & L. Lobmeyr, Number 26, has a superb line of crystal table sets and gift articles, including finely engraved and hand-cut crystal articles of an artistry comparable to that of the Steuben glass workers or the artisans of Orrefors. A thing of special grace and beauty that caught my eye was the line of thin-stemmed goblets. Lobmeyr has a shop in Salzburg, at Schwarzstrasse 20 near the Österreichischer Hof, and one in New York at 16 East 39th Street. A source of pride to the company is its crystal chandeliers, one of which was made for Washington's Kennedy Center for the Performing Arts—it is a brilliant "sunburst" that lights the opera house—and another, almost 20 feet in circumference, for the Lincoln Center "Met" in New York. Still another hangs in the lobby of the Met.

Kugler, Number 29–31, has a large stock of knitwear in various materials, wool and rayon, acetate, ribbonknit and straight wool knit. Many types and combinations are shown.

Resi Hammerer & Co., also at Number 29–31, is proud to display its stock of ready-made garments that have what it calls the Austrian Look, especially its sportswear for skiing. It makes tailored clothes as well, and its dirndls are in what the shop calls "modern style."

Trachten-Tostmann, Number 42, running through to a back lane and into the actual *Dreimäderlhaus* made famous by Schubert. He loved one of the three girls, Hannerl by name, but the family came down hard on the romance because young Franz was "only a poor composer," not suited to marry into such a family. The firm of Trachten-Tostmann is a specialty house for loden cloth, the heavy native wool fabric used for capes and coats, which is virtually windproof and waterproof—marvelous for mountain wear. The store also carries jackets and the like made by a fascinating "boiled wool" process. It all starts with the soaking of the wool for two or three days—this can be done in any convenient stream in the mountains where the wool is spun—then the knitted material is put together from a pattern cut to twice the desired size and shrunk by boiling it. This gives it such a tight firm weave that it is very warm and wonderful to feel. If you want to see one of these garments, and they are to be had in many shops in Austria, ask for *Walkjacke.*

Wilkens, Number 23, has a good display of silverware, pewterware and articles in horn.

Ö W, for *Österreichische Werkstätten,* (Workshops), Number 15, produces a wide variety of handicrafts, so extensive, in fact, that some enthusiastic shoppers have compared it to Copenhagen's famous Den Permanente.

Haute Couture is of considerable standing in Vienna and two well-known shops are those of *Berta Farnhammer,* who has her salon at Number 10 Kärntnerstrasse and *Franz Faschingbauer,* on Jasomirgottstrasse, the one-block street I have mentioned in connection with the city's history, that leads from Stephansplatz.

Leather articles, including first-rate wallets, are seen in many shops, two good ones being *Winkler,* on Himmelpfortgasse 7, and *Franz Schulz,* at Führichgasse 6, these streets leading east and west just off Kärntnerstrasse.

Wiener Porzellanmanufaktur Augarten, the last word being the important one, can be a fitting conclusion of our Kärntnerstrasse shopwandering, for Augarten procelain is famous the world over, certainly including America, where the line is known as *Royal Vienna Augarten.* The firm's chief shop in central Vienna is on Stock-im-Eisen-Platz, which is a sort of intermediary square between Stephansplatz and the Graben. Among its famous patterns are Maria Theresien and Wiener Rose, but perhaps the most famous of all Augarten products, at least in Europe, is its line of figurines of horses and their riders of the Spanish Riding School. The gleaming white procelain sets off the horses to the best advantage and the riders, authentically fashioned in their riding uniforms in the proper colors, make for a splendid contrast. No visitor, even if not shopping bent, should fail to have a look in the windows of Royal Vienna Augarten.

7 / Travel in the Provinces; First Burgenland and Styria

FOREGROUND FACTS

Going by Air, by Rail, by Road

PRELIMINARY NOTE: In plotting our course through the Länder we shall follow a general clockwise plan, starting with Burgenland and Styria; then Carinthia; then northward to Salzburg, City and "Land," together with the Salzkammergut lake region, where we shall catch up with our pre-Vienna Chapter 4; and finally the long western arm of Austria, with Tyrol and Vorarlberg, where we'll look, also, at the Principality of Liechtenstein. The chapters on Austria (and Liechtenstein) will be followed by one on Munich, with the 1972 Olympics, and one on the Bavarian Alps, which weld so smoothly with those of Austria.

Austrian Airlines serves more than a score of European cities, its lines fanning out from Vienna, but it does not, for the present, fly overseas, and within Austria its routes are limited, due to the fact that since a serious accident occurred at Innsbruck's airport a few years ago that airport has been declared unsafe except for small planes. The domestic network now includes, in addition to Vienna, the cities of Salzburg, Linz, Klagenfurt and Graz (with daily flights between Graz and Frankfurt). Graz is a sort of turntable, since Austrian Airlines flies domestically only between Vienna and Graz.

Train travel in Austria has improved substantially in the last few years, one of its greatest gains, to my mind, being the development of a fleet of TS trains, a sort of domestic Austrian application of the TEE (Trans-Europ-Express) idea that has been so great a success throughout Europe. The TS trains, and I will spare you the tongue-twisting German word for them, are fast intercity flyers that connect Austria's chief cities in shorter times than even the EX trains (for Express), because of fewer stops. Also, they are the *smoothest* fast trains I know, starts and stops being completely jerkless. The ÖBB (for *Österreichische Bundesbahn,* Austrian Federal Railway) has an excellent record of safety and it has shown itself ingenious in solving the problems created by Austria's mountain scenery. The *Autotransport* service through the *Tauern Tunnel* that connects Carinthia with Badgastein and the rest of Salzburg Province, or vice versa, is one of the marvels of modern railroading, enabling motorists by the tens of thousands to "drive through the 5½-mile tunnel by electricity." By this I mean that the driver and all occupants of the car remain within the vehicle while it goes through the tunnel on a railway flatcar. A similar tunnel service is maintained through the 6½-mile Arlberg Tunnel and this has special significance in winter when the road over the Alberg is sometimes blocked by snow. In the broader picture of European rails, the ÖBB takes pride in the international *Autoreisezüge* (Car-carrying Trains; called also Sleep Trains) that take on cars in Holland or Belgium or in Germany's northern cities like Hamburg and Hannover and carry them to Salzburg and Carinthia or to Bregenz, while their owners sleep their way to their destinations in berths or couchettes. From many northern points such trains roll to Munich as terminus. *Mountain rail routes* of special scenic appeal number at least a dozen and some of these will be encountered in the ensuing text, but cable railways, aerial cableways, chairlifts and skilifts, some of which are owned and operated by the ÖBB, are so numerous that we'll take a separate look at them below.

Road travel, by bus or by individual car, is a mighty and manifold subject, and also an intimate subject, for rolling tires offer a closer intimacy with the land and the people on it than does any other form of locomotion except walking. They weave into one's experience the little things of daily native life that fast, impersonal trains must necessarily ignore. They allow the traveler to feel the heartbeat of a nation, to see a country as the roads see it, to hear the pastoral symphonies of the upland, to smell the fragrance of hay field and flower-covered meadows, to pass within the distance of a handshake of quaint, rustic homes whose occupants may never have seen a city or a train. They lead you directly to the people of the soil, the forest and the dairy, people who sharpen your wits because you cannot talk with them unless you talk their language. For all these reasons, in addition to the basic reason that roads give access to many a choice spot untouched by rails, every traveler in Austria lacking a personal or rented car, and lacking also the time or energy for cycling, should acquaint himself with the possibilities of motorcoach travel. We'll consider that first, and then the roads as the motorist sees them.

Bus travel in Austria should *never* be thought of merely as a means of getting about available to the budget traveler. It can provide a summer (or winter) of thrills for the well-heeled quite as logically as for the traveler of modest means. No motoring worries or thoughts of parking problems mar one's sense of "excited peace." Let the driver worry—but he never does. Austria's Postal Motorcoach System, whose big, cream-colored coaches are modern, powerful, comfortable, expertly handled, are seen in all parts of the Republic. This far-spread fleet consists of some 400 giants of the road, deploying on more than 200 routes for a total of 7500 kilometers. They laugh at steep grades, and despite their bulk, are unafraid of narrow, serpentine roads. I have been impressed many a time with the skill of the drivers. They are never reckless, but they do astonishing things because they know exactly what space they have in which to maneuver their big vehicles. On one occasion, near Gosauschmied, in a lofty valley of the Salzkammergut, the driver of a coach in which I had come from the Lake of Hallstatt, encountered another monster of the road as big as his own. Passing

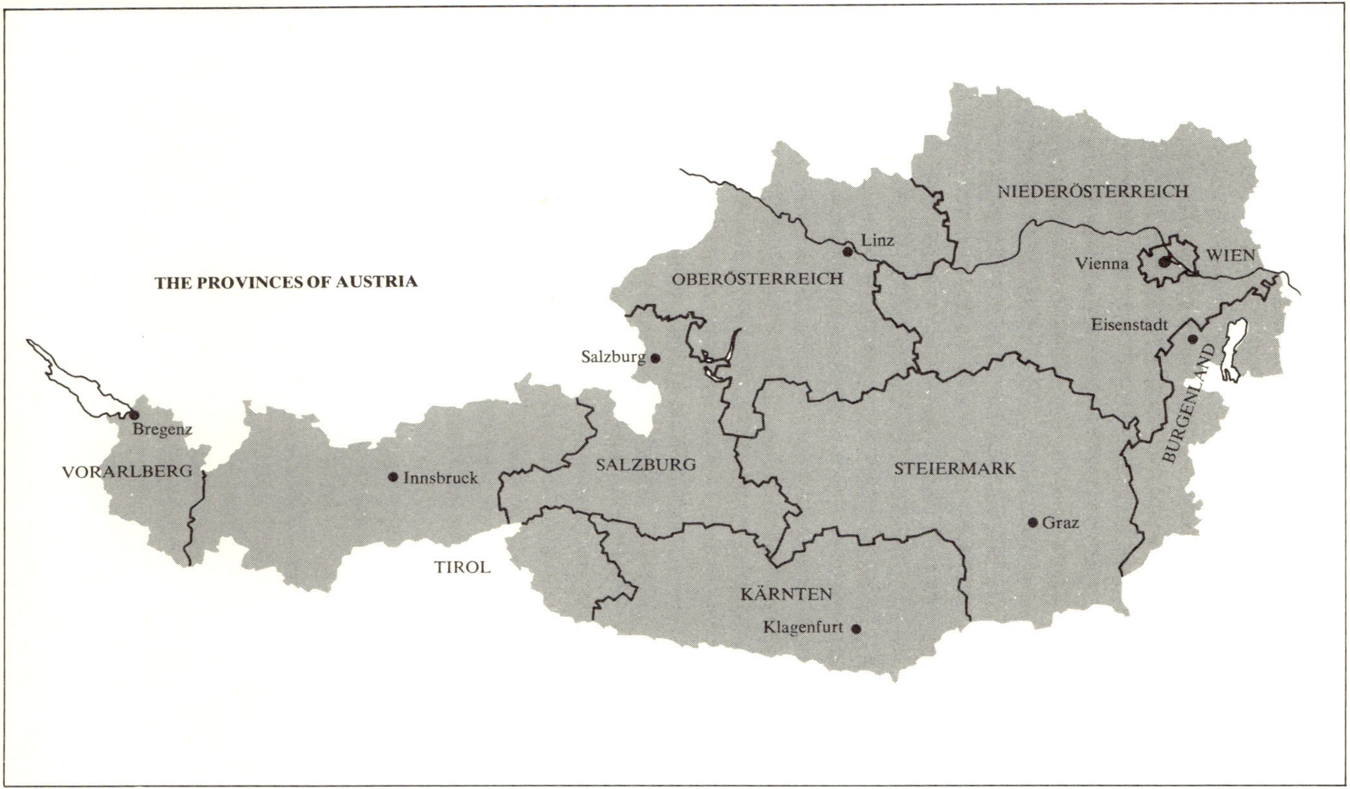
THE PROVINCES OF AUSTRIA
NIEDERÖSTERREICH
Linz
Vienna
WIEN
OBERÖSTERREICH
Eisenstadt
Salzburg
BURGENLAND
Bregenz
VORARLBERG
Innsbruck
SALZBURG
STEIERMARK
Graz
TIROL
KÄRNTEN
Klagenfurt

seemed to me impossible, but without much slackening his speed he sailed smoothly to the side and came to a halt beside a granite fence-post. The other bus edged by with half an inch to spare. I gazed out of my window on the fence side and saw with amazement that there was scarcely room for a hog's bristle to be squeezed between the granite post and our fender. It was on the offside of the driver and he could only estimate, not see, the space. "Um Gottes Willin!" I gasped. The driver, hearing my exclamation, smiled good-humoredly and said, "I know. We have to do that sort of thing all the time. Roads are a bit narrow in this valley."

Many smaller buses—a considerable army of them—are operated on branch routes by private companies and their quality varies with the prosperity and ambition of their owners. With all services combined there is scarcely a hamlet or a lonely farmhouse in all Austria that is not kept in touch with the world by some adventurous bus line, and by the same token there is scarcely a spot that cannot be reached, even without self-driving, by those persons who come from the outside world in search of "untrodden ways."

The fares for motorcoach travel, even within any single system, vary somewhat according to the steepness of the roads and the volume of traffic which the route commands. Principal fares may be easily ascertained from the timetables, but in general it may be said here that the cost on most routes is hardly higher than second-class rail travel. On a few routes, such as the skyscraping Grossglockner Road, it is, of course, substantially higher.

Europabus, "the Motorcoach System of the European Railways," operates various routes from Munich to Salzburg, to Innsbruck, and to Landeck, plus some important routes within Austria, but its big appeal to tourists who want to shed *all* responsibilities and just take it easy, is the system's Red-White-Red Tour of Austria, already mentioned as a seven-day weekly offering. To amplify this, let me say that the tours depart from Salzburg every Sunday morning from early May to late September. The route extends through the Salzkammergut to Ybbs-on-the-Danube, to Vienna, to Graz, to Carinthia and its warm lakes, to Kitzbühel, to Innsbruck and finally to Salzburg. Alternatively, you may commence the trip in Vienna or in Innsbruck. This is a magnificent tour and it can be 100 per cent carefree. The cost for *everything* is at present about $225, including the extra charge of about $25 for guaranteed single room at each halt. Couples sharing double rooms pay approximately $200 apiece.

Motorists revel in Austria, but unless they stick to the main routes they must be prepared to coax their cars up many a steep hill and to travel many a road too narrow to pass another car easily, these difficulties being mere breath-on-the-mirror compared with the scenic rewards offered hour by hour and day by day. As for main scenic routes, the motorist should be aware that in addition to the famous Grossglockner Road there are some newer roads of almost or quite equal scenic splendor. One is the *Felbertauernstrasse,* which takes off from Kufstein, Tyrol (reached by autobahn from Munich), passes through St. Johann in Tirol, Kitzbühel and Mittersill and then threads the 3.22-mile *Felbertauern Tunnel,* which pierces the Gross Venediger mountain massif at an altitude of 1 mile above sea level, to emerge in East Tyrol, continuing to Lienz, its capital, and so to and through Carinthia and a corner of Yugoslavia to Venice. Obviously, this new route makes it easy to reach many points that were formerly almost inaccessible, notably in the grand stretch between Mittersill and Lienz. Another new route is the lyrically called *Traumstrasse* (Dream Street), or more soberly the Tyrol autobahn over the Alps that runs from Innsbruck to and over the much-photographed Europabrücke to the Brenner Pass and Italy. A third new route is the toll road over the *Timmelsjoch* (Pass) from the Ötzal, and Obergurgl, the loftiest parish village in Europe, to St. Leonhard and Meran (Merano) in South Tyrol, now a part of Italy. The highest point of the pass is 8230 feet above sea level and consequently it is open only for a few months in summer. The Austrian Automobile Club, with headquarters in Vienna, at Schubertring 3 and with branches in Salzburg, Klagenfurt, Graz and other cities, has an excellent reputation for its friendly aid to motorists. For information and help one should phone 72–21–01 if calling from Vienna, or the same number preceded by 0222 if calling from any other point within Austria. Frontier offices, as I've said, are maintained by the AAC at the main points of entry by road to aid incoming motorists.

Lakes and Lake Boats

Propellers and paddlewheels churn the pellucid waters of many an Alpine lake in Austria, providing movement of a restful type to complement the more strenuous travel on wheels. Two of the country's chief portals, as mentioned in Chapter 1, are water gates entered by large passenger steamers. One, the Danube Gate, has been covered in Chapter 4 and here we'll view the Gate of Lake Constance (Bodensee), whose steamers, of three nationalities, Austrian, German and Swiss, tie Bregenz, the only Austrian port, to the various German ports, including historic Constance itself, and by connection at Lindau or Friedrichshafen, to the Swiss ports on the southwestern shore (Romanshorn and Rorschach). There is always a special quality of sophistication about an international lake and I think this Bodensee heads the list in such respects, for it is the only one in Europe that imperturbably touches three countries with its lapping wavelets. It serves as a silver-voiced statesman, playing down animosities, inviting fraternization. It is a holiday lake unsurpassed, and echoes on every summer day with the gay chatter of people having holidays. Beautiful in every part, it is bold and stunning only in that small Austrian segment on the south shore where the young Rhine empties icy water into it. No paddlewheels or propellers do a greater service to travel than do those which drive white craft into Bregenz.

The smaller fleets of the smaller lakes of Austria will appear and reappear throughout this book. For the moment I need record only that there are 13 lakes served by public steamers or motor launches. They are the following:

ON AUSTRIA'S WESTERN ARM

Achensee, in Tyrol, a lake whose blue is a special color, one of the most intense blues of the whole race.

Zellersee, one of Austria's smarter lakes, but no less lovely because it is known by the *haut monde*. It lies on the shoulder of the long arm. Zell am See is its great resort.

IN CARINTHIA

Wörthersee, the chief holiday lake of this holiday province, whose waters, probably warmed by subaqueous hot springs as well as by the sun, are a field of sport for all nations. Velden and Pörtschach are its leading resorts, Maria-Wörth its historic namegiver. For a good preview of this dramatic spot you may look at the first Austrian 50-schilling note that comes into your hands. On it you will see a pleasant picture of Maria-Wörth.

Ossiachersee, more rugged and less populated than the Wörthersee. From its port of Annenheim, at the western end, a basket swings you through the sky to the Kanzel peak. At the eastern end is Ossiach, whose great Benedictine abbey is the setting for Carinthia's Summer Festival.

Millstättersee, a soft and civilized body of water into which a thousand pagan statues (*Mille Statuae,* hence the name) were said to have been thrown by a zealous Christian knight who lived in the 8th century. Millstatt is the chief town. The lake's color is between blue and green and the water is nearly as warm as that of the Wörthersee.

IN THE SALZKAMMERGUT

Mondsee, a neighbor to Salzburg city. This lake is touched with a special culture emanating from its abbey town, which is likewise named Mondsee, but "Moonlake on the Moonlake" and its lesser sisters along the shore enjoy various watersports too.

Attersee, a large but somewhat less interesting lake, almost contiguous to the Mondsee.

Wolfgangsee (called also *Abersee*), a lake of outstanding glamor. St. Wolfgang, its chief attraction, is thrice famous, for the medieval masterpieces in its church, for the "White Horse Inn" on its shore and for the mountain railway to its guardian peak, the Schafberg.

Traunsee, a marvel of beauty. Only Gmunden, at its northern end, has pretentions to social smartness. Traunkirchen, midway on its western shore, is a picture of romance.

Hallstättersee, scenically the most spectacular in the Salzkammergut, if not in all Austria. Hallstatt itself is a village of enchantment untouched by time and hardly damaged by motor travel, since a high cliff road carries much of the traffic harmlessly past it.

Grundlsee, Toplitzsee. These two, with the minuscule *Kammer-*

see solely for ornament, have been already mentioned in Chapter 4.

IN BURGENLAND

Neusiedlersee, a thoroughgoing anticlimax, mentioned only in the interest of completeness. As stated earlier, it is broad, shallow, brackish, reedy, unexciting except for its incredible wealth of wildfowl of more than 200 varieties. If this counter-encomium stirs you to go there, be advised that a motorboat crosses it in something less than two hours from Rust to Podersdorf or vice versa.

The 13 lakes whose waters are thrashed by public propellers or paddlewheels are not necessarily the finest in scenery, though several of them are in the very front rank. If I were to mention the little lost lakes of the high places I would be in danger of running at a tangent far away from the subject of this chapter, for these remote jewels of lakedom are a subject dear to my heart, and body. I have dived (in the costume of Adam before his fall) into many of them.

Austria's 400-plus Mountain Lifts

Basket or chair locomotion, meaning the ascent to mountain tops by aerial cableways, is a great specialty of Austria. Other countries, notably Switzerland and the Alpine part of Germany, have lots of these delightful conveyances that swing you through space to lofty peaks, but none, I think, has developed the idea so far, in proportion to the total number of peaks tamed for the public, as has this land. All but a handful of Austria's more than 400 *Seilbahnen* (cableways) and Sesselbahnen (chairlifts) are of the Seil*schwebe*bahn type, *schwebe* indicating suspension, the very few exceptions being cableways where the conveyance runs on rails but is drawn up by a cable. This swinging company includes an extremely lofty conveyance that hoists its daily quota of passengers to a height of 9200 feet, whence a smaller cablecar hoists them another 530 feet to the summit of the Zugspitze at 9731 feet, this summit being squarely on the frontier of Austria and Germany.

"Suspension airways" are as *clean* as they are thrilling. That is one of their charms. Perfect visibility is another. Old-style rack-

and-pinion steam railways, their valiant engines sometimes breathing out threatenings and slaughter to the purity of the mountain air—four of these are still left in Austria—seem definitely outmoded, and even electric railways, plodding painfully up steep slopes, seem utterly clumsy by comparison with the cabins and chairs that soar above treetops with all the lightness of mountain eagles. Suspension travel is one of the safest forms of transportation because of the simplicity of its operation and the effectiveness of its brakes, yet the first-timer sometimes shudders with apprehension. It *is* weird to see the earth dropping from under one into the depths of limbo, and the trees leaning against one's vision at such incredible angles. Also there is often an appalling little shudder as the basket reaches its ultimate goal and then settles back a yard or two to its anchorage. My first suspension trip was to the top of Sugar Loaf in Rio de Janeiro more than 40 years ago and the memory of the mechanical shudder at the summit lingers with me yet. My heart must have skipped three beats. "There always has to be a first time for accidents," I thought, with a quick stab of terror, but I was quite as safe as if in my hotel, safer in fact, for a skylight fell into the hotel lobby that same evening and crashed into a thousand shivers of glass—just after I had left the spot.

To summon some statistics, by way of conclusion, Austria now has 163 major cableways, meaning suspension cableways, earth-clinging cableways and double chairlifts; 240 single chairlifts; 1926 skilifts; and, to repeat, 4 rack-and-pinion railways, but that is the count *as of now.* If I were to check it next year, or even next month, I am sure the count would be higher.

Spas for the Ill and the Well

Spas and health resorts abound in Austria and some of the spas are extremely rich in medicinal springs. We'll pause in one of the chief ones, *Baden bei Wien,* when this chapter travels to Styria, so I shall mention here only some of those that are at quite a distance from the capital. *Badgastein* is the most famous of these, with *Bad Ischl,* once the favored watering place of Kaiser Franz Joseph, next. Others are *Bad Hall* and *Gallspach* in Upper Austria and *Schruns* in the Montafonertal of Vorarlberg and a newer and excellent installation in *Mitterndorf,* Styria. Sumptuous, last-word installations and equipment are available for those who wish to "take the waters," and Badgastein is a sight for even the disgustingly well to marvel at. In that resort there are about a score of warm springs, of temperatures ranging from 98 to approximately 116 degrees Fahrenheit, and they are of help in curing almost every ill. Having no crucial ills, I once penetrated the heart of a mountain to see the *Franz Josef* [so spelled here] *Quelle* (Spring) just for fun. It was a raw winter's day outside, but in that tunnel I quickly became drenched with perspiration. It was terrific. Also, it *was* fun to have the experience, but upon emerging to the cold outer air I thought I should surely be a prospective customer for this or some other Quelle.

Winter and Its Sports

Winter sports are practiced with enthusiasm in every one of the nine Länder, including even Vienna, with its Woods, and Burgenland, whose big lake is perfect for skating and ice sailing, but the great centers are in Tyrol and Vorarlberg, so we will await Chapters 10 and 11 to explore that subject, though not neglecting other places in other provinces, notably Styria and Land Salzburg, where the sports are avidly practiced.

BURGENLAND AS A TANGENT TOUR

Burgenland is a queer-looking province on the map, its odd shape, a little like an hourglass, being due, as I have explained in Chapter 1, to a political amputation that took place after World War I, when the province was separated from Hungary and transferred to Austria. Prolonged negotiations at that time resulted in the allotment of Burgenland's capital, then named Ödenburg, to Hungary. The city adopted its Hungarian alias, Sopron, and has remained Hungarian, though this is geographically fantastic, since it sticks like a blunt instrument into the flank of Burgenland, as now shaped, leaving the province, at this point, only *three miles wide* and making it a two-part province, the northern part, wrapped around big (130 square miles), shallow (4 to 7 feet) Neusiedlersee, the southern part, much greater in extent, running 60 miles along the border of Hungary, and then Yugoslavia to a wedge at the extreme south. Eisenstadt, having at the time of the transfer less than one-tenth as many inhabitants as Ödenburg (3300 as against 35,000) became Burgenland's new capital and has now increased in population to almost 7500. Fortunately, Eisenstadt makes up in charm and in background what it lacks in size.

Burgenland is so different from the rest of Austria that the tourist within its borders sometimes feels he has been placed there by Lewis Carroll for the entertainment of Alice, but in that case he gladly accepts his assignment and enters into the spirit of his role.

One should not assume that when one crosses the line the aspect of the region will change at the turn of a tire. It's not that quick, but the change is sure and it becomes much more pronounced as one approaches and then reaches the enormous plain known as the Puszta, which begins in Burgenland and extends eastward, seemingly without limit, far into Hungary. In this area the villages, the road life and the people do certainly have that other-world look that you may have come to Burgenland to see, though I have to say, in all candor, that "progress" begins to threaten the picture. Small whitewashed houses, often thatched with straw, become the rule rather than the exception and they usually rise straight up from the street or square, without benefit of curb, sidewalk or steps. Oxen with twisted horns and endlessly chomping jaws plod along at the dizzy pace of 2 miles an hour drawing squeaky carts, battalions of geese may deploy in main squares and streets, and storks stand one-legged on their chimney-top nests, unless the first chills of late August shall have set them in motion for the "flight into Egypt," where they spend their winters.

Two days could well be used by the motorist in exploring this two-part province—whose roads, by the way, are rather good—one day for the northern part, one for the southern; but on the assumption that you may have only one day at your holiday disposal I will outline, in the syllabus style used above, a one-day tour from Vienna, out and back, that will give you, I think, the maximum satisfaction for the hours spent.

Enter Burgenland by crossing the range of modest, forest-covered hills melodically called the *Rosaliengebirge,* some 10 miles southeast of Wiener Neustadt, approaching it through the village of *Wolkersdorf* (find *Hochwolkersdorf* on your motor map) and crossing the line at *Neustift an der Rosalia,* which is in the narrow corridor that connects Burgenland's north and south. This is by no means the shortest or simplest means of entrance and you will have to give close study to a road map and perhaps even make some roadside inquiries, but I urge it, especially if your visit is in the spring, because *die blühende Rosalia,* as it is called, will make an instant impact on your senses, one that will surely endure as long as you endure. On a wooded knoll is the *Rosalienkapelle,* an Esterházy chapel, and from the knoll you may see the very color and substance of Burgenland. All around you, if the season is spring, you'll see what Burgenlanders proudly call their *Blumenmeer,* or Blossom Sea, the blossoms of cherry, peach, apricot and almond trees combining in a color scheme of unforgettable beauty, but if you are too late for the Blossom Sea, the countryside will still be magnificent with its ranks of orchard trees, its *Edelkastanienbäume* (chestnut trees) and its forested hills, dressed in all the greens that nature knows. Directly beneath the Rosalienkapelle, only a mile or two distant, is the moated *Burg Forchtenstein,* a historic Esterházy castle-fortress of the first importance (see below), and in a deep valley below the Burg you'll see the straggling village of *Forchtenau,* which is Esterházy-owned in its entirety. To the northeast, clearly visible, is the shimmering *Neusiedlersee* and beyond that the steppes. On very clear days you may even see Lake Balaton, in Hungary, Europe's largest lake with the exception of Russia's Lake Ladoga. I urge again that you use the Rosalia gate to Burgenland instead of the direct humdrum highway from Vienna to Eisenstadt. That may very well serve as exit, but not as entrance.

Burg Forchtenstein is an absolute must, I would say, of any visit to Burgenland, however brief. It embodies the Esterházy motif as nothing else does and the name of Esterházy is woven so closely into the whole fabric of the province that one cannot get the feel of it at all without knowing something about that famous family.

The first Esterházy of princely stature was Paul Anton, who acquired Burg Forchtenstein in 1626 and completely rebuilt it. He was a busy man but found time to beget 25 children, by two wives! A more recent head of the family (by three centruies), also named Paul, was, with his wife, in "protective custody" in Hungary for several years from the beginning of the Red occupation of Burgenland in 1945. His great crime was in being *rich,* for it is always dangerous to be rich when Communist armies approach. He was arrested, I have been told, on charges of having associated with Cardinal Mindszenty, but his wealth, fairly crying for confiscation, was his real fault. Much treasure of the Burg had been stolen long previously by the notorious Red Bela Kun, but there was plenty left. Regardless of any pilferings, it must be said, to the Russians' credit, that they did not damage Burg Forchtenstein during their 10-year occupation, though they did neglect its art works and let them deteriorate for lack of care.

Burg Forchtenstein may be visited any morning or afternoon in a guided tour that takes about three-quarters of an hour and the tour is immensely worth while. First you cross a bridge over a wide, grassy moat in which an outdoor theater flourishes, where historical *Burgspiele* (Castle Plays) are presented annually on five or six nights in July. Within the massive walls surrounding the Burg your guide takes over for the tour. In the building's inner courtyard he'll show you an odd equestrian stone statue of the original Paul Anton and in various salons several portraits of the Great Progenitor and his two wives. In one of the rooms there is a representation of the Esterházy family tree, which grows, uncomfortably, straight out of *Adam's* naked flank. Cain, Seth and Enoch are all there in the tree, as are hundreds of other notables from their day up to the 17th century. The Burg is an enormous, ramifying affair whose walls are 15 to 20 feet thick, with a big Rittersaal, with room after room of portraits, with an armory, with an artillery gallery and with—*a well.*

The well is the climax of every tour and it seems to me far and away more interesting than the deep well of Nürnberg's hilltop castle, which tourists flock to see. This one is 470 feet deep, 270 from the wellhead to the water and 200 from the water's surface to the well's bottom. This colossal work of engineering was done by Turkish prisoners during a period of 30 years from 1660 to 1690 and it is said that several thousand of them lost their lives in the process. A tremendous treadmill that was trodden by weary prisoners' feet is seen beside the well and this, too, took its toll of lives. It was used, of course, to draw up water from the well by means of buckets attached to a long iron chain. The guide drops bits of burning paper into the well and we watch the flares of them flutter down and endlessly down to the water. This is interesting, but the well's *echo* is the thing that invariably causes wide-eyed, or "wide-eared," wonder. I have never heard anything to approach it in clarity, clear ring and repetitiveness, unless perhpas in the Syracuse cavern called The Ear of Dionysius. At the wellhead the guide snaps a newspaper sharply and you her at least *eight* pistol shots of diminishing power from below. Or you may talk to the well and it will answer back, or sing to it and it will sing back. You've heard impressive echoes before in lots of places but I'm almost ready to "promise" that you've never heard one the equal of this.

Reluctantly you will conclude the castle tour with a walk on the grassy parapet, peering through gun slits at the magnificence of nature below you, and so across the moat and into your car. Or perhaps you will delay for a visit to the colorful wine tavern found within the castle and have a meal or a snack, accompanied by Oggauer or Ruster wine from vineyards on the edge of the Big Lake. Oggau and Rust, or Rust-am-See, to use its adoptive tag, center the wine production of Burgenland and Rust is its center of centers. Furthermore, Rust is a "free city" (of about 1800 inhabitants), having won its freedom from the Esterházy overlords in the 17th century by delivering 800 barrels of its choicest wines to the princely cellars. It has, even today, a special status of civil freedom, being subject, I am told, only to the governor of Burgenland personally and to the Austrian Federal Chancellor in Vienna. A generous sampling of *Ruster Spätlese* left me with the conviction that the Esterházys made a shrewd bargain when they swapped their suzerainty over one of their many communities for such a large store of the precious wine.

Mörbisch-am-See is another wine village just south of Rust and

I would vote it the most photogenic of them all, but it is in a sort of cul-de-sac, less than a mile from the Hungarian frontier, so the motorist should retreat to the north and west to visit Eisenstadt, Burgenland's small but growing capital.

Eisenstadt is a city of unfailing appeal, centered and dominated by a former Estherházy castle which now serves as the provincial seat of government. In its courtyard you'll enjoy a double row of very imaginative grimacing faces, seen in the plaster work (one row high under the eaves), this being, I suppose, the whimsy of an Esterházy architect, and in a main corridor of the four-square building you'll find—I hope—a gigantic green vase of so-called *Halbedelstein,* or semiprecious stone, ten feet tall and decorated with much gold, this being a gift from a Russian czar to an Esterházy prince. Perhaps you will also catch a glimpse of the *Haydnsaal,* a 17th-century hall seating 1200 persons where concerts, of course stressing Haydn's music, are occasionally given. Across the street from the castle you may remain in the Esterházy atmosphere by entering the *Weinkosthalle der Fürstlichen Esterházyschen Weinkellerei,* as it is lengthily called, to down a glass of good local wine. There is a huge tun, or cask, here holding about 15,000 gallons when full and until 1953 you could have had your wine drawn directly from the tun, for it was still in regular use, but since that date it has been only ornamental.

Haydn's home for 12 years (1766–1778) is found at Number 21 on the little street named for him Haydngasse, and the composer's body lies in an elaborate sarcophagus of white marble, a tribute given by Prince Esterházy, in the crypt of the Kalvarienbergkirche in the town.

There is one product of Burgenland that should not be overlooked, namely Serpentine Stone, sometimes called *Edelbernstein,* and sometimes also Bernstein Jade. This dark green stone, a specialty of this province and not found in any great amount anywhere else, lends itself to fashioning in handsome jewelry, as also in larger ornamental works. Its color, to me at least, seems so unique that it ought to sponsor a special shade of green, Bernstein green. Brooches, pendants and the like are purchasable in shops of Eisenstadt and also, of course, in Vienna. I have seen and bought such articles, for instance, in a shop in the much-mentioned Opernpassage.

The return from Eisenstadt to Vienna, and incidentally, to our clockwise plan of travel, may be made in about an hour if you are driving your own car, but in case you have elected to visit Burgenland's capital by public transportation, be advised that there is a regular postal bus service that ambles from Vienna to Eisenstadt, Rust and Mörbisch and in the reverse direction, the total transit time taking about two hours each way.

STYRIA; GRAZ, ITS CAPITAL CITY

To Graz by the Semmering Pass

Graz, the capital of Styria and the second city in Austria, is 126 road miles from Vienna, and it can also be a very easy and pleasant train ride via Bruck an der Mur *if* you are careful to take one of the smooth-as-silk TS trains from the capital's Südbahnhof (South Station—not to be mixed up with the East Station, which shares the same structure).

Baden bei Wien is the first place of interest encountered by the motorist, only 16 miles from Vienna, and it is, in fact, one of the very important spas of Austria, its 16 hot springs, of highly sulphurous water, gushing 1½ million gallons a day, most springs at about 99 degrees Fahrenheit, but one or two as high as 116 degrees, to help those ailing from rheumatism or kidney troubles.

The Römerquelle, or Roman Spring, reached by a Roman-built tunnel passage, is one of the spa's chief sights, but many other springs may also be visited, and by permission one may see the intimate workings of underwater therapy without taking the cure. Men and women bathe together, scantily but adequately clad, and have long done so, as is candidly revealed by Baden's armorial symbol, dating from the 1500s, a man and woman sitting together in a wooden bathtub! But don't think that *only* men and women benefit from these waters. Not too long ago a racehorse named Pythagoras developed a rheumatic lameness in one leg that prevented him from running. The ailing leg was faithfully bathed in the radioactive water daily for four months and Pythagoras then emerged to run faster than ever, winning race after race.

An odd fact of history and geology is revealed in the story of Baden, namely that at the time of the terrific earthquake which destroyed Lisbon in 1755 the waters of this watering place *ceased to flow.* For several days the copious springs didn't gush at all. Then they gradually came back to their normal output, and with them came a new spring that had never gushed before.

Baden has the biggest gaming casino in Austria and a beautiful Kurpark with a handsome floral clock. It has also a lot of hotels, large and larger and an interesting three-part thermal swimming pool of great dimensions, whose waters are warm but not too warm for comfort. The smell of sulphur pervades the air around them.

Wiener Neustadt, 14 miles due south of Baden, is an industrial city of interest only to the history-minded tourist and to him only for one thing, the Georgskirche, the chapel of the castle built by Duke Leopold V, where, under a large red marble slab in front of the high altar, lies the body of Emperor Maximilian I, "the last of the knights." It seems odd to many visitors, as it does to many Austrians, that his bones should lie in so simple a grave here instead of in the magnificent tomb that he built for himself in the Hofkirche of Innsbruck, but he was born in this castle and it was his last wish that he should be laid away in its chapel.

Semmering is the big name on the trek from Vienna to Graz for motorists who take the more westerly (and more interesting) route via Bruck an der Mur. Its fashionable resort hotels have long been big favorites, both summer and winter, of Viennese vacationists. Since 1955, when the Russians finally cleared out, this lofty resort, with an average altitude of 3300 feet, has attracted more and more foreign holiday patronage, for its air is superbly fresh, stimulating and normally sunny, and its Alp-and-valley views are as stimulating as the air. Attractions and diversions of various gay sorts are available, including heated swimming pools, and there are two chairlifts that carry passengers, respectively, to the *Hirschenkogel* (4100 feet) and the *Sonnwendstein* (5000 feet).

If, perchance, you should wish to stop over for a night or two or more on your way to Graz I can think of no more charming and unusual goal than *Schloss Rabenstein,* near the village of Frohnleiten, some 20 road miles north of Graz. This can be your first introduction to castle living, and the informality of it, amid many treasures of art and of historical significance, may surprise you. I have recently made my second stay in Schloss Rabenstein and its appeal "grows on me," as I think it will on you. Owned and personally run as a summer inn by Sigurt and Ruth Reininghaus, of an old baronial family, this 12th-century castle-into-inn is a dreamer's dream of what a medieval castle should be. From its terraces (for breakfast and sunbathing) and many of its windows the far-down view to and acorss the broad, green Mur River Valley, through which went the old Roman road from Italy to Vienna, is stupendous, and I blush for so weak an adjective. There is now a 9-hole golf course and a motel called *Murhof* in the valley, but it's a quiet and lovely course and I don't think the Romans would find it an intrusion. The woodsy and meadowy walks to be taken from Rabenstein are as numerous as they are lovely. The Reininghaus couple, both of delightful personality and both speaking English, make no secret of their catering, almost exclusively, to *American* guests, especially unhurried ones who can relax and enjoy the family atmosphere of the castle. Realizing that most Americans, however romantically inclined, relax better where there is good prosaic plumbing, they have installed private bathrooms with most, if not all, of their bedrooms, numbering seven. The presently quoted tariff for "room with bath, including breakfast and dinner" is about $18 per person. Many guests do not desire a formal lunch. They go on motor excursions or perhaps take long walks and find lunch or snacks in some rustic Stube.

Special features of Rabenstein are occasional chamber music concerts by top Austrian groups offered in the Tower Room of the castle, June being a favored month for them. They are community affairs but Mr. Reininghaus gives the use of the castle as his contribution. If you contemplate visiting Rabenstein and wish to know the current dates of such concerts or if you wish to make bookings for any date you may call up Mr. or Mrs. Reininghaus at the number Frohnleiten 170. Your hotel porter will help you make the call.

Don't overlook the pleasant village of Frohnleiten, 4 miles from the castle, and above all try to see the tiny and very old (11th-century) pilgrim church, remade into the baroque style in the 17th century and meticulously restored in 1955, in connection with the 650th anniversary of Frohnleiten, in the neighboring hamlet of *Adriach*. Why this church, among so many? Because Empress Maria Therese herself made it famous. She came here and brought a priceless sacerdotal robe that one of her daughters, Princess Maria Josefa, had made and upon which the empress herself had done much work. The robe is *in* this church and it is unique in Austria. To restore it to full perfection skilled embroideresses from all over Austria were engaged in the 1950s, so that the work could be completed for the anniversary. One of the charms of Austria is that historical treasures beyond price often remain just where they originally were instead of being taken to some great museum to be "lost in the shuffle."

Highlights of the Second City

Graz has been little exploited for general tourism, far less, in my opinion, than its historical significance and its beauty of setting warrant. Planted astride the wide, hurrying River Mur, guarded by the dramatic Schlossberg, superbly parked and gardened in every quarter, it is a city of quality with a pedigree extending back to the 12th century. It is on the so-called Pack Highway, a part of the highway from northern Italy by way of Carinthia to Vienna, and is thus on a main stream of traffic. This has helped to make Graz the large and important city that it is, with a population now nearing the quarter-million mark.

The important sights of Graz are marvelously bunched for the visitor who likes to see them the walking way, and always the Schlossberg, or Castle Hill, accents it. This is called by geologists a leftover of a sunken range of Dolomite hills. It was an early stronghold of the Styrian burgraves and later a fortress against the Turks, but in 1809 the conquering Napoleon required that its fortifications be blown up. This was done and it proved a blessing in disguise, for 30 years later it was converted into the lovely park that it is today, enhanced by a splendid view of the city and of the River Mur, centering its garden valley.

One mounts to the Schlossberg by any of several winding paths, by a stairway of 500 steps (!) or—to our relief—by a venerable funicular from Sackstrasse at the point where this street merges with the quay on the left bank of the Mur. Adjoining the upper station of the funicular is a café-restaurant, where the food and drinks are enhanced by the view, and near this is a feature of special loveliness, the Bastion Flower Garden, changed in color scheme every few weeks. The last time I saw it the flowers were engaged in a "tamed riot" of yellow.

Two conspicuous towers adorn the Schlossberg, namely the *Clock Tower* and the *Bell Tower,* and both are greatly loved by the citizens. In 1809 they showed their affection in the most practical way. In that year Napoleon proposed to destroy the towers, along with the wall, for the sole purpose of humiliating the city, but he "had his price" and was bought off, as an inscription states, for the odd sum of 2978 gulden and 41 kreuzer. Perhaps he saved the 41 kreuzer for the son whom he so eagerly desired.

The Clock Tower, on the southern slope a little below the summit, was built in 1561 and ever since then it has been the landmark and emblem of the city. It is 90 feet high and has a clock dial of colossal size on each of its four sides. The 115-foot Bell Tower is on a plateau at a higher level and contains, as its chief treasure, a 4-ton bell named Lisl, made in Graz some four centuries ago. Its big mouth is 6½ feet wide and it bellows its cheerful greeting to the citizens three times a day, at 7, noon and 7.

At all times, in all lights, the Schlossberg is symbolic of Graz. It looks its magic best at night, when strong floodlights make it a pillar of radiance above the city.

A Five-point Saunter Through Town

In two or three hours of easy footwork one may see, or at least glimpse, all the more important sights of Graz that are grouped around the base of the Schlossberg on the left bank of the Mur and I shall make bold to outline a suggested pattern for this walk, with five "stopovers" ranging in length from half a minute to half an hour.

The *Burggarten,* reached from the eastern quarter of the city by walking through the tree-lined Johann Allee, is practically a part of the Stadtpark. It is beautiful in itself and gains added popularity as the setting for lively pop concerts. On its west side are the *Burg,* a former castle now housing provincial government offices, the *Burgtor,* one of two ancient city gates still intact (the Paulustor is the other), and the big *Civic Theater,* fronting on Freiheits-Platz. The *Wendeltreppe,* or Double Stairway, of the Burg is a 15th-century curiosity that I cannot put into technical words. It enables two persons to start climbing in opposite directions and meet at each floor. I have been told that only two other such stairways exist in all Europe, one in the Château de Chambord, on the Loire, the other, a smaller one and inferior, in the St. George Church of Nördlingen, Germany. I have seen both of these, but am inclined to vote for this one of Graz as the best of the three.

The *Cathedral* and the *Mausoleum of Emperor Ferdinand II,* just to the south of the Burg, adjoin each other almost as two parts of the same structure. The former is mostly Gothic, the latter insistently baroque, with three time-greened copper domes, one topped by an angel swinging in the wind. The outer wall of the cathedral is ornamented with a curious painting made in 1480 by an unknown Carinthian artist. It is called the *Landplagenbild* and shows three plagues sent by God to chasten the citizens for some offense. One plague is locusts, another pestilence, a third the Turks, who are committing dreadful atrocities right before our eyes. God looks on from above, watching the effect of His grim corrective measures. In the Mausoleum Chapel there is a high altar by Fischer von Erlach, who must have been one of the busiest men of his era, but the sarcophagi win the visitor's principal attention. That of the emperor lies in a vault to the left of the altar, but the central spot is reserved for the double sarcophagus of his parents, Archduke Karl II and Duchess Maria of Bavaria, this tomb being a masterly work in red marble with the royal pair sculptured in chaste piety upon it.

The narrow Sporgasse, skirting the Schlossberg at its southern base, is worth finding for the quaint old houses that line it. It leads to the Hauptplatz, on which the Rathaus stands, and also the Luegg House, with unusual arcades and a 17th-century stucco façade, and from this important square one may stroll north on Sackstrasse, to admire some 18th-century mansions of the aristocracy, or south on Herrengasse, to see the *Erzherzogshof* (Archducal House), at Number 3, which is covered from street to eaves with frescoes painted in 1742 by Johann Mayer. This is more commonly called *Das Gemalte Haus* (The Painted House).

The *Landhaus,* farther along on Herrengasse, was the former House of the Styrian Estates and is now used for government offices, including those of the very efficient Styrian Tourist Office, whose nine-syllable name in German works out as *Landesfremdenverkehrsabteilung*. This office, if you don't let its name throw you, can be your very good friend in court during your stay in Graz and for all your journeyings in the province. The historic building, with a panther on a shield, the Styrian coat of arms, sculptured on its façade, is of architectural interest to the veriest layman. Its portal is strikingly beautiful, its flowered balconies are charming and its 3-storied arcaded courtyard, graced by an exquisite iron wellhead, is one of the finest things of its kind. The courtyard becomes an open-air theater at the time of the annual festival and here some of the attractions are staged, including symphony concerts and that favorite of the festivals, *A Midsummer-Night's Dream*.

The *Provincial Armory* (Landeszeughaus) adjoins the Landhaus and its interior is truly an amazing sight, for here is *the complete armor for five thousand soldiers,* chiefly of the 16th century, the total pieces of armor numbering *thirty thousand*. We see muskets, blunderbusses, light cannon, thousands of common suits of armor for men and horses, cuirasses and shields, each weighing up to 30 pounds and more, and even the instruments, chiefly fifes and drums, for 16-century military music. In completeness few armories in Europe can vie with this one of Graz, though its display has less of knightly elegance than some. The reason for this great buildup of arms is that Graz, like Vienna, was engaged for decades in defending itself, and Austria and all Europe, from the marauding Turks.

Boxing the Styrian Compass; Graz as Hub

There are many satisfying sorties to be taken from the hub of Graz, some mere suburban jaunts, some to the middle distance goals and some, especially in the north and northwest, calling for a substantial trip. In boxing the compass I shall start with the northeast and veer clear around to the northwest, due north, with Mariazell having been already covered in the Styrian mountain approach to Vienna in Chapter 4. First, we'll view four suburban attractions of Graz, all of them so near as to be easily reached by train or bus from the city's Jakominiplatz.

Mariatrost, northeast, is a pilgrim-and-holiday resort like a miniature Mariazell. Its *Pfeiffer Restaurant* is very good and its Franciscan pilgrimage church, a twin-towered one on the summit of a 1500-foot hill just above the tram terminus and the restaurant, is of striking character. Like Mariazell, Mariatrost has its miraculous image of the Virgin enshrined on the high altar.

Hilmteich, east-northeast, is a pleasant summer goal, with a little lake for boating and with a popular restaurant. *Rosenhain,* with its good *Café Rosenhain,* on a wooded hilltop, is within easy walking distance.

Schloss Eggenberg, west, lies only half an hour distant from the center by tram from Jakominiplatz or the Hauptplatz, and only a quarter of an hour by your car or a taxi. It is a sumptuous royal castle of Renaissance design built in the 1600s for Prince von Eggenberg and now a civic property of Graz.. Magnificent is the word for Eggenberg, with its 26 halls of state and banqueting rooms and with its large paintings and superb furnishings. The lower floor contains a Museum of Hunting Trophies and Old Weapons. It could go without saying that such a Schloss would be surrounded by its own well-kept park, and this park of Eggenberg is exceptionally large, with a free gamepark added. In the October Festival weeks, some of the concerts, especially of chamber music, are given in the castle courtyard.

Fürstenstand-on-the-Plabutsch, northwest, is a mountain restaurant-viewpoint, scenic climax of Graz's immediate environs, its 2500-foot level being reached by a chairlift. For all who love scenery this trip is the best in the city's vicinity.

We'll repeat the boxing of the compass for goals farther from Graz, starting with east and southeast points.

Riegersberg, Bad Gleichenberg and *Radkersburg* may be combined in a motor trip that may consume the better part of the day, or it may be combined in a long day with the *Weinstrasse,* almost due south of Graz. This present comment will, in fact, attach the Weinstrasse as a rider, and when we get there I will tell just what it is, and why a goal. The logical route from Graz is as follows: Leave the city by Elisabethstrasse; drive east on Highway 65 to Gleisdorf and then Ilz; turn right (south) to Riegersburg; then via Feldbach to Bad Gleichenberg; and from there due south to Radkersburg.

The *Fortress of Riegersburg,* dating from 1613, is built on the crest of a 1600-foot rock rising so steeply, some 350 feet, from the village of Riegersburg that the Turks, in many attempts, failed utterly to capture it. It is a castle-fortress, now owned by Prince Liechtenstein, and it is not *too* arduous a job to climb to it, by a path that penetrates seven gateways, for its grand view over the East Styrian plains. So starkly dramatic is this castle that even Hoch-Osterwitz and Burg Eltz, my two measuring sticks of castle drama, must look to their laurels.

Bad Gleichenberg, which is not far from the point where Austria, Yogoslavia and Hungary meet, is by far the chief spa of Styria, with waters specially beneficial to the heart and respiratory organs. Of course the place has plenty of social and musical gaieties to entertain you while "taking the waters."

Radkersburg is a frontier town if ever there was one, and in the centuries when it served as a Styrian outpost against attacking Turks and Hungarians it was in the odd position of having the town on the left bank of the Mur and its protecting Castle-Fortress of Ober-Radkersburg on the right bank. So it is today, except that time and wars have obliterated the castle, which has been Yugoslavian property, as is all of this stretch of the right bank, since the treaty settlement of 1918.

The point from which the motorist makes his way to and along the Weinstrasse is *Ehrenhausen,* a village on the right bank of the Mur at a point just before the river takes off to the east to Radkersburg, forming the boundary between Austria and Yugoslavia for some 20 miles. The Weinstrasse parts company with the river and takes off to the southwest to Glanz, Langegg and Leutschach, which villages, with Ehrenfeld itself and with Spielfeld on the frontier and Gamlitz a bit in (north), form the heart of southern Styria's wine region. On several stretches, each of 2 to 4 miles, the road *forms* the frontier and one would think it a smuggler's dream, since there are no customs stations or guards on it. The reason for this, I learned, is that there is no need for them, since there is no real reason to try to smuggle. Both sides of the border are contented regions just as they are.

A great attraction of this street (road) and the whole vineyard area is the existence of many a roadside *Buschenschank*. A Buschenschank is a "bush tavern," indicated always by a small bush or tree as sign. The keeper of such a tavern is entitled to remission of most taxes on what he sells, but he must grow, make, or in some way produce *all* the food and drink that he sells. He may not offer the guest any sort of food or beverage that he has *bought* "or otherwise acquired," as customs folk say. If he sells milk he must have a cow or two to produce it. If he sells wine he must grow his own grapes and make the wine. If he sells ham or bacon he must raise the pigs and produce it. Any cheating, but that is not in the heart of such tavernkeepers in such an area, could result in his being fined or losing his tax-easy status.

At Gamlitz, having worked up a most hearty appetite, I partook of an outdoor meal in a little Gasthof called *Das Alte Winzerhaus,* The Old Vineyard House, and wonderful it was, both in the food and the setting. *Backhendl,* fried chicken, was the heart of the meal, and the dessert was *Stanitzel mit Schlag,* which was a sort of super ice-cream cone topped lavishly with whipped cream. The Old Vineyard House has some very presentable, if unpretentious, guest rooms and the charge is about $6.00 for two, with breakfast! The vineyards of the region we're examining produce widely known and extolled red wines and also a very good rosé called *Schilcher Wein.* (North of this area, in a hamlet called Hochstrasse bei Stainz, is a somewhat similar rustic inn called *Igelwirt* [Hedgehog Inn], a humble place known for its very good food and good rosé.)

Piber, near Voitsberg, due west of Graz, is famous as the place where the celebrated white Lippizaner horses, so much admired in

Vienna's Spanish Riding School, are born and bred, and it is a fascinating place to see, a small village completely dominated by its equine industry, if that's the right word. The Stud may be visited in an hour's guided tour *except* during the breeding season, which is half the year, from mid-April to mid-October, but Piber fascinates anyway, and when the mares, with their foals are let out to pasture late in the afternoon it's a truly emotional sight, one tender part of it being that every mare knows her foal and every wobbly little foal knows its mamma. The value of a single Lippizaner is from $3000 to $4000. The Lippizaner, by the way, have been booked to perform at the Summer Olympic Games in Munich in August/September 1972.

Other features of Piber than the horses are the Carriage House —Queen Elizabeth used one of the carriages for a drive when she visited Piber—and the castle, *Schloss Piber,* with a lovely flowered courtyard, and with a welcome café-restaurant.

Northern Styria, from its small corner of the Salzkammergut at Bad Aussee to Mariazell, has been covered in Chapter 4, but the *young* Mur River, with the Upper Murtal (Valley), far to the west in Styria, has not, and that area has a great deal to offer. Near the very frontier of Salzburg Province are the important summer and winter resorts of *Gröbming* and *Schladming,* with ski runs recognized as valid for world championship competitions, and very near Schladming is the resort of *Ramsau,* the takeoff point for the ultramodern *Seilschwebebahn* (suspension cableway) opened in 1969, to the *Hoher Dachstein,* this peak reaching the altitude of 9820 feet, almost 100 feet higher than the summit of the Zugspitze on the Tyrol-Bavaria border, but the Grossglockner is more than 2500 feet higher still. This cableway from Ramsau is of the *Gondelbahn* (cabin) type, the cabin holding a whopping load of 70 persons, and it is a speedcabin too, making the long ascent in about six minutes. Another peak of the same Hoher Dachstein is reached, also by suspension cableway, from a point near Bad Ischl, in Upper Austria.

From a point near Gröbming a road, which becomes a toll road, heads south to climb up and over the 6000-foot Sölker Pass (I have thrown snowballs here in July), thus connecting the young Enns with the young Mur, a favorite goal of the Murtal (Mur Valley) being the village of *Murau.* This is a most appealing and typically Styrian village, a worthy goal in its own right, but its chief claim to *tourist* fame is the *Murtalbahn,* a narrow-gauge railway that celebrated its Golden Jubilee, its 75th year of operation, in 1969. It exists now only to give railway buffs and tourists in general the fun of operating the engine. The stretch of track is about 7 miles long, running from Murau to its terminus in the village of Frojach-Katschtal. Like other tourists I "drove" the old locomotive, belching smoke and cinders, and found it a barrel of fun, carefully following the instructions of the genuine engineer, who constantly stoked the engine with shovelfuls of coal. "Regulieren," he would instruct (although it sounded like Regulaten, maybe a Murtal dialect), and I would "let her go" full speed, maybe 15 miles an hour. From time to time he would caution me with the word "Bremse," brake; and when a tiny road crossing loomed ahead he would call "Pfeifen," whistle, which I did with great gusto. In fact, at every little lane I would pfeifen long and loud, giving the traditional ──── ──── ── ────── for anything bigger than a cart path. With that brief experience I became a "licensed engineer."

From *Predlitz,* a border village lying about 15 miles west of Murau almost on the border between Styria and Salzburg Province, a road heads south for another up-and-over climb, this one over the *Turracher Pass,* which is only 27 meters less high than the Sölker Pass (1763 versus 1790). At the top of the pass there is a little lake directly on the border between Styria and Carinthia called the Turracher See, and on both sides of the line there are summer and winter resort hotels, one of them on the Styrian side, the *Seehotel Jägerwirt,* being impressive, with a fine terrace above the lake and with a new swimming pool inside. The chief hotel on the Carinthian side is *Hotel Hochschober.* A good but *steeply* descending road leads the motorist to lower levels of Carinthia, and so to Klagenfurt, its capital.

HOTELS, RESTAURANTS AND SHOPS OF GRAZ, A PERSONAL REPORT

Hotels

My own first choice would be *Grandhotel Wiesler,* on a right-bank quay of the Mur, specially if I could get a room on the 4th floor, which has been recently built, or rebuilt, in very good modern style, and which has a most interesting view across the river to a row of old houses and rooftops, with the Schlossberg looming up to the left. Almost adjacent to the Wiesler is *Hotel Weitzer,* the largest hotel in Graz. Both have first-class rating, but are by no means deluxe. A bit more pretentious, possibly the best hotel in the city, is the *Steirerhof,* on Jakominiplatz. Another hotel, this of about the same standing as the Wiesler and the Weitzer, is the *Parkhotel,* on a corner of Leonhardstrasse, very close to the Stadtpark. I once stayed here and thought the courtesy quotient high. I hope this standard has been maintained. Still another hotel of about the same good rating proudly bears the name of the "Beloved Prince of Styria," *Erzherzog Johann,* the Archduke who married the postmaster's daughter of Bad Aussee and thus won affectionate immortality. A lesser hotel, and less expensive, or *still* less expensive, for Styria's hotel rates are all notably moderate, is the *Drei Raben* (Three Ravens), well maintained and recommendable of its type.

Restaurants

Restaurants are fairly numerous in Graz and some of them have special color. Two wine restaurants where you may expect to find good food are the *Keplerkeller und Weinstube* and the *Steiermärkische Weinstube,* the latter serving its own snails from its own snail farm. A restaurant of special character, not to be missed, is the *Krebsenkeller* (Crab Cellar), at Sackstrasse 12. Its courtyard "Osteria" (meaning Tavern in Italian), a place of beery and studenty leanings, with vine-clad arches and yellow walls, is the sort of "bit" that lures artists half way around the world. The Krebsenkeller is situated at the base of the Schlossberg, whose looming clock tower adds a sort of exclamation point to the scene. If crabs, crayfish and other crustaceans fail to call you, various excellent fish dishes are to be had in this popular Keller. Its main dining room is enlivened by music. The upper station of the Schlossberg funicular has an attractive open-air restaurant.

Cafés abound in the city, else it would not be really Austrian. The *Café Kaiserhof* and the *Café Europa* are big, bright, animated places, where illustrated magazines and current newspapers are to be had. The Europa, an upstairs place with a terrace above the street (Herrengasse) seems to me especially interesting. Another very good traditional café on Herrengasse is the *Herrenhof.* Still other good cafés are the *Pinguin,* the *Arabia* and the *Erzherzog Johann,* and in the Stadtpark there are two open-air cafés, the *Promenade Café* and the *Baby Bar Eiscafé,* this one serving no alcoholic drinks, but lots of pleasing ambience. The people of Graz enjoy good food and drink and they have a pleasure recipe that is worth passing along, namely *Ein Pipperl, ein Papperl, ein Pupperl,* which is, being interpreted and amplified: Something good to eat, something good to drink and a girl to share it all with.

Shopping

Shopping in Graz reaches its peak on *Herrengasse* and its continuation, *Sackstrasse,* and it is worth noting that these shops and department stores are *not* primarily aimed at foreign tourist purchasers, as many frankly are in Salzburg, but at average big-city Austrians, whose income is presumed to be much less than that of touring Americans. Perhaps this will have a special allure for you, shopping as the Styrians do. A dirndl specialist is *Mothwurf,* on Herrengasse, near the Hauptplatz. The city's largest department store is *Alpenland Kaufhaus,* on Sackstrasse, and this emporium, incidentally, has a good shoppers' restaurant. Two outstanding pastry shops of Graz are *Strehly,* off the Hauptplatz, and *Zaffita,* near Jakominiplatz.

Some notes on hotels in a few widely scattered towns and villages that are mentioned in this chapter may conclude this personal report, and please remember that the hotels of the Styrian Mountainway, from the Styrian Salzkammergut to Mariazell are covered in Chapter 4. In *Burgenland,* if you should elect to spend a night or more there, be advised that there are few hotels that can be called first class, even if one is in a generous mood, but there are good hotels of acceptable standing, such as the *Park Hotel* in Bad Tatzmannsdorf, a small spa, and *Hotel Burg Bernstein,* in Bernstein, both communities in the south. In Eisenstadt, the best hotel is the *Schwechaterhof,* a place of medium quality with a cheerful Keller.

In Styria's Piber, if the magnetism of the Lippizaner horses overpowers you, you will have to make do in a humble pension, the *Fritze,* where the going rate for room and board is—six (6) dollars a day! Better hotels, in case you don't feel in a make-do mood, are to be found in the nearby town of Voitsberg, the *Gussmack* being the best.

In Murau, that valley village of the puffing Murtalbahn, a place that I have enjoyed, chiefly for its excellent food, is *Hotel Brauhaus,* which suggests beer, and is indeed owned by a Murau brewery.

Finally, let me emphasize the attractiveness of the *Seehotel Jägerwirt,* on the Turracher Lake at the top of the Turracher Pass, mentioned earlier. It is a goal hardly known at all to American tourists, but well worth the effort to discover it.

8 / Carinthia, the Land of Warm Lakes

KLAGENFURT, CAPITAL OF LAKELAND

The word "Land" in this chapter title is, I think, a forgivable play on words, for Land, as we've seen, is the Austrian word for Province, and Klagenfurt is the handsome and progressive capital of the Province of Carinthia, whose German name is Kärnten (recalling Vienna's chief shopping street, Kärntnerstrasse, named for it). I will talk about Klagenfurt "in a minute," but first I feel an exhortation coming on. Why, I ask myself and almost anybody else who will listen, *why* do American tourists neglect Carinthia when it is so easy to reach and so rewarding when reached? By the thousand and ten thousand they pour into Salzburg, and with very good cause, of course, but in 45 minutes, with two daily flights available, they could fly from there to Klagenfurt by Austrian Airlines on the line that connects Frankfurt (and even London twice a week) with Klagenfurt by way of Salzburg. And if you're motoring, please note that Klagenfurt is a focal point in the design of Austrian traffic. It is a point of takeoff for, or arrival from, Graz, Vienna, Badgastein (by the Tauern Car-carrying Rail Tunnel), Lienz, the capital of East Tyrol *and the great Grossglockner Road* to and from Salzburg and its Land, Lienz being the road's southern "distributor."

Klagenfurt lies near the eastern end of the Wörthersee, being connected with it by a 2-mile canal, and is thus in intimate touch with the head of the family of lakes.

Klagenfurt calls itself "the Garden City of Carinthia," and the tag is not cloying, as such tags so often are; it is well deserved. The Theaterplatz, the Neuer Platz, center of modern life and site of the huge Dragon Statue, symbol of the city, and three adjoining parks named for Schiller, Goethe and Schubert are among the many parks and parklike squares. Add to these several very pleasant new pedestrian walkways lined with shops and centered by shrubs and flowers (and benches)—one of them, Kramergasse, is entered from the western end of the Neuer Platz—and the well worth seeing *Minimundus Park,* where famous buildings of the world, including Independence Hall of Philadelphia, are seen in miniature replicas, and confirmation of the city's garden character piles up. This miniworld, let me say, is extremely well done, rivaling the famous Madurodam Lilliputian World of The Hague, and an added attraction is its Europe Park, with floral features that are presents to Klagenfurt from various European countries.

Klagenfurt can be a stroller's city and very pleasant if one starts at the right place and strolls in the right direction. I would suggest starting in the Alter Platz, strolling to the Neuer Platz; then a few steps west to the Heiligengeist Platz (Holy Ghost Square), around the corner past the Landhaus and north to the park area around the City Theater. This splendid theater, to interrupt myself, is like a big city opera house to our eyes, yet it is typical of small cities all over Austria and Germany. In it, I recently enjoyed that delicious operetta *Im Weissen Rössl* about the White Horse Inn in St. Wolfgang in the Salzkammergut, and was aglow with admiration for the high quality of the performance and the obvious sophistication of the full-house audience, this in a city of some 70,000 population.

To get back to our stroll, the *Dragon Fountain,* a big, eye-filling affair in the center of the Neuer Platz, was designed by one Ulrich Vogelsang about 1590 and then carved out of stone. Basically, it is a 27-foot dragon spouting not fire and brimstone but an absurdly thin steamlet of water. Some 50 years after he was fashioned a sculptor by the name of Hönel made a fine big Hercules, complete with massive club, who has stood before the dragon for more than three centuries, getting set to slay him, though never quite going about it. This whole thing serves as the emblem of Klagenfurt, for it recalls the legend that a fierce dragon once devastated the region and devoured all the stalwart knights who dared engage him in battle. Finally, a peasant boy killed him with a club and was therupon rewarded with the hand of the grand seigneur's daughter in marriage. If you feel that practical aid for your tour is more important than legendry you may precede your walk by visiting the Carinthian Provincial Tourist Travel Office, *(Landesfremdenverkehrsamt Kärnten),* which is alert to your needs and will give you a friendly hand, along with lively literature, for your exploring of Klagenfurt and the lakes.

The Fürstenstein, or Princes' Stone, is a sight to be seen on the ground floor of the Provincial Museum. It is a sort of stone table, actually the base of a Roman column, on which a quaint ceremony of investiture of the Carinthian dukes, a ceremony quite unique in Europe, took place as early as the 9th century, continuing to the 15th. It went like this: A Carinthian peasant seated himself, cross-legged, on the Fürstenstein and the hereditary duke, dressed also as a peasant, then approached him in the spirit of an applicant for a job. The peasant subjected the duke to an examination as to his identity and his intentions. The duke, after passing the examiniation, as he always did, mounted the Stone in place of the peasant, flourished his sword to the four points of the compass, indicating his determination to defend the land against all enemies, and then received the acclaim of his subjects.

This was only Act I of the rite of investiture. After having thus secured the symbolic assent of the people the future duke hastened to a pilgrimage church at *Maria-Saal,* some 5 miles north of the city, where he changed his clothes and repaired to the nearby *Herzogstuhl,* or Ducal Chair, a huge stone throne in a clump of trees, and there took his seat and swore fidelity to his nobles, shaking each one's hand in solemn confirmation of his oath. The church of Maria-Saal is still a sight to see in Klagenfurt's environs, and so, even more importantly, is the Herzogstuhl. It is close to the road, on the right side as one travels north from Klagenfurt on Route 17, and should not be lightly passed by. This massive chair of stones, with many inscriptions in Latin, was set up in the year 834 and the portion of the rite centering here lasted until 1597. This Herzogstuhl, let me emphasize, is of great historical significance, almost like Wiltshire's Stonehenge or the Druid menhirs of Brittany from still earlier eras.

Klagenfurt has on its records few names of international celebrities but I recall a tablet to one citizen who certainly deserves the heartfelt gratitude of every tourist. I refer to Emanuel Herrman, whose name and service to humanity can be noted on a tablet on the inner wall of the main entrance to the post office. Emanuel Herrman first dreamed up the idea of the *postcard—Der Erfinder der Postkarte,* says the inscription—from which the picture postcard developed, and managed to get it introduced into Austria on October 1, 1869. The touring world should erect a monument in place of this modest tablet, for Herr Herrman has saved, in the aggregate, millions of hours of tourists' time by substituting for laborious letters of verbal description a visual appeal to wanderlust. He should be sculptured in bronze, writing with a bronze pen, the first "Having a fine time. Wish you were here."

CLIMBING TO HOCH-OSTERWITZ

Hoch-Osterwitz seems to me the most dramatic hilltop castle in Austria, if not in all Europe, a judgment to which I still cling even with the picture of Riegersburg fresh in my thought. It lies less than 12 miles from Klagenfurt and is reached by a side road from St. Donat, a village on north-going Route 17. It may be clearly *seen* from the windows of the train, on the left side as it approaches Klagenfurt from Vienna.

This castle, still in a very remarkable state of preservation, was built in its present form as a family stronghold by Georg Baron von Khevenhüller in 1586 and it is still owned, and very carefully kept up, by the Khevenhüller family, which has owned the hill continuously for some 500 years. The present head of the family, Franz Fürst (Prince) Khevenhüller, lives in a nearby château called Nieder-Osterwitz (Lower Osterwitz) on the plain, within clear sight of the upper castle, but he frequently drives his jeep to the summit—the steep, corkscrew road is not open to general motor traffic—to supervise things up aloft.

You and I and all visitors except house guests of the prince must hoof it from the base of the hill to the crest, a climb of about 500 feet in altitude, but the going is very interesting and not really arduous. We pass through 14 successive gates on the ascent and can picture the problem that faced any medieval attacker. The hill was, in fact, never taken by storm, though strenuous efforts were made by hostile forces on several occasions. The reward for the climb, in these tourist days, is worth many times the effort involved. The view, axiomatically brilliant, is only a part of the climber's reward, for there is plenty to see "up top" besides scenery. There is also a wonderfully cheerful restaurant (for light meals) that is set up in the courtyard and on the terrace at the edge of the parapet, where the world falls away sharply to a wealth of green meadows and darker patches of forest. The waiters and waitresses all wear the brown and green Carinthian folk costumes and on Sundays, when as many as 3500 visitors make the climb, there is music and even dancing in the courtyard.

Prince Khevenhüller maintains a small museum of family memorials in one wing of the castle and in it are items of interest to all. One is a letter from Maria Theresa to one of his forebears. Another is a full set of armor built for a giant soldier of olden times and now worn by a dummy exactly the giant's size. He is 7 feet 3¼ inches tall and his hands and feet are proportionally huge. No General Issue uniform of today could ever fit this Goliath, but he looks well in his armor.

The grandeur of the castle's outlook is indescribable, but I may mention two features of it, namely lots of wild red deer grazing in the fields below and falcons flying everywhere about the castle. It seemed to me like a scene from a historical novel, but then it became more an operetta, as the stirring *Khevenhüller March,* broadcast through a series of loudspeakers, filled the courtyard and the hillcrest air.

GURK AND ITS ANCIENT BASILICA

Gurk, lying about 32 miles north of Klagenfurt by Route 17 and a branch route numbered 93, arouses the intense interest of travelers who sincerely love ancient architectural masterpieces, but the trip holds little lure for those who can take such things or leave them alone. The basilica, completed in the year 1220, is all in all, so far as this excursion goes, but it is truly a masterpiece, and in some ways a curiosity.

The big church, generally considered Carinthia's greatest architectural monument, didn't just "happen" in this remote hamlet but grew naturally as part of a rambling abbey founded by the Blessed Hemma, a 12th-century Countess of Friesach. This lady, who is commonly called St. Hemma, lost two sons in battle and thereupon, about the year 1140, turned to piety, assembled her great wealth and dedicated her means and the rest of her life to the erection of the abbey. She died about the year 1170 and now lies in the crypt of this abbey church. Gurk had been the seat of a bishop even before her time, from 1072, and it remained so up to 1786, when this honor went to Klagenfurt. The buff-colored exterior of the church, with the twin towers, is disappointingly plain but its interior is full of wonders. They begin in the narthex, or galilee, which is adorned with famous 12th-century and 14th-century frescoes, still clear and well preserved. On the story directly above this are other ancient paintings, Biblical scenes done in 1339–43, that call forth ecstatic praise from critics, being called the finest Romanesque paintings now extant in Austria.

At the end of the nave is a leaden *Pietà* which was the last work of Raphael Donner. It depicts the Virgin holding her crucified Son in her arms while an angel attempts to console her and baby angels, their eyes streaming tears, hold a hand and a foot of the dead Jesus in an effort to show their grief.

The high altar (1631), of great proportions, was nibbled for centuries by industrious worms, whose efforts finally reduced it practically to wood-powder, held together only by paint and gilding, but masterly renovation work, backed by a great deal of money, saved it and it is sound today. Over 150 faces may be counted on the vast thing, including the twelve apostles and dozens of cheerful little angels. During Holy Week each year the whole altar is covered with a Lenten Veil called the Sheet of Youth, a rare 15th-century work of art containing about one hundred separate squares, each with a Biblical scene painted on the cloth. In front of the altar, in glass cases, are a 16th-century lady's shoe and a 12th-century lady's hat, whose religious significance, if any, I have been unable to learn. The shoe, with open toe and high heel, is strangely similar to those worn today.

The crypt where the Blessed Hemma rests is the most surprising thing about this surprising church, for it is a *forest* of one hundred marble columns, inevitably reminding travelers who have visited Córdoba of the many-columned Mezquita in that city. The crypt is so *cold,* even on a hot day, that you feel like blowing on your fingers to keep them from being frostbitten. The countess-founder-saint who is the reason for everything about this church lies in a simple grave, with an altar, on the western side of the crypt.

AND NOW THE LAKES

Carinthia has all the graces of the south and its warm lakes, numbering about 200, large and little, are powerful magnets to those who love swimming. A cold plunge in a cold lake is good, but a long swim in a warm one is better. The largest, and one of the warmest, of them, and by far the most developed, is the Wörthersee, whose surface temperature sometimes reaches 82 degrees and is always in the 70s in summer. Then, trending westward and mountainward, come the Ossiachersee, the Millstättersee and the Weissensee. These four I shall present in some detail.

The *Wörthersee* is the favored play-lake of Vienna's vacationists and attracts also a great many visitors from Germany, Switzerland and other foreign lands, but so far it has not been sought by Americans to anything like the degree that its advantages warrant. Velden (pronounced Felden) is the most important resort on it and this lies at the lake's extreme western tip, the opposite end from Klagenfurt. It may be reached from the Carinthian capital in 10 or 15 minutes, for there is, surprisingly, an autobahn along the north shore, extending to the neighborhood of Villach, Carinthia's second city. Velden may be reached far more slowly and charmingly by lake steamer, taking about two hours for the 10-mile trip, since it zigzags back and forth across the lake, making stops en route at nine or ten ports, the most important of which for holiday pleasures, are Pörtschach and Maria-Wörth.

Pörtschach, on the north shore, is the most fashionable place on the lake, running well ahead of Velden in this respect, for it is really nothing else than hotels, at least seven of them being first class or deluxe, with over 1200 beds. Park Hotel, to name one of them here, though this and others will be in the roundup at the end of this chapter, fills a peninsula and is completely surrounded by lavish flower gardens and a Park Promenade.

Maria-Wörth, on the south shore, sounds the quiet note of venerability, though it has some very lovely tourist hotels, too. For well over a thousand years it has had ecclesiastical significance, and its two churches, one of which, now of Protestant persuasion, was last *re*built in 1355, still dominate the little peninsula. The cemetery of the loftier and newer parish church, which is an architectural stripling of scarcely 400 years, contains a curious charnel house into which one may peer to see its neat piles of skulls, ribs, tibiae and fibulae. There is very little room in the hilltop graveyard and the occupants of it must be prepared for removal to this charnel house when time has reduced their bodies to dusty bones. Newer bodies need their places. Many of the gravestones bear Slavic names and inscriptions (Marija Samonig, Mici Paulic, Paul Šušu, etc.) to remind us of the mixed population on the south shore of the Wörthersee. A very strenuous effort was made by Yugoslavia, right after its creation as a new state, to secure for itself this lake littoral, with hinterland to the south, but in the plebiscite of October 1920 Austria secured 60 per cent of the votes and retained the whole of Carinthia except two small parings on the southern frontier, which the treatymakers snipped off and gave to Italy and Yugoslavia respectively. (A marker in the center of Velden records: *Bis hierher und nicht weiter kamen die serbischen Reiter, Anno 1919,* meaning "To this point and no farther came the Serbian cavalry in 1919.") International lakes have a certain appeal for the traveler, but everyone who loves Carinthia is glad that this lake does not have to divide its allegiance but is Carinthian in its entirety.

The Wörthersee has a satellite lakelet, the *Faakersee,* still nearer the Yugoslav border and a lovely thing it is, with an islet in its center and hotels both on the shore and on the islet. And more or less between Velden and the Faakersee, actually almost a suburban area of Velden, is the *Wildpark Rosegg,* a sanctuary for deer of various types. The *Rosental,* near here, is said to be the only *valley* in Austria where snow roses, those large narcissuslike early spring flowers with white petals and yellow center, are able to grow. As I have stated in the Styria report, they normally grow only on wooded slopes at higher, cooler altitudes, but here in the Rosental they somehow dare to push up through the snow in March, or even late February.

Swimming, sailing, boating and water-skiing are the chief delights of Velden, and one can also watch some of the bolder sports enthusiasts competing in water-ski kite flying events, in which a speedboat tows the skier as he clings to a huge kitelike contraption. With sufficient speed he becomes airborne, sometimes as high as a thousand feet. When the boat slows down again, he settles once more, skis and all, back on the lake. But despite the spread of available water sports on the Wörthersee, swimming is certainly the main one, indulged in by hundreds or thousands every summer day. Nowhere in Europe, unless in Scandinavia and Finland, do bathers of both sexes permit themselves greater freedom in bathing attire, or the lack of it, than in Austria. The men wear almost nothing, the girls and women a little more. The stout ones, of course, are a bit depressing to the eye, but the slim ones, the young athletes, are bronzed gods and goddesses.

I well remember my own first dive into the lake decades ago, from a springboard in front of a small pension. The air was distinctly chilly, for I took the plunge just as the setting sun was touching up with misty purple and gold the distant Karawanken Mountains, the range that separates Yugoslavia from Austria. What a wonderfully pleasant shock the water gave me. It was warm—*warm.* Hot subaqueous springs are said to feed the Wörthersee and keep its temperature higher than that of any other Alpine lake in Europe, except, perhaps, Carinthia's tiny *Klopeinersee* east of Klagenfurt. Even in May and October, when frost sometimes descends to the Klagenfurt basin, the Wörthersee maintains a 70-degree temperature. It was early June when I was first there and I made it a practice to go in about sunset and then loaf a long time in the water, watching the mysterious *Alpenglühen* fade gradually from the Karawanken peaks. Even at dusk the lake was always alive with countless tiny sailboats, sometimes manned by a single small boy, and with darting motorboats drawing gliders or water-skis on which trim young girls displayed not only their shapely tanned bodies but remarkable adroitness in keeping their balance.

On the hilltops above the lake half a dozen tiny, sharp-spired churches break the sky line, seeming to have selected the most unlikely places to perch, some of them almost inaccessible. One day I climbed to one that attracted me on the Kathreinkogl, 1500 feet above Velden. That one little white church, a bit the worse for neglect, half a mile from the nearest lone farmhouse, must have cost enormous, backbreaking toil, for the trail to it is very steep, but scores of others like it throughout Carinthia stand on lonely hills for no other purpose, apparently, than to remind the peasants below that there is a God.

The *Ossiachersee,* or Lake of Ossiach, lies only 6 miles northwest of Velden as the falcon flies, but human beings generally reach it by road via *Villach. Warmbad Villach,* a suburb, is one of Austria's important spas, with radioactive springs gushing 90 degree water, and with large indoor and outdoor pools, excellent hotels and all the trappings of a popular watering place.

The Ossiachersee, when reached, proves to be a relatively quiet lake, visited by tourists chiefly at the bathing resort of *Bodensdorf* (indoor and outdoor swimming pools) on the north shore, and at the lake's western end for the purpose of ascending, by road from St. Andrä, to the ruined *Landskron Castle,* a superlative viewpoint (café-restaurant), and ascending, much higher, to the 4920-foot Kanzel peak by a cableway from Annenheim. The name-giving hamlet of Ossiach, near the eastern end of the lake, is reached by a road along the southern shore from St. Andrä. It boasts a huge old Benedictine abbey where a *Carinthian Summer Festival,* mostly of music, fills the months of July and August, the concerts and other events being held in the rococo church of the abbey. Many top artists and orchestras participate.

A northward sortie may be made from the Ossiachersee's western end to a remarkable new spa—new to American tourists but not to Austrians—called *Bad Kleinkirchheim,* at an altitude of 3500 feet. The surge of this place is really something of a phenomenon, and so popular is it with those in the know that the 4000 beds in its more than a score of hotels and pensions do a brisk business virtually all through the year, except in the month of November when the spa closes up to catch its breath and prepare for the next onslaught. It is about equally popular in summer, and for sports, in winter. To help visitors the resort places a panel or bulletin at the entrance point of the road which lights up any and all hostelries that have rooms to offer. If, in any given hotel, no space is available the light is out. Incredibly, *all* the mineral water that makes this spa comes from one spring that is under the little Church of St. Catherine. There are two large indoor thermal pools, one with water temperature at 88 degrees, the other at 84 degrees and there's a splendid outdoor pool whose warmth is 75 degrees and this is maintained the year around. Carinthians are extremely proud of Bad Kleinkirchheim and to give it color all those who serve you in any of the hotels wear the brown and green Carinthian Trachten, enhancing whatever degree of good looks nature has vouchsafed to them. And the hotels keep the spirit of it by being of country (Bauer) style both outside and inside.

MILLSTATT AND THE MILLSTÄTTERSEE

Millstättersee, the third of Carinthia's four major lakes, lies 30 miles northwest of Velden close to the valley of the River Drau. The rail and road traffic point for approach to this lake is Spittal an der Drau, which sounds unlovely to our ears as a name but is, in fact, very lovely to the eye. The rushing Drau is an important river, since it carries millions of logs annually from the forests of East Tyrol and Carinthia to the sawmills and pulp mills scattered along its route. It also has important political duties to perform, for later on it marks the boundary of Yugoslavia and Hungary for a hundred miles. So it must always be hurrying, but we need not follow its example. At Spittal, for instance, we should halt to enter the arcaded courtyard of one of Austria's most beautiful castles, *Schloss Porcia.*

Everyone, from the most untutored tourist to the most critical architect, grows lyrical over the Renaissance perfections of this castle. An early owner was a medieval prince and chancellor of the Holy Roman Empire named Porcia, though he sometimes spelled his name Portia, like Shakespeare's legal-minded heiress. The Venetian architect Scamozzi may have built this castle, though there is some doubt of this, but whoever built it reached pinnacles of skill. In three tiers the arcades make their graceful way around three sides of the courtyard. Prince Porcia's coat-of-arms proclaims him a descendant of Trojan and Sicambrian kings. The prince's bones are dust and his boastful claims forgotten but his marvelous home lives on with a freshness that must be due to Carinthia's kindly climate.

After a 4-mile climb by car or toiling bus from Spittal we are on the edge of the Millstättersee, a "family lake" of great loveliness and one that is winning more and more attention from the holiday world, one feature being the ascent to it along the bank of the River Lieser, for on this madly tumbling stream "white water regattas" are held, the contestants using kayaks, and these races have won international fame.

Old Millstatt, situated midway on the lake's northern shore, owes its name to the legend of a pagan temple that stood above the present town. In this temple were a thousand pagan statues, *Mille Statuae.* A Frankish knight named Domitian, contemporary of Charlemagne, came here aglow with Christian missionary zeal, saw the temple and destroyed it in his wrath, hurling the thousand statues into the lake. Domitian's bones rest in a reliquary in Millstatt's church and though the authorities of the Roman Catholic Church declined to canonize him, Millstatt itself did canonize him, at least in effect. He is Millstatt's patron saint and his day is February 5th, a day assigned elsewhere to St. Agatha.

One of Millstatt's hotels, the *Lindenhof,* is in an ancient monastery, most of which dates from pre-Renaissance times. The Benedictines occupied it for four centuries, then the Knights of St. George, then the Jesuits, and now it is Austrian state property. The Benedictines built it in massive Romanesque style, the Knights added some fine Gothic vaulting, the Jesuits superimposed much baroque ornamentation and the Austrian state has permitted the addition of a restaurant and beer garden as well as the transformation of the monkish cells into hotel rooms. These latter-day concessions to the gods of commerce do not seem a calamity, particularly to those persons who profit by them. I regaled myself in that fine old courtyard with a *Rostbraten mit geröstete* and a *Krügl helles* and felt that the Austrian state had done well. In the center of the courtyard is a gigantic tree called *die tausendjährige Linde* (the thousand-year lime tree). I paced around this tree and found it 23 paces. Its trunk at the bottom is a good 12 feet in diameter. The linden casts its shadow over a goodly portion of the courtyard. If this tree gives its age correctly it must have been planted a century or so after the time of the Knight Domitian, but it has now remained for many decades the thousand-year lime, and refuses, like a magnificent spinster, to admit that it is well *over* a thousand now. However, and I hate to close this tribute with a "discouraging word," tree experts tell me that the splendid old veteran really is feeling its years at last and will be lucky to live another ten. Perhaps we can take comfort in the knowledge that in an outer court of the abbey there is a young linden barely five hundred years of age.

For hours, on my first of several visits, I loafed around the abbey admiring its varied architectural splendors and its embellishments, from the timid carved lions, which could not harm a baby, to the tablet bearing the names of Millstatt's war dead. Finally I took my leave and strolled through the old town down to the lake. There, at the public bathing establishment, on a fine, well-kept beach, I hired a bit of cloth courteously called *Hosen,* and plunged into the lake, being careful first to peer down through the green-blue water to make sure that I should not bump my head against one of the thousand statues. The statues are indeed there, local inhabitants tell us, and perhaps they are.

How different are Millstatt's bathing installations today. There is a splendid covered indoor heated swimming pool on a level a bit above the beach, and the whole bathing establishment has gone modern. For information about Millstatt and its lake, you would do well to visit the tourist office, which is handsomely ensconced in the Rathaus, a building worth seeing in its own right.

The *Weissensee*, its chief settlement, Techendorf, lying about 40 road miles west of Villach, is the last of Carinthia's large lakes; but before starting out from Villach you should take thought of a very special type of excursion road, the one that leads you from Villach to and along the *Villacher Alpe*, a dramatic cliff above the Gail Valley that has had its moods of savagery, as when it once let loose a vast avalanche of soil and rock that buried alive 17 villages and hamlets. The road has been meticulously engineered and you may feel quite safe in driving it to enjoy its series of thrilling views, the best of them carefully provided with car parks. This road, you should know, is an out-and-back one, built for excursion purposes only, for it leads only to a dead end on the clifftop.

So we'll move on to the *Weissensee*, still largely a *lacus incognitus* so far as Americans are concerned, though many Austrians, and some holiday seekers from neighboring countries are giving it more attention every year. I first visited the Weissensee more than 40 years ago and I was greeted with amazement by a local cobbler whose shop I entered. He asked from what country I came and I said, *"Ich bin ein Amerikaner."*

"Ein Amerikaner? Um Gottes Willen!" This was almost too much. *"Ein Amerikaner!"*

He assured me I was the very first American who had ever come to Techendorf. His next question was disconcerting.

"Are you from Mexico?"

I explained that I was from the United States.

"Ach ja! And what language, pray, do they speak in that country?"

I began to think I must be a most extraordinary specimen of the human race, like a tourist from Easter Island or a professor from Greenland. I report all this not for the sake of relating a curious conversation but in order to paint the village of Techendorf as I saw it then.

And what a contrast when I saw it "just now." It has certainly been discovered, and I understand that the count of American visitors who spend a night or more in one of the fine new hotels on the northern shore of the lake at Neusach, the last village before the road gives up at a dead end, approaches 2 per cent. And furthermore, I am quite sure that the Weissensee now knows that visiting Americans speak—American. This lake is a summer and winter resort, the winter sports enthusiasts being aided by a double aerial cableway that hoists them from the lake's altitude of about 3050 feet to the Naggler Alm at the 4500-foot level. The lake itself is surprisingly warm in summer, its waters averaging almost 72 degrees, but in winter it is, of course, a solid sheet of ice, on which various ice sports are enthusiastically practiced, including that fascinating one of curling.

A ROUNDUP OF CARINTHIA'S HOTELS, RESTAURANTS, SHOPS

Explanatory Note: The areas covered in this chapter cannot be treated in this roundup as Vienna was treated, or even Styria, with its big capital Graz, for there is no big city in Carinthia where separate restaurants, not in hotels, call for separate mention, or where special shops likewise need individual reporting. Therefore, throughout the following pages any separate restaurants or shops, or shopping streets, that warrant mention shall be reported incidentally to the hotel coverage. This *personal report* of hotels shall start with Klagenfurt and continue through the lakes and resorts in the same order in which they have been taken up in the previous pages.

Hotels of Klagenfurt

Four hotels of Klagenfurt seem to capture most of the American trade, namely the *Moser-Verdino,* the *Sandwirt,* the *Musil,* and for those wishing attention to any health problems, the *Kurhotel.* The *Moser-Verdino,* the largest hotel in the city, with 175 beds, is in the very center of centers, on a corner of the Alter Platz within a few steps of the Provincial Tourist Office. It is a busy hotel, able, because of its size, to accept guests by the busload, but it doesn't forget its individual guests. For them it provides a special Stöckl restaurant, with good food and service and enlivened by continuous evening entertainment. Due to the hotel's supercentral location some of its bedrooms are necessarily noisy, so if noise bothers you unduly you should request one of the quieter rooms. I have stayed twice in the Moser-Verdino with satisfaction, choosing it partly because I happen to enjoy living in the heart of any city I'm visiting. *Hotel Musil,* on 10-Oktober-Strasse, which leads south from the Neuer Platz, is a small hotel of 30 beds, but of such elegance in period furniture and fine decor that it is sometimes classed as deluxe. *Hotel Sandwirt,* on Pernhartgasse leading west from the Neuer Platz, is a first-class hotel of considerable charm, whose dining room is esteemed for its dependably good cuisine. The *Kurhotel,* bearing the name of Dr. Reichel, speaks for itself by its name. Other good hotels are the *Dermuth* and the *Airport Hotel.*

As for nonhotel restaurants, I may state that the *Landhaus* (Provincial Government House) has a lively Bauer-style cellar restaurant called *Landhauskeller,* and to go from basement to rooftop, there is a café-restaurant with a fine view on top of the *Hochhaus* (High House). A ground-level restaurant that is worth mentioning is the *Tigerwirt* (Tiger Host) on Paradeisgasse, leading off the Neuer Platz. *Shops* are abundant in the west-central part of town, which I have suggested for a stroll, and I urge, again, that you look up some of the delightful walkways that make window shopping and the real thing pleasanter. Perhaps the handiest walkway is Kramerstrasse, mentioned above. It connects the Neuer Platz with the Alter Platz.

Hotels on the Shores of the Wörthersee

North-bank hotels are led by the group in and around Pörtschach, which is led in turn by the luxurious 360-bed *Parkhotel,* already mentioned in a sneak preview. In addition to its magnificent floral-peninsular setting it has a large and most inviting open-air terrace, as well as its own private beach and tennis courts. Every room has bath and balcony, and every room views the lake. *Hotel Schloss Leonstain,* with an ambience of gaiety, and the *Sonnengrund,* with roof terrace, are other good hotels, as is *Strandhotel*

Europa, but the really different hotel of the Pörtschach area is the *Werzer-Astoria,* which has 500 beds and a wide-open price scale ranging from 190 schillings to 390 for a twin-bedded room. In other words, its rooms are scattered about among a main building and some 15 satellite cottages, and they greatly vary, one from the other. At a part of the lakefront called Töschling bei Pörtschach there is a castle-hotel called *Schloss Seefels,* beautifully furnished in an old Carinthian style.

South-bank hotels. As you drive along the south bank of the Wörthersee toward Velden the first place you pass is Reifnitz, with the good *Hotel Schloss Reifnitz* and several others—and then *Maria-Wörth,* with many hotels under its aegis, so to speak, and they are not "just hotels," but like individuals. *Hotel Linde,* with a lake terrace on two sides for meals or drinks, is a sheer delight, as is the lakeside garden restaurant of the veteran *Seehotel Pirker.* Beyond Maria-Wörth, but often counted among its hotels, is the excellent *Strandhotel Harrich,* and beyond that is *Golfhotel,* at Dellach, adjacent to its splendid 18-hole golf course, called the only one in Carinthia. The hotel, of chalet style in architecture, has its own stretch of private shoreline for its private Seebad. *Hotel Wulfenia,* first class, bears an interesting name, being that of a blue flower found in Tibet and—surprisingly—on some of the hills in Carinthia above the Gail Valley.

Velden Hotels at the Lake's End, plus Faakersee Hotels

Velden has a round dozen first-class hotels, led in standing and glamour by that deluxe castle-into-inn, *Schloss Velden,* baroque in style, dating from the early 1600s. It has 150 rooms, two-thirds of them with bath, and the whole hotel fairly exudes charm. Its main gate, dating from the 16th century, bids you enter the hotel from a flower garden, and upon entering your gaze is sure to note the main terrace restaurant, which pushes so close to the lake that part of it is actually *over* the slapping wavelets. Of other top hotels, one with a too-long name, *Seehotel Velnerhof-Mösslacher,* is certainly among the best. Three others of about the same rank are the *Parkhotel,* the *Seehotel Europa,* with an indoor swimming pool, and the smaller *Yachthotel.* One from the unpretentious "good middle-class" category that I like is *Haus Dr. Rauchenfeld,* a bit around the corner from Schloss Velden on the south side of the lake. It has only 28 beds, and only one bath and four showers, but it has a friendly something, and not only for the budget. This humble place has its own small private Seebad.

The *Faakersee hotels* need consideration here since that scenic lake, so near the Yugoslav border, is a sort of satellite of the Wörthersee, as I've said above, and particularly of Velden. Hotels dot the shores in the villages of Egg, Drobollach and Faak am See. *Strandhotel Faakersee* is at Egg (you remember that Egg means corner, or edge); *Strandhotel Karnerhof,* spacious and rural restful, is at Drobollach; and *Strandhotel Fürst* (Fürst means Prince) is at Faak am See. You will note that all of these are Strandhotels, which is not to be taken too literally, but they all do at least overlook the lake and each has its portion of the strand.

Hotels on the Ossiachersee

Persons who are in search of pure holiday, and let cultural advantages take their turn, will enjoy the little village of St. Andrä, where they will find the good *Hotel Lido,* a special goal for all who love water sports. Those who look for a bit of cultural stimulus with their holidays will take great joy in Ossiach at the other end of the lake, with its *Stiftshotel,* connected with the abbey where the *Carinthian Summer Festival* occurs. In some ways it is a barn of a place, even in summer—I once wandered about in it for minutes trying to understand its geography—but one comes across a cheerful dining room and then the Princes' Hall, for this was a castle, and the view of the lake restores one's directional sense. This is a special hotel for a special type of guest.

Hotels of Bad Kleinkirchheim

Kurhotel Ronacher is probably the leader of the many good hotels of this Jack-in-the-beanstalk-growing upland spa, and it has a cousin, so to speak, *Hotel Alte Post,* owned by the same Familie Ronacher. Another excellent hotel is the *Trattlerhof* and others of very good standing are the *Pulverer,* the *Sporthotel,* the *Berghotel Putz* and *Hotel Prägant.* Of course the number of small pensions and of homes taking in guests is legion. My text describing this resort mentioned three thermal pools, but a fourth is now taking form close to the entrance of Hotel Ronacher.

Hotels on the Millstättersee

There are two communities on the lake that are of special holiday appeal, Seeboden, at the western end, and most emphatically, Millstatt, the name-giver, on the northern shore. The leader in Seeboden is the *Royal-Hotel Seehof,* perfectly located in its own lakeshore park and with an indoor swimming pool. In Millstatt, two hotels vie for the top choice, the *Seehotel Löcker,* which is the life of the party, with a great big restaurant overlooking the lake and nightly dancing, and the quieter, but to me utterly alluring, *Hotel am See Die Forelle,* which means The Trout. In its lake-edge restaurant, shaded by a bower of trees, it suits its action to its name by providing a tank from which your trout, if you select that dish from the menu, may be netted and cooked before the creature knows what's happening to him. Die Forelle inevitably makes us think of Schubert and the haunting melody he wrote and named for the trout. Well, anyway, this 110-bed hotel, spang on the lake, is one of my favorites in all Carinthia. There is a *Hotel Lindenhof* in a wing of Millstatt's venerable abbey, and it has an outdoor restaurant surrounding the 1000-year linden (now eking out its last decade of life), and this hotel has also its Klosterkeller. All of these things have their magnetism, but the hotel is not up to the two others I've named, and anyway, when I'm in a lake resort I like to be on, or at, the lake. So—Die Forelle.

Hotels on the Weissensee

One doesn't have to worry about selection in this case for there are just two quality hotels on the lakeshore, both in the village of Neusach and both owned by persons related to each other, hence a friendly family rivalry. They are the *Strandhotel am Weissensee* and *Hotel Enzian* (Gentian). Of course they both have their own Seebad, and both are first class. I have a personal leaning to the Enzian because of its more Carinthian *Bauer Stil,* but really there is little to choose between them.

9 / LAND SALZBURG AND SALZBURG CITY

A PLAN OF APPROACH

Land Salzburg is one of the most difficult of Austria's Länder upon which to base a plan, for its key, Salzburg City, is far to the north by northwest of what may be called a rough triangle or a face of a pyramid. Badgastein and the long Gastein Valley are at the center of the base, with the Grossglockner Road to the west, and the newer Felber Tauern Road to the west of that, both roads clambering up and tunneling the Alps to reach Land Salzburg. Because of the general clockwise plan by which this book is circling Austria, it makes sense, I think, to present Badgastein first, and then go north by road, with a look at Heiligenblut on the first highway, Mittersill on the second, and Zell am See by either.

A TUNNEL TO BADGASTEIN

It is not possible to approach Badgastein from the south by road because there are no roads over the High Tauern Range except the Grossglockner and the Felber Tauern and they are well to the west. It *is* possible, however, and very easy, for the motorist to drive his car aboard a flatcar of one of the special "transport trains" at *Mallnitz,* the southern entrance to the *Tauern Tunnel,* which is 5½ miles long, and ride in it through the Hohe Tauern Alps by

172 /

electric power instead of over them by gasoline power. Many thousands of motorists do this every year. The northern end of the tunnel is at Böckstein, only 3 miles from Badgastein. Before traversing the tunnel this report should mention, in passing, that Mallnitz is more than a mere transshipment station. It is a finely situated health resort at the 4000-foot level, with several pleasant hotels, the quiet *Pension Bellevue* and the lively *Alber's Alpenhof* being the best.

BADGASTEIN, AUSTRIA'S SUPERSPA

Badgastein, which was spelled as two words, with two capital letters, until a few years ago, is situated at the head of the long and lovely Gastein River Valley, centered also by Bad Hofgastein and Dorfgastein. The "head of the family" is the smartest and most widely advertised spa in Austria. Big stone hotels leaped up at the turn of the century and especially after 1905, when the Tauern Railway reached this resort from the north, and 1909, when the tunnel connected it with Carinthia and Italy. Half a century before these openings it was a favorite resort of many of the sovereigns of Europe, particularly Emperor William I of Germany, who was a frequent visitor during a quarter of a century. In 1905, Emperor Franz Joseph came here to help celebrate the opening of the railway—the red carpet was wrongly placed, and dreadful confusion ensued—and he too was often seen in this spa, staying always at *Hotel Straubinger,* or in a property across the street owned by the Straubinger family, whose successive generations have owned and operated the hotel for more than 300 years. The emperor's 4-room suite in the main hotel is still proudly pointed out, just as he left it. Bad Ischl was his more customary summer retreat, but he loved Badgastein too.

It is fair to say that for a century and more, kings, nobles and assorted fashionables of many races have lent an air of sophistication to the scene. Today, Badgastein rates fourth in Austria's official tourist count, following Vienna, Salzburg and Innsbruck. More than a hundred hotels and pensions flourish and in some of them it is possible to pay about $24 per person per day, which borders on the fantastic in provincial Austria. Concert halls and a gambling casino flourish and every conceivable sort of thermal installation. The central part of the resort is strung along one main street and across the stone bridge under which the Gastein River plunges. Here there is a small Congress Hall, with reading room, and back of it blasted from the rock mountain a garage that can take 460 cars. A splendid, and far larger new Congress Hall, ingeniously constructed on a series of descending levels down the hillside, so it will not obstruct the view, is expected to open in the spring of 1973, housing up-to-date convention facilities and a new casino. The present one occupies cramped quarters opposite the existing Congress Hall.

Badgastein is full of well-to-do invalids recovering from this, that and the other, for at least 18 types of disease, including a mysterious one called *morbus basedowii,* are curable here, or can be kept from worsening, by the spa's 18 hot springs, some with temperature as high as 116 degrees, which are called the most strongly radioactive ones in Europe. And if these aren't enough there is a still newer thermal establishment at nearby Böckstein, where rock galleries in an abandoned gold mine have temperatures of up to 107 degrees and are full of a gaseous element called radon that works wonders on rheumatic complaints, circulatory diseases and many allergies. The potential of the Böckstein galleries is said to have been discovered by a stout gentleman—let's call him that —named Hermann Göring, who was trying to reactivate the abandoned mine. A special feature of Badgastein is a *public kindergarten* where guests of any of the hotels may park their kiddies.

I like Badgastein, and not sort of, which calls for a bit of personal explaining, for I confess that, generally speaking, this sort of resort, in any country, is something which I instinctively avoid. Badgastein must have some special appeal to induce me to visit it as I have now done five times. The first time, many years ago, I was lured by photographs, which called me irresistibly, and I found that the reality surpassed the photography. In two vast cataracts the *Gasteiner Ache* leaps at and through the town, plunging under the main street right between the luxurious hotels that hem it in. The effect is magnificent and the thunder of these glorious falls drowns my carping. For one dollar (and no other "valuable considerations"), on that long-ago first visit, I secured a room in the humble *Hotel Moser*—it would be more like three today—directly alongside the lower cataract. What an outlook from my window! Thousands of tons of mountain water thundered past, day and night, and with the windows open the uproar filled my room so that I could scarcely make myself heard with anything less than a shout. The Gesäuse of the Enns is a mere whisper compared to this. But I loved it and could hardly induce myself to leave the room. Each evening the cataract was (and is) illuminated with greenish floodlights, producing a weird, theatrical effect. In spite of myself I liked Badgastein. I liked it very much, and still do.

On subsequent visits I have come to love it as a winter sports center, even though I am chiefly a spectator of such sports, and as a place "to get up in the world," for there are two suspension cableways, four chairlifts, plus almost a dozen skilifts. As a practical note I may state that a season ticket valid for seven days may be bought for about $26 in the high season, $20 in the low season, providing unlimited use of all the lifts, plus one free entrance into the *Felsenbad* (Rock Bath). There are also one-day tickets giving unlimited use of all lifts, plus the Felsenbad. This public bath, near the station, is a most interesting one, for there is a hot pool, about 90 degrees Fahrenheit, indoors and there are two pools outdoors, on a grassy slope, one of them 90 degrees, the other 77 degrees. Bathing here is an experience not to be missed, and there are spacious grassy slopes in case you wish to sunbathe.

Now for a more specific word about the lifts.

From near the Schillerhof the so-called *Höllbrunn Lift,* and then the *Graukogel Lift,* carry up to the Graukogel Mountain Station (5950 feet); and from that point the Hüttenkogel is reached in a short climb.

From a hillside point above Kaiser-Franz-Joseph-Strasse the *Bellevue Lift* carries up to the *Bellevue Alm,* for the lovely chalet-type *Almhotel,* a mountain inn open in summer (swimming pool) and winter (crackling fireplace). A corkscrew road also climbs to this Alm.

The *Gondelbahn* (suspension cableway) to the *Stubnerkogel*

(7288 feet) operates in slack times once an hour, on the hour, the ascent taking 20 minutes, but on crowded days it operates continuously and can transport as many as 500 passengers per hour, with little waiting. There is a restaurant at the summit. The Gondelbahn, to explain the word, consists of an endless chain of small "gondolas," or "bubbles," hanging from a moving cable.

The *Jungeralm Lift,* a chairlift, ascends to the Stubnerkogel from a base station *behind* that crest and thus makes possible a "skiing seesaw," as local promoters proudly call it. This is unique in Europe, so far as I can learn. Badgastein's two lifts enable the skier and the plain "lifter" to go up-and-over. The Stubnerkogel is far above the tree line, so there are no growing obstacles in any direction, a fact which can be of prime comfort to the beginning skier.

Bad Hofgastein, about 12 miles down the valley (north) toward Salzburg, is also a watering place of some size and would receive much more attention were it not so blanketed by its big and famous neighbor. An insulated pipeline brings the radioactive water to this spa without any loss of its strength or warmth, so if a quieter place, but equally effective, is your desire, then Bad Hofgastein may be the answer. It has a cogwheel railway to *Kleine Scharte,* at the 6725-foot level, a double chairlift from that point to *Hohe Scharte,* at 7555 feet, and other single chairlifts and skilifts.

From Bad Hofgastein the distance is only 3 miles to *Dorfgastein,* the last and littlest of the Gastein family, and from that village the motorist reaches, in 25 miles, the junction point of Bruck an der Grossglocknerstrasse, joining the tourist stream that has ridden the sky from Lienz. This Bruck is less than 4 miles from Zell am See, which is a major turning point of traffic. We'll have a look at Zell, but first we'll travel the two Alpine highways that open the way to it from Carinthia, namely the Grossglocknerstrasse and the Felber Tauern Route. Both of these start, or may start, their climb from Lienz, the capital of East Tyrol, so we will halt at that engaging little city before heading north.

LIENZ AND ITS RING OF VALLEYS

East Tyrol is an integral part of the Province of Tyrol, though it has been cut off from the rest of it since the treatymakers did their heavy-handed work on boundaries after World War I. It *was* the most neglected part of Austria by foreign tourists from that time until the construction of the Grossglockner Road in 1935, and the subsequent construction of the Felber Tauern [Tunnel] Route in 1967. The obvious reason for its temporary disappearance from the tourist scene was that when the Treaty of St. Germain awarded South Tyrol to Italy in 1919 it largely isolated East Tyrol. The whole system of communications that had joined it to the rest of the province was now in a foreign land and Lienz was a dead end, reached only from Carinthia and Italy. The two roads have changed all this and made Lienz the southern gateway to two spectacular highways.

Lienz is a small city of 13,000 inhabitants but endowed with great charm, especially in its central main square, where the best hotels and the City Tourist Office *(Fremdenverkehrsverband)* are located, and along the banks of the River Isel, which brawls through the town in great volume on its way to join the Drau. The Isel is so turbulent and strong, being actually three times more of a river than the one of which it is a tributary, that it gives the impression of a sort of citybred Gesäuse.

Sights are quickly seen in Lienz, since the only things that really matter are the central square, the St. Andreas Church, with the grave of Egger-Lienz, the region's best-known artist, and the lovely walk along the left bank of the Isel, with a succession of clear views of the Lienz Dolomites, but every visitor should save time for the quarterhour climb to *Schloss Bruck,* on an eminence at the western edge of the city. This was the seat of the Counts of Gorizia from very early times until 1500 and it now houses the *Municipal Museum* of Lienz. This goes in strongly for all things connected with local folklore, but its chief treasures are some 50 paintings by Lienz's gifted son, Egger-Lienz, who was a pupil of another local artist named Defregger but who quickly excelled his teacher. From a point near the base of the hill on which Schloss Bruck stands, a chairlift ascends to a high point called *Venedigerwarte,* but there is a cableway from Lienz to a much higher point, 6030 feet, called *Zettersfeld.*

The ring of valleys around Lienz affords wonderful opportunities for the explorer-on-foot who is not afraid of exertion. Mostly they are ascending valleys, where roads grow rough and rougher and finally shrink to paths, but there is no more dramatically stunning region in all the Alps. The Dolomites, both Austrian and Italian, rise in a curtain of peaks to the south and the snowy High Tauern Alps, with Austria's two loftiest mountains, the Gross-Venediger (12,008 feet) and the Grossglockner (12,457 feet) loom in white majesty on the north. In the upper reaches of all these valleys there are huts and shelters owned by various Alpine clubs and information about their use is to be had from the Tourist Office in Lienz. The chief villages have simple mountain inns, where four or five dollars will do a lot of buying.

The six chief valleys (Tal is German for valley), to name them in clockwise order, are the Gailtal; the Drautal, by which travelers reach Lienz from Carinthia; the Defereggental, whose people, incredibly, became itinerant peddlers in the 17th and 18th centuries, hawking clothes, hats and blankets all over Europe, including Scandinavia and Russia; the Iseltal, being the valley whose river rushes so boisterously through Lienz, this same valley being the one up which one drives to use the Felber Tauern Road; the Virgental, with the village of Virgen, straight out of an operetta stage set; the Kalsertal; and finally, the Mölltal, which is the valley of the Grossglockner route.

GROSSGLOCKNER, WHERE YOU RIDE THE SKY

The Grossglockner Skyroad, that masterpiece of man-amid-the-mountains that leads from one valley floor to another over an extremely high pass—it tunnels through the Hochtor at 8218 feet—is called by its sponsors "the greatest and most modern piece of Alpine road construction of the present time," which is to say anywhere in the world. I doubt if Switzerland, Norway or even Argentina and Chile, with their trans-Andean highway, would seriously challenge this claim. Even where the road is nothing but an endless series of corkscrew turns, and even at its highest levels, it is broad, smooth, civilized, as though it were a turnpike commissioned to unite two populous cities of the plain. Instead of that it unites Lienz and Zell am See, passing through a corner of Carinthia, and in a broader sense it unites East Tyrol with all northern Austria, at least in summer. From mid-October until June the highest parts of the road are blocked with snow, the drifts being sometimes over 30 feet deep!

Commenced in 1930 through the initiative of the governor of Salzburg Province, it was so nearly completed by the summer of 1934 that Chancellor Dollfuss motored to the top of the pass to bestow his personal and official blessing upon it. A memorial was later erected here in token of this visit, for ten days after it the Austrian leader was assassinated.

I shall not attempt curve-by-curve description of the rides which have thrilled me on two occasions, once by bus and once in my own car, but will call your attention to a few of the major features of the journey in the order seen as one goes from south to north. If you ride the road from north to south I trust it will not be too awkward to follow these notes in reverse.

The road takes off from Lienz and has almost immediately to zigzag over a pass of moderate height to reach the *Mölltal* at Winklern. At the top of this pass, only 9 road miles from Lienz, the road crosses into Carinthia, and just beyond the line lies *Iselsberg*, a summer and winter resort of some importance. About 20 miles north of Lienz the road comes to *Heiligenblut* (4300 feet), perhaps the most-photographed village in Austria and well deserving the camera attention that is heaped upon it. Heiligenblut is famous as a pilgrim village, its special sanctity revolving about a phial of Holy Blood (hence the name) preserved in a monstrance in the church. A Danish knight named Briccius brought this phial many centuries ago from Constantinople. The fluid had gushed from a picture of Christ when stabbed by an unbeliever. Briccius, on his way home to Denmark—a path over the mountains had existed since Roman times and remains of it are still to be seen— was caught here in a blizzard. He died and was buried on the spot, since even a pair of oxen could not drag his body away. Soon he thrust a leg up from his grave to the open air and behold, in a gash in this upraised leg was the sacred phial, which he had heroically hidden there, to preserve it. That is the story of Carinthia's village of the Holy Blood, or at least one version of it, accepted, I suppose, without question by thousands of pious folk. The church that grew up at this spot is a 15th-century Gothic structure with a strikingly tall, slender spire and with a rich interior, featured by an elaborately carved and gilded altarpiece attributed to Michael Pacher, or his school.

The busses always make a halt of about three-quarters of an hour at this town, whose dramatic aspect would warrant a halt even if there were no pilgrim fame connected with it. There are half a dozen pleasant hotels, and there used to be another—until January 21, 1956, when "the white death," as a memorial inscription tells us, destroyed it and claimed 12 victims. The white death was, of course, an avalanche.

A few miles north of Heiligenblut, a side road takes off for *Franz-Josefs-Höhe,* a height that commands an immense and thrilling prospect of the Eastern Alps, including the towering Grossglockner itself, with its two peaks, the higher one, and it is the highest peak in Austria, soaring to 12,457 feet. There is a large hotel at this viewpoint, named similarly Franz-Josefs-Haus. One special item in the panoramic view from here is of paramount interest, namely the *Pasterzenkees,* which is the greatest of Austria's glaciers, being 6 miles long by 1 to 3 miles broad. It is on the Pasterzenkees that the annual June ski meet is held as soon as the road is opened to traffic.

At the highest point of the main Grossglockner Road is the aforementioned *Hochtor Tunnel,* in the middle of which is the frontier between Carinthia and Salzburg provinces. Carved over the entrance to the tunnel are the pious and appropriate words: IN TE DOMINE SPERAVI (In Thee, Lord, have I placed my hope), but Austria did not rely solely on the benevolence of God. When she opened her mighty skyroad she knew that everything humanly possible for its safe operation had been taken care of by the engineer (Oberbaurat Wallack) in charge of the whole construction.

One more lofty viewpoint, reached by a short branch road, is the *Edelweiss Spitze* (Peak) whose parking space, almost at the 8500-foot level, is the highest in Austria. From this point (restaurant and small hotel) an unimpeded view in *every* direction gives one a sense of the primeval in nature rarely to be experienced in the overcrowded Continent. This scene could not have been much different ten thousand years ago, will not be much different ten thousand years hence.

North of the Edelweiss Spitze the main road rapidly "unwinds," to descend to a little town with a big name, *Bruck an der Grossglocknerstrasse,* which has an interesting 500-year-old inn, and so to the softly civilized resort of Zell am See, "at the corner of holiday traffic."

(Note: The Grossglocknerstrasse does not connect East Tyrol with North Tyrol and Innsbruck, that task being left to the much newer (1967) Felber Tauern Route, several times previously mentioned. This does not touch Carinthian soil but goes directly north from Lienz to the resort of Mittersill, in a far-western valley of Land Salzburg formed by the young Salzach River but always known as "the Pinzgau." From Mittersill a fair-to-middling road carries over the Thurn Pass, at half the altitude of the Grossglockner, to reach Kitzbühel and all the rest of Tyrol. The Pinzgau will be covered in the ensuing section, starting with its chief resort, Zell am See.)

ZELL AM SEE, HEAD OF THE SCENIC PINZGAU

A glance at any railway or motor map will show what a turning point of traffic is Zell am See. It is an important halt on the main railway route from Switzerland and Innsbruck to Salzburg and Vienna (and Gastein and Carinthia), and it is the starting point of a scenic narrow-gauge line that ambles up the valley of the Salzach to Mittersill and finally to its head at Krimml. Here the finest waterfall in Austria releases the discharge of the Krimml Glacier in three grand leaps totaling 1250 feet.

Zell is a very lovely resort town on an equally lovely lake, the Zellersee. It is a goal of international holiday seekers, with a lively way of life and a great roster of hotels, some of them deluxe. A launch trip by motor ship around the Zellersee can be a rewarding experience. The tour totals about 5 miles in length and takes 45 minutes. At the south end of the lake is one of the most modern youth hostels in Austria, a hostel built and owned by the township of Zell, which, indeed, includes *all* of the lake edge on *all* sides. On the east side rises the *Honigkogel* (Honey Peak), which is said by Zellers to be the loftiest timber-covered peak in Europe. The normal tree line in Austria is 5600 feet, but this mountain rises 500 feet higher than that.

A second experience of any stay at Zell should be the ascent of the *Schmittenhöhe* by cableway. This Schwebebahn is one of the veterans of the Austrian Alps, for it was constructed almost 40 years ago. A bus carries passengers to the base station in 5 minutes and the ascent then takes 13 minutes in good-sized cabins holding from 20 to 25 persons. The upper station is at about the 6500-foot level, enabling the tripper to look down even on the timbered Honey Peak. A hundred other peaks are also visible, in the Tauern Range to the south, the rugged Kaiser Gebirge on the Bavarian border to the north, and other ranges on the east clear to the Dachstein, and of course Zell and its lake are spread out down below as if on a relief map. The Schmittenhöhe could well serve as climax to any stay in Zell, however brief.

SALZBURG, THE LOADSTONE CITY

Salzburg has its special place in the affections of travelers. This Rome-north-of-the-Alps, this shrine of Mozart, saturated with memorials and music, this city of hills and vales and snowviews "riding" an Alpine river, the Salzach, as if on a saddle, this festival city of world stature, certainly needs no introduction. But it does need to trumpet a caution, for it is so popular that in the summer season it is often very hard to secure accommodations unless one has engaged them well ahead. For the high-summer festival period you should make your booking *months* ahead. Up-to-the-minute help on this problem may be had by writing to Salzburg's official *Stadtverkehrsbüro* (City Tourist Office) at Auerspergstrasse 7. Perhaps I should note here that the City Tourist Office maintains an Information Center at 10 Mozartplatz, and in the same building is the *Landesverkehrsamt in Salzburg,* which is the head office for Salzburg *Land.*

The aspect of Salzburg is a clear reflection of its history. The

Church of Rome, in the era of its proudest temporal power, built the city which we see, bringing the architecture of the Eternal City across the Alps to this lovely site on the swiftly flowing Salzach. A churchman of vague origin, by name Rupert, founded the city about the year 700, and eight to nine centuries later a succession of hard, ruthless, art-loving prince-archbishops took the community in hand and made it architecturally important.

Four names are enough to remember: *Leonhard,* called the Turnip Bishop in deference to his peasant origin (he was proud of it and had a turnip in his coat of arms); *Wolf Dietrich,* an architectural zealot who vigorously introduced baroque; *Markus Sittikus,* who built Hellbrunn; and *Paris von Lodron,* who carried on various architectural developments started by his predecessors. With some intervals they covered the period from 1495 to 1650. Fischer von Erlach, by his bold genius, continued the architectural development of the "German Rome" in the 18th century.

The lives of the prince-archbishops do not always bear scrutiny but their very defects often contributed to the glory of the city. Leonhard was harsh and cruel. With utmost severity he crushed the spirit of his people and forced Salzburg to obey his arrogant behests, but to that spirit the city owes its greatest landmark, the Fortress of Hohensalzburg, where Leonhard entrenched himself. Wolf Dietrich was openly unsavory in his personal morals, but to his empurpled desire we owe the Schloss Mirabell and its glorious gardens. He built this place in 1606 as a "country retreat" for his mistress, Salome Alt, and impudently called it Altenau, thus flinging his amour into the city's face. Subsequent changes to a more florid style have greatly altered the castle's appearance (along with its name) but it might never have existed as a gracious pleasure center in the city had Wolf been morally austere.

Wolf hated both Romanesque and Gothic architecture and did his best to eradicate these styles from Salzburg and substitute baroque. When fire slightly damaged the Romanesque basilica he snatched at the chance to condemn the whole structure and call in the Venetian architect Vincenzo Scamozzi to design a baroque cathedral. Santino Solari, another Italian, soon succeeded Scamozzi and built the beautiful and impressive structure which we know. It is considered the purest bit of architectural Italy ever to have "crossed the Alps," its façade of rose-colored marble from the quarries of Untersberg being particularly admired. Paris von Lodron greatly advanced what Wolf Dietrich had commenced. He made Salzburg a city of domes rather than spires.

Like Graz and Innsbruck, and for that matter Paris, Salzburg has its Left Bank and its Right Bank. The Left Bank is the old city, containing the greatest monuments of the past, including the Fortress Hohensalzburg, and one 20th-century achievement, the Festival Play House. The Right is the chief pleasure bank and has theaters and business buildings, good hotels, banks, the Mozarteum and Schloss Mirabell, with their fine gardens and parks, a modern Congress House for conventions and a health center called Paracelsus Kurhaus. Holding all Mozartiana in abeyance for a separate section of this chapter, I will mention in abridged form six traditional attractions of the Left Bank.

The *Cathedral,* Santino Solari's masterpiece, is surprisingly simple in its interior, but its exterior is magnificent and its arcaded square (scene of the *Jedermann* performance on fair Sundays of the festival season) is always a pleasant strolling ground.

The *Residenz,* adjoining the cathedral, was the palace of the proud princes of the church who altered the face of Salzburg. Magnificent halls and a gallery of paintings attract many visitors.

St. Peter's abbey, church and cemetery, landmarks of a former era, are made particularly venerable by hermit dwellings and chapels of the very early saints carved in the adjacent cliff. St. Maximus and 50 companions are supposed to have been hurled from one of these chapels to martyrs' deaths in 477.

The *Franciscan* church, an interesting architectural combination of Romanesque, Gothic and baroque, the three basic styles developed over the centuries in Europe, is famed for Fischer von Erlach's high altar and Michael Pacher's carving of a Madonna.

The *Festspielhaus* is the magnificent modern Festival Hall, one of whose perennial themes is "Everyman." A bronze bust of its author, Hugo von Hofmannsthal, holding a pensive pen, adorns the lobby. In the great auditorium the story of the Rich Man's Death is played on Sundays when the weather is unsuitable for outdoor production. Goethe's *Egmont* is another festival favorite, and of course there are operas, ballets, symphony concerts, celebrated choirs, Lieder recitals, chamber music concerts and grand church music, though these are not all given in the Festival Hall but in various appropriate settings, especially the Mozarteum, Schloss Mirabell and the Residenz. All in all, the Salzburg Festival, conceived in 1917 by Max Reinhardt, Richard Strauss and Hugo von Hofmannsthal, is one of the greatest cultural events of Europe.

I cannot leave the subject of the Festspielhaus without telling of its history and structure. In July 1961 Salzburg, with a city-wide, even nation-wide, glow of pride, opened its new *Festspielhaus* (Festival Hall), just in time for the Summer Festival. Far surpassing in every way the former hall, which was no mean building, this structure has to be seen to be believed, and tens of thousands of visitors do see it every year. Built under the direction of the famous architect, Professor Clemens Holzmeister, it seats 2300 persons, and unlike Europe's traditional horseshoe opera houses, including the glittering one of Vienna, it provides a full view of the stage from every seat. The entire stage was designed by Professor Karl Unruh and what a stage it is! Since a vertical cliff crowds this part of the old town almost to the Left Bank of the river there was no room at all for *any* stage, much less a large one, so the whole thing, 55,000 cubic meters of it, had literally to be blasted out of the limestone face of the cliff. Every device for raising, lowering and revolving known to stage designers was incorporated, and the curtain is also a wonder of modernity. Made of hammered steel rubbed to a high polish, it is 105 feet wide yet it can be raised or lowered in 5 seconds. The acoustics of the main hall are as perfect as any in the theatrical world, this being due in part to an arrangement of uneven wood paneling on the walls that breaks up the sound waves. From the remotest corner of the gallery a stage whisper or a stage bellow is heard with the same clarity as from orchestra seats.

Hohensalzburg is reached by a funicular from the Festungsgasse near the cathedral. Features of it are the splendid rooms of the Turnip Bishop (Leonhard); the Golden Room, with a green and buff majolica stove of vast size for which Salzburg City is said to have refused an American offer of $600,000; the Rittersaal (Knights' Hall), with gold-starred blue ceiling and several curious pillars of red marble weighing 10 tons each (the pillars were raised to this hilltop in two years by prisoners, using the toilsome rope-and-spool method); the "Great Horn" of 1502, really a barrel organ with 180 pipes, whose bull voice formerly sounded the alarm in times of stress and is now heard in the city thrice daily, at 7, 11 and 6, following, in each case, music from the city's carillon, installed in its own separate tower; and finally the glorious view, both far and near. Below the fortress is the loneliest house in Salzburg, the *Henkerhaus* (hangman's house), entirely isolated in a meadow shunned by other dwellings. In the middle distance to the south is a lakelet dominated by *Schloss Leopoldskron,* the spacious mansion that was acquired by Max Reinhardt, whose genius played so large a part in elevating his chosen city to its present level of artistic fame. The castle is now the seat of the Salzburg Seminar for American Studies, as mentioned in the summer courses roundup in Chapter 2.

I must not quit the Left Bank without mentioning two newer attractions, complementing the old. One is the *Haus der Natur,* which can be translated only as Natural History Museum, but this is perhaps the most modern and ingenious "House of Nature" in Europe, with 80 rooms of extraordinary exhibits and dioramas. The other new sight to which I refer is the *Carolino Augusteum Museum* directly across the street. In addition to its art collections, with some remarkable old porcelains, it presents the cultural history of Salzburg from prehistoric times—Bronze Age finds have been unearthed at Rainberg on the city's edge—to the present time. These two unusual sights are close to the Franz-Josef Quay a few steps downstream from the bridge called Museumssteg.

The Right Bank is not *merely* a center of hotels, business offices and assorted pleasures. The *Mozarteum,* Salzburg's famous Music Academy, which has space and time also to offer many public concerts, is here, as I've said, and so is the famous *Marionette Theater* of Professor Aicher, where daily performances are given in summer—I'll have more to say about this in the chapter's concluding "Roundup" section—and so is *Schloss Mirabell.* This castle, originally built, as we have seen, by Archbishop Wolf Dietrich and later rebuilt in more lavish style, suffered a dire disaster in World War II, when bombs partly destroyed it, including its magnificent marble stairway, but it has been faithfully restored and is again a major sight of the city. At festival time its large hall is used chiefly for special concerts, but its lovely little Marmorsaal (Marble Hall) is the setting throughout the year for frequent concerts of chamber music and Lieder. In the handsome castle garden, graced with fountains and statuary—note especially the Pegasus fountain —there is a tiny open-air theater, close to the river, where performances are sometimes held. It dates from Mozart's time and is still just as he knew it. Back of this theater, in the garden of the Mozarteum, is the *Mozart-Häuschen,* a miniature summer house in which Mozart wrote his last opera, *The Magic Flute.* It once stood in the grounds of the Theater-an-der-Wien in Vienna but was transported to Salzburg in 1874 in order that the city which had treated him meanly in life might grant his memory increased honor.

About 3 miles south of the city lies *Schloss Hellbrunn,* the baroque pleasure-castle built by Santino Solari for Archbishop Markus Sittikus, and surrounding it is the prankster's garden that so delighted the prelate. Its water-powered mechanical devices are as numerous as they are devious, from singing and whistling birds to a mechanical theater, nearly half of whose 256 figures "act" by water pressure, and from a water organ to a great array of squirt tricks which the playful guides are now happy to demonstrate, though they will *just* miss giving visitors a real drenching.

To be specific about some of these many tricks, which throw such light on the customs of Salzburg's 17th-century churchmen, I will mention a few items: a statue of Neptune that grimaces weirdly when the water is turned on; a statue of Venus, who steps on a dolphin in such a way that water spouts from the dolphin over a surrounding flower garden in a wide *dome* resembling thin, clear glass; statues of various celebrities such as Barbara Mabon, a favorite girl friend of the archbishop, and of mythical personages such as Orpheus and Eurydice, all of which spout merrily upon demand or are spouted upon by surrounding jets (Eurydice wears a medal bestowed upon her by Markus Sittikus); a deer that squirts streams of water from his antlers; a series of chairs in the garden so rigged that at the turn of a lever all of the chair seats send up a strong douche stream in the style of a bidet, all, that is, except the chair meant for the archbishop. This trick must have been a real screamer when Sittikus was entertaining fashionable women guests.

By way of contrast to these fantastic follies Hellbrunn has a pleasant little *Monat-Schlösschen,* or Month Castle-let, so named because it was built in one month, namely August 1615, as a surprise for a prince who was to visit the archbishop. Hellbrunn also has on its grounds a small open-air theater, built in 1618, where Italian opera was first presented in Austria. Now there are concerts, with current entertainment, at Hellbrunn every Wednesday and Saturday evening in July and August, and several times each summer elaborate performances are given of music or ballet.

THE MOZART STORY

Joannes Chrysostomus Wolfgangus Theophilus Mozart was born in 1756 at Number 9 Getreidegasse (Corn Lane), the main street of Salzburg's Left Bank. Of the four baptismal names, Wolfgang stuck to this boy and man through life. The Greek name Theophilus (God-love) was Germanized by the boy's father to Gottlieb and later Latinized by the boy himself to Amadeus. As Wolfgang Amadeus Mozart he became one of the most admired and beloved composers of all time, a true immortal. The year 1956, the second centenary of his birth, was celebrated all over the civilized world, and not least in Austria itself, by special Mozart concerts, festivals and glowing tributes of every kind. In his lifetime, however, his native city, impersonated by its archbishop, treated him meanly, and his adopted city, Vienna, behaved most shabbily in the matter of his funeral, but both cities have long since repented and made eager amends in tardily recognizing his incomparable contribution to Austria's musical prestige. Salzburg, in particular, can hardly do enough to honor this native son. A Mozart motif runs through the whole life of the city, particularly at festival time, when the composer becomes a veritable patron saint of the gathering multitudes.

Unhappiness seemed to cling tenaciously to the short life of this man who brought such pleasure to succeeding generations. His nature was gentle, honest and lovable, but he did not know how to play the grim game of life and he often invited the troubles that came to him. In Salzburg, he was appointed court organist to Archbishop Hieronymus and that meant that he was in the social position of a servant in the great man's household, for this was the invariable custom of the day. He had to wear a red livery and sit at the servants' table, above the cooks but below the valets. To a sensitive young man who had been feted as a child prodigy in half the capitals of Europe this was exceedingly galling and he made no secret of his reactions.

Finally escaping this hated service, with the help of a vigorous kick from the archbishop's chamberlain, Mozart settled in Vienna and spent the last years of his life there. The cultured metropolis took notice of his talent, and sometimes lionized him, but his ill luck seemed to follow him and he was neither happy nor in good health. He married a woman who was never able to appreciate or cherish him. One day a stranger of cadaverous appearance who refused to identify himself sought him and commissioned him to write a *Requiem Mass,* whereupon the composer was convinced that Death itself had given him the commission. And this, in effect, proved to be true. The stranger was, as a matter of fact, merely a servant of the court who wished to remain incognito, but Mozart never found this out. He died before his *Requiem* was finished and this noble work is thought of as the musical expression of his own prayer for rest—*Requiem aeternam dona, Domine.* (On the occasion of a great memorial service for President Kennedy, following his assassination, Mozart's Requiem was movingly performed in the cathedral of Boston.)

On a day of rain and sleet in December 1791, public pallbearers carried through the streets of Vienna to the cemetery a plain wooden coffin containing the frail body which the flame of genius had burned out in three and a half decades, leaving to posterity nearly 700 varied works, many of which are acknowledged masterpieces. A few devoted friends (but not the widow) fell into line behind the coffin, but the weather soon discouraged them and one by one they dropped away, leaving only the paid pallbearers. These bearers, mechanically doing their job, left the coffin in a mortuary chapel and next day it was lowered into a common grave unmarked. It took the widow 17 years to stir herself to the point of visiting the cemetery with the intention of erecting a gravestone, but by that time Mozart's resting place could not possibly be identified. His body still fills a pauper's grave, unknown.

Recompense comes better late than never and the story has a happy sequel which flavors the life of a nation devoted to music. Without Mozart Vienna would not be Vienna and Salzburg would by no means be Salzburg. So dominant is the Mozart theme in that city that the Festival is sometimes popularly called the Mozart Festival. Mozart dominates also the Easter Concerts, the Musical Spring Concerts, held in May, and often the Salzburg Castle Concerts, which continue all year long.

Memorials to the composer are numerous on both banks of the Salzach. Schwanthaler's statue of him centers the Mozartplatz. The musician's birthplace at 9 Getreidegasse is now a Mozart Museum. Among items of interest one notes his first violin, a very small one suited to the six-year-old prodigy who played it; some Mozart manuscripts published in Paris when the child was but seven and eight years old; a diploma from the University of Bologna given when he was fourteen; a program of the opening performance of *The Magic Flute,* in which the librettist, one Schikaneder, takes star billing and the name of W. A. Mozart, in small letters, is scarcely noticed; the clavichord, with 36 broad brown keys and 25 narrow white keys (as against the 52 white and 36 black of today), on which he composed *The Magic Flute* and the *Requiem;* a watch given him by Maria Theresa, with the likeness of the empress enameled upon it; an enamel brooch bearing miniature portraits of young Wolfgang and Nannerl, the sister who accompanied him on his concert tours; and several letters to his wife Konstanze, who scarcely deserved the endearments he heaped upon her.

On Makartplatz there is a Mozart *Wohnhaus* (dwelling), long occupied by Leopold Mozart, Wolfgang's musically gifted father. Leopold was a native of Augsburg, and even though he left that Bavarian city before Wolfgang was born his Augsburg home is still pointed out to tourists, for something of the son's fame inevitably clings to the man who sired him.

FOUR-PART ROUNDUP: HOTELS, RESTAURANTS, EVENING ENTERTAINMENT, SHOPS

NOTE: In this chapter the only places where evening entertainment and shops are of enough importance to warrant separate discussion are Badgastein and Salzburg City. In the villages and along the great highways only hotels and restaurants will be treated separately, and in some cases only hotels. The different areas will be taken up in the same sequence as in the preceding text, starting with Badgastein.

Hotels of Badgastein, a Personal Report

Of Badgastein's hundred-and-more hostelries I will present only those that are clearly the best, plus others that have some special points of interest, plus a handful of lesser hotels that seem to warrant mention. Of the leaders, three stand out: the *Elisabethpark,* at the center of the main street; the *Bellevue,* on a street one lift higher; and *Hotel Der Kaiserhof,* on the edge of town but magnificently placed and not requiring any climb or descent to reach it. The supercentral Elisabethpark fairly invites the stroller-by to drop in. There's a large crescent dining room, this primarily for guests, where every guest, even if a singleton, is assured of his own table at every meal; there's a *Prälatur* (Prelacy), which is a series of little dining rooms charmingly decorated; and there's a *Causerie,* which is a café, entered directly from the street; and a well-stocked bar opening off the lobby. The Elisabethpark is quite literally "in the pink," being styled in a delicate pink throughout. In a separate building it has an impressive thermal swimming pool, with complete medical facilities. Nonguests, by paying an entrance fee, may use the pool, and it is so central that I found it temptingly easy to "drop up" to it. The temperature of the water is about 90 degrees, as is true of the public Felsenbad and five other hotel pools. The radon element has been removed from all of them, since the intake of this is to be regulated by physicians only, but the mineral content remains.

Parkhotel Bellevue, to give it its full name, is on a higher level than the main street but conspicuously visible from it. Its dining room and grill have grand views, but even better ones are to be had from other points in the Bellevue complex, for there is an annex (across the street) and another one, the aforementioned *Bellevue Alm,* high up the hillside, the Bellevue property extending to an altitude of 4300 feet. The Bellevue Alm, a small, 20-bed chalet in charming rustic style with its own little outdoor heated pool, is reachable by chairlift or by road, and it should not be missed by any visitor to Badgastein for at least a meal or a snack on its view terrace. This can be a memorable thing, as I can testify in tribute to a *Kaiserschmarrn* (Emperor's Delight) that I enjoyed here, a delicious sort of thick pancake full of raisins and roofed by whipped cream.

Hotel Der Kaiserhof caught me in a weak spot, so utterly perfect is its view down into the Gastein Valley, but it has much more than view, and is, in fact, preferred by some well-heeled Americans as the best of the best. It has every luxury, including, of course, its thermal swimming pool and full medical facilities, and there is an assured air of quality that you feel the minute you enter it. Under the same management is the *Habsburgerhof,* highly recommendable as a first-class hotel, and with a view to match that of its more luxurious "relative." The *Weismayr* is another first-class hotel directly opposite the Elisabethpark. I have stayed there recently and found it most satisfactory, an enhancement of the "Main Street Group."

Hotel Straubinger, mentioned in connection with Emperor Franz Joseph's "addiction" to it, is first class and it still has an almost imperial atmosphere, due to the fact that the present proprietor, meaning the present Herr Straubinger, devotes extraordinary attention to knowing every guest and to giving each one a feeling of having been personally invited. Franz Schubert was a satisfied customer of the hotel, so much so that he wrote two of his famous Lieder while living in it. This hotel is directly beside the Big Roar of the Gasteiner Ache and on its fallside open-air café terrace you literally have to bellow in giving your order to the waiter or in attempting to make your companions hear you at all. This, even for me, is a bit much and for comfort I would prefer something like the old-fashioned *Grandhotel Gasteinerhof,* with its friendly Stiftskeller, or the unpretentious *Kurhaus Jedermann,* from either of which you may have a stirring view of the thunderous cataract without *sitting* on the view. If you would like to get as far from the roar as you can, give thought to the *Mozart,* on a curve of the road leading up to the station, or to the hotels in the neighborhood of the station and the Felsenbad. The first-class *Söntgen* is one, the first-class *Salzburger Hof,* with pool and sauna at the top of the house is another, and there are two places of lesser standing, the *Krone,* which is one of the relatively few hotels whose view is *up* to the mountains rather than down the valley, and *Sporthotel Wührer, under* which a brooklet races to join the Gasteiner Ache.

While I'm still about it, I will name three other far-from-the-roar hotels, all first class. The *Schillerhof,* on the mountainside, just below the lower station of the Höllenbrunn chairlift, generates equal appeal for its location, dramatized by huge picture windows, and for its first-rate ambience. The *Miramonte,* often classed as a deluxe hotel, is on the slope just below the Schillerhof, and a 9-hole golf course is just below that. *Hotel Grüner Baum* (Green Tree), in the Kötschach Valley a mile and a half below the main part of Badgastein, is a sort of self-contained village, very popular with young and old. It has various Stüben and open terraces at three or four levels for eating and drinking, and it has its own thermal pool. Major elements in its charm are its rural setting, with a stream flowing between its buildings, and its architecture, which is *Bauernstil* (peasant style) throughout.

Finally, let me say that in requesting a room through an agency or by writing to the *Kurverwaltung,* which is the resort's tourist administration, you may specify "with or without waterfall."

I have neglected many good hotels but I can only say that I have a fellow feeling for the author of a popular handbook who suggests that his readers lodge in "any one of twenty hotels." That was his escape hatch, but perhaps a try at selectivity is better.

Restaurants of Badgastein are virtually all connected with hotels, so we need not list them again, but I would stress that for a good informal time the *Hotel Grüner Baum* can give you a sense of having "eaten out" in pleasant surroundings. And in the field of nonrestaurant eating let me mention the shop of *August Mayer,* calling himself, cutely, "Zuckerlmayer" (Sugarmayer), where you will find among its temptations chocolate balls half way in size between a marble and a Ping Pong ball called *Mozartkugeln,* which have some sort of indescribable core that will ravish your taste buds. You will come across Mozartballs in shops like this all over Land Salzburg, this being one more tribute to the composer who was called in his youth "Wolferl," a diminutive of his given name, or, just as affectionately today, "Mozartl."

Evening Entertainments in Badgastein are announced in posters and calendars and there are a good many to choose from, including operettas, folklore evenings, special concerts by groups brought in, and of course concerts and cabaret shows. I recently heard the *Sängerknaben vom Wienerwald* in a concert hall of Badgastein, and thought the youngsters from the Vienna Woods formidable competitors of the more famous Vienna Choir Boys.

Shops of Badgastein are in many cases branch shops of the famous big-city shops of Vienna's Kärntnerstrasse. Among these are *Hügler,* a high-grade jeweler, and *Adlmüller* for ladies' and men's fashions, though this shop, in the Hotel Straubinger, bears, also, the disconcerting name Stone & Blythe as successor to Adlmüller. Other fine shops conspicuous on the main street, are *Henns,* for ladies' fashions; *Wiedermann's,* for dirndl clothing and skisport clothing, plus sport articles in some variety; *Kirchlehner,* for a considerable choice of Austrian souvenirs; and a small shop of *Erika Rösser,* for *Folk Kunst* (handicrafts).

Hotels and Restaurants on the Approaches to Salzburg City

On the Grossglockner Route there are several points where hotels and mountain restaurants are encountered. We'll try them as needed, but in this portion of the chapter Lienz will not be included, since it belongs more properly to the Felber Tauern Route. The first point of importance met on the Grossglockner ascent is Iselsberg, barely within East Tyrol at the border of Carinthia, where several hotels that look like outsized chalets are found, the *Wacht* and the *Iselsberghof* being the largest. At Heiligenblut there are several good hotels, one of them, the largest, being the first-class *Rupertihaus,* a resort hotel with a grand-view terrace. A well-appointed indoor swimming pool is a welcome feature of this pilgrim village at 4300 feet altitude. At the *Franz-Josefs-Höhe,* that thrilling tangent from the highway, but still within Carinthia, we come upon the big *Franz-Josefs-Haus,* a motorists' and bus riders' hotel par excellence. It's a big place of over 200 beds with a panoramic view for which the word stupendous is too weak. Fernleiten and Fusch, both within Land Salzburg, have modest hotels where one can eat well enough. At Zell am See, which we may consider the end of the Grossglocknerstrasse, though Bruck, 4 miles to the south, is the technical terminus, the *Grand Hotel am See* is the deluxe leader, trailed by *Hotel Latini,* in the Schüttdorf section, and then by many first-class and economy hotels, for this is a big resort.

Hotels in Lienz and on the Felber Tauern Route

The leaders in Lienz are the *Traube,* on the main square, a hotel with considerable style and a most cheerful dining room, and the up-to-date *Sonne,* with a gemütlich Stube in the Tyrolean style. I recall having stayed in the Traube a dozen years ago, when it had not grown up to its present status, but I liked it even then.

The hotels on the Felber Tauern stretch are less developed than on the older Grossglockner, but the *Rauter,* in Matrei-in-Ost-Tirol (to be distinguished from Matrei-in-Brenner) may be mentioned, as may the *Schlosshotel Mittersill,* in Mittersill. Other hotels worth considering in the Pinzgau (Valley) are the *Post* in Krimml (all rooms with bath), at the Pinzgau's western tip, and in the east, the humble *Orgler* at Kaprun, which brings us close to Zell am See, covered on the Grossglockner Route.

Hotels of Salzburg, a Personal Report

The many good hotels of Salzburg City can best be envisaged by sorting them into three areas of the city, the Left Bank (Old City); the Right Bank (New City); and the hotels on the surrounding hills, most of them genuine castle hotels.

Left Bank Hotels should really be put in the singular, for the only high-quality hotel in the Old Town is the *Goldener Hirsch* (Hirsch is Stag, or Hart), on Getreidegasse, not far from the Mozart Birthplace House. This has been an inn for more than four centuries, and it was a patrician house for four centuries before that. It was reconstructed 25 years ago, and of course modern plumbing was introduced. The cuisine has been long celebrated, but there is a danger in such fame, the temptation to live on reputation. Not long ago the hotel was purchased by the wealthy owner of Schloss Fuschl (see below), but the son of the widely known *former* owner, Countess Walderdorff, is its manager, so let us hope that its pristine aura as of *the* traditional best hotel of Old-Salzburg style will not dim. So far it still has *Holiday Magazine*'s coveted award annually. (I wish there were more quality hotels on Getreidegasse, but the only others are of the third-class category, namely the 100-bed *Blaue Gans* [Blue Goose], and the small *Mödlhammer,* both very near the Goldener Hirsch. As a budget hotel I think the Blue Goose would get by all right.)

Right Bank Hotels are led, I would say, by the 100-room-and-bath *Österreichischer Hof,* frequently called by tongue-saving American guests the Ö-Hof. It is on Schwarzstrasse, parallel to the river, and its several glittering dining rooms, together with many of its bedrooms, look squarely out upon the hurrying Salzach. Its 4th floor, called the Panorama Floor, makes the guest think that he lives in a glass house (and shouldn't throw stones) for the picture windows deliver the view at its total best. I have recently enjoyed a stay in the Ö-Hof, though not on "the 4th," and have loved everything about it, including the food in any of its restaurants. It was *so* taste teasing, with wondrous specialties of game and with rich Austrian desserts, that it threatened to make me a "gourmandic."

The *Bristol,* on Makartplatz near the Ö-Hof, may not have the glamour of its neighbor, but it is a deluxe hotel, very handily situated within close strolling distance of the Landestheater and the Marionettentheater, the Mozarteum and the Mirabell Castle. *Hotel Stein,* a first-class hotel of 134 beds on the Right Bank quay directly at the main Staatsbrücke, capitalizes on its commanding site with a 9th-floor penthouse restaurant and on the roof above that a newer open-air café with close view of the Salzach and a great part of the city.

Parkhotel Mirabell, a deluxe hotel on Auerspergstrasse close to the City Tourist Office, stands between the Congress House and the Kurhaus, with the Schloss Mirabell Gardens close behind it. After a talk with the management I am trying to understand a change that is now being made, and I'm sure it will be all to the good. In short, a new ground-floor dining room is taking form in the rear, in a building adjacent to the present hotel. It will have huge picture windows that can be opened to the garden view in summer and closed in winter. Government offices will fill the floors above it.

Grand Hotel Winkler, on Franz-Josef-Strasse near the Mirabell, a modern place and rather appealing to the eye, is a big hotel, officially rated in the luxury class. I hesitate to comment on it, since I have not stayed there, or even eaten there, but I have heard so many complaints about Winkler charges, especially for meals— and the same about the enormous *Grand Café Winkler,* with a terrace as big as all outdoors, that is so conspicuous on the Mönchsberg, a bright sight at night from down below—that I must believe there can't be all that smoke without some fire, and I'm sorry about that. I wish the Winkler would think it over.

Of the hotels officially rated first class, as against deluxe, and there are 20 of them, I have stayed in 2, the *Europa,* on the Right Bank near the station, and the *Pitter,* on Rainerstrasse, one block from Auerspergstrasse and the City Tourist Office. The Europa rises, matchboxlike, a full 15 stories, and by many Salzburgers this was considered an affront when it was being built. It does indeed cause indisputable damage to the many-domed skyline of the city, but it is a very good hotel, with every comfort and convenience and it is reasonably distant from the center, so—there it is; and if it is an intrusive building to look *at,* it is wonderful to look *from,* especially if you are in its top-floor café-restaurant. The Pitter, with 420 beds, is Salzburg's largest hotel. I found it quite all right for what it is, a hotel of mass tourism, handling its crowds efficiently.

In the second-class category there is a hotel that I think well worth mentioning, namely the *Bayrischerhof,* on Elisabethstrasse near the station. It is clean, cheerful, and with excellent food. Friends of mine have recently stayed there and can't praise it enough.

The Castle Hotels on the surrounding hills are a marvelous asset to Salzburg, unmatched by the outlying hotels of any other Austrian city. All but one of them (the Fondachhof) are on or beyond the Left Bank and we'll look at these first. The nearest of them, and the most expensive and exclusive in atmosphere, is the *Gastschloss Mönchstein,* on the hill whose name it bears. Its bedrooms consist solely of elegant suites and the whole place has an ambience of aristocracy.

Two lovely castle-inns on the road to Hellbrunn south of the city are the *Schlosshotel St. Rupert* and the *Maria-Theresien-Schlössl* (Castle-let). The St. Rupert is quiet, beautifully furnished, and altogether good, in a park setting. The Little Castle (Schlössl) named for Empress Maria Theresa (Theresia in German) can accommodate only 30 guests, so it takes on a sort of family atmosphere.

The last of my Left Bank castle-inns is *Schlosshotel Klessheim,* on the western fringe of the city, in a country setting that offers unusual opportunities for such sports as tennis, swimming and golf, which last is a talking point in Austria, since the mountainous terrain makes golf courses difficult to achieve. This castle was once used by the Isadora Duncan School of Dancing.

On the Right Bank of the Salzach is one castle-inn, or perhaps more properly a mansion-inn, called *Fondachhof,* a place that fits well into the baroque nature of Salzburg. A new summer dining room, very recently built, is in a pavilion on the terraced lawn and this should add a sort of picnic touch to the Fondachhof. And here I must sneak in a mention of a noncastle-inn that has greatly delighted me, namely *Hotel Kobenzl* on the Gaisberg heights a few miles to the east of the city at an altitude of about 2500 feet, with a wonderful distant view over the Salzach to the Bavarian Alps, including the Kehlstein on which Hitler's Eagle's Nest perches.

Schloss Fuschl and Schloss Sighartstein, Two Supreme Castle-Inns in the Environs, some 13 miles east and 10 miles northeast, respectively, of Salzburg, call for more than a swift listing, for although each one is very different from the other, each is at the very top of its type. We'll first consider *Hotel Schloss Fuschl,* on peaceful Lake Fuschl (it was here that I first became acquainted with Austria's noiseless electric motorboats, strictly required on some lakes), which is a perfect goal for persons in upper financial brackets in any country, and lots of them come—from lots of countries. They include "the beautiful people" and the international play-people, but the inn is also full of guests who have no pretensions except to enjoy this superlatively lovely place. To outline its properties, it has a main building, the former hunting castle of Salzburg's prince-bishops; a neighboring Jagdhaus, or hunting lodge, whose every room is enhanced by a Dutch-tile bath; a Gästehaus, also close to the main building; a boathouse and a lakeside bungalow, both with one or two guestrooms; and a mile or so away, a Jagdhof, with inexpensive rooms in country style, this building having, also, an extensive Hunting Museum, as well as bowling lanes and a shooting gallery! The main hotel has a large open (but roofed) dining terrace and below it a glassed-in, Wintergarten-type bar-lounge. The bedrooms are all individually furnished and decorated with flawless taste. And just about every summer sport you can think of on land or water is available, including hunting, appropriate to its nature, and golf on a 9-hole course. Guests are sometimes startled to note that a building close to the front door of the main building announces that it is occupied by the Consul General of Ecuador, but do not suppose that throngs of Ecuadorians-in-trouble will be trooping into the building, for this is an *honorary* consulship—old Austrian custom smiles on such arrangements—and the consul is a wealthy salt king of Munich, by name Carl Adolf Vogel, who bought the whole property from the titled Walderdorff family, and at the same time, as we've seen, Hotel Goldener Hirsch of Salzburg. Consul Vogel takes great personal pride in his property and we may be sure that Schloss Fuschl will tend to improve rather than deteriorate. As one item of maintenance I may state that there are ten full-time gardeners to keep the extensive property up to snuff, and two or three fishermen always on duty to catch trout and pike for the guests.

Schloss Sighartstein, in the area of Neumarkt, about 10 miles northeast of Salzburg close to the Wallersee, is as different as can be from Schloss Fuschl, but in one respect it is the same, perfect. Fuschl is an outright hotel, seemingly without flaw, while Sighartstein is a genuine *castle,* having been owned by the same family of Uiberacker for more than five centuries. I have recently enjoyed a stay in this castle that was as perfect as the place itself. I will allow myself, perhaps rashly, to set forth here, verbatim, a portion of a letter I received in 1967 from a lady living in Chevy Chase, Maryland, for it expresses, in spirit and in word, exactly what I would like to report from my recent visit. It is written longhand on Sighartstein stationery and the passage reads as follows: "We have had the great pleasure of staying here at Schloss Sighartstein, mentioned—oh, so briefly!!—at the beginning of your twenty-two pages on Salzburg. May my husband and I, also interested in history as we travel, mention that you might add a bit when next you go to print? This is to mention that this remarkable castle-inn is now the residence of the most gifted and charming of people, Count Uiberacker's daughter, Countess Gabrielle Pálffy and her husband, Count Wolfgang Pálffy. They have rooms to accommodate 12 guests [it is now 14 to 16, Ed.], each with its private bath, some with private sitting room and outside balcony. Schloss Sighartstein also has lovely terraces and gardens as well kept as the beautiful, in-good-state-of-repair interior of the castle, so full of armor, exquisite furnishings and mementos of the Uiberacker and Pálffy families. And above all, there is here a splendid warmth and joy in the atmosphere, reflected from the personalities of the old Countess Uiberacker and her daughter Countess Pálffy and her son-in-law Count Pálffy, who manage the Schloss and take care of the guests of the old castle." Well, dear reader, "Them's my sentiments," to use the crisp pronouncement of Fred Bullock in Thackeray's *Vanity Fair,* "Them's my sentiments," and I could add plenty more. Guests and owners have tea together, often as the first get-acquainted round; they—we—sit together for meals at a long table; and after dinner we gather in one of the living rooms in front of an open fire if it is cool, for a feast of good conversation, quietly opened and steered by our host and hostess. I have stayed in at least half a dozen ancient castles in Austria, and as many in Germany, and for atmosphere geared to comfort I can think of none to surpass Sighartstein. There is even a surreptitious elevator in an inconspicuous part of one of the corridors. Said Count Pálffy to me as he and his wife took me to my room, "I only fell for this contraption recently and now I love it—better than I love my wife," and he gave her a most contradictory little love pat on the shoulder. Nearly all of Sighartstein's guests are Americans and usually they are of the discerning and appreciative kind who enjoy the fine meals and wines that are served (without extra charge for the wines), but enjoy still more the rich bonhomie that infuses every gathering of hosts and guests, a contributor to it, when he can be there, being the scion of the host family, young Martin Pálffy.

The Restaurants of Salzburg City

Salzburg has quite a number of good restaurants in addition to those in the quality hotels, and "first off" we'll explore four of the most interesting: *Weinhaus und Grill Restaurant Eulenspiegel* (page Richard Strauss!); the *Weinhaus Lenz Moser;* the newer *G'würzmühl* (Spice Mill); and the still newer *Die Goldene Sonne.* The Eulenspiegel, occupying several floors in a building of 10th-century aura, hides away in a passage leading from busy Getreidegasse, across the street from the Mozart Birthhouse, its forte being grilled specialties. The Weinhaus Moser, on the central Marktgasse, is so limited in space and so popular that getting a seat without advance reservation may be difficult. I had a Salzburger Nockerl here that was straight out of—Salzburg. The G'würzmühl, whose name is a mouthful in itself, to Americans anyway, is an upstart as Salzburg restaurants go, but is doing just fine with its steaks and other hearty dishes aimed at the palates and wallets of the well-to-do. It got off to its rousing start in the late 60s. It is located on Leopoldskron Strasse on the far side of the Hohensalzburg Fortress. Die Goldene Sonne on the Left Bank in the lee of the Mönchsberg, near the lift that hoists you to it, is in a building that dates from 1418 but has been a restaurant only since 1712. It was redone in its present enlarged form in 1968, occupying various rooms on various floors. The proprietor is proud to point out some relics worked into the building, a small pillar for one thing, that were found here during excavations and date from Roman times. I must mention a fifth eating place, and newest of all, the *Restaurant zum Krug* (Mug), on the 4th floor of a building in a tiny lane opposite the Österreichischer Hof, and also a café-restaurant that you couldn't miss if you tried, namely the *Glockenspiel,* on a conspicuous balcony overlooking the Mozartplatz.

Other restaurants of good fare or good atmosphere or both are: *Peterskeller,* big and beery (also vinous) with several interesting Stüberln; and the *Stieglkeller,* on a steep street leading up to the Fortress, an enormous *summer* café-restaurant capable of serving 800 guests at a time, which Salzburgers have been enjoying since 1491. Its face was lifted some years ago.

A very good place for Yugoslavian and other Balkan dishes, though the name doesn't reveal this, is the *Weisses Kreuz.* And if you're short of time and need some quick nourishment give thought to *Dom-Stuben,* on Goldgasse just off the Residenzplatz, which has a full larder of *Schnellimbissen* (quick snacks), though it calls itself, also, a Café und Weinrestaurant with grilled specialties.

The *hilltop* restaurants consist chiefly of two remarkable places. The *Winkler,* on the Mönchsberg, is the larger, a three-ply place with two separate restaurants and an extremely large café. You mount to the Winkler by one of three elevators that were originally ordered for a building in Zagreb but made their way here instead. The prices in the Winkler, as I've said, are *high* and the spirit seems commercial, but the great panorama makes you forget these faults.

The other hilltop place is the *Festung* (Fortress) *Restaurant,* on top of the dramatic hill of Hohensalzburg, towering above the old town. It has its colorful and historic halls, among them the *Wappensaal,* or Armorial Hall, and also scores of garden tables set out on the terrace clear to the walled edge of the perpendicular fallaway. One of this restaurant's specialties is a delicate crepe-thin pancake called *Schmarrn,* not to be confused with the thick one called Kaiserschmarrn. Hohensalzburg is served by a funicular. Both the Winkler and the Fortress Restaurant have views of overpowering impact, but the Festung has much longer afternoon sun than does its competitor.

In addition to its excitingly various restaurants Salzburg has a number of cafés of great appeal. One is *Café Tomaselli,* an upper-veranda place overlooking the interesting Alter Markt. Another is the *Café Bazar,* with garden, a riverside place that formerly catered to a very smart clientele and still has an air of old-line aristocracy. Still others are the *Garden Café Posthof,* on Kaigasse; *Café Mozart,* an upstairs place on Getreidegasse; and the animated *Café Wernbacher,* on Franz-Josef-Strasse near Hotel Pitter.

Evening Entertainment in Salzburg City, on the high-grade musical side and on the lighter, laughing side, is to be had in a big way, though late-night fun doesn't flourish much, nor should it in such a city. The evenings are made merry by two folk-dance groups that stage infectiously gay shows six nights a week in the season. The *Alpinia* group puts on its show at present on Monday, Wednesday and Saturday evenings at 8 o'clock in the big Stieglkeller and the younger (20 to 30) *Salzburger Stierwascher* group on Tuesday, Thursday and Friday evenings in the smaller but elegant *Wappensaal,* mentioned just above, of the Festung Restaurant on Hohensalzburg. These groups pride themselves on *not* being professionals. They are simply young and younger people of Salzburg who dance for their own fun, and ours, and have become very expert indeed.

A show by the younger group that I once enjoyed seemed to me as sparkling and varied a folk show as I have seen in Europe. In addition to the usual *Schuhplattler, Watschenplattler* and *Bandeltanz* there were strange dances that had a story to tell, like the *Stelzentanz,* or Stilt Dance, a weirdly effective number that "drives out winter," songs of many types, from yodeling to lovely choral folk songs, all beautifully done, and solos on several instruments, from the harp to the singing saw. In an intermission, and after the final number—there were 18 numbers in all—the dancers charged up to the tables of diners and insistently pulled us from our chairs to do folk dances with them. This sort of urgency can be a risky thing, displeasing to guests, but the youngsters put such charm into it that literally nobody did or could refuse to participate. The girls, seizing male guests, were so fresh and lovely, the young men, seizing feminine guests, so strong and athletic, that the venture was a howling success and everybody entered into the folk spirit.

An evening that I enjoyed with the Alpinia group very recently was a bit different but every whit as good. Perhaps it was less impetuous but there were some *excellent* singing, yodeling and bell-ringing numbers.

Night life, as I have implied, seems quite "beside the point" in a small, cultural city like Salzburg that offers so much of special character, yet it is to be had by those who want it. There are various bars such as *Astoria-Bar, Casino Alm* and *Casanova,* an innocuous striptease cabaret on Linzergasse, and there are *Tanzlokale* for discothèque dancing, but night life belongs to *big* cities. Salzburg is a city apart, a special goal of travel sought for its special self.

One thing that gives the city its own unique flavor, and I have purposely saved this for the end, is, of course, the celebrated Marionette Theater. The summer program, with something offered almost every evening and many afternoons, includes two that I have seen as if entranced, *The Barber of Seville,* and, this a two-part show, *Mozart at the Piano, in a Hofkonzert in Schönbrunn; Eine Kleine Nachtmusik,* the taped music and spoken parts synchronizing perfectly with the action of the half life-sized marionettes. Others that I have missed and want to see are *The Magic Flute, Don Giovanni* and *Rumpelstiltzchen.* Another evening feature, quite as distinctive of Salzburg, is the program of evening concerts and entertainment at Hellbrunn, but this has been already mentioned in connection with the sightseeing trips.

Shops of Salzburg City are as tempting as those of Vienna, and the shopping area is quite as concentrated and "walkable." In the Old Town, the most important street—you guessed it—is Getreidegasse, continued "upstream" by Judengasse to the Waagplatz. Griesgasse, parallel to Getreidegasse, is another good shopping street, and several of the important squares, including the Alter Markt and the Residenzplatz, have their due quotas. In the New Town (Right Bank), Schwarzstrasse, running downstream from the Staatsbrücke parallel to the river, and Makartplatz are full of good shops, as is Linzergasse, a Right Bank continuation of the Staatsbrücke.

We'll start with the Old Town and let me say that one of its great fascinations both to shoppers and plain roamers is its narrow passages, with shops on both sides, running through from Getreidegasse to its parallel streets on either side. A modern one, the Salzach Passage, almost as interesting as the ancient ones, runs through from the Alter Markt to the riverside quay. It has a hat shop, a gift shop and a first-rate shoe shop, *Reiter*. One of the most colorful of the Getreidegasse passages, leading "inland" in this case, you will find opposite the Mödlhammer Hotel at Number 25. In the passage is a little old courtyard surrounded by four levels of flowered balconies and having on its pavement, and inside, a little café-restaurant called *Kaffeehäferl* (Cup of Coffee). You'll be well rewarded if you find this passage.

Leading shops often have places on both sides of the river, so we'll have to put on our Janus faces and look both ways. Dirndls and *Lederhosen* (leather pants) lure women and men shoppers and many shops offer them. For dirndls, *Wenger,* on Münzgasse, "downstream" from Getreidegasse, has a good stock, as does *Seifert,* on Judengasse, but the best known is *Lanz,* a firm with shops also in Vienna and Innsbruck, conspicuous on Schwarzstrasse, opposite the Österreichischer Hof. Lanz calls itself "The Founder and Creator of the Austrian Look for Fashionable Clothes," a resounding claim indeed. It is, at any rate, very high grade and its stock includes loden wear and *Wildleder* (wild leather) garments for men and women. Salzburg, not Vienna, is its home base. A specialist in leather goods, of course including Lederhosen, is *Schaller,* on a conspicuous corner of Judengasse, with a Right Bank shop on Linzergasse. Quite as well known is *Jahn-Markl,* at Residenzplatz 3.

Petit point embroidery, discussed at some length in the Vienna shopping coverage, is a product that fairly calls out to me from shop windows, so very Austrian is it, and so weirdly demanding of the embroideresses who make it. The shop I know best for this is *Slezak,* on Makartplatz—the owner is a relative of actor Walter Slezak—and from his stock I'm sure his clerks can pick out articles from Jolles in Vienna, one of the greats in this industry. Other shops selling petit point are *Fritsch,* on Getreidegasse, and *Ennsmann,* on the same street, the latter also with a good supply of gloves and belts. Porcelains are displayed temptingly in the *Porzellan Augarten* shop on Schwarzstrasse, near Lanz; and for fine gift items in porcelain, ceramics and glass a top shop is *Rasper,* on the Waagplatz. And for peasant handicrafts made in Land Salzburg in very wide variety, from furniture to silk brocades to articles of hardwood and even to domestic utensils, don't overlook *Salzburger Heimatwerk,* in Residenzplatz "under the chimes," as it likes to proclaim.

To return briefly to Getreidegasse, take note of the following: *Thalheimer* for ladies' clothes, especially for younger women and girls; *Opferkuch* for clothes for both sexes, also with a kiddies' shop; *Gebrüder Roittner* for souvenirs, and also for kitchenware and cutlery; *Denkstein* for shoes; *Springer* for furs; and for costume jewelry look for the word *Schmuck,* which means ornament, at the entrance to one of the passages—I believe they call it Passage '70 —running "inland" from Getreidegasse. You'll find a great array of costume jewelry in the windows and more inside, including, as the shop emphasizes, *Dirndlschmuck.* Finally, in another "inland" passage at No. 3 Getreidegasse, very near the Mozart birthplace, look for *F. Weber,* a candlemaker whose shop has been in the same family since 1583. All the candles are handmade and hand decorated and they are exquisite. A few gift shops in the United States, hand picked by Herr Weber, carry them.

10 / THE SALZKAMMERGUT, HALCYON LAKELAND OF THREE PROVINCES

THE SALT CROWN LANDS AND LAKES

Salzkammergut means Salt Crown Lands and the name was once commercially significant, since the salt mountains of this region, centered by Bad Ischl, with its curative sulphur and saline springs, long provided a principal source of imperial income, and even now, in these republican times, they produce nearly a million pounds of common salt per annum and about 100,000 pounds, of coarser type, for cattle and for fertilizing purposes. Three principal mines are now worked, plus the separate mine at Hall, near Innsbruck. One is near Hallein, south of Salzburg, one above Lake Hallstatt and one near Bad Aussee, all three being in the Salzkammergut, though each is in a different province, namely Salzburg, Upper Austria and Styria respectively.

The Salzkammergut is a "geographical expression," as Metternich once called Italy, and its boundaries are hazily defined. Loosely speaking, it is the whole lovely district of lakes and mountains, and salt, stretching east of Salzburg but not including that city. Originally and strictly, it referred to the saltworks in the upper portion of the Traun Valley, in the neighborhood of Ischl, but it has expanded in meaning, and our travel spirits are sure to expand

/ 207

when we visit it, even though its weather is not as mild or dependable as that of the balmy Carinthian lakes. It is a region of dramatic beauty and of holiday rampant.

The Salzkammergut, as stated above, belongs to three of Austria's Länder, which often comes as a surprise to American tourists. Because the word starts with *Salz,* as does the word Salzburg, it is natural to assume that the region is a playland belonging to Land Salzburg, but this is far from true. Actually, Salzburg has an important stretch of shoreline on only one of the major lakes, the Wolfgangsee, and by no means all of that, since St. Wolfgang itself, the most famous lakeside village in the whole region, belongs to Upper Austria, and therein lies an illuminating fact of politics, for there is *no direct road* connecting St. Wolfgang with St. Gilgen, Land Salzburg's sophisticated resort on the same lake. Just west of St. Wolfgang the road dwindles and dies. St. Gilgen is in no hurry, say the St. Wolfgang people, to make it easier for tourists to reach the rival resort, so the motorist coming from Salzburg must drive 19 kilometers clear around the eastern end of the lake instead of 8 or 9 to get to St. Wolfgang. This must, however, be an isolated case, for certainly the Salzkammergut is a single unit of travel, and for the most part it works and plays as a unit. There is, in fact, a Salzkammergut Coordinator, with office in Bad Ischl. To clarify the area's geography, Upper Austria has by far the largest part of the lakeland, with the whole of the Traunsee, the whole of Hallstättersee, with the three small but superscenic Gosau lakes, and almost all of the Mondsee and the Attersee, only tiny snippets of these two lakes adhering to Salzburg. Styria has only the resort of Altaussee, on its like-named lake, and the important spa of Bad Aussee, plus the insignificant appendages of the Grundlsee and the Toplitzsee. Leaving provincial boundaries to whom they may concern, we'll explore this marvelous holiday area, setting out from Salzburg City.

A SIX-LAKE CRESCENT TO THE SOUTH

The Salzkammergut Lakes are so spread out that they need to be sorted into two swings, south and north, with Bad Ischl, though

THE SALZKAMMERGUT / 209

it is on no lake, as the turntable, a logical place to spend a night or two—or more. This greatly flourishing spa-resort is so centrally located that *any* of the lakes can be comfortably reached from it. The six lakes of this southern crescent are: Mondsee; Wolfgangsee; Hallstättersee; and the three Gosau Lakes. The lakes of the Styrian Salzkammergut (Altausseersee; Grundlsee; Toplitzsee) have been covered in Chapter 4 in following the Styrian mountain route to Vienna.

I cannot resist harking back, for a moment, to the old days when I first explored the Salzkammergut by the *Kleinbahn* (light railway) that struggled for 40 miles through glorious scenery from Salzburg to Bad Ischl, a line that warred against progress but had to surrender about 15 years ago. It was the best-loved and most jokeworthy railway line in Austria, and inevitably reminded Americans of the cable cars of San Francisco in that it was impractical, archaic, but dear to the hearts of natives and visitors alike. It was a very costly plaything, piling up scandalous deficits every year, yet whenever there was talk of abandoning it the talk was drowned by howls of protest. So the Kleinbahn toiled on, the butt of wits and wags, the darling of holiday tourism, both Austrian and foreign, till it finally passed away—R.I.P. Busses and motorcars replaced it. The roads, in general, are good and will be better when new roads connect various towns and resorts with the main Salzburg-Vienna autobahn. This major turnpike passes through Mondsee Town, and for two or three miles along the northern shore of its lake, then skirts the Attersee and passes not far north of Gmunden, the most important town on the Traunsee.

Mondsee town lies on the western tip of the westernmost of the region's large lakes, which also is named *Mondsee*. The town's parish church and Benedictine abbey give it a cultural flavor, its occasional summer entertainments give it a festival flavor, its locally made cheeses give it a pungency that you may relish, and its lake of summer sports gives it an aura of water holidays that almost suggests Carinthia. There's a Schloss as part of the vast old abbey and in it a very special restaurant, but that will be described in the Roundup at the end of this chapter. Mondsee town is one with genuine character and charm. An avenue of lindens leads you to the like-named lake, whose waters are the warmest in all the Salzkammergut.

St. Gilgen, lying at the western tip of the *Wolfgangsee,* has a Mozart flavor, for the composer's mother was born here and her house, the "Mutterhaus," is conspicuous near the lakefront. Mozart's sister Nannerl married the governor of the district and then settled in St. Gilgen, adding an extra strand to the Mozart tapestry. St. Gilgen is so near Salzburg (20 miles) that it could almost be classed as a wealthy suburb of the city, but it is also a lake-sailor's paradise, the waters in front of it being dotted, on any fair day, with white and lemon-colored sails. Its view of the mountains backing the lake is deservedly famous.

St. Wolfgang, as we've seen, lies just barely within Upper Austria on the northern shore of the lake to which it lends its name, or its saint's name, and is reached by circling the lake's eastern end, passing through Strobl, a town that has been mentioned in Chapter 2 as the setting for some of the summer courses offered to foreign students by the University of Vienna.

The resort village of St. Wolfgang is almost as celebrated as it is beautiful, for it was the retreat of St. Wolfgang, converter extraordinary of the heathen, protector of the faithful against fire and hail. A Gothic church was built here and in it Michael Pacher of Bruneck (in lost South Tyrol) erected a winged altar that is the finest thing of its kind in existence. Pacher was equally great as a woodcarver and a painter, and on this altar he lavished his most loving skills.

The interior of the church tells us, too, a fine story of artistic sportsmanship. Gothic had its day and baroque came in. Thomas Schwanthaler was one of the exponents of the latter style. He was commissioned to make a new baroque altar for the St. Wolfgang church, for it was felt that the pious could not worship properly before any altar that savored of the outmoded Gothic. Schwanthaler made his altar but obstinately insisted that Pacher's altar should stay where it was in the place of honor, and his own take a secondary place. "Absurd," said the authorities, but Schwanthaler stood his ground. If this story is true, as local folk insistently say, Schwanthaler should receive a gold star in the Book of Conduct. Such sportsmanship during the baroque period was very rare indeed. He saved for us one of the greatest art works of Austria, knowing that his own altar would always suffer by comparison. Outside the church is a 15th-century fountain of bell-metal with an inscription dedicating it *"Zu nutz* [use] *den armen Pilgrump, die nit haben gelt und wein, die sullen pei diesen Wasser frellich* [merry] *sein."* If you have even a little knowledge of modern German you will enjoy this. Without any at all you may enjoy that word Pilgrump, for we are all Pilgrumps now to the hospitable Salzkammergut, though persumably not without some *"gelt und wein."*

From St. Wolfgang one should, of course, ascend the Schafberg on foot or by rack-and-pinion railway, and in doing so you may use a train powered by an old-fashioned steam engine or a modern one powered by electricity. The authorities have tried repeatedly to junk the old steam train, but each time a great outcry arises and they give in.

The Schafberg is often called the Austrian Rigi. Why? I think it is bad advertising, as it certainly directs the tourist's mind to the original, which is by implication a little better. Perhaps, after all, Lucerne's Rigi should be known as the Swiss Schafberg. Certainly it would be hard to choose between their two views. From the summit of the Schafberg we see the whole of the Salzkammergut, with more than a dozen of its lakes, large and small. We see as far as the Bohemian Forest to the north, as far as the faintly shimmering Chiemsee in Bavaria to the west. To the south and east stretches a wild, tossing sea of peaks, some of them interspersed with glaciers and covered with perpetual caps of snow. At our very feet is a trio of the green-blue lakes, being the two named above plus the *Attersee,* and another tiny lake, seeming black as ink, the mysterious *Krottensee,* which, though only a pond in area, is said to be the deepest lake in the whole Salzkammergut.

This Schafberg prospect will never let us go unless we dominate it by a steely stare and go anyway, just as if it were any ordinary view. We must descend to the village and lunch on the lake edge, perhaps on the terrace of the Weisses Rössl, which, as I've said, is the original White Horse Inn, the setting for the old stage and screen operetta hit of that name. If romance calls you, be advised that this famous inn asks only $20 to $24 for a twin-bedded room and bath, with all meals for two, service and taxes included. (In the high summer season it would be about $2 more per person.)

Bad Ischl, though lakeless, is the heart of the lake-strewn Salzkammergut. What it lacks in lake intimacy it makes up in majesty, by which I mean His Majesty, Emperor Franz Joseph, whose aura fills this spa, his favorite summer home, even though his physical presence disappeared from earth more than 50 years ago. Pictures, postcards, memorials of every kind, fairly saturate Ischl's shops, and the Imperial Villa is its chief tourist sight. Visitors are shown through the Villa by devout guides who point out everything connected with His Majesty, from the antlers of some 3500 chamois and stags he shot to the depression in the seat of the favorite imperial easy chair left by the imperial buttocks. A second celebrity of Ischl is Franz Lehár, whose home is now a museum of Lehariana. The composer of *The Merry Widow* and *Gypsy Love* would, of course, rate top billing were his fame not so blanketed by that of the benevolently whiskered monarch.

Before leaving His Majesty I should mention that his very existence is firmly believed by Ischlers to be due to the curative waters of their spa. His parents, Archduke Franz Karl and Archduchess Sophie, were childless—until they took the waters of Bad Ischl upon advice of the imperial physicians. "The cure was successful," reports the sobersided town chronicle. "The child was given the name of Franz Joseph." I might add here a point of "social history" that sometimes astonishes visitors, namely that this spa was for more than half a century a focus of the most brilliant and fashionable life of the Continent. The fashionable glitter has long since gone, but the "cure" has gained enormous prestige, and a life of concerts and entertainments has replaced the old court life. As for the curative program, a visit to the *Landeskuranstalten* reveals the effective work that is being done. In the summer season some 1300 treatments a day are often given, and the annual tally is at least a quarter of a million. Ischl is proud of its saline waters, which Badgastein does not have to any extent. There is a pool open to all, whose waters, gushing right from local springs, have an average of 2½ per cent salt content, about the same as the Adriatic waters off the Lido in Venice. In a park at the base of the Imperial Villa's property there is a public pool of nonmineral water, heated to about 77 degrees, where anyone, male or female, may rent a *Badeanzug* (swimsuit) and enjoy a dip.

As for music, there are actually a dozen musical organizations that make their summer homes here, and one or more concerts, or perhaps an opera or operetta, can be enjoyed any evening in the week. I saw Lehár's *Paganini* here in the big auditorium of the Kurhaus, which is also a café and restaurant, and thought it impressively well done. In the music field I was really thrilled to hear a long concert in the Kurhaus by "Young Americans in Concert." The participants, filling the central stage and two high balconies, right and left, included in an ambitious concert an "Iowa Mixed Chorus," a "Chicagoland Chorale," and the youthful "Des Moines Chamber Music Orchestra." The concertmaster, or concertmistress of the orchestra, was a 15-year-old girl and she also played, with orchestral accompaniment, a Mozart concerto. She played well, *very* well, and this despite the fact that she had just had an accident to her foot and had to limp painfully onto the stage, her foot in a cast. Later, in Innsbruck and in Igls I heard other concerts, by other American youth groups and all were downright *good,* including, for example, The Concordia Youth Wind Ensemble at Igls, sponsored by the Council on Intercultural Relations, with seat in Chicago. Ischl has a lot more than its past to recommend it, for it is a top pleasure spa of today, as well as a top *Kurort.*

The *Hallstättersee,* with Hallstatt as its great drawing card, is the southernmost lake of our south-trending crescent and a marvelous climax it makes. Hallstatt clings precariously to the edge of a salt mountain on the west side of the lake and is reached by a good road, partly tunneled, that now cuts through and along the cliff above it, somewhat relieving the dreadful car congestion that used to clog its narrow streets and small Plätze. Those who come by trains of the Federal Railway get off at a station on the opposite side (east bank) of the lake and cross by a small and busy steamer. This small village, which is so overshadowed by mountains that the sun does not touch it for three winter months, is of enormous interest to historians, for it has furnished archeological finds of the first importance. On the hillside half way up the Salzberg (salt mountain) above it, is the celebrated Celtic Cemetery, whose contents have proved beyond doubt that iron was *first used* in this district, whence it spread to Greece, Egypt, Italy and western Europe. You may find learned dissertations on the "Hallstatt Age" in any encyclopedia. Homer, whether one or many men, lived in the Celts' Hallstatt period of development, though probably later than these of Hallstatt. The cemetery is now a hillside cabbage patch. A sign on it has amused me: "Digging for finds here most strictly forbidden. Besides, there is nothing here, as all has been removed to museums." The last statement leaves the beholder unconvinced of the first. One of the former occupants of this burial plot is pictured in a large painting on the side of a building by the lake's edge. His name is given as "Rä Ingo II," his age at the time of exhumation as 3720. He is now in his 39th century and has taken up a permanent residence in a glass case in the little Hallstatt Museum, where I went to see him. All the more valuable finds have been taken to Vienna and Linz but this museum of Hallstatt is full of interest.

I wonder if Rä Ingo II went swimming in Hallstatt Lake. I did anyway, once or twice every day, diving from the garden of a little lakefront house where I had secured a furnished room. Past me chugged the steamer, weaving like a shuttle between the village and its railroad station, and all about me were the queer water transports of Hallstatt, high-prowed boats rowed gondola style. On Corpus Christi Day they form a religious procession that draws pious folk from all the villages of the lake.

To the Salzberg above Hallstatt I went one day by lift for a tour. At the salt-mine entrance I joined a group of tourists and each of us was given a protective cloak and hat. Then, herded along in the wake of a guide, we walked through a long corridor into the heart of the mountain. The roof and walls of the corridor, which were of claylike appearance, though strangely mixed with salt, gleamed dully in the rays of the guide's lamp. Sometimes the basic color seemed to be gray blue, sometimes yellow brown and occasionally there were conspicuous streaks of red. Touching fingers to walls and then to lips gave a strong harsh tang. At a halt far in the mountain we were all seated, toboggan style, at the top of a chute, given heavy leather gloves with which to cling to guide ropes, and then shoved into an inky black abyss. So steep was the grade, so bullet-swift the pace, that it seemed we should presently start smoking from the friction (our personal upholstery was not padded with leather or asbestos), but presently we all tumbled out in a heap on matting at a lower level of the mine. The fearsome ride was wonderful fun—after it was over.

The mountain is honeycombed with large reservoirs which are filled at intervals with fresh water. This is allowed to stand for six or eight weeks until thoroughly impregnated with brine, then drawn off through a brine conduit to the evaporating works at Ebensee, 20 miles to the north.

Emerging finally to the almost unbearable brilliance of day we walked along the glorious sylvan path *(Soleleitungsweg)* which surmounts this brine pipe line and voted that nature was more desirable outside the mountain than inside. Far below us, cupped by the walls of the Dachstein and other mountains, lay the deep blue lake, fed by the gleaming ribbon of silver which is the Traun River. All about us were various shades of foliage, at our feet were pink-purple cyclamens by the million, and overhead was that strange burnished disk of yellow that knocked our vision into myriads of whirling electrons. At Gosaumühle the path descended to the lake and we took a motorboat back to Hallstatt.

Gosaumühle needs further mention here, for it is the takeoff point for a bus or car trip to the *Gosau Lakes,* or rather to the Lower Gosau Lake, for there are three of them, Lower, Middle and Upper. Hikers may continue to the Upper Gosau Lake (Hinterer Gosausee) by a wonderful if arduous path in a climb that takes about 1½ hours. The fir-fringed path is dominated by the peaks of the Donnerkögel, as stunning to the senses as the Aiguilles above Chamonix.

The Upper Lake is in a setting of utmost splendor only a little under the Dachstein (Roofstone), whose double glacier sends frigid streamlets to keep the lake cold. Twice I have climbed to this spot for the two best-refrigerated swims I have ever enjoyed. Both times I dived off a rock and swam as fast as possible, *with the sunshine,* trying to keep ahead of the advancing shadows cast by the mountain peaks, but the shadows easily caught me, though the hour, in each case, was between 2 and 3 in the afternoon.

Obertraun, at the far southeastern tip of Lake Hallstatt, is about a mile and a half from the valley station of a cableway (capacity of the cabin 40 persons) that carries up to the *Dachstein Ice Caves,* at an altitude of 4400 feet, and in a second section, to the very lofty *Krippenstein,* at 7000 feet, where the 90-bed *Hotel Krippenstein,* with a good restaurant, is a most welcome refuge.

The ice caves of the Salzkammergut are a phenomenon quite as distinctive as the salt mountains and infinitely more beautiful. The largest in the world is the *Eisriesenwelt* above Werfen (just south of Salzburg), but even in the Dachstein Caves, to which one is so easily hoisted by the cableway, there are at least 20 miles of ice chambers and corridors. Outside the cavern known as *Rieseneishöhle* I waited a bit for the guide, with a growing group of sightseers, all German-speaking, since Anglo-Saxons are still surprisingly few in the Hallstatt area. It was hot in the sun even at that altitude of 4400 feet but a blast of polar air rushed out at us from the cave. Nature forms and maintains this Giant Ice Cave and all the others by refrigerating the rocks each winter to such a degree that they freeze the streams of melted snow that trickle into them each spring and summer, forming ever new and ever more fanciful decorative effects.

A world of fantasy, ingeniously lighted by electricity, is the Rieseneishöhle, with a frosty Gothic chapel, an adjoining "sacristy" adorned by a curtain of glistening ice many yards long, and with numerous domed chambers that have acquired Wagnerian names. The *Tristandom* is a brilliant feature and near it is a slender ice shaft named *Isolde.* On every hand are needles, pyramids and cones of coruscating whiteness. Even the bare rock walls have been painted with a thick coating of hoarfrost. As in so many parts of Austria nature has worked on a lavish scale to create her effects. Here in these lofty caverns she has found a material wholly worthy of her genius and it has stimulated her to achieve wondrous feats of artistry.

NORTH TO ATTERSEE, TRAUNSEE AND SOME MINILAKES

A good way for the motorist to approach the Salzkammergut's northern lakes from Ischl is to start north on Route 145, but after about 4 miles turn sharply to the west on Route 153. This brings you to the southern end of the Attersee, or Kammersee, for it has two names in equal use, which you round and head north along the western shore of that lake, a distance of 7 miles from south to north. The Attersee (Kammersee) is one of the less scenic lakes, except in its southern part, but the lakeside road makes pleasant driving as it leads to interesting goals. One of these is the circuit of the northern tip of the lake, with the communities of Kammer, Seewalchen and Schörfling. In Schloss Kammer chamber music concerts are given during the summer season.

Continue for a short distance east on the autobahn and then turn north on Route 143 and you come to the large lake town of Gmunden at the north end of the Traunsee, and a fine goal this is, certainly one of the most interesting towns in the Salzkammergut. Gmunden is justly proud of its lakeshore promenade, nearly 3 miles long and shaded by chestnut and linden trees. In the central portion of the promenade is the so-called Schillerlinde, around which folk dances are performed for the pleasure of tourists. Here, too, is a fountain and sculpture memorializing the salt carriers. One of them carries on his back an actual salt crystal that is claimed to be the largest in the world. Other features of the central waterfront are the highly appealing 16th-century Rathaus, with a café in and out of it, so to speak, some tables being indoors and some outside on the pavement of the Rathausplatz; and the new Kammerhof Museum, overlooking the lake. Even if museums are not on your list of musts you should not lightly pass this one, for it is different, beautiful, and with superb views from the windows that face the lake. In this building Emperor Maximilian I contracted, in 1493, to marry Blanca Maria Sforza of the famous Sforza family of Milan, his first wife, the gentle and beautiful Maria of Burgundy, having died. Music lovers will be interested in the special Brahms Room, with the composer's piano and some of his personal effects. Brahms greatly favored Gmunden.

A special product of Gmunden which has achieved international acclaim is a type of highly individual ceramics, some of it with an odd but pleasing "crackled" appearance. A feature of the town is a set of ceramic chimes, a carillon said to be unique.

The lake is alive with craft of many kinds, but the private motorboats, please note, are *electrically* powered, this by law, at least in summer, and are therefore nearly noiseless. It is fascinating to *see* them and not *hear* them. Some American lakes could well follow this tranquilizing idea. A lake steamer bears the name of *Empress Elisabeth,* while a similar steamer on the Wolfgangsee is the *Kaiser Franz-Josef I,* bearing the name of her husband. Both steamers are *paddlewheelers,* and for that reason they are held in deep affection by all lake dwellers, and tourists too. The *Franz Josef* had its *hundredth birthday* in 1971, but the veteran still paddles on, and the older it gets the more it is loved, reminding us of the affection felt for the old steam train toiling up the Schafberg.

There are two features of the town and its area that I especially like. One is the walk along the left bank of the swift, green River Traun, here an effluent from the lake, to the Marienbrücke, across this and up to the *Kronprinz Rudolph Anlagen,* on the heights above the right bank. The other is the idyllic *Seeschloss Ort,* filling an islet southwest of the esplanade. You reach this island castle by a long wooden bridge and a portal beneath an onion-domed tower to find yourself in a courtyard enclosed by a red-roofed hexagonal castle of 17th-century design now occupied by government offices. This is one of the Salzkammergut's most frequently photographed structures, and if I may inject a personal note, it was used for the jacket of the first book I ever wrote, a discursive travel book on Austria published in New York by Robert M. McBride & Company in 1930—and if that doesn't date me nothing will!

Perhaps you are wondering about the odd name of Schloss Ort, since that word means "place." The castle was acquired in 1878 by Archduke Johann Salvator, a nephew of Emperor

Franz Joseph, but he finally became bored with his royal role and adopted the name Johann Ort. Later, under conditions that have never been explained, he disappeared while cruising in South American waters. He is thought, or said, or supposed, to have taken with him papers that would have explained the mysterious double death, in 1889, of Archduke Rudolph, only son of Emperor Franz Joseph, and his 17-year-old inamorata Maria Vetsera in a hunting lodge in Mayerling, south of Vienna. Thus mystery was piled on mystery, and the two have never ceased to intrigue mystery followers, even to this cinema-and-television day.

The return to Ischl, or other parts of the Salzkammergut, should be made by the road along the west shore of the Traunsee and the first place of note that it leads to is Traunkirchen, a village that nestles on a promontory in the lee of the chapel-crowned Johannesberg. This is, I think, a dash of sheer perfection. More explicitly, I think that for romantic charm it is one of the supreme lake villages of the Salzkammergut and of all Austria. I have just now reviewed the case, allowing Hallstatt, Pertisau, Maria-Wörth and many other cameos of lake beauty to crowd upon my memory, and not one of them can surpass the jutting *peninsular* part of Traunkirchen. The scene is at its best in the evening, when floodlights play upon the hill. The "mainland" part is not of special interest.

At the southern tip of Traunsee is Ebensee, a considerable industrial village and also a resort, at the point where the Traun River enters the Traunsee. This was once an important center for refining salt and for transshipping it by lake to Gmunden and then the lower Traun. Today, for us, it may be the takeoff point for the cableway to the lofty (5300 foot) Feuerkogel peak, where there is a mountain hotel of some size, the *Berghotel Feuerkogel,* and also for a grand walk to the two Langbath lakes, formerly included in a vast imperial hunting preserve. Both lakes are pure gems and over them tower the Höllengebirge, or Infernal Mountains. It would seem that the brooks rushing down from these crags should be of scalding water, but this did not seem to be the case and certainly these Peaks of Hell looked bleak and half frozen. The Langbath lakes are full of trout, "and often," said a lumberman with whom I fell in, "they are as long as *that.*" He was vague in his gesture, but he did say definitely that he had caught *Forellen* (trout) weighing 8½ kilos (almost 19 pounds).

TWO-PART ROUNDUP OF HOTELS AND RESTAURANTS, A PERSONAL REPORT

NOTE OF EXPLANATION: The Salzkammergut, as far as tourism is concerned, consists largely of lake resorts, in which almost all the restaurants are connected with hotels, though there are a few exceptions; and as for shops, the only places where separate mention of them might be in order are Ischl and Gmunden. Therefore any stray restaurants and shops that call for mention will be presented in connection with the hotel coverage, and this, I may add, will be drastically pruned, for the number of them runs into many hundreds.

Hotels of Mondsee are surprisingly budget-typed for a place of such background and character, the *Königsbad,* a lake inn on the edge of town being the best, but what the town lacks in hotels it makes up in having a separate restaurant of more than local fame. This is the *Castello Bar-Restaurant,* in the castle portion, hence the name, of the Benedictine abbey earlier mentioned, a Schloss that was once owned by Napoleon's Fieldmarshal von Wrede. The place is bursting at the seams with atmosphere, but that's not what makes it so hard to get a table unless you've reserved in advance. It's the *food.*

Hotels of St. Gilgen —99 of them in the official list—are led without question by the *Excelsior*—all rooms with bath; lakeside terrace restaurant and private beach; all watersports; and tennis. The *Radetzky-Hof,* at the top of the town, near the pleasant Rathaus and its Platz, is first class; as is *Seehof Nebrich*; as is *Parkhotel Billroth;* and a high-grade pension that speaks for itself when seen is the appealingly named *Haus Evelyn* at and *over* the lake. (Who is Evelyn? What is she?) There's a separate, widely known restaurant in St. Gilgen, by name *See-Restaurant Fischer* where I, as one tourist, have eaten extremely well, the meal being enhanced by the portly presence of Herr Fischer, keeping a chef's eye on his guests.

Hotels of St. Wolfgang are more or less blanketed by the world fame of the *Weisses Rössl,* which has been drenched in publicity beyond any other hotel in Austria. This is not to say that its fame is undeserved. Far from it, but one has to agree that The White Horse has been shot with luck. I have never overnighted in it, but I *have* lunched, wonderfully, on its terrace, letting the romance of the place add flavor to the first-rate food. Other thoroughly good and attractive hotels of St. Wolfgang are the *Seehotel Cortisen;* the *Schloss Eibenstein,* in a castle-park of its own; and the family-type *Strandhotel Margaretha,* all three west of town. On the east, splendidly placed on a slope above the public Seebad, is the *Belvedere,* a chalet-type hotel garni, meaning that it offers room and breakfast only.

Hotels and Restaurants of Bad Ischl

Hotel Post on Kaiser-Franz-Josef-Strasse, squarely in the center of this great Kurort, is the traditional key hotel of Ischl and it is the largest. I have much enjoyed a stay in the Post, whose garden, in the rear, lends its cheerful touch, but the hotel's dining room is a bit cramped and plain for so good, and good-sized, a 6-story hotel.

Hotel Goldenes Hufeisen (Golden Horseshoe) on Pfarrgasse is quite as central as the Post and has a very good name. *Hotel Austria,* on the Esplanade overlooking the River Traun near the Elisabeth Brücke, is in a quiet location, but still very near the Kurhaus, with a good view of the mountains that surround Ischl. The Kurhaus is, of course, the center of Bad Ischl's social and entertainment life. There are several separate restaurants, by far the largest being that in the Kurhaus itself, with seating for 400 guests. This has an imperial touch, and the added advantage that the guest may dine in a spacious corridor of the establishment within easy ear-range of the concerts or other entertainment but without actually being inside the big quadrilateral. There is also an outdoor garden terrace café. Of several much smaller restaurants two to consider are the *Café-Restaurant Marmorschlössl,* located within the area of the park of the Imperial Villa and the *Weinhaus Attwenger,* on the Lehár Quay across the Elisabeth Brücke. Among cafés, consider the *Ramsauer,* on Kaiser-Franz-Josef-Strasse, and if your sweet tooth is *very* sweet, the *Café-Konditorei Zauner,* on Pfarrgasse. The Zauner is a name commonly linked with Vienna's Demel as one of Austria's two super-pastry-shops. It has been serving multicalorie marvels since the days of the empire. *Shops* abound in Ischl, the better ones being mostly found on Kaiser-Franz-Josef-Strasse, Pfarrgasse and other central streets within the half circle formed by the rivers Traun and Ischl.

Hotels of Hallstatt are dominated by the 64-bed *Grüner Baum* (Green Tree), located on the small but utterly fascinating central Platzl (squarelet) and with a garden-café directly on the lake. But for sheer charm consider the small and modest *Hotel Seewirt,* located at the "top" of the Platzl but with a view of the lake from some of its upper rooms. This is about as rustically charming a place as could be imagined, and its owner-manager is Sepp Zauner, magic name, a "grill king" who has held cooking classes and has written a cookbook that was translated into English, complete with photographs of Sepp's creations. Friends of mine who stayed there were glowing with praise of it, though the hotel is officially given only a C rating. On my next visit I propose to book there if I can secure one of its 30 beds.

Gosau has blossomed with several good second-class hotels, especially at the Vorderer (Lower) Gosausee. The *Jagdschloss Hotel was* a hunting Schloss and its character has been preserved. *Gasthof Kirchenwirt* is a modest but recommendable hotel, and the still humbler *Gosausee* has been recommended to me by a friend as a budget place, on the lake.

Hotels of Gmunden are numerous and good. The *Seehotel Schwan,* though perhaps not the best, is well situated on the Rathausplatz near the lake. The much larger *Austria* and the equally large *Parkhotel am See,* both with terrace restaurants facing the sea, are justly popular with Americans. The *Kurhotel,* on higher ground, has a broader view, which some prefer, but I have saved for the last Gmunden hotel the one I know best (and the one with the toughest name), *Schlosshotel Freisitz Roith.* It is on a level well above the lake near the base station of the cableway to the Grünberg, "around the corner" from Gmunden. A lunch on its wide-open view terrace is one not soon forgotten. The food is very good, and in summer you may likely have an American student waiter to serve you.

On the summit of the Grünberg, very comfortably reached, at about the 3300-foot level, by a suspension Seilbahn, is the *Grünberg Gästehaus,* a first-class hotel and restaurant with a heated outdoor swimming pool. A lunch or a stay here can be the high point, figuratively as well as literally, of any visit to Gmunden.

Hotels of Traunkirchen are few, suited to its much smaller size than Gmunden. The *Post*—a name borne by hundreds of hotels all over Austria—located on the chief square, is the largest (110 beds) and best; but one that I've liked for its lakeside stance is the *Traunsee.* It has only 40 rooms, 10 of which, on an upper floor, have bath or shower. Pleasing features of the hotel are a tiny lake garden and a miniature rose-bordered boat "harbor," crossed by a little up-and-over wooden bridge.

11 / Tyrol

APPROACH AND ENTER: A PLAN OF TRAVEL

I had thought to deliver a one-minute treatise on the glories of Tyrol, spelled Tirol in German, but I rescued myself just in time, for what is the use of commenting on something that speaks for itself in its own way. If gilding the lily is unprofitable, so is brightening the sunshine in Alpine valleys and whitening the snow on snowpeaks. So—we'll march right in.

A name and place that you will encounter early in your approach-and-enter program is Kitzbühel. The shortest way to reach it from Zell am See, which is a major turning point of traffic, lies through the valley of the Salzach to Mittersill and from there over the Thurn Pass, but most motorists elect to follow the longer, smoother route by way of Lofer and St. Johann in Tirol, which latter is a picturebook town worth seeking for its own sake. If you follow this course you come to the junction town of Wörgl, continuing from there either by Route 1, which extends all the way from Vienna through Salzburg to Innsbruck and clear to Bregenz, or by the now building Brenner Autobahn, if it is finished and open when you need it, climbing the Inn Valley westward for the remaining 40 miles to Innsbruck. From this stretch of highway tempting tangents lead north and south up smaller scenic valleys. At Innsbruck the autobahn takes off south over the spectacular Europabrücke to the Brenner—this part has been open for some time—and Italy, and from Zirl, a village 5 miles west of Innsbruck, one may go north to reach the popular mountainside resort of Seefeld in Tirol, or more ambitiously, up and over the Bavarian frontier to the violin village of Mittenwald. Farther west, the Ötztal leads south up to Obergurgl, the much-mentioned "loftiest village," and over the new Timmelsjoch Pass to Merano (once Meran) in South Tyrol, a province, now, of Italy. Other valleys sound their calls, but the main highway leads up to the Arlberg and beyond that mountain to the Province of *Vor*arlberg, meaning *Before* the Arlberg.

KITZBÜHEL AND ITS WHITE CARNIVAL

Kitzbühel means Chamois-Kid-Hill, a Kitz being a young chamois and Bühel being a hill in the local dialect of Tyrol. Appropriately, the town has the chamois as its emblem. Kitzbühel is a biseasonal or multiseasonal resort popular at all times of year but its vast popularity seems not to have seared its soul too badly. In other words, despite its luxurious hotels, its gambling casino, its emphasis on *après-ski,* and its patronage by the international play set it still manages to look like a Tyrolean village of the 16th century, at which period it was an important traffic center endowed with special wealth from its silver and copper mines. Gaily frescoed houses, aglow with flowers at every window, still brighten the main streets. Their hugely overhanging roofs suggest an operetta village. The Town Hall, though perhaps somewhat subdued by all the goings-on, is still a very jolly affair of buff walls, red shutters and gaudy flower boxes. One feels that the local magistrates must have a civic music box to entertain them while they discuss taxes. In 1935 the Prince of Wales, who was to become King Edward VIII and then the Duke of Windsor, put Kitzbühel on the map of world tourism as a winter-sports resort, with emphasis on social pleasures, and ever since then it has held its high place as one of Europe's chief skiing centers. From it many teachers of this sliding and leaping art have gone to all the corners of the earth. I met one of them in Yosemite Park, whither he had been summoned from

Kitzbühel to teach the finer points of skiing to snowy California. We'll look further at skiing hereinafter.

To clarify the subject of mechanical ascents, there are 4 cableways, 3 double chairlifts, 9 single chairlifts and a dozen or so skilifts. These last serve a system called the *Skizirkus* (ski circus) whereby skiers may make a chain of different skiruns without repeating any one. At least one major slope is lighted for night skiing. In hockey, Kitzbühel is Austria's unrivaled center and it is strong, also, in curling.

The four cableways mentioned above include *two* to the Kitzbühelerkamm, the highest one reaching 6549 feet, plus a double chairlift, and one to the Hahnenkamm at 5458 feet. The baskets can hold 32 to 40 persons and soar at the rate of 23 feet per second, making the whole ascent in seven and six seconds respectively.

These peaks are chief centers of Kitzbühel's "White Carnival," as the winter-sports festivities are collectively called. The season is at its height from Christmas through New Year's and from early February to mid-March, and the scene is then enlivened by international ski competitions and spectacular torch skiing at midnight, but the whole area around the town is also awash with gaieties, including costume parties under spotlights on slopes agleam with snow. In town there are lavish parades, Tyrolean evenings in the hotels and cafés, with Stimmung provided by well-known entertainers and with concerts in the main *Platz*. It is axiomatic that there are nightclubs too, headed by the casino, and of course there are crowded ballrooms and still more crowded barrooms, for Kitzbühel is a perennial favorite of those winter visitors who put evening gaieties at least on a par with sports. There are character restaurants to enhance all the other doings, the best of which will be reported in the Roundup at the end of the chapter.

I should not leave skiing without a general word on the subject. The Big Four in Austria are Kitzbühel and St. Anton am Arlberg in Tyrol, Zürs and Lech in Vorarlberg, with Badgastein, in the view of some, making it a Big Five. It is customary, at least in some resorts, to use yellow markers for tough runs, for experts only; red for average runs; and blue for gentle slopes suitable for beginners. Skiing competitions of championship events are ruled by the FIS *(Fédération Internationale de Skis)*.

Kitzbühel is not a mineral-water spa like Badgastein, but it does have a health specialty in the form of peat baths. The peat, or mud, is secured in limitless quantities from the bottom of the little Schwarzsee (Black Lake) and is piped from there directly to an establishment called *Moorbad,* meaning Mudbath. Here you may encase your body any day in luscious, healing mud, but I have a feeling that summer sunshine or winter snow will call you more urgently than mud.

CLIMBING UP THE INN

Wörgl is the first point where the west-going traveler in Austria encounters the River Inn and while this junction town is of little interest in itself, it suggests a couple of tangent trips, to the south for Schloss Itter, to the north for Kufstein.

Schloss Itter, a castle-inn standing on a ridge some 5 miles from Wörgl, has a curious story that is worthy, I think, of being set down here. During World War II, at the height of the Nazi ascendancy, Schloss Itter was the chief prison for captured French notables, including such key figures as Daladier, Reynaud, François-Poncet and General Weygand. In 1955 a hotel man of Innsbruck by the name of Willi Woldrich undertook to turn this castle into a first-class inn and he effected this metamorphosis in five strenuous months, from January 1 to May 28, on which date it was opened to the public. Mr. Woldrich, having a fine flair for publicity, cordially invited the celebrated ex-prisoners to visit Schloss Itter for its opening, this time as guests of honor, occupying the very same rooms they had occupied as POW's; but bitter memories were apparently still too strong for them and they did not accept.

The castle-prison-inn looks from below rather like an English castle in the "geometrical decorated" style, with crenelated battlements and a high, square tower, but its close-up look and its interior are more inviting. It is composed mostly of small suites, each with private bath and each with fireplace and private balcony. The tower, served by a small elevator, is 5 stories high, the bedrooms on its upper floor being 90 feet above the castle lawn and terrace. There is a 5-car garage *inside* an old wall and a car park for 25 cars on top of the wall! Schloss Itter has 44 beds, many of the rooms having private bath.

Kufstein, almost on the frontier of Bavaria, borders the River Inn 9 miles to the north of Wörgl on the main railway express route from Italy via Innsbruck to Munich. The town is quite overshadowed by the imposing *Fortress Geroldseck,* which belonged to the bishops of Regensburg in the Middle Ages and to the Bavarian counts after that, but passed into Tyrol's possession in a violent episode of history in 1504, when Maximilian I laid siege to it and took it. To accomplish this, the emperor had two giant cannons built, the Weckauf and the Burlepauss, these being the largest in the world at that time. It took 32 horses to drag each one to the Inn, where two huge rafts floated them, after infinite trouble, down to Kufstein. Maximilian set up these giants across the river from the fortress and they threw 300-pound iron balls a mile and a half, finally battering down the castle wall, which was "fourteen shoes thick." Such was the power of artillery in 1504. It seems incredible. A marvel of Geroldseck today is the *Heldenorgel,* or Heroes Organ, which was built to honor the dead of World War I and is acknowledged to be the largest open-air organ in existence. Brief concerts are given twice a day, at noon and 8 P.M. (but check at the time of your coming), and its vast voice can be heard for miles. About 10 miles up the Inn valley from Wörgl, on the river's right (south) bank, is Rattenberg, which looks like a 17th-century town (except for its congested traffic), a town where, in August every year, a knightly tournament is held, followed by a festival and torchlight procession. At all seasons Rattenberg is fascinating, but if you can manage to leave it and climb the Inn 6 miles more you come to a double junction point where you must do some hard deciding. To the south runs the long and lovely Zillertal to Mayrhofen, a valley that is the traditional home of the Tyrolean zither. To the north, on the Inn's left bank, is Jenbach, the takeoff point for the ascent, by road or cogwheel rail, to the Achensee. You have seen many lakes in Austria but this Lake of Achen is one by itself, which I humbly beg you not to miss. It is bluer than any of the others and that is fact not fancy. Perhaps algae at the bottom are the cause of this blueness as they are in the case of the Blausee at

Kandersteg in Switzerland, but whatever the scientific cause, it looks as if someone had colored the lake with a million barrels of indigo.

The chief town on the lake is *Pertisau*, and my own first arrival at this port, by the cogwheel railway from Jenbach and then a short steamer ride, was an experience never to forget. The sun had just broken through the clouds after a sharp shower and Pertisau wore an indescribable mantle of glory. Its far spreading fields, nearly level where all else around that 6-mile body of water is frowning crag or snowcap, were one great carnival of color. Solid patches of purple and saffron flowers alternated with pink clover and the sparkling green of grass lately flooded by rain, now flooded by sunshine. Typical Tyrolean chalets, their 2nd-story balconies running around three sides, dotted the meadows here and there. Pertisau has no center to speak of, though there are a few small general stores. It is always an event when the boat chugs up to its wharf, for the boat is Pertisau's only link with the world except a road of mediocre quality connecting it with the tiny port of Seespitze at the lake's southern tip.

I climbed one day to the Erfurterhütte on one of the mountains opposite Pertisau. It is typical of the shelters found everywhere in the Austrian Alps, often named and sponsored by some German or Austrian town. The D-Ö. A. (Deutscher und Österreichischer Alpenverein), which owns this Erfurt shelter, has 200,000 members and leads all other clubs of its kind. Because I was not a member I paid a little higher price for a bottle of beer and *Schinkenbrot* but the indescribable view, with the lake a mile or so below, cost me no more than it costs those who pay dues to the club. On the lake chugged a tiny waterbug down to Scholastika, at the northern tip, where a beetle, which was one of the Bavarian post busses, was waiting to take travelers across the frontier to Tegernsee.

Whenever I see the Achensee, close to or from some height, I feel the need for a powerful new blue with which to characterize it. Although a dictionary I have hopefully consulted lists 226 blues, from Chicago blue to Zambezi blue, from anthracene to ultramarine, none satisfies me. Achen blue will have to do.

230 / ALL THE BEST IN AUSTRIA

Solbad Hall in Tirol, only 6 miles east of Innsbruck, is so near that city as to be almost a suburb, yet it has an identity quite its own. Solbad means Salt-Water-Bath (in reference to the briny springs which make this a spa) and Hall is an obsolete word meaning salt, supposed by etymologists to be derived from the Greek halós. We have met the word in other towns of Austria and Germany (*Hall*ein, *Hall*statt, Bad Reichen*hall,* etc.), but this Hall is one of the oldest, dating from Roman times, and its salt mountain is still the mainstay of the town's economy. The brine formed in the mountain's salt chambers is brought down in conduits to the evaporating works, where it yields actually 30 per cent of its weight in pure salt.

The bulbous towers of Hall's churches, and even more, its *Münzerturm,* or Mint Tower, give it a typically Austrian appearance, which a closer approach does not belie. This Münzerturm was built in the 14th century by Duke Siegmund of Tyrol, who transferred the ducal mint from Meran to Hall so that it might be near the rich silver mines of Schwaz, a bit to the east of the town. It was in this mint tower that Andreas Hofer, the peasant hero of Tyrol who defied Napoleon, minted his *Kreuzer* and *Zwanziger* during his brief period of dominance in 1809, and that was the last occasion on which the tower was ever used.

Just outside Hall, at *Absam,* Jakob Stainer was born, perhaps the greatest violinmaker of Germanic extraction. He used to wander through the woods above the town, says tradition, for days on end, tapping various trees with a hammer until he came upon one whose "tone" satisfied him. Then he would have it felled and use its wood to fashion violins, which he himself sold in the streets of Hall for a top price of six florins, about two and a half dollars. After a life full of tragedy and haunted by continuous poverty he died in an asylum in Absam. A genuine Stainer sells today for a fabulous sum, not too far below the figure for a Guarnerius or an Amati. Stainer's art has been partially lost but the people of the violin village of Mittenwald, across the Bavarian frontier, have retained some of the skills learned from Stainer by their musical ancestor Mathias Klotz.

The wealth of Hall's neighbor town, *Schwaz,* has lain in mines not of salt but of silver. The fortunes of this village were at a very low ebb when one day in the early 15th century a bull lost his temper from some cause unknown to history, went raging over the hillsides above, and in his violent anger tore up big clods of grass with his horns. A herdsman, surveying the damaged turf, rubbed his eyes in amazement. Surely that shiny stuff was silver. So instead of cannily covering up the vein and buying the hillside he raced impetuously down to the village and told everybody. Yes, it proved to be an enormously rich deposit of silver. Instead of laying the fortune of the herdsman it laid the fortunes, eventually, of several Bavarian families, especially the Fuggers of Augsburg. They built a substantial, though now showy, castle in Schwaz and in their home city of Augsburg they became the financial leaders of Europe. The Fuggers were a curiosity of their time. They presented the anomaly of great wealth and no pedigree. Not a single robber baron could they claim as ancestor, yet they owned castles. In the 15th and 16th centuries their money virtually *ran* the world and its wars. They were the billionaire bankers of their time and—checkbook balancers take note—they *invented* the system of paying bills by checks. Schwaz grew to be a rich, bustling town of 30,000 inhabitants, but its mines were finally depleted and it reverted to the pleasantly somnolent town we see today.

INNSBRUCK, THE ESSENCE OF TYROL, AND TYROL'S CAST OF CHARACTERS

The story of Tyrol, keyed to its great and interesting figures, is quite as dramatic as the story of Vienna and the cast of characters is entirely different. Believing that any traveler will enjoy Innsbruck more if he has a "speaking acquaintance" with the leading personages of the past, I will present them in brief introductions, weeding out all names except those that greatly matter, those that the traveler encounters at every turn.

First about the name of Tyrol itself. It comes from the Castle of Teriolis, situated on a hill just above Meran (Merano), which was the historic seat of the Tyrolean court but is now a city of Italy, as it has been since the treatymakers of 1919 awarded South Tyrol to that country. To all Tyrolese of today the very name of their province is salt in the wound. A somewhat analogous case would be if we were to lose the state of Virginia, with George Washington's Mount Vernon, to a foreign power. We would not feel happy about it, nor do the Tyrolese feel happy about *Teriolis Irredenta,* but they have sorrowfully accepted it as a *fait accompli.* There is little public airing of their grievance and the average tourist is scarcely aware of it.

To come to the figures of history, there is, first of all, *Margareta Maultasch,* whose name has already crept into this book as the Ugly Duchess of Tyrol. She was "Pocketmug" (the translation of Maultasch) to contemporaries and has, cruelly it seems, remained so for historians ever since. Even the most serious works of historical research seem sometimes constrained to use the name, for her ugliness, partly caused, it is said, by an accident in her youth, was so formidable that it was harrowing to her subjects. At the age of 12, this girl, heiress to Tyrol, and Carinthia as well, came from Meran to Innsbruck to be married to the 10-year-old son of King John of Bohemia. She was even then cursed with a muddy complexion and an apelike mouth that startled the unhappy boy who found himself her husband. Through life she lived in rebellious mutiny against her fate, which always seemed adverse. When her only son (by a later husband) died she had to hand over the Duchy of Tyrol to her cousin Rudolf, Count of Habsburg, whose dynasty held it for more than six centuries until November 1918, when the Habsburgs themselves bowed to fate.

Some decades after Margaret's demise came *Friedrich-mit-der-leeren-Tasche* (Frederick-with-the-Empty-Purse [literally pocket]) to Innsbruck to dwell there as its duke. He was of the powerful Habsburg line and did a great deal to make Innsbruck a worthy capital. Whenever his purse was really empty it was because he was too humane to tax his subjects heavily enough to keep up his court and his public works.

Frederick came to grief through a curious and unfortuante quarrel with Sigismund, King of Hungary. The latter paid Frederick a state visit just before the famous Council of Constance. Frederick, to do his guest honor, staged a magnificent masquerade. Then began the trouble. Late in the evening a young Innsbruckerin was violated by a tall masked man "who wore a long beard." The description fitted both Frederick and Sigismund. Circumstances pointed the accusing finger at them. Public indignation was at fever pitch. Which one was guilty? Each stoutly asserted his own innocence and accused the other. The quarrel grew and grew. Soon Sigismund was elected Holy Roman Emperor at Constance. Here was his chance for venting his rage. He caused the church to excommunicate Duke Frederick and the duke even had to fly for his life from the emperor's displeasure. Sigismund was a faithless, licentious monarch and very likely it was *his* long beard that the girl of Innsbruck had tried to identify, but in any case the event grievously damaged the career of Frederick, who might have done much more for Innsbruck.

Frederick's grandnephew *Maximilian,* "the Last of the Knights," became the puissant Emperor Maximilian I. He united all the far-spreading Habsburg dominions of Bohemia, Hungary and even Spain. Yet Maximilian found time to build Innsbruck's fame on enduring foundations. He constituted himself its special patron, drew to it from all over the world leading armorers, bronze founders, glaziers, skilled craftsmen in every branch of the arts, and left it world famous. As a study in ingratitude we may read how Innsbruck rewarded its benefactor in his declining years. Because of some petty question regarding an innkeeper's claims the emperor's carriages and horses were left standing in the street without any attention or shelter one frigid December night. It was a small but significant affair. The emperor, peculiarly sensitive in his feelings toward this town which he loved so much, decided to return at once to Vienna. He embarked forthwith on an open barge to float down the River Inn. One of the few things he took with him was a plain wooden coffin, "the only prince's palace," he said, "for which nobody envies me." The exposure resulting from this severe December trip undermined his already enfeebled constitution and he died at Wels, in Upper Austria, on the journey. It seems that the narrow wooden "palace" was eagerly claiming its heartsore owner. Much of the glamour that is Innsbruck is due to the intelligent generosity of Maximilian, Last of the Knights.

Out of the welter of historical confusion following Maximilian we need select, for romance' sake, only the name of his great-grandson, *Archduke Ferdinand* of Tyrol. His two passions in life were collecting art works, especially fine old armor, and adoring his beautiful but unpedigreed wife, Philippine Welser of Augsburg. This match is one of the most romantic in history. The Welsers were a hardly less famous family of wealthy burghers than that other Augsburg family, the Fuggers, but for a burgher's daughter to marry an archduke, son of the Holy Roman Emperor himself, was unheard-of. The marriage took place secretly, but then Ferdinand took his bride openly to Innsbruck and there installed her in Schloss Ambras, a little outside of the town, where Philippine, removed from the spotlight of court functions, might not feel the embarrassment of her anomalous position. This situation gave Ferdinand the opportunity to gratify his two great passions simultaneously. He lavished on the castle and on the fair Philippine all the treasures of art which he could come by, including a large collection of armor, which was quite natural, for in the earliest days Innsbruck was one of but four places in Europe where good armor was made, the others being Milan, Augsburg and Munich. In spite of the fact that most of the armor and other treasures were later transferred to Vienna, this castle, because of its romance, remains one of the show places of Innsbruck.

In one leap I shall come to the beginning of the 19th century and present one last figure of Tyrolese history, whom some think the greatest of all, "a man who"—to use the political nominator's verbiage. *Andreas Hofer* is the man's name.

Why is not this name as familiar in America as that of Garibaldi? I do not know, unless it is that Hofer never became, like Garibaldi, a temporary New Yorker. Hofer is one of the outstanding romantic heroes of history. No man ever fought with more tenacity and courage against hopeless odds to free his native land from an invader. Tyrolese sometimes call their country Hoferland. Since 1919 the hero's tomb in Innsbruck's Hofkirche has been hung with black crêpe.

The story of Hofer can be briefly told. He was a shaggy innkeeper of South Tyrol's Passeier Valley, an intelligent and honest horse trader as well, and something of a connoisseur of fine wines. The year of his sudden appearance on the firmament of history was 1809. All Europe trembled before Napoleon. Bavaria and Saxony were allied with the French emperor. Italy was abject. Vienna cowered. Then Andreas Hofer saw his own beloved land overrun by the invaders. He tried to stir up distant Vienna but the Habsburgs were badly frightened. They were in favor of Hofer's putting up a stout resistance—by himself. Hofer took up the challenge. Incredibly, he built up a force of 15,000 peasants. The French had confiscated all arms but the peasants collected scythes, axes, billhooks, a few shotguns. On the night of April 10 signal fires blazed from a dozen mountain tops. The next day, in irresistible fury, Hofer and his men swept down to the Inn Valley. To Hofer's right and left were his faithful lieutenants (they lie buried with him in the Hofkirche), Josef Speckbacher and Joachim Haspinger. The latter, fiery red of hair, was a Capuchin friar. In one hand he carried a crucifix, in the other a sword. Innsbruck's streets ran blood, but Tyrol was delivered. The entire Bavarian garrison was astonished to find itself captured by a band of peasants. Next day, Napoleon's General Bisson surrendered unconditionally.

In a few weeks Austrian regulars, under General Chasteler, undid Hofer's work so effectively that the French and Bavarians were able to recapture the city. In May, Hofer again drove them out, furiously, magnificently. This time Vienna, in panic at the growing menace of Napoleon, signed the Treaty of Znaim in July. The French and Bavarians, and now the Saxons too, were back in Innsbruck, 40,000 of them, led by the redoubtable Marshal Lefèbvre. Then Hofer achieved his most dazzling feat of all. Briefly, he *drove them out again,* treaty or no treaty. Hofer signed no treaty with the Spoiler, nor would he ever.

Vienna, delighted but still frightened, ventured to bestow upon Hofer the title of Oberkommandant of Tyrol. He coined money (at Hall) to carry on the fight. He ruled with combined force and humility. But in a few weeks Vienna had lost all heart and concluded the Treaty of Schönbrunn, definitely ceding Tyrol to Bavaria. Even Hofer had to see that the game was up. He was forced to fly to the mountains, as a big price was on his head. In his mountain fastness a neighbor by the name of Josef Raffl, the Judas of Tyrol, betrayed him for 30 pieces of silver, more or less. Hofer was taken to Mantua, given a mock trial by his old foe, General Bisson, and executed at the express order of Napoleon himself during the interval between the latter's contract of marriage with the Austrian Louise and its consummation. As Hofer stood before the executioners an attempt was made to bind his eyes, but he refused to permit this. "Shoot straight," he said simply. They did, and thus died Andreas Hofer, as intrepid a hero as any land ever had. A terrific hue and cry was raised all over Central Europe at this execution, whereupon Napoleon, as glib a liar as the next man when it suited his purpose, "explained" that the shooting had been contrary to his wishes and due to the mistaken zeal of his underlings.

INNSBRUCK'S SIGHTS UNSCRAMBLED

The tourist's Innsbruck, and it is the Innsbruck of all who love the city, is easy to understand, for it is largely concentrated in one main stem, with the big Hofburg complex near its northern end and some museums "off to the right." The stem starts out almost as a Platz named Maria-Theresien-Strasse, with a Triumphal Arch at the point where Salurnerstrasse joins it. The arch, I may inject, is a strange happy-and-sad affair, for the south side celebrates the marriage, in 1765, of Archduke Leopold, who later became Emperor Leopold II, with the Spanish Princess Maria Ludovica, while the northern side mourns the death of Francis I, the beloved husband of Maria Theresa, which tragically occurred at the very same time as the wedding. The street-square continues north past the Column of St. Anne, surmounted, however, by a statue of the Virgin, and then extends in a very narrow and always crowded street called Herzog-Friedrich-Strasse to the famous Goldenes Dachl (Golden Rooflet). This continues, through an archway, along the Pfarrgasse, to the St. James Cathedral (called in German Dom zu St. Jacob); but to reach the Hofburg complex you must halt at the Golden Roof, or return to it. As you face the Roof turn right on narrow Hofgasse, and then left into the Rennweg, which brings you to the Hofburg's entrance. The Hofkirche (Court Church) and the Silberne Kapelle (Silver Chapel), all of these sights to be discussed below, are on the right of the Rennweg as you head north to enter the Hofburg. One more basic item: At the base of the Goldenes Dachl where (facing it) you turn right for the Hofburg, turn *left* for the historic and celebrated *Hotel Goldener Adler,* just a few steps along the street leading to the river, this being an extension of the narrow Herzog-Friedrich-Strasse. That's it for the sightseer. Lesser things will easily fall into place with a map, which your hotel porter or the tourist office (*Verkehrsverein Innsbruck-Igls,* Burggraben 3) will provide.

The cultural sights of Innsbruck need not appall even the hurried visitor. They are very numerous but I should say that barring those things like the world-celebrated *Goldenes Dachl* that "see themselves" one could properly resort to ruthless pruning and reduce the luxuriance to *one* unqualified must, namely the ensemble of the *Hofburg,* including the *Hofkirche* and the *Silberne Kapelle,* adding other sights according to taste and available time.

The Goldenes Dachl, or Golden Roof, is a two-decker Gothic balcony with a gilded copper roof adorning a former palace of the 15th century, by name the Fürstenburg. It confronts the stroller "unmissably" at a small square, or widening, where Herzog-Friedrich-Strasse, a continuation of Maria-Theresien-Strasse, to repeat this for the sake of clarity, turns sharply toward the river. Although there have long been scholarly arguments as to its origin most students of the times consider that it was built about the year 1500 by Emperor Maximilian I as an embellishment of the palace that had been erected by his great-uncle, Duke Frederick-with-the-Empty-Purse. The palace itself has lost all significance, its rooms being actually let to private persons, but the two-storied balcony and roof, visible from far down the main street, make a unique sight. The balcony was really designed as a stage box from which Maximilian and his court could watch the performances of players, jugglers and buffoons in the street below. Red marble pillars support the structure and it was from the loggia on the upper of the two stories that the court looked down. The reliefs, done with artistic skill and grotesque humor, actually picture the court watching the players and revelers.

But the roof, the *Dachl* itself, is the crowing glory, at least for the tourist. This is composed of some 3500 gilded copper plates shaped like large coins. Each plate is supposed to have cost nine ducats ($20) some 460 years ago. That brings the roof covering alone to $70,000, which is quite enough to build a balcony roof even today.

Interesting buildings are all around the Golden Roof. Across the way from it is the *Helblinghaus,* a patrician mansion in the most lavish baroque style where great visitors have been welcomed, and close to this, toward the river, is the world-famous Hotel Goldener Adler, while just to the east, in the Hofgasse, are the 16th-century *House of the German Order* (Number 3) and the *Burgriese* (Number 12), this being a house built in 1487 by Duke Siegmund for his favorite giant, one Nikolas Heidls, a life-size statue of whom decorates the façade. And to the east and north of the Dachl sprawls the whole complex of the *Hofburg,* which was the Tyrolean palace of the Habsburgs, built by Maximilian I but quitted by him when he undertook his tragic journey (in 1519) to Vienna.

The Hofburg was constructed at about the same time as the Dachl but was extensively altered in the 18th century by Maria Theresa. From then on it survived all vicissitudes until World War II, when a single badly aimed bomb—the airmen had been strenuously briefed to avoid such cultural monuments—fell on the north wing, destroying one room and a lot of fine furniture. The room has been restored and so has much of the furniture, but some valuable pieces were hopelessly ruined. On the other hand, the bomb served to reveal one excellent painting which had been covered and forgotten.

The guided tours of the Hofburg, with its huge gold-and-white *Festsaal* and the *Andreas-Hofe-Saal,* and of the adjacent *Hofkirche* (Court Church), one of the noblest sights of Europe, together with its *Silberne Kapelle* (Silver Chapel), seem to me distressingly mechanical and far too hurried, even though the full tour consumes two hours. The Hofkirche and the Silver Chapel may be visited on your own, so perhaps the thing to do is to take the full tour, for a basic understanding of the Hofburg, and supplement this by leisured visits under the personal guidance of yourself.

If the Hofburg is the nucleus of historic Innsbruck the Hofkirche is certainly the nucleolus, for it contains, in addition to the tombs of Andreas Hofer and his lieutenants, to which I have already referred, the sarcophagus of Maximilian, surrounded by 28 bronze statues, and the Silver Chapel (reached by a staircase from the right aisle), with the tombs of Ferdinand and Philippine, which had to be in a chapel separated from the Hofburg (*Court* Church) because Philippine was a commoner. Maximilian's tomb is one of the world's most remarkable art treasures, quite unmatched of its kind. The one unfortunate thing about it is that Maximilian does not lie in it but far away in Wiener Neustadt, which was his birthplace.

Of the 28 bronze figures surrounding the tomb all but 2 formerly bore torches in outstretched hands. As the torches have long since disappeared it gives the 26 an awkward appearance, grasping at empty air, that seems unfair in competition with the two, King Arthur of England and Theodoric the Ostrogoth, who do not labor under this handicap. Nevertheless, the superiority of these two statues is a tribute to the master who fashioned them, Peter Vischer of Nürnberg. Perhaps no bronze founder ever surpassed him in skill. These masterpeices, however, were pawned immediately after their execution to the Bishop of Augsburg and were not redeemed until long after Emperor Maximilian's death.

All of the 28 were real, or wishfully supposed, members of the Habsburg House, the most nebulous ones being Arthur, Theodoric, Clovis and Godfrey de Bouillon. Maximilian must have used emperor's license in including them. Most of the other figures, however, were of genuine and undeniable ancestors, relatives or wives. His two wives, as a matter of fact, now share, with fine impartiality, the same number (10) in the official listing. They are Maria of Burgundy and Bianca Maria Sforza of Milan. I cannot help wishing that the Burgundian wife had been given a place of special honor, for she was one of the most lovable characters in the annals of royalty, though Maximilian seems hardly to have recognized her worth.

The huge cenotaph itself, constructed of various colored marbles, is surmounted by the kneeling figure of the emperor cast in bronze. He was to have been surrounded by 23 saints, also connected in theory with the House of Habsburg, but for some reason it was thought more suitable to surround him with the Four Cardinal Virtues, so the 23 Habsburg saints have strayed out into the Silberne Kapelle to watch over the sleep of Ferdinand and Philippine. Before directing your steps to this chapel you will pause to admire the white marble panels, 24 of them, on the sides of the cenotaph. They were pronounced by Bertel Thorwaldsen "the most admirable and perfect" such works in existence.

The Silver Chapel owes its name to a silver statue of the Virgin and embossed silver representations from the so-called Litany of Loreto, but the visitor's chief interest is in the tombs of the royal pair, whose love for each other is a pleasant fact of history, and in the 23 little Habsburg saints who were so unceremoniously shunted here from Maximilian's tomb. They are a queer job lot indeed, including St. Gudule, the patroness of Brussels, St. Stephen, who was a fine old swashbuckling king of Hungary, St. Simpert, son of Charlemagne's sister Symporiana, St. Guy, St. Oda, St. Jodok, St. Pepin Teuto. Saints, by the way, abound in Austria and a few old country folk, even today, know the calendar only as a list of saints. Mention July 1, for instance, and it will mean vaguely little to such a person, but call it St. Theobald's Day and you will promptly strike a spark.

As a sightseer's footnote to the Silberne Kapelle I am pleased to record that one of its features is a small 16th-century organ of cedar wood and on this organ 16th-century music is now played *every Wednesday evening in summer.* For these concerts about one hundred chairs are placed in the chapel and those who occupy them are treated to an Innsbruck specialty they will always remember.

There are ever so many things for the leisured lucky to see and do in Innsbruck and its neighborhood. There is the *Ferdinandeum,* the largest and most varied Austrian museum outside of Vienna, with an important art collection, a natural history section and a historical section. This last proudly includes a Hofer Room, where many Hofer relics are displayed, including the original trilingual proclamation recording his trial and death and, near it, his simple tombstone from Mantua. There is the *Volkskunstmuseum* with peasant costumes, peasant art and peasant homes, and since 1970 there has been a new *Alpine Museum* in what *was* Emperor Maximilian's arsenal. This is located "across the tracks" on Zeughausgasse. Outside of town there is the riotously rococo Parish Church of Wilten, there is Schloss Ambras, greatest of Tyrol's castles, and there are the heights reached by cableways—church, castle and heights will be described below—but the one-day visitor will presumably spend most of his free time strolling the city's streets. These rambles should include a walk along the *Rennweg* or the *Inn Allee,* on the right or left bank of the river that is this city's first reason for existence. You can scarcely keep up with the swift current without running. If you enjoy speculative exercises toss a chip of wood into the stream and try to guess how many days hence the chip will emerge into the Black Sea and by which of the Danube's three mouths.

The *Parish Church of Wilten,* a section of Innsbruck south of the center, is a shrine of rococo-gone-mad. In its decoration shameless cupids, masquerading as cherubs, race madly over pillow-puff clouds and the angels seem flushed with good Heuriger. One feels that God must have been in a very tolerant mood, in 1764, when the artist (named Günther) did these paintings, and one feels, without undue flippancy, that Gilbert and Sullivan ought to have composed music to be played and sung in such a church. I like Virginia Creed's comment, in her engagingly written guide *All About Austria:* "Here is revealed completely the Austrian concept of heaven. The Austrians have no patience with the heaven of the ascetics. That which they hope to achieve is another Austria, only much more so."

Schloss Ambras (sometimes spelled Amras) is situated 2 or 3 miles to the east of the city. Originally built in the 11th century for the Counts of Andechs, it came into the possession of Archduke Ferdinand II in 1563, and as related earlier in this chapter, he made it first of all a sort of shrine to his beloved bride, Philippine Welser, and second, a museum of art and armor. Even though these treasures have mostly been removed to Vienna the castle, or double castle, as it actually is, abounds in interesting things to see.

There is a Lower Castle, with what is left here of the armor, there is a lovely park and there is an Upper Castle (Hochschloss), containing all sorts of oddities. In the armory of the Lower Castle we see the original armor of Maximilian I and that of five of Ferdinand's small children, also, by way of contrast, the armor of a *nine-foot* giant. Perhaps he was Nikolas Heidls or perhaps a giant of imagination. I could not find out. If he was *really* that tall the giant of Hoch-Osterwitz must feel a bit puny by comparison.

The park is exceedingly beautiful and romance still dwells in it, for it is peculiarly a feminine park, Philippine's park, embellished with an artificial waterfall amid the trees where, one assumes, she could take an open-air shower bath whenever she wanted, though her bath *tub* is also on exhibit (in the Upper Castle), a colossal affair in which she could stand upright in water to her chin!

The Upper Castle contains more curiosities than treasures, one of them being noted just above. Others are a hat of Philippine, with a little phial of perfume on top; a picture made solely of butterfly wings; a perfect crucifix of mandrake root grown by nature and never altered by human hands; and a 16th-century *Wechseltisch,* or Exchange Table, with a list of the foreign exchange rates then being quoted.

Schloss Ambras is certainly a goal worth saving half a day for if you can. It may be reached by bus or by a one-hour walk on a forest path called *Fürstenweg* (Princes' Way) from Wilten and Berg Isel.

Innsbruck is a venerable modern city, the hearthstone of a people of strongly independent spirit. Sophistication has not spoiled this spirit, nor will it ever, I think, for the mountains stand guard to prevent this. It is true that important international railway lines cross paths here. It is true also that Maria-Theresien-Strasse resounds for many months of the year with the polyglot chatter of tourists. But under the arcades of Herzog-Friedrich-Strasse, or around the corner on the Marktgraben, these same tourists touch elbows with plump mountain girls still wearing country costumes and also the long, much-coiled hair that tradition demands. Bony men of the mountains, too, stroll the streets, sucking at long pipes with porcelain bowls on which are depicted scenes of Hofer's life. These men are faintly contemptuous, perhaps, of the highfalutin airs of the capital and will crack some good jokes at its expense when they get back home in the evening.

The foreign visitor's attitude toward a place like Innsbruck is always a contradictory one. He is so fearful of its being spoiled that he deprecates his own presence there. A city that is set in a valley cannot be hid, from tourists. But if the mountains loom close over its streets, as in Innsbruck, the city cannot forget them or grow ashamed of them. It is unbelievable how *close* the 8000-foot peaks do crowd in upon Innsbruck. They seem to tolerate the city and its mixed crowds with lofty good nature.

FOUR-PART ROUNDUP: HOTELS, RESTAURANTS, ENTERTAINMENT, SHOPS

Hotels in Kitzbühel and on the Approach to Innsbruck, a Personal Report
(EXPLANATORY NOTE: Virtually all the interesting restaurants in Kitzbühel and on the main route from Zell am See to Innsbruck are connected with hotels, and the same is true of entertainment. If any exceptions crop up they will be woven into the hotel report. There is no need to single out shops in the holiday resorts, but when this report reaches Innsbruck, in the succeeding section, special shops will, of course, be presented.)

Hotels in Kitzbühel are very numerous and they range all the way from the deluxe *Grand,* a goal of the international and titled set, to the humblest bed-and-breakfast pensions and guest-taking homes. There are three castle-inns and at least four mountain inns, and a new venture being undertaken by Mr. Falk Volkhardt, the dynamic proprietor of Munich's popular Bayerischer Hof, has Kitzbühel waiting and watching. He has taken over the Guido Reisch Hotel and great things are expected.

To be more specific about Kitzbühel's accommodations, the *Grand Hotel* is a large and rambling Tyrolean-style place in several gabled sections in a park on the edge of town. It has all the amenities looked for in an international grand hotel, including nightly dancing to its own orchestra, and in the high winter season entertainment as well. The hotel benefits by its lawn-surrounded pool, its private tennis courts and a nearby golf course. The pool is eclipsed by Kitzbühel's great modern pool with glass walls that can be lowered into the ground or raised according to weather and seasons. Another top hotel is the *Goldener Greif* (Griffin), in the center of town, with a well-liked grill-tavern and a Klause (literally cell or hermitage) where Tyrolean shows are given. The hotel has an indoor swimming pool. Other first-rate hotels are the *Sporthotel Hinterbräu*, in the heart of town, and the *Weisses Rössl* and the *Tennerhof*, both a bit out of town. The small *Postkutsche* (Post Coach) is liked for its first-class self and for its Tyrolean tavern. Two lesser hotels, and lower priced, are the *Tiefenbrunner*, with its Golden Goose Bar, one of the few local hotels that includes breakfast in its published prices, and the *Tyrol*, each with about 80 beds. The two best-known castle-inns are the first-class *Schloss Lebensberg*, recently and thoroughly renewed, and the small *Schloss Kaps*, operating as a pension. Mountaintop hotels are led in quality, though not in altitude, by the 100-bed *Hotel Ehrenbachehöhe*, at about the 6000-foot level. Of somewhat lesser quality as a hotel, but higher up and with a thrilling panoramic view that includes the Kaisergebirge and also the Grossglockner and the Gross-Venediger, is the *Kitzbühel Horn*, on the Hahnenkamm at the level of 6550 feet. On the *Bichlalm*, at about 5600 feet there is a third summit inn, all three being reached by cableways. On quite a different level and different subject is the bathing lake of Schwarzsee, 2½ miles from town, where you'll find a pleasant *summer restaurant* connected with the bathing establishment. The lake's waters, said to reach 75 degrees in summer, rival those of the Carinthian lakes.

Hotels on the Way to Innsbruck do not need extensive coverage here, but some of the leaders may be mentioned. St. Johann in Tirol has several unpretentious but good hotels, the 160-bed *Goldener Löwe* being the largest, followed by the 100-bed *Sporthotel Austria*. A smaller one, with 60 beds, bears the name of the Olympic champion *Christl Haas*. It is much the newest of the three and its public rooms and bedrooms have the appropriate Tyrolean decor. In Kufstein, if you make that northern tangent, you'll find the good-sized *Andreas Hofer* and the small *Egger*, both on the same Platz. Pertisau, in case you visit the cerulean Achensee, offers the *Kristall*, which, however, operates only on a pension basis. Two other places are the much larger *Hotel Pfandler*, with a variety of rates, and the *Strandhotel*, situated on the lake's edge, as its name announces.

Mayrhofen, nestling in its scenic site far "up south" in the Zillertal, has the big 200-bed *Neuhaus*, the *Kammerwirt* and *two* hotels named for the post office, the *Alte Post* and the *Neue Post*, the Old Post in this case being the better, and higher priced. On the highway stretch that leads to Innsbruck from the junction points for Pertisau and Mayrhofen you are unlikely, I think, to make any overnight halts, so we'll turn our explorations to the sizable Tyrolean capital, whose population has just eased over the 100,000 mark.

HOTELS, RESTAURANTS, ENTERTAINMENT AND SHOPS OF INNSBRUCK AND IGLS, A PERSONAL REPORT

Hotels of Innsbruck and Igls

Innsbruck has a trio of hotels, good, better, best, under the same ownership and management and on the same square, Südtirolerplatz, named for the lost province of South Tyrol. The square, very broad and always full of traffic, lies directly in front of the main railway station. The three hotels, in an ascending scale, are the *Arlbergerhof*, the *Europa* and the *Tyrol*. I have stayed twice in the Europa, and I can say with enthusiasm, for the present management, headed by Mr. Erwin Gutwinski, has done a great deal for all three hotels. He is that rare type of big-hotel manager who is *visible* to his guests much of every day. The Europa, which is the largest of the trio, with 208 beds, receives tourist busloads almost daily in summer, but the hotel is so large, as is its main dining room, that the bus trippers, usually staying just for one night, are easily absorbed. They do not dominate even the lobby except, perhaps, for the short periods when they are arriving and leaving. The Europa has built up an enviable reputation for its service, both in the dining room and to the guestrooms, one evidence of it being that if you leave your laundry with the maid in the morning you'll get it back late in the afternoon of the same day, and *without being charged extra.* The hotel has a nice Stüberl, opening on Brixnerstrasse but reachable, also, by a circuitous route, from the hotel lobby, where regular guests may lunch or dine. The food is excellent in both restaurants. Hotel Tyrol is Innsbruck's only deluxe hotel and its quality is self-evident as you enter the lobby. It is almost as large as the Europa and its rear rooms, quiet and elegant, have a magnificent view of the Nordkette (North Chain) mountain range that hangs in the sky like a background curtain on a majestic stage. I have not overnighted in the Tyrol but I have enjoyed meals there and the cuisine is magnificent, as is the dining room itself, with a famous glassed-in veranda. One special dish stands out in my memory. You may say that a chicken is a chicken is a chicken, but when you have tried the Tyrol's *Geflammtes Masthähnchen Tirol* you will say that *this* chicken is a culinary *chef d'oeuvre.*

Hotel Maria Theresia, on Maria-Theresien-Strasse in the very heart of town, has about the same general rating as the Europa but is 25 rooms smaller. Its atmosphere is tourist-plus, which may be a good thing if you're in the mood for it but could be too boisterous if you're not. Both hotels have large halls reserved for entertainment features, Tyrolean Evenings of song and dance (Schuhplattler style) and assorted entertainment features.

Hotel Goldener Adler, on Herzog-Friedrich-Strasse between the Goldenes Dachl and the river, will be 600 years old a couple of decades from now, but it has been restored and renewed countless times and is a first-class 80-room hotel of today, a fact that is sometimes forgotten because of the sustained deluge of publicity its restaurants have enjoyed. In the published prices for lodging, breakfast is included and the management is careful to say that the guest "may choose whatever he likes from the buffet." This is highly unusual in Austria. The Golden Eagle is almost unrivaled in Europe in illustrious patronage of former ages. Kings, queens, emperors, dukes and duchesses almost without number, and notables, too, in all walks of life, are listed on tablets outside the building as having stayed here. The impressive list seems to include everybody who was anybody, from ex-Queen Louise of Haiti to Andreas Hofer to Prince Metternich, and of course Napoleon. Many an artist, musician, poet and author has been attracted to this inn at the crossroads of Central Europe. Among them, Heinrich Heine alone trumpeted sour notes about the "immeasurable imbecility" of the Tyrolese. Almost all others have sung polite paeans, most of them obviously sincere. Paganini scratched his name with a diamond on the window of his room in the manner of Bobbie Burns, who was always doing this (but not in the Goldener Adler). Of the hotel's several restaurants, the best known is the *Goethe Stube,* a place of mellowest tradition. Here a Tyrolean zither player, aided usually by a contra-guitarist, entertains tirelessly with folk songs, in which the guests often join. The place is of exceedingly gracious atmosphere and dismisses all somber moods and worries. The walls are hung with paintings and assorted Goethe memorials, including valuable autographed letters, for the poet-dramatist did actually stay in this inn for substantial periods. You may dally in the Goethe Stube over a full meal, climaxing it, if you like, with an *Inntaler Hochzeit* (Innvalley marriage), a rich egg soufflee, with nuts, fruits, chocolate-cream and whipped cream (!), or you may order a mere Krügl of beer and stay as long as you like. The spirit of minstrelsy is stimulated by a portrait of Walther von der Vogelweide which hangs on the wall amidst the various Goethe portraits, and the poetic instinct, dormant in most of us, by a very large portrait of Schiller as a youth with long golden hair. Hofer is not forgotten by the Goldener Adler, for there is a *Hofer Stube* as well as a Goethe Stube. From one of the windows of this room, on the second floor, the Tyrolean hero addressed his fellow citizens in August 1809, after he had driven out the French for the third time. The speech, commencing in true Tyrolese fashion *"Grüss euk Gott, meine lieb'n 'Sbrucker!"* is set forth on a pyrographic plaque on the wall. The hotel has a *Kaiser-Josef-Stube,* honoring Emperor Josef II, an Adler Bar, a *Batzenhäusl* for quick lunches, a Konditorei, a kiddies' library on the 2nd floor and—

"that's enough," you're saying, and it is, but this vast array manages to keep its cool due to the watchful eye of the Cammerlander Family, who own it, and Manager Karl Pokorny, who runs it.

Other recommendable Innsbruck hotels are the big, 260-bed *Grauer Bär,* and the modern 80-room *Clima,* both in quiet locations. A very unusual hostelry is the *Hotel-Café-Restaurant Villa Blanka,* on high ground (Weiherburggasse) overlooking the city. This is a *Tiroler Hotelfachschule* (Tyrolean hotel training school) and if I may judge from the wonderful meal I had there, concluding with a superb Salzburger Nockerl, the training is *good.* A newcomer to Innsbruck's roster of hotels is *Holiday Inn.* Soaring skyward for 12 stories on Salurnerstrasse at the corner of Maria-Theresien-Strasse, this invader from overseas has aroused as much concern from Innsbruckers as the rising of Hotel Europa some years ago aroused from the Salzburgers, and this hotel, unlike Salzburg's tall one, is in the very center. Anyway, it's there, with the comforts and modernities that so many Americans yearn for and if it clashes, as this certainly does, with the traditions of Innsbruck, not to mention its skyline, well, it was erected with the full consent and cooperation of the city fathers.

The *hotels of Igls* (pronounced Eagles), Innsbruck's smart hotel and residential suburb at the 3000-foot level, are a sophisticated group, two of them, the big, 150-bed *Sporthotel Igls* and the small, 30-room *Schlosshotel Igls,* under the same ownership, being clearly deluxe. The little castle-hotel, snow white, is a gem, with gables, turrets 'neverything, one of its surprise features being a 33-foot-wide picture window that opens as a unit onto the hotel's garden and pool. *Golfhotel Iglerhof* is one of four first-class hotels, but the golf course that it incorporates in its name is a mile or two away in the village of Lans.

Quite a bit beyond and above Igls, on the old Roman salt road, is an inn of a special type, the *Grünwalderhof.* This is a family-type hotel but it has a pedigree four or five centuries long, having been a mansion of the noble Thurn und Taxis family, whose descendants *still* own it. This family, which had the postmaster-generalship of the Holy Roman Empire, a hereditary office, for hundreds of years until the middle of the 19th century, is widespread throughout

Europe. I have had the pleasure of an afternoon hour with a Prince of Thurn und Taxis in his castle in Duino, a suburb of Trieste. One of the quaint eating rooms of the Grünwalderhof, in a part of it that is over 400 years old, is called the *Thurn und Taxis Stube.*

Other high spots around Innsbruck with hotels atop are easy to understand, for there are only two that demand consideration, though one of these is a tripleton.

Hungerburg-Seegrube-Hafelekar, immediately north of the city, is the tripleton and the altitudes of the three halting places are, respectively, 2830 feet, about the altitude of Igls, 6250 feet and 7400 feet. At the base station for the Hungerburg funicular railway there is an interesting and realistic diorama of a Hofer triumph, but present eagerness to mount the hill, which can be done, also, by car, is stronger with most visitors than any historical urges. The cogwheel railway ascent to the Hungerburg takes about ten minutes and there we find *Hotel Mariabrunn,* perched on the very edge of a cliff that falls away sharply to the center of Inssbruck. From this eerie one has a bird's-eye view never to be forgotten, particularly the nightly spectacle of the lights of a large city as they come on, the whole scene being backed by the "Altar of Tyrol," as the peak of the *Serlesberg* is called. The terrace restaurant and tree-shaded garden of the Mariabrunn fill a considerable stretch of the Hungerburg's rock shelf, and while I am on the subject of the restaurant I must mention a specialty of the hotel's cuisine, namely a melt-in-the-mouth cherry-and-strawberry cake. I hope for you that you can visit Mariabrunn during the season of this specialty, from May to July. (A smaller but attractive inn of the Hungerburg is *Hotel-Pension zur Linde,* with two or three Tyrolean Stüberln.)

At the Hungerburg, if you consider this a waystation you change to a cableway for the swing up to Seegrube and at that height to another cableway for lofty Hafelekar, these two final stages taking about 25 minutes. Do not be content, I urge, merely to drink in the view, along with a beverage, from the café of the small (8 beds) *Berghotel Hafelekar,* at the upper station, but climb up a path just a hundred yards or so beyond and above the café—take it easy at this altitude—for the view "over the top" to the north. This reveals an endless savage tumble of jagged, pinnacled peaks, one after another and range after range, to Bavaria, each range a little hazier than the one before it. From this same sky-bruising ridge you see also the Inn Valley to the south and range after range to Italy. To get the full benefit of this double view you really need a swivel neck. No more stunning point is reached by any cableway in Austria, and in saying this I do not forget the Dachstein or the Austrian Zugspitze, both of which are higher.

The *Patscherkofel,* immediately south of Innsbruck, is reached by a two-stage cableway from Igls. The altitude of the upper station is about 6400 feet, which is 1000 feet less than its rival across the valley, and it is therefore less rugged in temperature and wildness. In high summer the slopes below it are densely carpeted with Alpenrose flowers, *so* densely, in fact, that it becomes literally a glowing red mountainside. *Berghotel Patscherkofel,* on this mountain, has this special and beautiful feature to offer. If you don't elect to make a sojourn here try, at any rate, to stay for an unhurried snack and beverage on the hotel's open-air terrace, and may you have sunshine with your snack. Let it illuminate the red carpet spread out on the slope below you.

Restaurants and Entertainment of Innsbruck

Innsbruck is a good-time city of the first order, not in the sense of Paris but in the sense of—Innsbruck. There are lots of good places to eat and drink, to watch folk dancing and mingle in it, and to hear Tyrolean songs, usually accompanied on the zither.

Among food items typical of Innsbruck and its region are *Gröstl,* being beef cut into small bits and oven-roasted with potatoes; *Tiroler Knödeln,* which are dumplings with minced ham in them; *Schmarrn,* which are pancakes, much like those of Salzburg but served here with whortleberry sauce; *Hupfauf* and *Schutzauf,* which are concoctions of local cream cheese. For lubrication of such fare one should by no means overlook the red wines of South Tyrol, even though these are now imported.

The best restaurants of Innsbruck and Igls are, of course, in the top hotels, but there are plenty of good gemütlich ones to enjoy. Restaurants of general nature that function also as cafés are the *Schindler,* on the Maria-Theresien-Strasse; the *Stadtsaalkaffee,* on a broad parkside terrace diagonally across from the Hofkirche; and the *Hofgarten-Café,* these last two places both providing entertainment and dancing in the evening.

Restaurants emphasizing wine are the *Ottoburg,* in a 13th-century castle directly beside the Inn; the big old *Stiftskeller; Weinhaus Happ; Weinhaus Jörgele* and so forth, while those stressing beer include *Alt Innsprugg* and *Breinössl,* both on Maria-Theresien-Strasse across the street from Hotel Maria Theresia.

One further establishment calls for mention. That is the *Hochhaus,* where good eating and good fun "rise to the top." The building has 8 stories, the 3 upper ones being occupied by a variety of restaurants and music cafés. An attractive part of this three-layer goal is the open terrace on the 7th floor, with an interesting close-up view of the city.

To clarify the matter of evening entertainment I should state that Tyrolean dances and songs, including very beautiful and tender ballads of country life as well as thigh-slapping hoopla, are offered nightly in summer, sometimes in *Hotel Europa,* sometimes in the *Hotel Maria Theresia* and the *Breinössl,* and frequently, also, on an improvised stage in the open air on the street widening immediately below the Goldenes Dachl, while floor shows of more international type, with intervals of dancing, are given in the *Hofgarten-Café* and the *Stadtsaalkaffee.*

Shops of Innsbruck

Shopping (hours 8–12, 2–6, though some places stay open through the noon hours in summer to catch the tourist trade) goes its eager way along Maria-Theresien-Strasse and its alley-width continuation Herzog-Friedrich-Strasse, where the most tempting articles are dirndls and Lederhosen, Loden sport clothes, various knitted articles, woodcarvings, ceramics, fancy candles and even wrought-iron articles, though these may pose problems in getting them home. Two marts of special interest *not* on the main stem are *Lodenbaur,* at Brixnerstrasse 4, strong on peasant attire, and *Tiroler Heimatwerk* at Meranerstrasse 2, offering many interesting articles of authentic Tyrolean handicraft. I have been impressed with the wide choice available in the Heimatwerk shop, for it includes woodcarvings, linen and wool articles, glass, especially ruby-red glassware with the designs engraved in white, wax candles, painted furniture, wooden flower pots, pewterware, doilies, runners, painted napkin rings, and much more. To return to the main stem, if you're looking for peasant costumes and dirndls you'll find *Trachten-Konrad* in the narrow Sparkassenpassage, opening from Herzog-Friedrich-Strasse 27, with a good stock, as also *Lanz,* the firm you may know from Salzburg, on Wilhelm Geilstrasse, running more or less parallel to the main stem. *Ennsmann,* at Meranerstrasse 7, has good leatherware and also petit point embroidery. A specialist in candles only is *Marius Retti,* on small Kiesbachstrasse in the old town near Herzog-Friedrich-Strasse. This *Wachswarenwerk* (work in wax) shop sells both traditional and modern candles in imaginative designs, including fancy torches to be stuck in the ground for garden parties. In *Schmuck* (costume jewelry articles) you'll find interesting displays in the arcade shops on Herzog-Friedrich-Strasse, garnets from the Zillertal mountains often being used. Innsbruck seems to me the very special city in which to shop for handicrafts, for Tyrol makes many and varied eye-catching articles.

Hotels in Seefeld, an important mountainside resort previously mentioned for a tangent trip north from Zirl, west of Innsbruck, are numerous and unusually interesting, even outstanding. No less than four of them are officially rated deluxe and at least eight are first class. I suppose one reason for Seefeld's great popularity is the existence of a fine 18-hole golf course, whose construction was quite an achievement for Alpine Austria. Of the deluxe ones I vote for the *Karwendelhof,* since it makes such an ultra-Tyrolean spectacle with its dark brown woodwork and its many, many balconies, every one, on every floor, aglow with flowers. The interior is equally pleasing to the eye and must be so to the guest who stays here. The others rated deluxe are the *Astoria,* the *Schlosshotel* and the big, bouncing *Klosterbräu,* whose deluxe quality seems to me a bit less assured. A first-class hotel that I like is the centrally located *Lamm,* whose name in English would end in mb instead of mm. Perhaps it's the hotel's name that gives me a charge.

At Mösern, a little lower down the mountainside than Seefeld, stop, if you can, to take a look at a hotel named *Inntalerhof*—and at its view. Of all the countless fine views I've enjoyed from above the Inntal down to it I think this is the one that will linger longest with me, for its gentle beauty, as against the savage scenes, equally beautiful, of the high Alps, has a durable quality.

Hotels of Ötztal and Westward to the Arlberg

Tyrol has a wealth of valleys and branch valleys, most of them stretching south, like tentative feelers, up to eternal snow and blue ice along the frontier of Italy (South Tyrol). Of them all, my personal favorite is the *Ötztal*, about midway between Innsbruck and the Arlberg. An Ötzal prospectus before me claims, probably without exaggeration, "100 mountain lakes, 100 glaciers, 100 mountains over 10,000 feet" for this valley's immediate sphere of influence. My eyes, all but wrenched from their sockets by such sublimities, have been my own prospectus.

The Ötztal has grown up, touristwise, since I first knew it, when I drove up to "the highest parish village in Europe," Obergurgl, on a frighteningly narrow road with a cliff on one side and a car-swallowing fallaway on the other. Now the route, numbered 186, is almost like a boulevard, with sectional points, but no tolls, at Ötz, Umhausen, Huben, Sölden, and so to Obergurgl. You hardly realize that you're ascending until you take out your fountain pen to make a note and find it leaking like a sieve. Hotels of the town of Ötz are led traditionally by the good Tyrolean-style *Drei Mohren* (Three Moors), whose garden restaurant is a good place for lunch, with the *Posthotel Kassl* as a worthy competitor, but a new hotel, the 80-bed *Alpenhotel Ötz*, has won its share in the Ötztal sun. Another hotel that I've liked, budget minded but charming, is the *Alpenrose*. At Umhausen, *Gasthof Krone* (Crown) issues its welcome as one of the valley's most typical inns, simple and nearly bathless, but very good in its modest bracket. At Längenfeld, *Gasthof zum Hirschen* (To the Deer) does its unpretentious and pleasing best to serve you. At Sölden we find a split-level village, the old lower one at the 4200-foot level, the upper one, virtually consisting of half a dozen resort hotels, at 6800 feet. In the main village, the best hotels, and "pushing first-class" are the *Tyrolerhof* (spelled with a y possibly in deference to English-speaking tourists), the *Sporthotel Central* (uninspired name in a valley village) and the *Alpina,* but some of the less ambitious ones like the *Sölderhof* have plenty of eye appeal. I haven't yet visited Hochsölden, the upper village, but the names of its hotels invite me: *Alpenfriede* (Mountain Peace), *Edelweiss* (having indoor pool) and *Schöne Aussicht* (Beautiful Prospect). Actually, *Hotel Hochsölden* may be the best of the group. It is, at any rate, the largest, with 160 beds. Sölden is the takeoff point for the two-section suspension cableway to the Gaislacher Kogel at the official altitude of 9974 feet. Söldeners, not content with this near miss of 10,000 feet, put the altitude at 10,091 feet. This is, at any rate, said to be the highest of all the cableways of Austria. At Obergurgl, the two big conspicuous hotels are the *Hochfirst* and the *Edelweiss & Gurgl.* In the latter's Stube I have enjoyed a memorably excellent meal, or was it just that I was ravenously hungry?

About 18 miles west of the base of the Ötztal is Landeck, near where the Inn tumbles into Austria, this being the Swiss unit of our "Seven Gates to Austria" in Chapter 1. From Landeck you climb over the Arlberg or bore through it by rail and both means provide thrill upon thrill. Road and rails climb together to the famous skiing center of St. Anton am Arlberg, whose name is sometimes misleading, for the resort is in the Province of Tyrol, but on the Arlberg Mountain. At St. Anton, the train plunges through the mountain, a third of a mile beneath its crest, to emerge at *Langen,* on the Vorarlberg side, while the road toils up and over. At the highest point of the pass (5900 feet) is the winter-sports station, with government-sponsored school for skiing teachers, of *St. Christoph am Arlberg,* whence a cableway, built in 1952, ascends the Galzig Peak (7144 feet). It was on the slopes of the Arlberg that the celebrated pioneer ski instructor Hannes Schneider first started giving lessons to tourists in 1907.

To pause for a swift review of the hotels of St. Anton, the *Post,* well up near the railway station, is the clear leader, goal of moneyed international visitors intent upon a gay social life along with their sport, followed by the Tyrolean-style *Schwarzer Adler,* with 99 beds (couldn't they put in *one* more?) at a lower level of the village. A central hotel with a lively life is the *Alpenrose.* In St. Christoph, *the* hotel to seek, and refreshingly different, is the big 160-bed *Hospiz,* first class and with private bath for most rooms. This historic inn of refuge, a modern "edition," since the old one was destroyed by fire in 1957, has much in common with the more famous Hospiz of St. Bernard, on the Simplon Pass from the Rhone Valley to Italy, for it was intended as a shelter for hard-pressed travelers making the passage, in this case, between the fertile Danube lands and Lake Constance. For centuries trained dogs, canine cousins of the Swiss St. Bernards, were used to bring succor to travelers bogged down in the snow drifts. In the Middle Ages, the Hospiz sheltered many a mighty prince and prelate, especially at the time of the Council of Constance (1414–18), when half of Europe's celebrities were passing back and forth between Vienna and Constance. An enormous wooden figure of St. Christopher, now really an ex-saint, but still revered by travelers even though he was "decanonized" in 1969, *was* a special sight of the Hospiz chapel, but it was destroyed in the fire and has been replaced by a modern statue. The old one had a hard life, for it was a much-sought item of the Hospiz chapel and thereby hangs a tale. It was believed that this image of the Christbearer with the Infant on his shoulder had miraculous powers to cure homesickness, so countless travelers whittled off tiny chips of it to carry with them for this remedy. Finally, so much of the base was whittled away that St. Christopher had to be enclosed in a stout wire netting.

The Arlberg Railway is of such prime importance to the life of St. Anton, and indeed of all Austria, that perhaps a few words of recapitulation and further description are in order. Opened as long ago as 1844 and electrified in 1924, it is a masterwork of engineering that deserves almost as much fame as the St. Gotthard and Simplon routes. Just a few miles west of Landeck the two wild tomboy rivers that I've mentioned, the Trisanna from the south and the Rosanna from the Arlberg, meet and merge into one. At the point of meeting is a single-span 400-foot bridge by which the railway leaps over the Trisanna Gorge, 280 feet deep, and gets set to climb the Stanzertal, with the Rosanna, to St. Anton. There, as

I've said, it enters the Arlberg Tunnel, grandest achievement of this mighty engineering job. The tunnel is almost 7 miles long, which is but 3 less than that of the St. Gotthard, and travelers are *in* the Arlberg from 12 to 15 minutes during the transit. As in the case of the Tauern Tunnel to Badgastein there is an *Autoverladung* (automobile shipment) here for motorists who do not wish to drive over the top.

12 / Vorarlberg, with the Principality of Liechtenstein

VORARLBERG'S HIGHWAY NETWORK

It is easy to motor around Vorarlberg, when even making a complete circuit by what is called in German the *Bodensee-Arlberg Rundstrasse,* or in English, Lake Constance-Arlberg Highway Circuit. Using the Bodensee, which is Lake Constance, as the starting point it means driving from Bregenz through the whole Bregenzerwald (Bergenz Forest), Lower, Middle and Upper; over the Hochtannberg Pass (5500 feet) to Warth; then south over the famous Flexenstrasse, a marvelous feat of engineering, passing through Lech to Zürs to Stuben; then west down the Klostertal to Bludenz to Feldkirch, on the edge of the Principality of Liechtenstein; and so, paralleling the young Rhine, north, back to Bregenz and the big lake. A lesser but important loop, or crescent, is formed in the southern parts of both Tyrol and Vorarlberg by the *Silvretta-Hochalpenstrasse,* which opens up the great Montafonertal from two directions.

The major circuit, like the lesser one, may, of course, be started at any point in either direction. If you have come from the Arlberg you will find the junction of the Flexenstrasse and the Klostertal at a point just east of Stuben. This book *has* come from the Arlberg and will therefore proceed *up* the Flexenstrasse (north), and then west, to and through the Bregenzerwald to Lake Constance.

THE SKIERS' HOLYLAND

In a glowingly penned article by Frederic Morton, published in a very-far-back issue of *Holiday* (June 1956) there was a sentence that I've never forgotten and think worth resurrecting here: "As long as snow will fall from heaven the Arlberg remains the skiers' Holy Land." Well, the snow will fall on the mountain for a very long time, piling up to 15 or more feet every winter and enabling the resorts to announce "unconditional guarantee" of snow. Many other places in Austria, Bavaria and Switzerland can guarantee plenty of snow, but the Arlberg remains the highest heaven of the dedicated, simon-pure zealot. Three resorts compose this rarified heaven, St. Anton, on the Tyrol side of the mountain, Zürs and Lech on the Vorarlberg side. These last two centers are reached, as I've said, by the Flexenstrasse, second in fame as an Alpine name-road only to the Grossglockner. It climbs northward over the Flexen Pass in many a zigzag, through many a tunnel of rock and often of snow, under the protective roofs of many an avalanche-gallery, the high point of the pass, 5853 feet, being only 52 feet lower than the Arlberg Pass itself (5905 feet). From that saddle the Flexenstrasse descends slightly (about 200 feet in altitude) to Zürs and more (about 900 feet) to Lech. Both of these resorts are among the most dependable in Europe for ski weather and the season lasts from November to May. Zürs is above the tree line and Lech about *at* the tree line, but numerous cableways and chairlifts, plus many skilifts in both places, carry skiers far up the slopes. Lech has also a cableway to Oberlech, a resort a thousand feet higher. And since the 1969 opening of the cableway from Lech to the Rüfikopf, at the 6800-foot level, it has been feasible, and popular, for skiers to make a long "ski circus," quite as good as that of Kitzbühel, from Lech's snowfields to those of Zürs and back to Lech without any climbing whatever.

THE FOREST ROAD FROM SNOWFIELDS TO LAKE CONSTANCE

The road from lofty Warth over the Hochtannberg Pass and through the Bregenzerwald is not used by overseas tourists nearly as much as its intrinsic interest and unspoiled charm warrant, for it is thought of as "the back way." We will follow it now, with a few words about a few points.

The lofty Hochtannberg Valley is one of four valleys in Austria to which refugees from the Canton of Valais, in the Upper Rhone Valley of Switzerland, retreated in the 13th and 14th centuries, the others being Brand, in the Brandnertal, the Grosswalzertal, these two being respectively south and north of the Klostertal road, and the Kleinwalsertal, to be covered hereinafter in Chapter 14, with the Bavarian Alps, since that high valley can be reached, except by skilled Alpinists, only through Oberstdorf in Bavaria.

Schröcken, the first community you encounter on the forest route to Bregenz, was reached only by a cart track until the building of this road, but for all that it is a fine little mountain hamlet crowding for warmth around a tall white church. Across a forbidding range of the Allgäu Alps but scarcely 4 miles distant if one could pierce the range, lies the Kleinwalsertal, completely cut off from the rest of Austria, though owing allegiance to it. Helicopters form an aerial path in case of special need. Schoppernau, the next village along the route, is well within the Bregenzerwald. It rises beside the Bregenzer Ache, a stream that finally makes its way to Lake Constance a bit west of Bregenz. The next village is just plain Au, which calls for a little explanation. Au is a shortened form of Aue, meaning meadow, and we find in close proximity not only Schoppernau and Au itself but Mellau, Bezau and Bizau. Au, with the smallest name, has the biggest hotel in the Bregenzerwald *(Hotel Krone)* and in it I recently had one of the biggest meals, and best, but I'll come to that in the chapter-end roundup. From many Bregenzer Ache villages, but more especially from Mellau, you have a *grand* view of the Kanisfluh, a towering mountain cliff reminiscent of the dramatic and seemingly unpredictable mountains of the Dolomites, as seen from the heights above Bolzano

(Bozen). At one point it looks like a table set out for use of the Alpine gods. Beyond Reuthe, and Bad Reuthe, the latter a minispa where you may treat your arthritis, lumbago or other ailments in a thermal bath or a rich mud bath, you reach the milder orchard country around Bezau and Schwarzenberg, and so to Egg, one of numerous Austrian Eggs, singly and in combination, which has the Tourist Travel Office for the whole Bregenzerwald area, bottom to top. It is located across the street from the chief hotel and is called *Verkehrsamt Bregenzerwald*. I made a few inquiries here and learned some interesting facts. For one thing, 45 percent of all the habitations in the Bregenzerwald, and indeed throughout Vorarlberg, are single houses, mostly of wood, and many of the peasant houses are imposingly big. Trachten, the peasant costumes, are still worn by women on the shady side of 50 but deplorably seldom by the young fry except on very special occasions. Another fact, and this of prime interest to your pocketbook, is that Vorarlberg is one of the least expensive areas of Austria, and even of all Europe. In Egg, for instance, you can have a clean room (but no private bath), with all meals, including service and taxes, for a trifle over $5 a day, or possibly $6, depending upon the exchange of your U.S. dollars. The Bregenzerwald has 20 communities equipped to receive tourists, and all are full of "guaranteed charm." I have overnighted, or have had at least a meal, in five or six of them and haven't been disappointed yet.

DOWN THE KLOSTERTAL AND UP THE MONTAFONERTAL

If the road we've just taken is the back road—and there is *much* to be said for it—we'll now take the front road, meaning from the Arlberg, at the Stuben junction point, down the Klostertal to Bludenz and then, as a side trip, up the long Montafonertal to Schruns, the valley's most important community, and far up to Partenen on the Silvretta-Hochalpenstrasse where the 15½-mile-long Silvretta Toll Road carries up to Bielerhöhe, at about 6700 feet altitude, here entering Tyrol and descending the Patznauntal, beside the Trisanna River, to Landeck.

Schruns, the Montafon capital, is important in the medical world, for it has one of the finest cure establishments, though not very large, in either Germany or Austria, namely the deluxe *Kurhotel und Anstalt Montafon.* This Cure-Hotel-and-Institute stands directly beside the small River Litz, near where it flows into the Ill, and I can think of no pleasanter place in which to be cured of anything. The Anstalt does not accept patients requiring hospitalization, but short of that it aids in the cure of many internal ailments and one visible one—obesity. The Kurhotel is open to all, whether or not desiring treatment, and there are, of course, many other hotels, of simpler type, in the village. For those wishing thrills aloft there is the cableway called Hochjochbahn, in two sections, carrying to 6100 feet, while a single-seat chairlift carries up to the Sennigrat at over 7500 feet. About 40 more lifts of all types ascend from Schruns, Partenen, Gargellen and other villages, so you'll have the widest possible choice. A 7-day Skipass is available in the Montafonertal, similar to the one I have mentioned in Badgastein. It costs less than $7 and gives you a *lot* for a dollar a day.

About 6 miles up the valley from Schruns there is a Y. One road leads south, to Gargellen, the other southeast up the main Montafonertal to St. Gallenkirch and Partenen. At Gargellen, to take that valley first, the mountains, with apologies to Job, announce: "Hitherto shalt thou come, but no farther; and here shall thy proud wheels be stayed." Mountain climbers of the eager and expert kind look upon Gargellen as the takeoff point for ascents to various points of the Silvretta Range, which separates Austria from Switzerland's Engadine and serves as watershed between streams headed for the Danube and the Black Sea and those headed for the Rhine and the North Sea. If one could bore straight through this range to Switzerland one would reach Klosters in 7 miles and Davos in 12. Since hotels play such a key role in resort areas like the Montafonertal I will save further comment for the roundup concluding this chapter.

BRAND AND THE BRANDNERTAL

The Brandnertal leads south to the name-giving resort of Brand, only 8 miles distant. Brand has a chairlift that can hoist you up to the Niggenkopf, at 5740 feet, but the resort's challenge is to mountain *climbers,* of the serious sort, and the challenger is the Scesaplana, sometimes spelled Schesaplana, the highest peak (9700 feet) of the Rhätikon Range.

The road continues from Brand 3 or 4 miles more to the Schattenlagant Refuge, from near which a cableway lifts you up to the Lünersee, at 6300 feet, a lake that was made into a big reservoir about 15 years ago, its water level being raised by a hundred feet. On the rim of the lake you will find a good-sized Alpine shelter named the Douglasshütte, in menory of John Sholto Douglass, a much-loved mountaineer and cotton mill owner of Vorarlberg who was president of the local Alpine Club. He bore exactly the same name, except for the extra "s," as the Eighth Marquis of Queensberry. He loved, however, not pugilism but almost unscalable mountains, roaring cataracts, chamois, shrike, scarlet tiger butterflies—Vorarlberg's great out-of-doors. He was killed at the age of 36 while climbing a treacherous mountain. He fell from a height of "many, many church steeples," say the natives.

His son was the author Normal Douglas (one *s* in his case), whose most enduring book was, and is, *South Wind.* Another of his books, *Together,* was about the home of his youth, Vorarlberg. It is rather a gem and can give you a vivid and authentic picture of that simple land, for Norman Douglas, like his father, knew from experience all that anyone need know of mountains and marmots and garnets and gentians, if not of "cabbages and kings."

FELDKIRCH, WITH A SIDE TRIP TO LIECHTENSTEIN

Feldkirch, at the "corner" of lower Vorarlberg, is a mellow old town, its streets heavily arcaded, its market square whispering of the past. Immediately above it looms the 12th century Shattenburg (Shadow Castle), built for Hugo I, Count of Montfort, a castle that dominates the whole city and its surroundings. In 1971 a new and highly important cultural feature gave Feldkirch added prominence, namely the opening of a first-class art gallery by Prince Adam Alexander Liechtenstein, of the same family as the prince who reigns in the neighboring Principality of Liechtenstein. The paintings fill several floors of the Liechtenstein Palace, and they include masterpieces by Rembrandt, various other Dutch and Flemish masters, including Hals and Van Dyke, and Spanish paintings by Goya and other artists. The art works are well lighted by a soft overhead lighting system.

Perhaps you are wondering if the Schattenburg Castle has also an art gallery or museum within its wide-spreading walls. The answer is "Sort of." It does have a small museum, but much of the imposing Schloss is given over to restaurants and cafés, in which Tyrolean *Schrammelmusik* enlivens the scene, being the kind of music offered in Grinzing and in the general run of Weinstuben. I have spent a long, gay evening in two of the four eating and drinking places that are found at different levels and was amazed and amused to find a crowd of teenagers in one of them dancing exactly as kids of the same age would dance in any American café or discothèque. Ample carafes of red wine, Austrian I'm sure, were being carried to the tables in all the eating places, though possibly not so much in this youthful dance hall.

Feldkirch is neighbor-across-the-fence to the Principality of Liechtenstein except that there is no fence. Nothing in all travel could be easier than to go by your own car or by bus to Vaduz, the principality's village capital. If there are any border formalities at all you'll hardly be aware of them as you roll across the line and so to the village of Schaan and 2 more miles to Vaduz.

Lying as a geographical wedge between Switzerland and Austria, Liechtenstein is a country, a nation, a proud and independent state of Europe, a constitutional and hereditary monarchy. It is, in fact, the only surviving state of nearly 350 that once comprissed the Holy Roman Empire. The House of Liechtenstein is eight centuries old, but it acquired the Principality only in 1719 by purchase from a hard-up nobleman, the Count of Hohenems. It was a minor item in the wealth of the then ruler, Prince Johan-Adam von Liechtenstein, who already owned a great palace in Vienna, plus more than forty castles and two thousand square miles of land in Austria, Bohemia and Saxony, with eight hundred communities. Amid all the turmoils of war and near war for two and a half centuries Liechtenstein has maintained its independence and neutrality, even managing to shrug off Hitler's poisoned attentions. Since 1924 it has been, for convenience' sake, affiliated with the Swiss Customs Union, and for money it uses Swiss currency, but it has its own postage stamps, its own elected parliament *(Landtag),* and decidedly, its own identity. Though one of the political curiosities of Europe, it has not been overly publicized as a tourist goal.

I can claim to have grown up with the Principality, for I have been a frequent visitor during the last four decades. The times have caught up with Liechtenstein to such extent that some communities are geared to modern industry while the little capital, Vaduz (pronounced Va*dootz*), centers a growing tourist trade, but this does not mean that there has been any noticeable lessening of the unstudied friendliness of the people. In short, this winsome miniature is still Liechtenstein, still the land where everybody greets everybody with a hearty "Grüss Gott" (God's greeting).

Some brief practicalities about Vaduz need mention here. The name, to start with, is a contraction of the Latin *Valle Dulcis,* Sweet Valley. Since most visitors lodge in the capital, I will name a few hotels. *The Sonnenhof* and the *Waldhotel,* but more especially the former, both located on the hillside above Vaduz, are clearly the leaders, but the place where I usually stay, if I can get a room, is the *smallest* hotel of all, and to my mind one of the most appealing in its family atmosphere, namely *Hotel Real,* which is on the main street of Vaduz, frankly in the very heart of the tourist hubbub. I don't happen to mind street noises at all, but if you do, then try to get a rear room. The Real has only 8 bedrooms, 4 of them doubles, and because of the exceptionally high standards of its French dining room, one flight up from the street, it is far more widely known as a restaurant than as a hotel. Its cuisine, indeed, is rivaled, if at all, only by that of the Sonnenhof, and thereby hangs a tale. The Real is owned by Felix Real and his Zillertal-born wife Theresa, while the Sonnenhof is under the wing of Emil and Jutta Real and—here's the point—*both* brothers studied cooking for extensive periods in Paris under none other than the celebrated Louis Vaudable, maestro of Maxim's. As for tiny Hotel Real, Felix and Theresa run it, and the two restaurants, in a notably personal and "visible" way, Felix devoting much attention to the kitchen where he holds sway, in season, over a staff of *twelve* assistant cooks. A Real dinner, perhaps with a bottle of Vaduzer Rosé, which is a wine to know, can be a memorable event on any tourist's calendar. On the ground floor is a Stube entered directly from the street, but the same kitchen serves both restaurants. Emil and Jutta Real achieve a cuisine approximately equal to that of Felix and Theresa, and of course their domain is several times as large. The outlook from the Sonnenhof's dining-room windows down to the Valle Dulcis and beyond to the young Rhine is peaceful, enchanting and altogether consonant with the hotel's fine fare.

To stimulate the tourist trade there is a wide-awake National Tourist Office, *Landesverkehrsbureau,* conspicuously located on the main street, long directed by a born Liechtensteiner, Herr Banzer. Cooperating closely with the Bureau is an energetic travel agency called the Quick Tourist Office, owned and directed by Baron Edward von Falz-Fein, whose daughter Ludmilla was the inspiration for one of Paul Gallico's best-loved stories, called simply *Ludmilla.* The Baron is very much of a personage in Liechtenstein, his travel agency being only one of his many activities. This is, in fact, embedded in his shoppers' mart called the Quick Shop, located almost next door to the Hotel Real.

The life of Vaduz centers in three or four blocks of its main street. Here are some of the tourist inns, the post office, the mart, various small postcard and postage stamp shops—stamps are big business—the Picture Gallery, with priceless paintings from the Prince's collection, the Rathaus and the Princely Government Building *(Das Fürstliche Regierungsgebäude),* this last containing portraits of all the reigning princes from Johan-Adam on. Up the climbing street called Hintergasse, and then Schloss-Strasse, one mounts to the Royal Castle, which is a beautiful and dramatic sight, standing on the edge of a cliff and seeming almost to hang in the sky above Vaduz. Its oldest portion, the so-called Heidenturm, dates from the 13th century.

The "hinterland" of the Principality offers great attractions to the motorist and there are good places to stay outside of Vaduz. One such place is *Motel in Liechtenstein,* a modern motel scenically placed on a slope above the village of Triesen. Another place, called *Alphotel Gaflei,* is in the mountainside hamlet of Gaflei higher up. It is a government-owned hotel that some Liechtensteiners think far too pretentious for a mountain inn. A developement that has aroused wide interest and enthusiasm is the rapid growth of the once tiny community of Malbun as a new winter-sports resort, already with eight good-sized hotels, and more sure to come. The Principality, as a whole, has a dramatic "backdrop" of serrated peaks soaring up almost to 10,000 feet and culminating in The Three Sisters *(Drei Schwestern),* which here form the frontier with Austria. Malbun is located as if clutching at the skirts of the stony trio, but there is another community, way down on the valley floor, that has aspirations. I refer to Nendeln in the northern part of Liechtenstein only 2 miles from Feldkirch. A plan is now going forward to construct a suspension cableway from Nendeln to the very brow of one of the sisters, or perhaps to her coiled hair, reaching a point that is actually just within Austria, which country is expected to take a hand in the action. And here's the climax: Liechtensteiners say that there *must* be a television mast or some other form of tower on the crest, *with a revolving restaurant up aloft.* It seems incredible, unworkable, but who knows what ambition can do when a minuscule country sets out to do something majuscule.

DORNBIRN AND BREGENZ

Dornbirn is Vorarlberg's largest city, with a population of 28,-000, as against Bregenz, the provincial capital, with about 25,000 and Feldkirch with 18,000. Dornbirn is widely known in business circles for its *International Trade and Sample Fair,* stressing textiles, which occurs early in August and is always synchronized with the Bregenz festival. Dornbirn's Fair is of astonishing scope and spread for such a city and actually it is rated among Central Europe's most important ones. Statistics show that more than 50 countries are represented, including the United States, about a dozen big U.S. companies exhibiting. The visitors number over 300,000, of whom some 50,000 are from foreign lands.

Regardless of trade, don't fail to halt in Dornbirn at least long enough to visit the *Rotes Haus,* conspicuous in the Marktplatz, for this is a tavern known throughout Austria. Built in 1633, it is typical of its times, and although it is a Gasthaus, where you may treat yourself to good food and good wine, it is also a repository of many lovely antiques. One could almost call it a museum that works for its living.

Bregenz is a two-way, swinging gate. It has been briefly described in Chapter 1 as the 7th gate *to* Austria, but for the purpose of adhering to a clockwise plan of Austrian travel it could here be considered—reluctantly—a gate of exit, perhaps by one of the two fine new ships in service on Lake Constance, the *Vorarlberg,* which is the pride of the fleet, and the *Österreich.* However the gate swings, in or out, be sure that Bregenz is much more than merely a place to pass through, heading for somewhere else.

A thousand years and more, according to *The Maid of Bregenz,* that ballad by Adelaide Anne Procter which is still dear to British travelers but is rarely known to Americans, has the Vorarlberg capital stood at the base of the Pfänder, but the word "more" does not even hint at the fact that *two* thousand years ago Brigantium was a Roman town and that even the Romans had taken it over from the Celts, who had dwelt there for several centuries prior to the Christian era. The Pfänder has stood guard a lot longer than the town over which it broods but I will not insult it by calling it "a million years young," in the well-meant way of people attempting to flatter an oldster, for it *is* young, and peppy, as you'll find out by swinging up to it by cableway (altitude 3350 feet) and enjoying the amenities of the *Pfänderhotel* and the beauty of the woodsy walks that can be enjoyed at that brisk level. The view down to the city immediately below you and out over the shimmering lake, with the German island town of Lindau in plain sight, is one of the greats of the scenic world.

It is to be hoped that you can visit Bregenz at the time of its increasingly popular midsummer Festival and it is further to be hoped that *if* you plan to do so you will plan also to secure accommodations *long* in advance. It has sometimes been said that the Bregenz Festival is to operetta what Salzburg is to opera, though this is a loose generality. It is, at any rate, a dream of a festival centering on a vast stage built on piles in the harbor. Actually, it is said to be the biggest stage in the world. Such operettas as Johann Strauss's *A Night in Venice,* Carl Millöcker's *Der Bettelstudent*—this has been announced as the major lake-stage show of the 1972 Festival—and Otto Nicolai's *The Merry Wives of Windsor* are handsomely presented by the festival management, and rapturously received by the large audience in the 30 rows of seats, but dramas such as *König Ottokar, Glück und Ende,* by the great Austrian dramatist Franz Grillparzer, are also given, as well as ballet performances, and in the city's gleaming opera house, homespunly called Theater am Kornmarkt, grand opera— I once saw Donizetti's *Daughter of the Regiment* splendidly done there—symphonic concerts and choral concerts by the leading organizations of Europe. In the 1971 Festival the United States got into the action with *Porgy and Bess* done *in English* on the big lake stage by U.S. actor-singers. William Warfield did a magnificent job as Porgy and so did Joyce Bryant as Bess, James Randolph as Crown and Robert Guillaume as Sportin' Life. The scene on the lake stage was absolutely unforgettable as Catfish Row came to life in highly realistic fashion. For the hurricane scene the palm trees bent and waved madly and for the picnic scene there was a tremendous display of fireworks. For the big ballet scene a small lake ship of two decks was used and then it sailed away out of the harbor of—Charleston, South Carolina! To make the scene even more dramatic the big lake passenger steamers berthed and went out-to-lake from time to time; the train from Lindau made a moving streak of light along the shore; and Lindau itself was a huddle of light in the lake only 4 or 5 miles across the Bregenz Bay. On a level below Catfish Row the Vienna Symphony players, the Chorus of the Vienna National Opera and the ballet corps of the Volksoper of Vienna gave their musical support. I think it is eminently fair to call the Festival of Bregenz unique in its setting. Its quality matches its setting and I can think of no harder way of preparing to wrench oneself from the holiday splendors of Austria than to devote a last evening to one of these festival events. It's like leaving the beach in September on a perfect summer day.

HOTELS, RESTAURANTS AND ENTERTAINMENT IN VORARLBERG, A PERSONAL REPORT

Hotels and Restaurants of the High-snow Area

(NOTE: The hotels of Vorarlberg will be set forth in exactly the same order that the traveling took. Only in the "Side Trip to Liechtenstein" will the few hotels mentioned in that Principality be covered directly with the touring and sightseeing text. As a note on personnel, let me say that Vorarlberg and Liechtenstein are among the few places left in Central Europe where the hotel waiters, chambermaids and porters are largely natives, blond, charming and seemingly happy in their jobs. You don't have to learn Italian, Spanish or Turkish in order to talk with them.)

The winter-sports resorts along the Flexenstrasse are mostly run on a seasonal basis, and despite the beauty of the area in summer some of the top ones are open *only* for a few months in winter, which goes to show the power of these villages as winter wonderlands. Zürs, the first resort encountered, has the finest, most exclusive and most expensive hotel in winter-Austria, namely the *Zürserhof,* which is owned by the current president of the Austrian Hotel Association. What do you do for the hotel that has everything? Well, you lodge there if you can afford it and can get a room. The rest you can imagine, including the ice bar, the sun terrace and the free sauna for guests, but you might not guess that one of its refinements is suites with open fireplaces. Other top hotels are the *Alpenrose-Post,* biggest of them all; the one-fourth-as-large *Albona;* the medium-sized *Lorünser,* oriented to youthful sport; the *Edelweiss,* perhaps more slanted to British guests than the others; and the somewhat less expensive *Hotel Flexen.* The Lorünser, open only in winter, and the Flexen both operate on the full-pension plan only. As for the winter season, it is at its peak through the Christmas-New Year's holiday period and then again from early February to mid-April, as is the case generally in Austria's other socially smart winter resorts.

Lech has seven top hotels, five of them with indoor swimming pools, and a veritable multitude of lesser ones. The *Post* with an *outdoor* heated pool, is possibly the best, but the *Schneider,* the

Arlberg and the *Krone* are all excellent, the last-named being owned by the present Mayor of Lech, Robert Pfefferkorn (Peppercorn).

Hotels on the Bregenzerwald Route

Au-of-the-short-name has the largest hotel on the forest road, namely *Hotel Krone,* with 100 beds but not many baths. It was here that I enjoyed the Gargantuan meal I mentioned in the touring section. Its mastermeat was *Wiener Zwiebel* (onion) *Rostbraten, mit Pommes Frites und Salat,* followed by a noble dish of strawberries covered with a dome of whipped cream. The owner of the Krone is the president of the Bregenzer Verkehrsamt. Mellau's leading hotel is perhaps the *Gasthof Kreuz,* not strictly first class but very good, and well known. The humbler *Sonne* is liked by many for its lively evening Stimmung. Bezau, the Bregenzerwald's largest village, looks with pride at its *Hotel Post,* which has very recently opened a smart new section called *Kur-Sport Hotel Post,* whose name speaks for itself.

Hotels in the Montafonertal, with Gargellen

Schruns has already been partly covered by the earlier mention, in the touring part, of the *Kurhotel und Anstalt Montafon,* a place of genuine luxury. I have stayed contentedly in the much more modest *Schäffle* (Lambkin). Other good hotels of no great pretensions are the *Taube* and the *Alpenrose,* while the *Krone* should be visited for its good restaurant, enhanced—and I hope this will long be true—by the really remarkable song-and-zither artistry of Fritz Födinger, who entertains at dinner time. He is internationally known, and for myself I can say that he is *the* best artist in his field as a singer-zitherist that I have ever heard. For one number, on the night I was there, he sang *The Battle Hymn of the Republic* with great verve. I could not resist adding my tenor to his air. It went well and we did it again. Tschagguns, a suburb of Schruns—the name of the village is typically Romansch, as are so many names in this valley—has a first-class hotel in the 70-room-and-25-bath *Cresta.* Gaschurn's top hotel is the almost-first-class *Sporthotel Epple,* with private baths in many of its rooms, but the somewhat lesser *Posthotel Rössle* has a widely admired Montafon-style dining room with a large and very striking mural that depicts the entire Austrian Silvretta Range. It was done in 1899 by one of the hotel's early guests and given outright to the hotel. Have a meal there if you can, to feast your eyes on this mural as you feast your palate with good food. A separate restaurant of Gaschurn—and such places are rare in Austrian resorts—is *Restaurant Alt Montafon.* The place has special character and special food, its decor including such ornaments as a huge cowbell and a still huger burning candle that is always growing fatter. I enjoyed an excellent lunch here of fresh-caught trout from the River Ill, which is the Montafonertal's stream, flowing clear down to and through Feldkirch and finally to the Rhine. The Ill Forelle was followed by a local sharp cheese called in the local dialect *Räser-Kas.* It went well with the restaurant's open wine. Gargellen, heading its own side valley, which is increasingly popular with Americans, has one first-class hotel, the lengthily named *Alpenhotel Heimspitze,* its special attraction being its atmospheric cellar Stube called, in the dialect of the valley, *Maises Stöbli.* I found it a fun-Stube, full of Schrammelmusik. Other Gargellen hotels are the *Madrisa* and the *Silvretta,* this a hotel garni, each of them with an indoor swimming pool. As for that other side valley, from Bludenz, the Brandnertal, with Brand as center, the leading hotel, and I have lodged there with special pleasure, is the *Scesaplana,* with its own indoor pool, and also with a heated open-air pool near by, this a public one.

Hotels and Restaurants in Feldkirch, Dornbirn and Bregenz

Feldkirch has three first-class hotels, two of which I know and like. The big *Central-Hotel Löwe* has an interesting oddity in that its proprietor collects unusual clocks as a hobby. Two or three dozen of them, all ticking away busily and keeping more or less correct time, fill the lobby and the hallways. The Löwe is so directly *under* the Schattenburg that you feel the castle is going to fall into the parking lot and perhaps even crush the "Lion" itself. The other hotel, in a quieter location, is the far smaller *Alpenrose,* a delightful miniature, charming outside and in, and meticulously managed.

Dornbirn's top hotel is the *Parkhotel,* a first-class place if you decide to spend a night in Vorarlberg's largest city. I have already mentioned Dornbirn's colorful *Restaurant Rotes Haus.*

Bregenz has many hotels but since the closing, as a hotel, of the luxurious and very lovely castle-inn Schloss Hofen, in the suburb of Lochau—it is now, I understand, a hotel-and-cooking school— the city has no hotel that could possibly be called deluxe. Of the more than 30 listed hotels the best is probably the *Weisses Kreuz* (White Cross), with a very good French restaurant and a popular Brasserie, followed, I should say, by the *Messmer,* then perhaps by the *Kinz,* and then the *Central,* whose quality is far above the impression one gets upon entering it. Actually, the Central is a good hotel, the trouble being that it has no lobby at all, and the dining room is reached through a tiny and congested barroom. The hotel has 27 private baths, which is a good showing for Vorarlberg hotels. I have stayed both in the Weisses Kreuz and the Central and have found the courtesy rating high in both.

If Bregenz lacks a group of hotels worthy of its importance, it certainly does not lack for a restaurant of special luxury. I refer to the *Burg Restaurant Gebhardsberg* on a cliff high over the city. This mountain restaurant is a newcomer, having been opened only in 1971, but it has established itself as something quite out of the ordinary, a place to be sought. It is reached by a good winding road. It is the sort of top-luxury restaurant that Vorarlberg's capital will surely match some day with an equally impressive hotel.

13 / Munich and Its '72 Olympics

Munich is a "personality" and the established cliché of comment, true, like most clichés, is to refer to it as essentially a 19th-century city. To be cautiously personal, I may state that I, too, am a 19th-century product and first visited Munich, as a very youngster with my parents, soon after that century gave way to the present one. We stayed three months and from that day to this I have loved the city. It has its detractors, for those who are keen on 16th-century Nürnberg or 20th-century Berlin sometimes have difficulty falling in with Munich's pace, which is neither of one nor the other. I have to say here, however, that the 20th-century has thrust an imperious knee in the door, for high-rise American-powered hotels are sprouting, thankfully not in the very center, and an elaborate subway system is taking shape. This trend is stoutly resisted by one splendid gesture, for Munich's main west-east shopping thoroughfare from the traffic hub of Karlsplatz, popularly called Stachus (the name will be explained later), to Marienplatz, the very heart of the city, with the old and new town halls, is being converted into a half-mile promenade for pedestrians only, graced by fountains, flower gardens and assorted seating places, including many sidewalk cafés and beer gardens. The battle of the centuries may continue but Munich's popularity is steady and undimmed. Few cities on the globe have so many devoted admirers coming from such widely ranging regions and financial brackets. They come from many an established citadel of culture such as London in the Old World and Boston in the New. They come, also, droves of them, from American universities. This city on the Isar does have a distinctive magnetism and nearly all visitors, from old-line Brahmins to young men studying chemistry, sooner or later succumb to the pull of it.

To me Munich's spaciousness and its versatility are two of the chief elements in its charm. It is located on a great plain a third of a mile above sea level and has all the room it could ever desire in which to spread out. It does not exactly "make big," like a comfortably settled railway traveler trying to discourage other travelers from entering his compartment, but it does, like London, appropriate to its uses a great deal of the earth's surface. Its boulevards are wide and long and well kept. Its buildings, if they fail individually to excite rapture, form an effective ensemble, and its parks, headed by the large and well-loved Englischer Garten, are just what city parks should be, cool strolling grounds in summer, cold skating grounds in winter. I also like its shopping arcades, with restaurants and cafés.

The impact of the 1972 Olympic Games upon Munich, the host city, is and will continue to be significant, but this subject will be discussed in a separate section hereinafter. Here, it is enough to say that the Olympics are not merely a giant sports event that builds up and breaks on the city like a great comber. Rather, they add a new and permanent dimension to the Bavarian capital, dramatized by the 950-foot Olympic tower, with its revolving restaurant at the 560-foot level. The various stadia and nearly all the other structures have a bright and worthy future.

As for Munich's versatility, one may say in a sense that any large city is versatile, but one does not often find love of art and love of science equally strong, as is the case here, nor love of heavy study and light conversation, nor love of vintage wines and beer-by-the-liter. And as for music, that of Munich is suited to every "brow," high, middle and low. Museums abound, and the one called the German Museum of Masterpieces of Natural and Technical Science (invariably shortened to the first two words) is called the greatest of its kind in the world. Among popular festivals, the city's *Fasching* (carnival), lasting from Epiphany (January 6) until the beginning of Lent, is among the liveliest in Europe and its *Ok-*

toberfest has hardly a match as a folk festival. And finally, Munich is *closer* to the sort of scenery that really knocks you breathless than any other city of its size in Europe. Only Milan, perhaps, could challenge this statement.

THE ESSENTIAL SIGHTS OF MUNICH

The German name of Munich, München, is a puzzle to most foreigners, as it long was to me until a scholar explained its meaning. It derives from the words "*bei* den *Munichen,*" an ancient form of Mönchen, meaning Monks, the sense of it being "at the Monks' [place]." The name-giving monks came a full thousand years ago, in the 9th or 10th century, from a Benedictine monastery at Tegernsee, a lovely lake town south of Munich. The monastery in that town, founded in 711, still exists, though it has been converted into a Schloss, and in its *Braustübl* you may quench your thirst with a stein of Tegernsee beer. From the founding monks comes the familiar symbol of Munich, a child in a monk's robe of black and gold holding an *Eidbuch* (book of city laws) in one hand and, very often and irreverently, a mug of beer in the other.

The city of the little Monk now has almost a million and a half inhabitants, the count, at the moment, increasing by several thousand annually, and its historic, artistic and scenic sights are legion. For quick orientation, many short-time visitors start out by taking a city bus tour *(Rundfahrt)* under the direction of a multilingual guide. The standard tour, consuming about an hour and a half, starts morning and afternoon from in front of the Hertie department store opposite the Central Station, and I will outline, seriatim, its main halts and quick pauses. Perhaps you have a map in your hands.

The Neptune Fountain, surrounded by the massed flowers of the Old Botanical Garden, starts things off.

The Wittelsbach Fountain, at the western end of Maximiliansplatz, is a showy affair built in 1895 to mark the opening of the city's modern water supply. This fountain's name is that of the Bavarian royal family, whose fortunes finally collapsed with World War II.

Königsplatz was Munich's most magnificent prewar square and

most important center of art, but it was very heavily damaged during the war. Now largely restored, its main objects of interest are two galleries of antiquities and sculpture (the more famous Alte Pinakothek is two blocks to the north) and the great unmissable Propyläen, a 19th-century gateway of noble dimensions designed in imitation of the Propylaeum that serves as entrance to the Acropolis of Athens.

On the same square, opposite this supergate, stood the national headquarters of the Nazi party, Hitler's grim Braun Haus, which would account for the heavy bombing of the area. The building is only a bad memory now, but next to it, on Arcisstrasse, stood the *Führerbau,* which has been reconstructed as a high school for music. For a few years it was the Amerika Haus, which now has its own modern building on the Karolinenplatz. On the second floor of this conspicuous building "Munich" occurred, on September 30, 1938. Chamberlain and Daladier met Hitler and his servile Axis partner Mussolini and agreed to let the Führer have his "last territorial demand," the Sudetenland. If Nazism can be said to have had a shrine, it was the mausoleum that stood here and which contained the bronze coffins of the 12 men killed in the Beer Hall Putsch of November 9, 1923. The structure has been destroyed and the bodies hidden in unmarked graves so that it shall not become a pilgrimage for any die-hard Nazis still "at large" in Germany.

The *Alte Pinakothek,* mentioned above, is Munich's entrant in the great art gallery competition of Europe, on a level to be discussed with Paris' Louvre and Florence's Uffizi, though it is not on so great a scale. It is replete with masterpieces of German, Dutch, Flemish, Italian, Spanish and French paintings. It is in an impressive building that fills a whole block between Barerstrasse and Arcisstrasse just a bit north of Königsplatz. All of the paintings are splendidly lighted, as a reward, it would seem, for visitors who must climb 80 steps to reach them.

Ludwigstrasse (which the guide painfully translates as Louis Street and rue Louis!) is the most important of the many architectural embellishments of the city undertaken by Ludwig I,

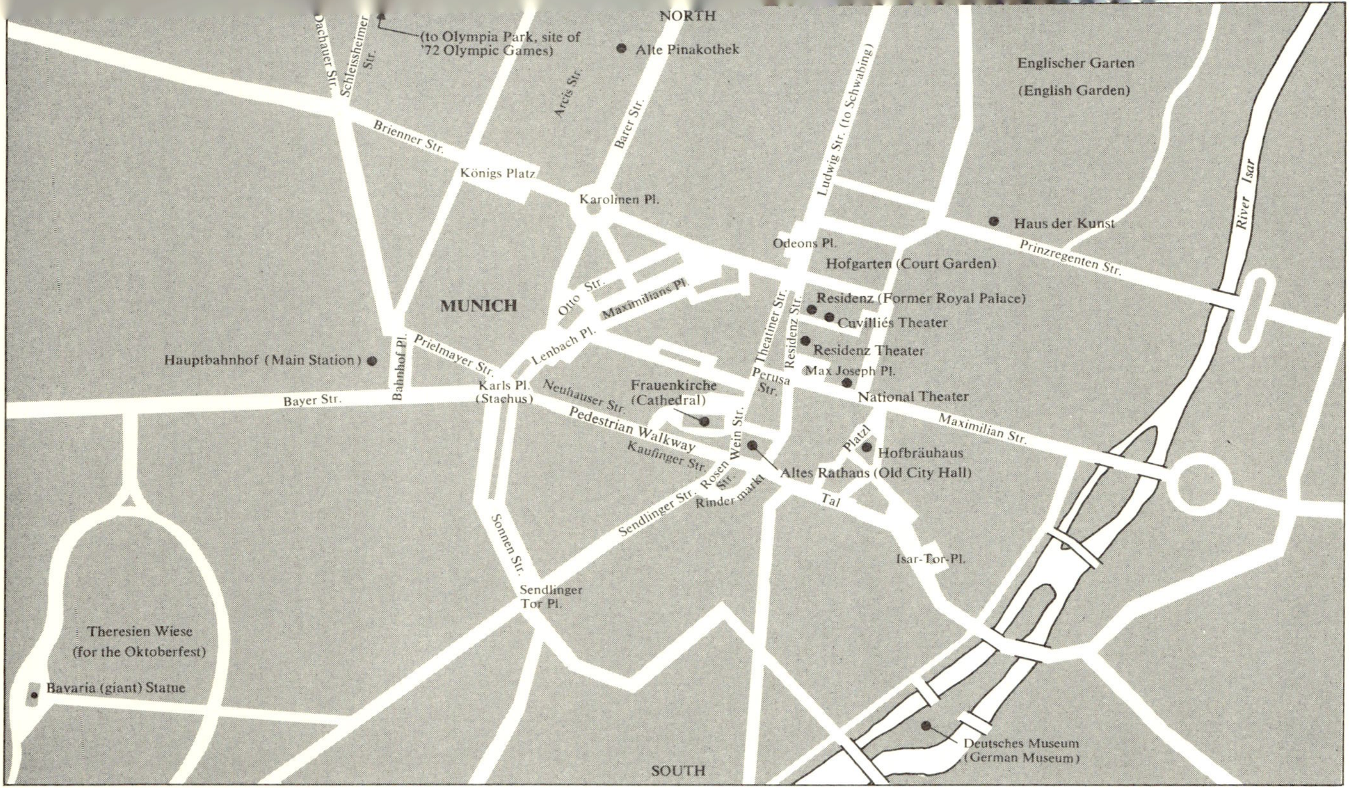
NORTH
(to Olympia Park, site of '72 Olympic Games)
Alte Pinakothek
Englischer Garten
(English Garden)
Dachauer Str.
Schleissheimer Str.
Arcis Str.
Barer Str.
Brienner Str.
Königs Platz
Karolinen Pl.
Ludwig Str. (to Schwabing)
River Isar
Haus der Kunst
Prinzregenten Str.
Odeons Pl.
Hofgarten (Court Garden)
Residenz (Former Royal Palace)
Cuvilliés Theater
Residenz Theater
Max Joseph Pl.
National Theater
MUNICH
Otto Str.
Maximilians Pl.
Lenbach Pl.
Prielmayer Str.
Hauptbahnhof (Main Station)
Bahnhof Pl.
Bayer Str.
Karls Pl.
(Stachus)
Neuhauser Str.
Pedestrian Walkway
Kaufinger Str.
Frauenkirche
(Cathedral)
Theatiner Str.
Residenz Str.
Perusa Str.
Wein Str.
Rosen Str.
Rindermarkt
Sendlinger Str.
Platzl
Hofbräuhaus
Altes Rathaus (Old City Hall)
Maximilian Str.
Tal
Isar-Tor-Pl.
Sonnen Str.
Sendlinger Tor Pl.
Theresien Wiese
(for the Oktoberfest)
Bavaria (giant) Statue
Deutsches Museum
(German Museum)
SOUTH

who was the "father of 19th-century Munich." For three-quarters of a mile, from the Odeonsplatz to the Arch of Victory, it is a broad, grandiose street of buildings of uniform height and style.

Prinzregentenstrasse is another grand avenue and a relatively recent showpiece of Munich, dating only from 1890. It competes with the Königsplatz area as the art center of the city. Ranged along its north side are several galleries of art and architecture, including the Bavarian National Museum, one special attraction of this being a fascinating collection of crèches (nativity scenes), and the Haus der Kunst, built by Hitler, now showing a fine collection of 19th-century French paintings as well as contemporary art exhibitions.

This thoroughfare is flanked by the delightful 600 acres of trees, lawns, rivulets, flowers and shrubs called the Englischer Garten. This was laid out by the American known as *Count* Rumford, a rather fantastic character. Born in Massachusetts, he went to England at the outbreak of the American Revolution and served in the British Civil Service. Just as he was about to join the Austrian army to fight the Turks, the Elector of Bavaria persuaded him to join his government. He served as Minister of War and Police for 11 years. In the meantime, he had been knighted by George III and had been made a Count of the Holy Roman Empire; he chose the name of Rumford from the township whence came his wealthy American wife. On his return to England his wife soon died, whereupon he went to Paris and married the widow of the famous French chemist Lavoisier. He died in the French capital in 1814. He is remembered today as a scientist who experimented with the explosive force of gunpowder, firearms, and signaling at sea, but his most important work concerned the nature of heat caused by friction.

The Maximilianeum, on the far side of the Isar, was built in the middle of the 19th century by Maximilian II as a home for outstanding student aspirants to the higher civil service. Even today there are "Maximilianeum-Studenten," the best of whom are eligible for a state-financed higher education.

The Feldherrnhalle, or Hall of the Field Marshals, a forthright copy of the famous Loggia dei Lanzi in Florence, was built in 1840–44 largely as a city ornament. In 1923 it attained dubious fame as the scene of Hitler's first effort to seize power in the Beer Hall Putsch. Seven of the twelve Nazis mentioned above were shot down here on the adjacent Odeonsplatz. During the Hitler era a plaque on its wall on Residenzstrasse was one of the most sacred Nazi memorials, guarded night and day by honor guards. All Germans passing it were supposed to stiffen in salute and keep totally silent! Almost across the street from the Feldherrnhalle is the restored Theatinerkirche, a church of the 17th and 18th centuries, largely baroque and with a 19th-century façade by an architect whose name is worth mastering, François Cuvilliès. Munich's well-loved rococo theater designed by him and bearing his name is devoted especially to Mozart operas.

The Frauenkirche, or Church of Our Lady, is Bavaria's Metropolitan Church. Its 325-foot towers, capped by onion-shaped copper "turbans," constitute a symbol of Munich almost as much loved as the Münchner Kindl. The inside is extremely plain, with walls of white plaster. There is a modernistic pulpit and behind the altar there is a *very* tall stained-glass window to relieve the plainness of the walls. Visitors may ascend one of the 325-foot towers by elevator, though it takes a considerable climb to reach the elevator's base point. Near the Frauenkirche is the Michaelskirche, where over 30 Wittelsbachs, including Ludwig II, the castlebuilder, are buried.

The so-called New Rathaus, built in quasi Gothic style from 1867 to 1908, is a copy of Brussels' Hôtel de Ville, except that the Münchner Kindl, high in the sky, replaces St. Michael. The building is noticed by tourists chiefly for this child-surmounted, 280-foot tower, which is adorned by a mechanical clock. At 11 A.M. daily figures seen on the front of the tower at a conveniently low level do a medieval coopers' dance, while other figures, representing knights, enter into a jousting tourney, both these efforts being watched invariably by knots of tourists gathered below on the pavement of Marienplatz.

The Residenz is a *wonderful* complex. It has the Residenz (Cuvilliès) Theater, a place of rare, rococo splendor; the big Herkulessaal for concerts; and the National Theater (Opera House), with a most cheerful interior of light gray and rose colors and a five-level "horseshoe." Within the Residenz are no less than seven courts or patios, some of them beautiful with greenery. The Residenz Museum and the Treasury (Schatzkammer) have treasures beyond price. Among the things I noted was the crown of Empress Kunigunde, the prayer book of Charles the Bald from the year 860, a spectacular travel service given by the city of Paris to Empress Marie-Louise, and most valuable of all, a St. George of 1590, done in gold and encrusted with many rubies.

There are few pleasanter places in which to stroll or relax than the adjoining Hofgarten with cafés, shops and art galleries.

The Isartor, a restored 14th-century gate, is reached by a tangle of old streets and then the tourist chariot passes across a branch of the Isar to an island in the river. (*In* the Isartor is the Valentin Café, where huge cups of coffee, with cakes, can be had, though perhaps not on the bus tour.)

The colossal German Museum is on this island and fills nearly all of it. To stroll through the various halls and corridors of this behemoth, without looking at anything, would take a good stroller at least two hours, for the total distance is some 6 miles, but the displays, and the various machines, many of which actually do their assigned work if you press a button, are truly marvelous and I shall tell something about them later. The visitor to Munich with more than an absolute minimum of time should surely make a separate visit, for the guided motor tour allows time for only passing glimpses of a few rooms.

The newly opened Stadtmuseum (City Museum) is also a "must," being a lovely and well-arranged 5-story building with some 50,000 items, but it isn't the number that appeals. Rather, it is the many, many things of interest even to museum dodgers. For example, there are musical instruments of the past 3000 years, a superb collection of marionettes, with a marionette show, and bronzed wood morris dancers dating from 1580. Recently, a photo- and-film section has been added, and also, very appropriately, a brewing museum.

The Gärtnerplatz, in the southern part of the city, is a small "round square," or *étoile,* of exceptional charm, with a garden in the center, yet it is hardly ever mentioned, even in blow-by-blow handbooks that tell all, except for the Theater am Gärtnerplatz that fronts on it, now a stage for operettas. I, for one, am grateful to the rubberneck tours for routing their coaches through this unsung Platz.

The Theresienwiese (Wiese means meadow) is the final item on the standard itinerary, for this is the locale of Munich's world-celebrated *Oktoberfest*. This master festival fairly dominates the city's life during a full fortnight at the end of September and the beginning of October. It dates from 1810, when it was first held in celebration of the wedding of Prince Ludwig (who became Ludwig I and gave Munich its architectual character). Throngs mill about having fun in the big beer tents and the assorted sideshows, and mass feasting is an intrinsic part of the fun. On the first Sunday a big procession brings the fun to its peak. This features national costumes *and* teams of dray horses drawing trucks with huge loads of beer. No one who has seen these glorious brewery horses can ever forget them, for they are like ambassadors of labor from the land of the Houyhnhnms, their tremendous haunch muscles rippling under velvet hide that's as lustrous as a general's boots.

The Theresienwiese is not a negligible thing even when nothing is happening there, for it is the setting of the Bavarian Hall of Fame and of a colossal bronze statue of Bavaria, designed by Ludwig Schwanthaler over a century ago. Bavaria is a hefty young woman of 80 long tons holding a wreath high in one hand and a grounded sword in the other, while a peaceful lion stands beside her. She is 98 feet tall, with her base, and permits visitors (though there is no time for this on the prepared tour) to mount by 130 steps to the inside of her 7 foot head. For all the room within it—for five persons at a time—we so no sign of brains, but the lady has eyes and through them we may peep for a glimpse of the big meadow and much else. She grows very feverish under the rays of a summer sun, so it is advisable, if your Munich stay is in summer, to visit Bavaria in the forenoon. Her head is open from 10 o'clock.

THE PORCELAINS OF NYMPHENBURG

On the Western outskirts of Munich lies Schloss Nymphenburg, in other days the summer palace of Bavarian royalty, with its great formal park. This pretentious affair is, of course, "Munich's answer to Versailles," which castle and park were imitated by most of the kings and princes of Europe in the centuries following Louis XIV's reign. The castle, with its Marstall Museum of coaches and saddlery, is rather interesting, its park, with a very lovely rococo hunting lodge called Amalienborg, is more interesting and its State Porcelain Factory is *most* interesting. Castles and parks are everywhere in Germany, but Nymphenburg porcelains are in some respects unique.

This was a Wittelsbach enterprise, ducal and then royal, started about 200 years ago and early sparked by a Ticino Swiss artist named Franz Anton Bustelli, whose works, especially eight pairs of figurines, are among the most famous porcelains ever made in Germany. These and many other masterpieces of other artists are on display in the salesroom of the museum. The factory employs the same number of artisans, 150, that it did in 1790, for there is no mass production here and every piece is meticulously made by hand, on order only. The little factory is still powered by a flowing brooklet as it was in the 1700s, and by traditional methods even the most delicate work is being done, such as the fashioning of porcelain flowers by women artists. The principal materials are kaolin from Czechoslovakia and feldspar and quartz from Scandinavia. The firing, which is done only once a fortnight and takes about 48 hours, is, of course, an exceedingly tricky operation. The heat has to be checked every 6 or 7 minutes during all that time, for one single error of the firing men may spoil the coloring and thus ruin the effect of up to 9000 pieces.

I have mentioned the salesroom and you have inferred, correctly, that you may place an order here. As a matter of business fact a considerable portion of the Nymphenburg product is ordered by American visitors and sent overseas.

THE GERMAN MUSEUM, AN ISLAND OF HUMAN ACHIEVEMENTS

All the conventional museums and galleries of Munich must yield precedence to the really amazing Deutsches Museum filling its island in the Isar. This was founded in 1903 by an engineer named Dr. Oskar von Miller and all Germany has contributed to its growth of natural and technical sciences, and to this end hundreds of its machines and pieces of experimental apparatus can, as I've said, be worked by the visitor himself or by the attendants.

Three connected buildings display just about everything, it seems, that man has achieved and is trying to achieve. There are sections on pharmacy, musical instruments, cinema, radio and TV, mining and smelting, astronomy (there's a planetarium, with the sun, moon, planets and 4500 stars which move at the touch of a button) and meteorology, tunnel blasting, nuclear fission, watchmaking and many more fields of endeavor, but it isn't a jumble, like my listings here, for all is carefully arranged in sequences. It takes a good three hours to see even a few chosen departments with any real pleasure, so I am happy to say there's a restaurant on the ground floor where you may break up your research and take the weight off your feet.

For most nontechnical visitors, especially those who have not seen the Daimler-Benz Motor Museum in a suburb of Stuttgart, I think the transportation section is among the most fascinating. Even the layman can enjoy hours there. One can follow the development of the bicycle from its ungainly infancy to the sleek perfection of the latest motorcycles and scooters and then the automobile from its birth to the very last word in today's cars and tomorrow's prophecies. Steam and electric locomotives also grow before one's eyes from "Puffing Billy" (a full-sized replica of the original in London), which really puffs and whistles in solemn earnest, to the most approved electric giants of American and European railways. The section of sea and air transportation, with its varied contents, is enormously popular with Germans and foreigners alike. Another feature that captures the attention of all, whether musically gifted or not, is the large section of musical instruments. Most of the instruments, however ancient, can be played and often *are* played by a guard-musician. We hear music from instruments actually owned and played by such greats as Mozart, Haydn and Chopin.

Of the individual items in the museum, one, a heavy pendulum hanging from a great height, seems fairly to shout for Galileo of Pisa. Four times a day an attendant steadies the pendulum so that it hangs motionless, but within a few moments it is oscillating in an arc that measures over 3 feet.

The museum has a 210-foot tower which one may mount by elevator, and since no labor is involved every visitor should certainly do this, for the view of the city and of "Isar rolling rapidly," to quote Thomas Campbell's phrase from *Hohenlinden*. If the day is clear one also sees the magnificent background of the Bavarian snow peaks.

MUNICH AS YOU DO IT YOURSELF

This is a swift rundown of what you need to know in order to enjoy Munich on your own, and to the full, starting with a page of the past. Bavaria has been a part of Germany for just over one hundred years, the union taking place in 1871, when Prussia's King William was crowned Emperor William I of Germany, but more than any other state of the Reich it has maintained a sort of quasi independence. Bavarians are quite unlike the Prussians. They are more easygoing, more like Austrians, and a spirit of independence has always permeated the state, whether as a duchy, an electorate, a kingdom or a republic. This made amalgamation into the German Empire a difficult problem, but it was finally achieved and it was the Bavarian King Ludwig II himself who proposed that William of Prussia be given the imperial crown.

The *Kingdom of Bavaria* was created in 1806 and lasted until the end of World War I. Its six kings, one of whom, Otto I, never reigned because of insanity, were of the Wittelsbach Dynasty. Two of the Wittelsbachs have special interest for today's visitor to Bavaria.

Ludwig I (reigned 1825–48), to reemphasize this point, created the Munich that travelers ever since have known and loved. He was a powerful patron of the arts and of city planning and it is to him that posterity has owed the magnificence of the Munich scene. (The city was very heavily damaged in World War II, some 80,000 dwellings having been destroyed or hurt beyond repair, but at the present time the visitor has almost to be told of the destruction, for he hardly sees it except in the form of extensive hills near the Olympic grounds, hills of rubble long since turfed and landscaped as if they had "been born there.") Ludwig I was finally forced to resign, chiefly because of popular resentment at the power granted by the king to his celebrated mistress, the dancer Lola Montez. Her only bequest to Bavaria was her pretty name, which even today graces a prominent Munich nightspot.

Ludwig II (reigned 1864–86) was the king who built the glorious, or vainglorious, castles of Linderhof, Neuschwanstein and Herrenchiemsee, going mad in the process, though this is still doubted and debated by some. He brought Bavaria almost to financial ruin by his extravagances, but it is said that over the years since his passing the castles have brought in far more revenue from German and foreign tourists than they originally cost. Ludwig drowned himself, or was drowned, in Starnberg Lake on June 13, 1886. More will be told about him and his castles in Chapter 14, but it should be mentioned here that it was this king's patronage of Richard Wagner that brought out the genius of that master composer. The Bavarian monarchy, within the German Empire, came to an end with Germany's defeat in World War I, and amid the strife and turmoil that ensued, Hitler's Nazi movement was born in Munich and eventually took over the whole country.

Orientation needs comment here, for Munich's contours can be confusing. I have mentioned the new and priseworthy half-mile walkway straight through the heart of the city, which is a *blessing* both for the Münchener and the visitor. It replaces "Main Street," which starts at Karlsplatz, passes through the Karlstor (gate) and then bears, out of deference to tradition, the successive names of Neuhauserstrasse and Kaufingerstrasse, lined with many shops, including great department stores, but lined, too, with plenty of eating and drinking places of every type (22 by present count) and brightened by 8 fountains, so far, and a profusion of little and larger flower beds and nooks, with benches here and there for the weary. Any city that has such a central mall seems to me on the wave of the future. Pioneers were Rio de Janeiro, with its famous Ouvidor, Copenhagen with its Strøget and Amsterdam with its Kalverstraat. Then rather recently came Cologne, opening its mile-long Hohe Strasse and Schildergasse, and now Munich, with perhaps the most cheerful "strollway" of all. Surely other cities of Germany and other countries will follow suit.

Before leaving this subject I should explain something important about the mall's starting place. Karlsplatz is its official map name, but its universal spoken name, and very often written and printed too, even on traffic and streetcar signs, is Stachus. The name has a double source, for centuries ago a little church stood here dedicated to St. Eustachius and there was also a beer restaurant—the area was then just outside the city walls—kept by one Eustachius Föderl. So Stachus it is. One sees and hears it far oftener than its "right name." Underneath it is one of the largest subterranean shopping and parking plazas in the world, four levels deep and with some 16 escalators from and to as many entrances. The shopping part, which includes branches of some of Munich's finest surface shops, was opened in November 1970.

Stachus is the nucleus, or *a* nucleus, of the Altstadt Ring (Old City or Inner Ring), of interest to motorists, and it centers a crescent whose northern arc is a chain of very wide, parklike, well-fountained boulevards bearing long names that you need to know if you're a shopper, for the whole area abounds in fine specialty shops. They are Lenbach Platz, Maximilians Platz, Briennerstrasse, Wittelsbacher Platz and Odeonsplatz. From the last-named square broad Ludwigstrasse heads north to the student area of Schwabing, and two narrow but important streets, Theatinerstrasse and Residenzstrasse, "pried apart" by the earlier mentioned Feldherrnhalle, head south for Marienplatz, a name now familiar to you. Theatinerstrasse changes its name to Weinstrasse a hundred yards or so before it reaches Marienplatz. Connecting Theatinerstrasse with Lenbach Platz (see above) is a thoroughfare which blossoms, in the middle part, into a garden-park called Paradeplatz, on which is located the popular luxury hotel the Bayerischer

Hof. Residenzstrasse, passing the Residenz, borders the wide-open Max Joseph Platz, with the pillared opera house, from which, running east, is the boulevard called Maximilianstrasse, on which is located the luxury Hotel Vier Jahreszeiten (Four Seasons). Maximilianstrasse continues to, and across, the Isar River.

The above outline, followed on a good map, will give the do-it-yourselfer the essentials of central Munich. The motorist should know that there are three more or less concentric traffic rings. We've noted the Inner Ring but for the motorist the most important one is the Mittlere (Middle) Ring, connecting with the autobahn expressways from the north (Nürnberg) and the east (Salzburg). There is to be an Aussere (Outer) Ring but construction is as yet barely getting started. Motorists will be pleased to encounter (in the summer season) motor guides stationed at the chief points of entrance to Munich, ready to help them find their way to desired hotels or other destinations.

In the city's central area several addresses of information offices should be noted. In the building of the Central Station, at 2 Bahnhofplatz close to the main entrance, is the *Fremdenverkehrsamt München,* which is to say Tourist Traffic Office of Munich, offering leaflets, brochures and help on all your needs, including your need for immediate accommodations. There is a branch office in the arrival hall of the airport, and the head office is at Rindermarkt 5, near Marienplatz. An *Olympia-Informationszentrum* (center) is conspicuous at Weinstrasse 14, this street being, as I've said, the continuation (south) of Theatinerstrasse, only a few steps north of Marienplatz, and a few steps east of Paradeplatz and Hotel Bayerischer Hof through Maffeistrasse, a short but busy street of shops. Finally, there is the *Fremdenverkehrsverband Munchen-Oberbayern,* which is the Tourist Traffic Association of Munich and Upper [Mountain] Bavaria, an office of major importance to you if you plan to explore the Bavarian Alps (Chapter 14) by out-and-back trips with Munich as base. American Express can be a place of refuge for those who want the language comfort and familiarity of the home scene. The company's quarters are conveniently located at Paradeplatz 3, within a few steps of the Bayerischer Hof. Motorists may contact any of several automobile associations whose names are not *too* jawbreaking, two widely used ones being Algemeiner [General] Deutsches Automobil Club (ADAC), at Königinstrasse 9–11a, with a Southern Bavaria section at Sendlinger-Tor-Platz 9, and Automobil Club von Deutschland AvD, Bavaria section, at Prannerstrasse 30. Of course your home AAA office will inform you on everything about driving in Germany including your American international driving permit, which may not be necessary in Germany but may be in Austria.

Local Transportation within Munich is a subject not to be treated too casually, though conditions will improve enormously when the ramifying subway, whose construction has blocked off many points of the main streets, is finally completed, taking some of the burden from surface traffic. Taxis are reasonably numerous and can always be had at the doors of the chief hotels and of course also at the Central Station. Bold foreigners may wish to learn the intracacies of the subway and streetcar and bus systems, especially if staying a long time in Munich, but the average visitor will depend on taxis and footwork, since there are features about bus or streetcar travel that are quite strange to us. The passenger, for instance, must always *cancel* his ticket himself within the conveyance at one of the automatic canceling machines found beside each door. If he boards the *trailer* of a streetcar he must have a ticket in advance, bought at a private sales agency, a station booth or a streetside ticket dispenser, of which there are many, being conspicuous blue boxes. You put in two DM (marks) and get three tickets (which you must cancel, upon use, *in* the conveyance). Why do I go into all this detail when I am advising you to use taxis anyway? I'll tell you. A ticket is *travel insurance* to get you back to your hotel from the theater, concert or anywhere, if you simply can't get a taxi, Before I knew this I once attended an evening concert in the Congress Hall of the German Museum. I went by taxi. After the concert I waited for a taxi—and *waited*. In half an hour exactly *one* came and twenty people wanted it. In desperation I finally boarded a passing streetcar marked simply STACHUS. I entered the trailer, ticketless and innocent, and left it at Stachus. By good luck no checker happened to check that car. Had he done so I could have been fined, I believe, 10 marks ($2.85). I asked a fellow passenger who left the car with me "how come" I got a free ride and he explained the system and said I was lucky. I am certain that I could have waited *all night* for a taxi, so I urge you to invest two marks and equip yourself with three tickets, to keep handy "just in case." The only other alternatives in your effort to get back to your hotel, short of walking a considerable distance, are to engage a taxi for a given point at a given time and *hope* the man will show up, or else have him wait for you for two or three hours, or whatever.

Car rental firms (Auto-Verleih) are fairly numerous in Munich, Hertz and Avis, easily reachable by phone, being available at the airport and in town. A Munich-born firm that I have used with satisfaction, and it seems to be popular with the top hotels, including the Bayerischer Hof, is *Auto Sixt,* at Seitzstrasse 11 (telephone 22.33.33).

THE '72 OLYMPICS, AUGUST 28 TO SEPTEMBER 10

The summer Olympics of 1972 will be held in Munich, the winter Olympics in Sapporo, the capital of Hokkaido, Japan's rugged far-northern island. Oh, East is East, and West is West, *and in sports the twain shall meet.* Kipling's ballad has the gap eliminated "When two strong men stand face to face, though they come from the ends of the earth!" In the Olympics, thousands of strong men and women come from the ends of the earth to confront each other in 21 forms of sport, and what a marvelous soldering alloy the Games are. Black athletes from the new African countries confront white athletes from our deep south, Orientals from Thailand and Taiwan confront Occidentals from Britain and the European Continent, Scandinavians confront Argentines and Brazilians, Russians confront Americans. Peace, it's wonderful, Olympics—they're wonderful.

The incredibly elaborate preparations that Munich has made, and is making, for the Summer Olympics of 1972 give impressive evidence of the drive that has brought Germany to such a level of achievement and prosperity.

Before describing the various stadia and other buildings in

Olympia Park I should report here on how to secure tickets and lodgings, for Munich expects two million visitors during the two weeks of the Games. The American Automobile Association has been designated the official United States travel agent for the Munich Olympics and in its 855 offices it will act as sole agent for the sale and distribution of all housing accommodations and tickets allocated to the United States. Housing and tickets must be purchased as a package and are not available separately in America.

I have several times had, as you may have, a 360-degree tower's-eye view of Oberwiesenfeld and its Olympia Park, as it presses unceasingly on toward readiness. The five-syllable name, a mild one as German names go, provides an area of about 1 square mile situated 2½ miles from the center of Munich. Within this area 90 per cent of all the competitions will take place, no sports facility being more than a few hundred yards from any other. The tower's-eye view I've mentioned is had from the revolving restaurant of the 950-foot Olympia Turm (Tower), a television tower with two observation levels in addition to the restaurant, which is at the 560-foot level, reached in 30 seconds by two outsized elevators called the fastest in Europe. The restaurant turns, making each revolution in 36, 53 or 70 minutes, as the management may decide, these times being a bit more deliberate than those reported (Chapter 6) of the revolving restaurant of Vienna's Donauturm, 26, 37 or 52 minutes. The restaurant's windows are protected from glare and harmful rays by some sort of gold covering which I cannot explain but can endorse, for 2½ hours of staring out of my window left my eyes quite unwearied. Seating 230 guests, the restaurant provides a good meal, catered by Wienerwald (see restaurant section at end of chapter), while on a covered panorama platform above it there is a snack bar for those who are, unhappily, in a hurry. I was *not* in a hurry, in fact, anything but, for I dawdled over my dinner during four full revolutions at the 36-minute pace, enabling me to study, and largely identify, the numerous stadia, sports halls and other facilities, including the two Olympic Villages to house 12,000 athletes, 10,000 of them men and 2000 women, plus the necessary personnel.

Let me outline just one feature of what the Oberwiesenfeld

square mile holds, namely an Olympic Stadium seating 80,000 and a huge multipurpose Sports Hall that includes a swimming stadium with seats for 8000, the *whole thing,* except one half of the Olympic Stadium, being covered by a 260-foot-high translucent thermoplastic roof, with an area of 732,000 feet, said to be the only one of its kind outside the United States, though Japan, remembering the Osaka World's Fair, might challenge this. On the open side of the stadium will be the Olympic Flame.

Among other features of Olympia Park (Oberwiesenfeld) are: a 7000-seat covered ice rink; a 3500-seat volleyball stadium; a velodrome, or cycle track; the two Olympic Villages just mentioned; parking areas for 10,000 cars; a suburban transit railway station; a subway station and much more. [Taxis will be in great overdemand and you may need to learn something of the subway or bus system to feel safe in reaching the Games and returning from them. A subway station from which you may go directly to the east side of Olympia Park is almost adjacent to the Olympic Information Center I have mentioned at Weinstrasse 14, near Marienplatz.]

At Feld Moching, 5 miles from the city center, will be the regatta course, 1½ miles long and 150 yards wide. Within the borders of Munich will be the shooting ranges and the basketball stadium. Two Olympic events will be held in other cities, namely the exciting canoe slalom in Augsburg, 40 miles northwest of Munich, and the yacht races, for six classes, in Kiel, a long 550 miles from Munich in Baltic waters. The cost of preparing for the Olympics held in Munich alone is budgeted at about $325 million, or *was.* Prices mount in Germany, too, though not as fast as in the States.

All of the projects of the builders of Olympia were planned, to quote the official statement, "with an eye to their utilization after the Games are over. The Olympic Village for men is thus to be converted into modern flats for several thousand Munich families, while the women's section will later house students. The radio and television center will become a university sports center and the Press City will be turned into a housing estate with its own shopping center. The Olympic area will be a leisure haunt for the people of Munich and their guests."

FOUR-PART ROUNDUP: HOTELS, RESTAURANTS, ENTERTAINMENT, SHOPS, A PERSONAL REPORT

Hotels of Munich

A pre-note: In almost all hotel and restaurant bills in Germany two items are *included* (enthalten) in your bill, not added to it at the end, namely 15 per cent (sometimes 10 in the lesser hotels) for service (Bedienungsgeld) and 11 per cent for a government tax (Mehrwertsteuer), making a whopping 26 per cent. Prices are quoted with these charges absorbed in them, which most travelers greatly prefer to the old system of tacking on extra charges. Tipping over and above this 26 per cent is permissible—tips should be in *small* amounts, say 3 to 5 per cent—if the service warrants a bit of extra generosity. Since the German mark was cut loose in the spring of 1971 to "float" and find its own level in exchange for dollars, it has floated upward, and then in August, the dollar was cut loose and floated downward (though not alarmingly), so it is obviously impossible at this writing to figure where the dollar will ultimately find anchorage. The tourist, taking it philosophically, can only say "que sera sera."

The top hotels of Munich, as of Vienna and many another Continental city, are of two main types, those of traditional European inspiration and those of modern American inspiration, these being usually very large, very long on creature comforts and latest luxuries but necessarily far less personal in atmosphere and service. Both types have plenty of adherents and I shall try to be objective in describing them, taking those of European type first. To avoid complexity I will include each hotel's dining rooms with the description of the hotel itself. Separate, nonhotel restaurants will be described in their separate section below.

The two European hotels that I know best, from sojourns in each over the years, are the *Bayerischer Hof* and the *Vier Jahreszeiten*. The former is one of my own favorite hotels in all Germany, while the latter, with an illustrious past and a drastically changing present calls for reserve of judgment till the changes are completed. About the Bayerischer Hof, a 400-room hotel of luxury-at-ease, there is an atmosphere that has a strong appeal for me. It is on Paradeplatz, in the very heart of the city, where the action is, yet its "grand hotel animation" is by no means hectic, and the service, in my experience, has been of an unusually personal and smiling nature, though this may not shine through so much during the fully packed height of the tourist summer. The staff now benefits by the hotel's recent acquisition of the former reception manager of the Vier Jahreszeiten. The Bayerischer Hof's array of eating places is among the most varied and imaginative of any hotel in Germany. I will describe them below, but a special attraction of the hotel which includes an eating place needs first-off emphasis here, namely the roof-garden swimming pool entered from the 5th floor and reachable by a separate bather's elevator. Many hotels have pools but few have anything like this one. It has a sliding roof and is open from 7 A.M. until evening. Its pleasures are abetted by a really charming pool-grill, open from noon till 3 P.M., and on Sunday a big brunch from 10 to 3. It is abetted, also, by a complete sauna, with massage facilities for men and women. A little boutique is stocked with swim suits, sunglasses, tan oil and so forth, and near it is a small drinks-and-coffee bar. This topside swimming pool is really something, for it is astonishing to see bikini-clad girls lolling at the edge of the pool with the twin towers of the Frauenkirche close by and those of the Peterskirche and the Rathaus just beyond, a contrast made doubly strange since the various towers attain about the same level as the pool. Your lovely feminine body and stalwart masculine body are treats for the tourists who ascend the Frauenkirche tower for the view. The Bayerischer Hof's roster of features includes a large festival hall, a 500-seat theater, and in the cellar, what is perhaps Munich's liveliest nightclub. And there is another important thing. The proprietor of the hotel, Mr. Falk-Volkhardt, has recently negotiated the purchase of the adjoining Montgelas Palais, formerly a palace of the Bavarian government, and is doing big things with it, as will be recounted later.

Now let's see the hotel's restaurants. On the ground floor, leading from the reception area, is the lobby-lounge, with fireplace, and a few steps up from this the Spiegelsaal (Mirror Hall), a restaurant that doubles as breakfast room. On the ground floor there is a grill room, as well, open for lunch and also for dinner, with music from 6 o'clock till midnight, plus a garden terrace open on days of fair weather. In 1971 a Trader Vic Restaurant was launched in an area below ground and it has made an instant and sustained hit. Having eaten in several Trader Vics in Hawaii and the mainland States, not to mention London's Hilton, I would say that this one of the Bayerischer Hof, the first on the European Continent, fully attains, and maintains, the Polynesian atmosphere and cuisine that such a place demands. And finally, in the cellar of the hotel's Montgelas Palace a *Weinstrasse,* or European Wine Street, is being readied. On wooden tables, if present plans hold, wines of all countries, plus two favored Bavarian beers, will be served to accompany steaks and Bavarian country specialties. On the floors above the Wine Street two fine old halls are being restored, the one on the 2nd floor being the Königssaal, of historic value. Above that are two floors that will comprise new luxury apartments, promising to be among the best in Germany.

The *Vier Jahreszeiten,* as I've said, is undergoing great changes, for in 1969–70 it was bought by a consortium of hotel interests, 50 per cent by Berlin's Kempinski Company and 25 per cent each by Lufthansa and Inter-Continental Hotels, a Pan American Airways subsidiary. It will not be fully reconstructed till 1973 but enough of it will be ready, and is indeed now in operation, so that Avery Brundage and his Olympic cohorts will take over the whole hotel for three weeks in connection with the Games. The Vier Jahreszeiten was "founded" in 1852 by King Maximilian II and maintained a character of considerable elegance for over a century, but its chief claim to tourist fame was, is, and will likely continue to be, its *Restaurant Walterspiel,* brought literally to world attention by the cooking expertise of the late Alfred Walterspiel. It maintains its excellence due to having half a dozen cooks who have been right there since their youth and are now "pushing fifty." A youthful but highly experienced member of the Walterspiel family is now, and will remain, manager of the hotel under its new ownership. There will be a new Four Seasons Grill, entered directly from the street, and like its rival, a roof garden and 5th-floor swimming pool. It confidently announces that the mellow patrician atmosphere for which it used to be known will be restored.

Hotel Continental is located on Max-Joseph-Strasse at Ottostrasse, a street of art and antique shops parallel to Maximilians Platz, and I would say that its luxuries fully match those of either hotel I've named above, and that the "Conti," as it is called, has an abundance of artistic atmosphere that is all its own, with statuary and paintings and antiques, a tapestried Gothic room, a Barok Stube, a Tiroler Stube made from a 500-year-old farm, an attractive Conti Grill and on an upper floor a Dachgarten (Roof Garden) that is one of the loveliest restaurants I know, brightened by its blue-tile floor and a flawlessly kept little flower garden right there by the tables. The Continental is an altogether admirable hotel, heartily recommendable.

Near the Conti, at Maximilians Platz 5, is the *Regina Palast,* extensively rebuilt after destruction in the war, and providing three dining rooms. It has a big following of comfortably fixed but perhaps not wealthy Americans and is, in general, a successful and advancing hotel. I haven't yet tried it but hope to.

A recommendable European-type hotel of very good quality but not deluxe is the *Ambassador,* on Mozartstrasse half a mile west of the station, a homelike place conveniently reached by motorists and with its own 40-car garage. Its bedrooms, softened by Persian rugs, are equipped with TV and radio and with a "fridge" stocked with drinks ranging from cokes to champagne, plus small goodies to go with them. Milk if desired is also quickly available for kids and grownups. I liked very much my experience in this hotel, finding it an Ambassador of good will. Other hotels in this same general bracket are the very modern and convenient *Königshof,* on Karlsplatz (Stachus), the *Excelsior* (under the same ownership), opposite the main entrance of the station, and the *Deutscher Kaiser,* just north of the station, an 18-story "skyscraper," with dining rooms on the 3rd and 15th floors, the latter with a fine view of the Alps on a clear day. The *Eden-Hotel-Wolff,* just north of the station, is a former doubleton that has now unified itself as a single large hotel, moderate in rates and good. Two hotels in which I have stayed rather inexpensively are the *Bundesbahn Hotel* (Federal Railway Hotel) right *in* the Central Station and the *Drei Löwen* (Three Lions) south of it, at Schillerstrasse 44. Both give good value for their charges, the *Bundesbahn* being perhaps the better of the two because of a newer wing that is really first class. A special type of hotel where I've had an amusing stay, but you might not wish to try it if noise disturbs you badly (I'm impervious to noise), is *Hotel Platzl* opposite the main entrance of the seething Hofbräuhaus (see under restaurants). It has 200 beds, with more to come and rises directly above the roaring Bavarian nightclub called also *Platzl.* The sounds of hilarity penetrate the hotel very lightly though the show may be heard from the bedrooms by turning on a special intercom apparatus. The public rooms are very small and so, indeed, are the bedrooms, but they are compactly designed and many of them are with bath. They are modern, Americanesque, each with radio. And here are a couple of added points: Blankets, instead of the smothering featherbed, may be had at the drop of a hint; and express laundry can be taken care of overnight upon request.

A French-inspired hotel called *Maison Morizet* in the student quarter of Schwabing has caught my eye and I think it could have much appeal for young couples as well as for some older people. This does not mean that the hotel itself swings, for it is a quiet, well-ordered place on a side street (Hohenzollernstrasse 9), with several small dining rooms, its excellent grill being directed by Maître Pierre, a Gallic chef born to gourmetry. The hotel has 150 beds and there's a bath with every room. Each floor is identified by a color and this applies to the carpets, the drapes, the elevator markings and even the tassels on bedroom keys. I recall, for instance, that the second floor is orange, the fourth floor green. Give thought to Maison Morizet, which is certainly different. Finally, three 1971 hotels of very moderate identical rates but all rooms with toilet and showers are the *Imperial,* the *Bellevue* and the *Caravelle,* this in Schwabing. I haven't had a chance to examine them but they "sound good" and are gentle on the wallet.

Among new, large, Americanesque hotels, some are finished,

some are being hustled to completion and some will be too late for the Olympics. Among those already open and flourishing the *Holiday Inn* and the *Esso Motor Hotel* are conspicuous. Holiday Inn is a big place of 400 rooms and 600 beds, one of its talking points being its location at Leopoldstrasse 200, easily found by motorists and within not-too-arduous walking distance of Olympia Park. If you like bigness be advised that the Inn is a three-part affair with the longest lobby in Europe, 243 feet, with carpet of clamorous orange contrasting with overstuffed sofas of blinding blue. The main restaurant is the Sevilla, but there is also a Holiday Grill in Bavarian folk decor, two levels down, and for nightfun a three-level nightclub called the Yellow Submarine. The Swiss restaurant chain called Mövenpick (Möve means full) is part owner of Holiday Inn and runs the food department. Not satisfied with this big inn, Holiday plans to rush through another, of 300 beds, on the motor road Schleissheimerstrasse, to open just before the Olympics.

Esso Motor Hotel, in the trans-Isar residential section of Bogenhausen near the Middle Ring and therefore easily reached by motorists using the Nürnberg or Salzburg autobahn, is Germany's eighth Esso hotel or motel and Europe's fiftieth. I know several of them, in several countries, and I have a genuine liking for their first-class but unshowy style and their comforting way of life. This one has 150 rooms, mostly doubles but with some singles of studio type. Its main dining room is interestingly called the Titurel.

Motel Vitalis, at 24 Kathi-Lobus Strasse, near the southern side of the Oberwiesenfeld, is a first-class 115-room place of Bavarian inspiration that was built in 1964 but is now making many changes to gear itself to the Olympics. It has a pool on the 9th (top) floor and is completing a pleasant new lobby and also a new subterranean restaurant and bar under the parking area, where there's a filling station and car wash. The place may take a bit of finding but gives excellent value when found.

A *Sonesta Hotel,* using the adopted name of all new hotels of the American Hotel Corporation, is under construction and will be a big affair of a dozen or more floors costing some $15 million; and the restaurant chain of Wienerwald is building a hotel of several hundred rooms near the base of the Olympia Turm. Sheraton plans a large hotel but fulfillment will be some time off.

Restaurants of Munich

Bavarian foods are hearty, to say the least, as are the beers, but a good digestion can cope with them and of course there are many fine restaurants serving international dishes and some strongly wine-oriented ones that wouldn't be caught dead serving beer at all. *Garniertes Sauerkraut* is a typical dish, the garnishing consisting often of slabs of pork. *Semmelknödeln,* being stout dumplings, if placed in a plate of soup are so formidable as almost to constitute a meal in themselves. *Spanferkel* is perhaps the most typical of Bavarian dishes, being suckling pig, with fixings. If accompanied by plenty of Bavarian beer and topped off with an *Enzian* liqueur, which is made from the roots of yellow gentians, it can make a very pleasurable meal. Now for certain (nonhotel) restaurants, and I'll start with the two that I like best.

Humplmayr, on Maximilians Platz, is an intimate, elegant, candlelit place of tasteful decor and quiet charm, catering to a sophisticated clientele. It is one of those places where you feel wanted and don't have to wait ten minutes for a waiter to notice that you're there. It is one of those places where the waiter brings a warmed fresh plate for your second helping, a small service but significant. The restaurant provides piano music in its grill and it has developed an upstairs night club for dancing, from 10:30, called the Red Salon.

Schwarzwälder's Natur Weinhaus, on a short street called Hartmannstrasse that leads from Paradeplatz, opposite the Bayerischer Hof, toward the Frauenkirche, is a restaurant of ultravinous type, as you'd guess from its name. The waiter would "try not to notice" if you were to commit the faux pas of asking for beer. It is a three-level restaurant, basement, ground floor and second floor, the last named being your best goal. My mouth waters at this moment as I recall a dish of *Frischer Stangenspargel* (fresh asparagus) *mit Sauce Hollandaise,* plus *gekochte Schinken* (ham) accompanied by a smooth white wine. Don't miss "Blackforester's Nature Winehouse," to more or less translate the name.

Franziskaner Restaurant und Fuchsenstube is a big sprawling beer restaurant, in the very heart of the city, bordered by short Perusastrasse and running for a full block from Theatinerstrasse to Residenzstrasse, with an extremely large terrace section. So popular is it that despite its size I had to wander about on a recent occasion for a good five minutes before I could find a free place to park my weary self. It specializes, of course, on Bavarian fare and its own delicious Franziskaner beer.

The *Ratskeller,* in the "cellar" of the Town Hall, entered from Dienerstrasse, is a sort of all-bracket restaurant, where the waitresses wear black and gold uniforms, the colors of Munich. By all-bracket I simply mean that a businessmen's group may be eating at one table, a bevy of tourists at the next, and then a huddle of young office workers. The food is dependably good despite very moderate charges.

Gistel's Stube Zur Kanne (Jug or Mug), at Maximilianstrasse 30 not far from the Vier Jahreszeiten, caters to theater folk, and nightfolk generally. It consists of six small candlelit rooms whose walls are adorned with theater programs dating back as far as 1837 and it features—or did so on a night when I dined there—*Irish* specialties, including Connemara lobsters flown in from Dublin, and Irish coffee, complete with Irish whisky and a topping of sweet cream, not whipped, as in Austrian cafés. This is a character place of the first order, as you will see if you dine, for example, in the tiny Wagner room. And the food, too, has plenty of character. Herr Gistel, for example, produces a wonderful Salzburger Nockerl, with a caramel sauce, that should make Salzburg itself "sit up and take notice."

Three restaurants of quality near together in the heart of the city are *Boettner,* a seafood specialist in Theatinerstrasse, and two on Residenzstrasse roughly opposite the opera, namely *Ewige Lampe* (Eternal Lamp), catering to late theater crowds, and *Spatenhaus,* a good beer-inspired place accenting Saurbraten and various hearty Bavarian dishes. In this same neighborhood I have spent a wonderful evening in the *Feldherrnkeller,* a wine-oriented cellar restaurant, enlivened by a good combo, *under* the Feldherrnhalle. A friend and I amused ourselves trying to drip the traditional 18 drops from a bottle of wine that we had pleasurably emptied. We did it but had to hold the bottle upside down nearly 18 minutes to get the 18th drop.

A restaurant that I like for its location is the *Peterhof,* on Marienplatz directly opposite the mechanical clock on the soaring Rathaus tower. The *Café Glockenspiel,* on the 5th floor of Number 28, also right across from the clock, has the same advantage and even more closely.

In this same area, in what is historically Munich's oldest house, is the *Weinstadl Restaurant.* You'll find it on Burgstrasse, a short and interesting street that runs north from the eastern edge of Marienplatz.

The historic *Künstlerhaus,* on Lenbach Platz, was a gathering place for artists *(Künstler)* in the late 19th century and then became a goal for all who like to eat well (and rather expensively) in a superior setting, with an open-air garden for use on fine summer days. Mövenpick, of Switzerland, has taken over this restaurant and at first I had some personal apprehension, but I'm told, (*not* by Mövenpick) that it will still be, or perhaps already is when you read these words, a first-class restaurant. I have not yet had an opportunity to test this good news.

Café Luitpold, located at Briennerstrasse 11 amid some of Munich's most luxurious shops, was once called the Café de la Paix of Munich but its glory was shattered by the war. It has since been reborn in a smaller, but really interesting way, for it is a tripleton, Grill, Café and Confiserie (sweets shop) with comfortable counter chairs in one section. I have tried the Grill only, but found it excellent.

Germany's biggest chain of restaurants is *Wienerwald,* born in Munich, with more than 30 links in its native city, 180 in Germany, and almost 400 throughout the world. Ten of them, with more to come, are in New York City, the most conspicuous Manhattan example being in Times Square at 46th St. I've tried them in several countries, their traditional specialty being grilled chicken, and have found them "filling," even if providing no great thrill to one's taste buds. Some, I think, are excellent, others merely nourishing. Schwarzwälder's, about which I have just been reporting so favorably, is owned and operated by Wienerwald.

Among Munich's many huge, smoke-filled beer restaurants, which can be very enjoyable if you're in the mood, are the *Pschorrbräu Bier Hallen,* the *Salvator-Keller,* noted for its *dunkles,* or dark beer, the *Augustiner-Keller,* the *Löwenbräu-Keller,* and so on. To be singled out as a *Sehenswürdigkeit* (a sight worth seeing) is the *Mathäser Bierstadt* (Beer City), an enormous place with several *Stuben* ranging from the proletarian to the aristocratic. This is at Bayerstrasse 5, the busy street adjacent to the station on the South side.

It is inadmissible to leave Munich without having seen and visited that colossus of the people, the Hofbräuhaus, which H. L. Mencken once called "the Parthenon of beer drinking." It was founded in 1589 to sell the beer of the court (Hof) brewery, ducal at that time and later royal. The Hofbräuhaus is unique in my travel experience in that people of many social strata, literally from the lowest to, well, at least upper middle, patronize this three-level beer hall. Its street floor, called the *Schwemme* (horse pond), is an immense, uproarious, often malodorous and incredibly lowbrow beer hall, with a Bavarian band in the center adding all it can to the din. The place is sometimes compared to a fourth-class railway waiting room, of dark memory, but that hardly does its hectic squalor justice. Beer and pretzels are the fare, the beer, light (helles) or dark (dunkles), being drunk only in one-liter steins, just under a quart, and any guest who can't down at least three or four of these is a weakling indeed. Occasionally, after some guests have had their three or four, or five or ten, the squalor of the place isn't too cheerful, for fights can break out and on one visit I saw a dandy.

Upstairs, to raise our level by our own footwork, we find an equally immense and far higher-brow restaurant favored by burghers of modest social brackets.

On the top floor there is a big dance restaurant, with a big band on the stage. The guests here are solid and folksy—everybody dances with anybody—but by no means in the subearthy spirit of the Schwemme. Big commemorative events and dinners sometimes take place on this floor. The Hofbräuhaus can take care of 4000 guests without batting an eye.

Persons with a sense of history may wish to visit a beer hall of sinister overtones, where Hitler hatched his famous Beer Hall Putsch. It is the *Bürgerbräu-Keller,* at Rosenheimer Strasse 29.

Cafés and tearooms are naturally not as abundant as beer halls but there are plenty of them in evidence. Two of the most interesting are *Café am Dom,* on Marienplatz and the *Chinese Tower,* delightfully situated, especially for a summer afternoon, in the refreshing English Garden. The *Kreuzkamm,* on Maffeistrasse, is no upstart, for the house was originally founded in Dresden in 1825, where its owner was appointed pastry chef to the King of Saxony.

Two temples of fine food that we may take out, and I like to compare them with London's famous Fortnum and Mason, are the *Gourmet Restaurant,* on Theatinerstrasse, and *Dallmayr-Haus,* on Dienerstrasse across from the entrance to the Rathauskeller. Surely this extensive establishment is one of the world's most tempting houses of assorted groceries, delicatessen and every possible type of home-grown and foreign delicacy.

All the big department stores, such as Hertie, Oberpollinger, Kaufhof, and Karstadt, have restaurants and/or tearooms. On the top floor of a conspicuous Hertie on Leopoldstrasse, the main stem of Schwabing, reached by two elevators in an enclosure *across the sidewalk* from the big store's entrance, *Spatenbräu* maintains a beer restaurant that is worth the trip to Schwabing *after dark* just to see its view. From its windows you are looking, as if from a low-hovering helicopter, at a veritable firmament of lights, white, red-and-yellow for traffic, and multicolored neon.

Evening Music and Midnight Life

Munich is one of the two or three leading music cities of Germany and there are few evenings when some important events of opera, drama, musical comedy or concert are not offered. It has, again, its own opera house handsomely reconstructed, while the Theater am Gärtnerplatz is used chiefly for operettas. Symphony and other concerts are held in the Congress Hall of the German Museum and in the restored Herkulessaal, which was the former throne room of the Residenz, which was Bavaria's ducal and then royal residency from the 16th to the 19th centuries. The operas of Mozart and Richard Strauss are at home in the Cuvilliès Theater, which is the sparkling jewel of the Residenz. The music calendar of Munich is a full one, with a Bach Festival in June; a Nymphenburg Summer Festival in July, with chamber music in the "Stone Hall" of the main castle; an Opera Festival in midsummer; and glamorous concerts in the baroque castle of Schleissheim, 10 miles north of Munich.

Among nightclubs, one of the best is the one in the cellar of the Buyerischer Hof, which I have previously mentioned. *Eve* is good, expensive and, of course, sexy, and I have heard good words about *Intermezzo* and *Moulin Rouge*.

On the middlebrow side I should emphasize the Bavarian merriment of *Platzl,* alluded to above in connection with Hotel Platzl. You probably won't understand the rich Bavarian dialect and slang of the sketches but you'll shake with laughter anyway at the comedy of it all and you'll love the spirited Bavarian dancing, singing, yodeling, bell ringing and Alpine horn blowing, Munich's counterpart of Innsbruck's Tyrolean Evenings, as you down a Wurst and a stein of beer at one of the tables. And as for the beer, if you are one of a substantial group you may have a small *keg* of beer placed on the table and serve it to your table mates on draught from a tap. The Platzl is relatively inexpensive and very good fun. A real and full Bavarian meal is to be had in Platzl if you wish it.

And then there's *Schwabing* which is something very special, at least for "evening owls." It is a residential portion of the city lying north of the Siegestor, reached by broad Ludwigstrasse, which continues as Leopoldstrasse. This quarter houses some 15,000 of Munich's 24,000 students and student artists and it houses, also, a lot of night life, for young artists and would-be artists seem always to have plenty of night time at their disposal. The student bars and cabarets here are beyond counting and they are always changing, in name, character and location. The life in them before and after midnight is fascinating, being convivial, jam-packed, intimate and not too startlingly sexy. The students are traditionally short of cash and if they can muster money enough for a *Hühner-*

suppe and some beer they're doing pretty well. Schwabing *is* a lot of fun, and if you go there of an evening you will likely find that the students are interested in *you* as an American and will ply you with questions on American life and aims and politics. Some of the sharp questions may even embarrass you if you haven't done your homework lately. In case hunger besets you many restaurants-of-the-night are available in Schwabing.

Among the night restaurants and dance halls patronized by the young in droves are *Drugstore; Città 2000; Dadscha; Bretz'n; Blow Up,* this last, on Elisabethplatz, mobbed nightly by *thousands* of youngsters. Of much gentler nature is *Gisela,* presently flourishing because of its popular singing owner, whose name it bears. Gisela, the German equivalent of the French Giselle, is pronounced with a hard G, and the stress is on the first syllable.

I hear talk of a colossal new entertainment center to be called *Schwabylon,* characterized as "a sort of second Las Vegas." Such a project, to my mind, is something, to paraphrase Churchill's famous quip, "without which Munich could do."

Shops of Munich

Munich is one of the top shopping cities of Germany, aglow with temptations in several quarters. The leading and most extensive sector of luxury shops is the area starting at Lenbachplatz and then Maximilians Platz and its parallel Ottostrasse, this one strong on art shops, extending to Briennerstrasse and along it in both directions. Many of the finest shops are in a large block here called Luitpold Block at the point where Maximilians Platz merges into Briennerstrasse. I have talked with the managers of most of them in this block and in the whole area that it centers, giving them promptly to understand that I am not "the last of the big spenders." Here are some names to note: *J. Bierstorfer,* antique furniture, gold and silver articles; *A. Bauch,* fine furs, also "rainwear"; *Schiessl,* high-grade piece goods, especially silks; *Mädler,* handbags and luggage; *Plaschke,* also with a good variety of handbags, etc.; *L. H. van Hees,* men's clothes, also a maker of men's suits, many (said the manager) for Americans; *Menke,* women's clothes;

Adlmüller, also women's clothes, and, across a courtyard off Briennerstrasse, a *haute couture* section—we've encountered Adlmüller in Vienna; *René Kern,* jewelry; *Söhnges,* optical goods; *Kunstring,* an association of artists on Briennerstrasse; *Meissen-Kunstring,* chinaware (but *Staatliche Porzellan Manufaktur,* a few steps farther on at Odeonplatz 1, is the chief outlet for fine porcelains of Nymphenburg).

There are two big *Werkstätten,* literally workshops, one, *Deutsche Werkstätten* (De We), on Briennerstrasse and the other, *Vereinigte Werkstätten,* on the spacious Wittelsbacher Platz opening from Briennerstrasse. This last especially fascinates me, for it has an abundance of beautiful, *buyable* things on the ground floor, on the 2nd floor, which features fine furniture and is reached by a beautiful double stairway, and on a level below ground where there's a great variety of gifts.

Leaving this deluxe area let's take a look at some scattered eyecatchers in the heart of the city, by which I mean chiefly Theatinerstrasse, with the passages that lead from it, and Residenzstrasse. First of all, I urge you to explore the big 4-floor store called *Lodenfrey* on Muffeistrasse almost at the corner of Theresienstrasse. Loden cloth, as we've seen, is wool, but of a heavier mountain-and-sport nature. *Trachten* (folk costumes), Lederhosen (leather pants) for men and dirndl dresses for women, abound, but there is *much* else, sport clothes, youth clothes, rain clothes, gloves, ties, stockings and pantyhose in all the colors of the rainbow, plus a few that rainbows don't know. Wander up and down in Lodenfrey and be amazed.

Schreibmayr, at Theatinerstrasse 9, has everything that concerns writing, whether by hand or typewriter. *Dietl,* on Residenzstrasse opposite the opera house, is an important store for men's wear; *Henckels,* world famous for its cutlery, has its chief Munich outlet at Weinstrasse 12. *Andreas Huber,* on Rasidenzstrasse next to the Spatenhaus, is a widely known and trusted watchmaker. And finally, have a look at *Küster and Perry,* on one-block Perusastrasse, very near the Olympic Information Center. This is a 2-story shop replete with assorted small gifts in gold plate and silver plate, glass, enamelware, brass, wood, costume jewelry, petit point work, and "you name it." It's the sort of shop where you can really find those nice but not too costly gifts for the home folks. On request the firm will, of course, mail them for you.

14 / THE BAVARIAN ALPS, BLENDING WITH THE AUSTRIAN

LET'S CALL THE ROLL

I can think of no other frontier in the world, unless perhaps in some parts of the Andean mountain chain, where 200 miles of Alps manage to create so friendly a nonbarrier as do the Bavarian Alps as they merge with the Austrian. All the way from Bregenz and Lindau on Lake Constance to Land Salzburg and the outskirts of Salzburg City they are like a row of sentinels on parade, standing 6000 to almost 10,000 feet tall. From west to east the roll call reads: Allgäuer Alpen; Ammer Gebirge; Wetterstein Gebirge (with the Zugspitze, tallest sentinel of them all); Chiemgauer Alpen; Reiteralp Gebirge; Latten Gebirge; and I'll spare you the names of their Austrian counterparts across the nebulous boundary. So casual is the border that in two areas, the Kleinwalsertal and the little resort of Jungholz, Austria leaps the Alps and must be entered through German (Bavarian) soil, since there is no practical way to reach these points except through a technically foreign land. In both cases the villages concerned owe political and tax allegiance to Austria but are economically tied to Germany. Post and police are Austrian, but the money is German, all of which adds a chummy touch to the Alpine scene.

THE ALPINE NAME ROADS—AND A PLAN

The motorist will run into a Bavarian puzzle when he tries to figure out the best design of travel to and through the Bavarian Alps, for the pattern must be made to include so many and such various things, for instance: King Ludwig II's widely scattered castles; the great winter sports center of Garmisch-Partenkirchen, with the Zugspitze; Mittenwald, the violin village; Oberammergau, village of the Passion Play; Tegernsee, lake and resort village, with a lakeside hotel at Rottach-Egern that some consider the best in all the Bavarian Alps (see end-of-chapter roundup); Bad Reichenhall, Bavaria's greatest health spa; Berchtesgaden, with Hitler's Eagle's Nest; and a lot more. I have crisscrossed the whole region by car and train a good half dozen times trying to solve the Bavarian puzzle and I shall attempt to come up with something that makes sense.

The motorist would do well, I think, to make his start in the western part of the Alps, especially if he can tie his plan to the ending of his Vorarlberg touring. He can work his leisurely way east while the railbound traveler must operate in a fanwise pattern, making several out-and-back sorties from Munich's main station. Oberstdorf, Tegernsee, Garmisch-Partenkirchen and Berchtesgaden are all easily reached by rail. In either case the traveler will benefit by a point-by-point itinerary, worked out by one of the Munich travel agencies, or to repeat this name and address from Chapter 13, by the Tourist Association of Munich and Upper Bavaria, at Sonnenstrasse 15, Munich. Renting a self-drive car is almost as easily done as said, both Hertz and Avis (and many other firms) being ever ready. For tours by bus, again consult one of the agencies. American Express and Cook both have central offices, near the Bayerischer Hof. The central starting point for Alpine bus *tours* is on Lenbachplatz.

Bavaria has two important name roads, the *Olympia Strasse,* running from Munich to Garmisch-Partenkirchen, and the *Deutsche Alpenstrasse* (German Alpine Road) running along the whole "upperland" of the Bavarian Alps from Bregenz and Lindau to Berchtesgaden, though some parts of it are not yet finished. To the above highways we should add the so-called *Romantische Strasse* from (Würzburg and) Augsburg through Landsberg (easily reached by Route E 61 from Munich) to Füssen, for Schloss Neuschwanstein, the most spectacular of Ludwig II's castles; and the magnificent *autobahn from Munich to Salzburg,* passing close to the Chiemsee, with Ludwig II's most massive castle, Schloss Herrenchiemsee, on an island in the lake.

The west-to-east plan of tackling Alpine Bavaria, doing it as a touring motorist, not as a tripper using Munich as a base for out-and-back trips, involves, as I see it, at least four full days of roadwork. The *first day* carries through from Bregenz/Lindau to Immenstadt, and then, quitting the Alpine Road, heads due south to Oberstdorf, which is Germany's most southerly market town and one of the most-sought Alpine resorts, a chief center of the Allgäu Alps. Beyond and above (south of) Oberstdorf a run should certainly be made into the cul-de-sac of Kleinwalsertal, which is a geopolitical curiosity, but far more than that, being well worth this extension trip for its own beautiful self. If at all possible a night should be spent in one of the hotels of Kleinwalsertal, or if the better ones there are full, in Oberstdorf.

The *second day* is a long one, which could be broken into two by an overnight halt in Oberammergau *(Hotel Alois Lang; Hotel Wittelsbach; Hotel Alte Post).* It involves returning by the same route to Immenstadt; then driving east on the Alpine Road to Füssen for a visit to the Castle of Neuschwanstein; then north to Steingaden, with a 1½-mile side trip to see the Wieskirche, Bavaria's most remarkable rococo church; then to Oberammergau and a side trip to Linderhof, the mosh remote of Ludwig II's castles; and so to big, sophisticated Garmisch-Partenkirchen and its famous Zugspitze, which, believe it or not, is *owned,* lock, stock and snow peak, by Partenkirchen. Garmisch owns the much lesser Kramerspitze. The night could be spent in simpler but fascinating Mittenwald, or that could be a side trip to start the third day.

The *third day,* after leaving Mittenwald, and making the ascent of the Zugspitze, could be an easy one to the Walchensee, Bad Tölz, a flourishing spa, and the Tegernsee, which is my own favorite lake of them all, with my favorite hotel of all.

The *fourth day* should bring you first to Schliersee; then to, and briefly along the Munich-Salzburg autobahn to Prien on the Chiemsee, halting there to take an excursion steamer from nearby Stock to Herreninsel, for a visit to Ludwig II's Versailles-like Schloss Herrenchiemsee; then return to Prien and drive south by way of Marquartstein and Reit im Winkl to Ruhpolding and thence on a splendidly scenic portion of the Alpenstrasse to the important spa of Bad Reichenhall and then to Berchtesgaden, which is in close touch with the celebrated Königssee, guarded by the hugely towering Watzmann mountain. Good hotels are available both in Bad Reichenhall and Berchtesgaden.

Most, but not all, of the points mentioned above can be reached directly by rail, as I know from having done it—the hard way. But in the Bavarian Alps, of all places in Germany, *a car's the thing* and if touring costs can be split two or three or four ways it reduces them to very modest proportions.

THE CASTLES OF LUDWIG II, A ROYAL EXTRAVAGANZA

The three castles built by Ludwig II of Bavaria are such a composite and such a reflection of the character of the man who built them that I feel they should be presented here as a group, even though they are situated in widely separated settings.

King Ludwig II, of the Wittelsbach line, who acceded to the throne of Bavaria in 1864, was one of the strangest monarchs that ever lived. Madness ran in his family, some 20 of the line having been more or less tainted with it, and his own brother Otto being a hopeless lunatic. There seems far less reason to doubt Ludwig's madness than to doubt Prince Hamlet's, and yet people argue almost as much about the one as about the other. I have read a standard German biography and also that of Jacques Bainville, a Frenchman who reviews the facts impartially, and both do plenty of pro-ing and con-ing, but seem to conclude that the king really was mad and not the victim of evil machinations.

At all events, Ludwig's castles are mad as a hatter—and they are beautiful despite the dictum of Maurice Barrès that they are worthy of a parvenu banker. Their locations are the maddest thing about them, but that is a good part of the secret of their beauty.

To understand the castles even a little one must refresh one's mind on that strange youthful passion of the king for his protégé, Richard Wagner. On Ludwig's 16th birthday he saw for the first time a performance of *Lohengrin* at the Munich Opera House and the fact that the legends of the swan actually centered about the Alpsee, near whose banks his ancestral castle of Hohenschwangau was located, fired the boy's imagination almost to the fever point. The knight of the white armor appeared from *his* lake. *His* castle, Hohen*schwan*gau, was the Swan Castle, with the swan motif in many forms worked into its decorations and furnishings.

From that day the prince, who shortly became king, longed to meet Wagner. The composer likewise longed to meet some king or prince who would befriend him. He was over 50 and utterly discouraged at the bog of mediocrity into which he felt that he was sinking. When Ludwig was 18 the meeting of composer and king took place and a violent attachment sprang up. On Wagner's side it soon settled into a mere affection of expediency, for the king was lavish in his financial aid. But on Ludwig's side it was idolatry. One cannot read the boy king's letters without blushing for him. No lovesick swain ever penned more extravagant phrases to his sweetheart: "My only one," "Unique and dearly loved," "I live for you, for you alone!" "You and God. Till death, till the Kingdom of Shadows." "Let our love burn, flashing forth . . ." One cannot read these phrases (and dozens more) in the letters exhibited in the Ludwig II Museum of Herrenchiemsee without murmuring the irreverent word "tripe," and yet Ludwig's Wagner-complex ran all through his strange life. Even after Munich's burghers, who felt that Wagner exerted a baneful influence on their ruler, forced a separation, and the fires cooled somewhat, the king's weird theatrical outlook on life remained and lashed him on and on to new absurdities, which found their chief expression in castle-building.

Gertrude Atherton wrote of Neuschwanstein, the New Swan Rock, "The white Romanesque castle of Neuschwanstein, on a solitary peak above the old town of Füssen, confronting the ancient brown castle of Hohenschwangau on an opposite peak, lakes between, pine woods surrounding both, and three glittering Alps in the distance, dominates a scene of concentrated beauty equalled nowhere on earth."

This castle was his first great effort, begun when he was 24 and finished—more or less—six months before he died at 40. From countless plans submitted to the king and based to some extent on his momentary interest in France's Château de Pierrefonds, he selected one of the most fantastic, that designed by Herr Jank, decorator of the Munich opera. With its wild profusion of giddy crenelated turrets, its soaring watchtowers and its battlements it could have come, as one commentator has put it, from the pencil of Gustave Doré. Located, by royal command, on a sharp, high rock above the roaring torrent of the River Pöllat, its construction offered enormous difficulties. Twenty million gold marks were poured out on it, and the stream of gold was halted only by the king's death. But it had no toilets!

Ludwig, as his restlessness or madness grew, could not sleep o' nights and used to pace up and down in the frescoed galleries of Neuschwanstein, imagining himself to be Siegfried or Parsifal or perhaps some medieval landgrave. He admitted, even glorified these aberrations. His fancies leading him on, he would leave the castle and gallop rashly through the countryside while normal folks slept. Then, not even yet exhausted enough for sleep, he would command the illumination of his castle. Taking up his stance on a high bridge over the Pöllat, he would watch Neuschwanstein burst into brilliant "flame" with myriads of candles, with Bengal lights and even fireworks. Luminous fountains added their fairylike touch. This bridge over the Pöllat still exists, and like every other tourist, I have stood on it and looked at Neuschwanstein. The effect, even by unromantic daylight, is one of the most astounding one can possibly imagine. Yes, it must be a work of Gustave Doré.

Linderhof, begun the year after Neuschwanstein and actually completed in eight years, is plainly inspired by the Trianon of Versailles. Ludwig had been invited to France by Napoleon III for the Paris Exposition of 1867, and from that date began his passion to emulate Louis XIV. In 1874, almost before the embers of the

Franco-Prussian war had died out, Ludwig, under the name of Count von Berg, made a secret trip to Paris and spent many an hour at Versailles dreaming of the Bavarian Versailles he would create. Linderhof became his Trianon and Herrenchiemsee his grand château.

Linderhof, high up in the Alps where snow covers the ground six months of the year, often difficult of access, was a grotesque defiance of nature. Its formal gardens, inspired by Le Nôtre, its nymphs and cupids condemned to shiver amid icicles and snow, and strangest of all, its stalactite grotto, imitating the Blue Grotto of Capri, proclaim the jumbled qualities of the king's artistic nature. The castle is really very beautiful, the loveliest, by far, of all his mad creations, but in the grotto one sees the parvenu banker at his worst. At one end, behind the barque of Lohengrin, is a great panel which represents the Venusberg. Tannhäuser, surrounded by the Three Graces, a corps of Cupids and many ballet dancers (as in the first act of the opera), lies at the feet of the Goddess of Love. In this setting the king used to partake of his luncheon, seated upon a rock which he called the Lorelei, his viands spread upon a branch of imitation coral.

More than once ambitious women, attracted by the king's romantic manner, his flashing eyes, and his apparent wealth, thought to play the role of Bavarian Pompadour or du Barry, but Ludwig had nothing but scorn for the whole race of women. In his youth he had been betrothed to his charming cousin Sophie, sister of the Austrian empress, and all Munich was agog at thoughts of such a fine match, but Ludwig expected the impossible from Sophie. He wished her to use the phrases he had used toward Wagner, to send him impassioned poems in the middle of the night. Vexed beyond endurance by his eccentricities, the maiden once flung a bowl of water at him and that effectually quenched the royal ardor.

At Linderhof a celebrated *diva* named Fräulein Schefsky begged the king's permission to sing for his pleasure the air of Elsa in the setting of the Blue Grotto. The king was pleased and seated himself, perhaps on the rock Lorelei, while the *diva* stood in the swan boat. In the midst of the song she suddenly pitched forward into the water (2 feet deep) screaming, "Save me, my beloved!" The king beckoned to a footman and said tranquilly, "Take out that woman and have her dried off."

Ludwig's Versailles complex reached ridiculous heights at Linderhof. He dedicated the Yellow Room to Louis XIV's mistresses, a neighboring salon to the same monarch's ministers of state, and most deplorable of all, changed the beautiful name of Linderhof to "Meicost-Ettal." You would never guess the point of this clumsy name, but juggle its letters about and you will get this amazing result: *"L'état, c'est moi."* Thanks to Bavaria's solid citizens, who could not accept such nonsense, this name was long ago dropped into oblivion and Linderhof, dream of loveliness, reemerged.

Herrenchiemsee was begun in the same year that Linderhof was finished, and was to have been another Château de Versailles. Even more than the other castles this one shows the king's growing insanity, for it was insane, surely, to erect such a magnificent palace on a marshy island 60 miles from the capital. Versailles and Potsdam have an obvious excuse for existence, but of what use, queries a French writer, is such a vast palace devoted to the reveries of a solitary monarch "without a court, without admirers, without poets, without mistresses"?

Ludwig sought to outdo the Sun King at his own game. Magnificent enameled peacocks in the vestibule set the tone of the palace, and the lavishness of the interior staggers the beholder of today as it did the taxpayer of Ludwig's day.

Three hundred needleworkers are said to have labored for seven years on the handwork of Herrenchiemsee. The curtains are so heavy with gold and silver embroidery that it takes two men to draw them. The purple and gold bedroom, with its jeweled bed (which Ludwig occupied only a score of times), is said to have cost over $500,000, which would be millions in today's dollars. The ballroom, used only once, the Gallery of Mirrors, surpassing in every way that of Versailles, the genuine and costly woodwork and furniture all testify to the king's growing frenzy.

All this was of, by and for the king himself. He became more and more a recluse until he would see no one but his hairdresser, his major-domo and a few of his servants. He refused to see even his ministers except when he had to have money. Bavaria, exhausted by taxes and fearing hopeless bankruptcy, finally declared its sovereign officially mad. A committee of Munich doctors entered the king's apartments at Neuschwanstein and made a farcical examination, in which the king made a disconcerting show of sanity. Nevertheless, they declared that he was mad "for a year at least," since his Uncle Luitpold had already assumed the regency, and this could not be done constitutionally unless the ruler was incapacitated for a year. This cruel sophistry seemed to break the king's resistance as well as his heart. He went peaceably with his captors to Schloss Berg on the Starnberg Lake, where he had lived at the time of his courtship of Duchess Sophie. At dusk on the following day, which was Whitsunday, June 13, 1886, the captive king, still a young man of 40, went for a quiet walk in the castle gardens with one of his guardians, Dr. Gudden. They did not come back and finally another doctor, named Müller, sent out searchers for them. The search grew frantic. At last, late in the evening, the king's umbrella, hat, overcoat and jacket were found on the lake edge and the two bodies not far away, that of the doctor face down in the water at the very edge, that of the king in less than 3 feet of water. There were evidences of a terrible struggle and it would seem that Ludwig caused Gudden's death not as a planned murder but in order to free himself from the other's restraint so that he might take his own life. An impressive cross in the lake now marks the exact spot where the body of the king was found.

At Ludwig's funeral veritable mountains of flowers surrounded the royal coffin and women wept for their "virgin king." Bavarians have a strange, indestructible affection for the ruler who nearly brought them to ruin and whose mad castles now net them, from admission fees, a very handsome annual revenue. The affection seems not at all venal, however, as the above note might imply, but rather in the nature of a personal devotion to the last of the feudal monarchs. When one tosses off a stein of beer in some Munich *Bierhalle* one is likely to discover at the bottom of the stein a small picture, and this picture will display either the jolly little form of the Münchner Kindl or the Adonis face and flashing eyes of Ludwig II.

THE ALPS—WESTERN PART

Oberstdorf; Kleinwalsertal; Neuschwanstein

Oberstdorf, Germany's "farthest south," lies in a wonderful *cirque* of towering Allgäu Alps and is a holiday dream both summer and winter. As a practical note I may say that in summer there is always plenty of space in the hotels and in winter there may be —none, for it is one of the most famous winter sports resorts in all the Alps. Part of its fame in this respect rests on the fact that it has one of the four highest ski jump platforms in the world, the others being in Mitterndorf, Styria (see Chapter 4), Planica in Yugoslavia and Vikesund in Norway. Oberstdorf's *Skiflugschanze* looms a frightening 540 feet in the air, which is about 13 feet higher than the world's tallest church spire—at Ulm!

I have seen Oberstdorf both in deep-snow winter and in high summer. One of its summer charms consists of peaceful valley lanes from which motor vehicles are excluded, though not horse-drawn vehicles. No less than seven little valleys, each with its chattering brook and each with its good resort inns, converge here to form the headwaters of the Iller, a Danube tributary, and on at least four of them you may walk without thought of cars, motorcycles or the impudent scooters so common in Europe. One of the best of these walks is along the *Bergsautal* beyond the *Freibergsee* (with its terrace restaurant), which can be reached by a short bus trip. Incidentally, this lane leads past the giant Skiflugschanze.

I have mentioned above that delightful curiosity of this section of the Allgäu Alps, the *Kleinwalsertal.* This upland valley is Austrian territory but separated from the Vorarlbertg section of its motherland by mountains that are quite untraversable by the ordinary resident and visitor, though one or two rough trails can be negotiated by expert mountaineers. This little valley, however, only 9 miles long, is by no means a lost one for it has a very brisk tourist trade. It is tied in economically with Germany, by its inclusion in the German customs union and its use of German currency, all of which means, for visitors, a wide-open frontier. There are four villages in this Austrian valley, in this ascending order of altitude:

Riezlern (3666 feet), the chief village; *Hirschegg* (3866 feet); *Mittelberg* (4060 feet); and the hamlet of Baad (4166 feet). German folders of the region refer to the location of Baad as "im Talschluss" (in the valley end) and that it certainly is, for here the road ends abruptly and the hamlet is shut in by the 8300-foot Widderstein as by a stone slab erected by titans.

Some curious facts and figures about this valley are worth setting down, in part repeating. Its residents, being Austrian citizens, pay taxes to Austria, but their currency is German marks, and on products bought in their homeland and brought to the valley they have to pay taxes to Germany. The postage stamps are Austrian, but you pay in marks and pfennigs. Both countries have *inland* phone rates, and every phone in the valley has two numbers, a German and an Austrian. If a crime is committed and the guilty person caught, he cannot be taken to court through Germany but must be flown by helicopter to Bregenz, the capital of the province (Vorarlberg) of which the valley is a part, there to await trial. Kleinwalsertal has but one mayor for the entire valley, and it has but one industry, the manufacture of a facial cream, or perhaps it's a sunburn cream, called Pizbuin. You see it advertised everywhere in Austria.

The lift equipment of Kleinwalsertal is surprising, for there are 2 suspension cableways, 2 chairlifts and 24 skilifts. There are 8 ski schools, plus 1 bobsleigh school. *Pferdeschlitten,* which is horse-drawn tobogganing, is popular, as is skiwalking on special courses. For regular walking there are 100 miles of good and well-marked trails, and for those who can stay awhile there is a system of graduated walks, climbs and physical exercises, under medical controls, with honors for all as they gain proficiency—and health, this whole interesting system, in 20 advancing stages, being designated *Vita-Parcours.* For relaxation there are ten indoor pools in the hotels, plus two heated outdoor public pools. Perhaps you think Kleinwalsertal pulls up the covers and goes to sleep at 9 P.M., but this is far from the case, for it has a surprising evening life, spurred by many musical groups. This little valley is quite a lively number.

Füssen (Tourist Office: Kurverwaltung, Reichenstrasse 9), the terminus of the Romantische Strasse and a key point of the Alpine Road, is the chief castle town of the Wittelsbach dynasty, for here is *Schloss Hohenschwangau,* built for Maximilian II, the king who preceded Ludwig II, and on a rocky knoll above it Ludwig's own fantastic *Schloss Neuschwanstein,* which has been described in the Castle section above. Both castles admit visitors for guided tours of the interior, each tour consuming nearly or fully an hour. Motorcars are not allowed to mount to the newer castle and it takes about half an hour to reach it by an easy walk, mostly climbing. Neuschwanstein cost, as I have said, 20 million marks and the king was about to make some embellishments that would have cost 6 million more when he was deposed. He had had only 100 days (Napoleon must sympathize) to enjoy his "Swanstone" home in its completion, and the pathos of it is evident to every visitor, for this was Ludwig's shrine to Lohengrin and one sees the swan motif and the Wagner-worship everywhere in the castle's paintings and decorations. Even the water jug in the royal bedroom emptied its water into the royal silver washbowl through a swan's neck and bill!

THE ALPS—CENTRAL PART

The Wieskirche; Oberammergau; Linderhof; Garmisch; Zugspitze; Mittenwald

A little way north of Füssen on the Romantic Road, as outlined in the general itinerary, you come to *Steingaden,* where you should turn sharply east to reach the *Wieskirche* (by a short run on a side road) and then *Rottenbuch.* The first and last of these three little places have famous churches, a Romanesque minster in Steingaden a 15th-century convent church in Rottenbuch, but the Wieskirche *is* a church and *one of the finest rococo masterpieces,* religious or secular, in all Germany. It is modestly plain on the outside, but once you enter it you are bound to expand if you have any liking for this riotous style, for it is wonderfully *luminous.* The vestibule is shaped in a sort of crescent and the big nave in an oval and all of it is painted white with lavish gold trim. Even the big organ at the west end is white and gold. This "Pilgrim Church in the

Meadow" (Wiese), to give its full name, was the masterpiece of an 18th-century genius named Dominikus Zimmermann. So dedicated was he to his task that he spent eight years achieving it and then ten more, the rest of his life, living in a nearby house watching over the church.

Oberammergau is only 14 miles from the point on the main route reached, in 3 miles, from the Meadow Church. Once every ten years, on the dates that end with a zero, the villagers give their famous Passion play and then the world looks at Oberammergau and visits this Alpine village in hundreds of thousands—over half a million came last time—but out of season, and on the nine lean summers, the village cuts itself down to size as a community of woodcarvers and as a pleasant, biseasonal recreational resort. Cynics have said, and will continue to say, that Oberammergau puts on its decennial play solely to make a pile of money, but after three visits to the village when nothing was going on I am convinced that it is singularly free of commercialism.

I have made a stay there in midwinter, when deep snow blanketed the village, in spring, when the trees were beginning to bud, and again in late September, after the tourist season. I have talked with the Christus, as everyone does, and I have bought some picnic makings from Mary and Lazarus. I have spent a wonderful hour with Judas, and have been served a bumper of *helles* by one of the Disciples. The little contacts of village life are so simple and natural that it is impossible to think of these people as scheming for gain and gloating over fat profits. Even Judas, despite his sedulously cultivated black beard and capacity for crafty looks, can scarcely be thought of as jingling 30 pieces of silver in his hand, for it is a well-known tradition in the village that the man selected for the part of Judas must be above reproach in every way.

The picture of a noon luncheon hour spent in Oberammergau's main square lingers in my mind as typical of the place. To the accompaniment of a drum very busily but not very rhythmically beaten, a troop of dancing bears entered the square. I was lunching at a sidewalk table of one of the hotels and the bears came up and danced for me. Youngsters suddenly came running from all directions to watch the fun. A man wearing a wondrous virgin beard and a house-painter's smock rode up on a bicycle and joined the crowd, and then a little man whom I set down as Zacchaeus because he climed up on a trellis to watch the bears. A rare flash of memory recalled to me that "Zacchaeus, he did climb a tree, in order his dear Lord to see." My waitress, on the other hand, didn't seem to think the bears worth looking at. She was "cumbered with much serving" and I set her down as Martha, the sister of Lazarus.

Except for this busy "Martha," all Oberammergau riveted its attention on those clumsy, shuffling brown bears. Apostles, saints and martyrs mingled in the crowd with publicans and sinners, Pharisees and Sadducees with despised tax-gatherers. For all I knew, Nicodemus may have been present, and Barabbas the robber, and old Simeon "waiting for the consolation of Israel." Perhaps the "woman taken in adultery" was there, too, for some pious and devoted Frau must play even that part. To me the crowd was fascinating, and I only gave the bears an occasional glance. One can, after all, see bears in any zoo, but only in this lovely valley of the Upper Ammer can one see the street crowd of old Judea.

The mere facts and statistics of the Passion play constitute some sort of a record, I think, in human endeavor. It is the result of a vow made in 1633, at the time of the Black Plague. In the childlike, bargaining spirit of that period the villagers made a pledge that if the plague should be lifted they would give a play of the life and passion of Christ every ten years. The plague did quickly pass and they have kept their pledge ever since, except during World War II when it was impossible. The cast numbers about 1400 players, including 250 children, and about 125 of them have speaking parts. Only born Oberammergauers may participate. The adult female parts, with the exception of Mary, must all be taken by married women, but Mary must be a virgin and above suspicion of any blemish. She may not be over 35 years old. The play lasts all day, with a morning session from 8 to 12 and an afternoon session from 2 to 6, and there are 40 changes of scenery. It is given about 86 times and in each performance the Christ must hang on the cross for 22 minutes. The Passion-play house, seating 5200 persons, is covered by an enormous arched roof without view-obstructing pillars, but the stage is open to the sky, which forms a lovely natural background, enhanced by wooded hills. The play takes place rain or shine. The principals all have spare costumes into which they can change but if the stage crowds and extras get wet they just get wet. There are large costume rooms and prop rooms and below the stage there is a stable for the play's horses and asses. This simple but wonderfully complete and effective play house is used only for the play (and certain lesser productions in intervening years, such as Bach's *St. Matthew Passion*). For ordinary needs there is an *Übungstheater,* or Practice Theater, where tryouts for the parts are held.

Oberammergau, play or no play, is a place not to be missed. It is lovely just as an upland village, with the tiny River Laine flowing briskly through the center, and it is near many things of holiday importance.

Schloss Linderhof, another of Ludwig II's prodigal castles, has been presented above. It lies only 7 miles from Oberammergau by a fine stretch of the Alpenstrasse and the drive would be worth while even if there were no special goal to seek.

The *formal gardens* of Linderhof are as sightly as the rococo castle and they make a striking contrast in their frame of wild, dramatic scenery. Directly in front of the broad steps leading to the castle doors is a fountain that spurts aloft 105 feet in a single column of water and at its base, taking a perpetual showerbath, is a glittering golden Flora, enjoying herself without benefit of bikini. The royal taste went berserk in these extensive gardens, for in addition to the expected and numerous statues, several more fountains, a pretentious cascade, a Venus Temple, a Königshäuschen (Royal Hunting Lodge) and the absurd Blue Grotto mentioned earlier, there is, of all things, an elaborate Moorish Kiosk. This was built for a Bohemian nobleman and was exhibited in the Paris World Exposition of 1867 where Ludwig saw it, fancied it and bought it. It fits into the rococo ensemble of Linderhof about as aptly as a jukebox would fit into the Parthenon.

Garmisch-Partenkirchen (tourist office adjacent to the railway station) is a double star of tourism and of winter sports. In the former department it has several luxury hotels and many good ones, a *Spielbank* (casino) in its own new building, an unsurpassed array of available excursions and—the Zugspitze, highest mountain in Germany (9732 feet), which one ascends either by a swift cableway or by a cogwheel railway, recently much improved, that is a wonder of engineering. Both means will be discussed below, and perhaps I can sneak in mention here of a new cableway, the *Hausbergbahn,* this to a different peak, with a cabin that holds 80 passengers, claimed to be the largest swing-cabin in Europe.

In the department of winter sports this two-part resort is preeminent, quite equal in fame and facilities to Switzerland's St. Moritz. Its International Winter Sports Week draws the world's best skaters, skiers, and bobsledders. Its Olympic Ice Stadium, with a fascinating ice museum, seats 12,000 spectators and its separate Olympic Ski Stadium, into which a huge ski jump actually "debouches," seats 30,000. With various toboggan runs, including the Olympic Bob Run, with sleigh runs galore, with ski jumps both for novices and experts and ski runs of every type and gradient and with plenty of skilifts in the neighborhood, this is incontestably the leading winter sports center of Germany, even though its altitude is only 2360 feet. Meteorologists say that winter snow is assured because of special meteorological conditions, making altitude a lesser factor. And of course there are innumerable high spots for skiing, many of them reached by lifts.

The ascent of the Zugspitze by rail is in a class by itself in German mountain railways and is fully comparable to the Swiss railway up to the Jungfraujoch. Garmisch is the takeoff point, the train proceeding first by ordinary traction (20 minutes) to Grainau, and from there by rack-and-pinion (in 45 minutes, which used to be 90 until mechanical advances were recently achieved) on an 11-mile climb to a hotel up aloft called *Schneefernerhaus,* a cheerful and *warm* hotel (140 beds) at an elevation of 8700 feet. From that point a cableway lifts you, in five minutes, to the very summit, more than 1000 feet higher. From this summit you climb up to a view terrace and your feet will feel like stumps of lead while your heart pounds as if you had just finished running a four-minute mile. *Go easy* on this foot climb and don't go to this altitude at all if there is doubt about the soundness of your heart.

The view from the terrace, if the clouds don't blot it out, will take away what breath you have left, if any. In case you have any qualms about going to so great a height, you may take the cog railway only as far as Eibsee, at the modest altitude of 3200 feet, and the view is *plenty good* from that lake-in-the-mountains. There is a pleasant restaurant there, the *Eibsee Alm Café,* where a hungry man's lunch is available.

Since 1963 there has been a fast-climbing cableway from Eibsee to the Zugspitze summit—9 kilometers (5½ miles)—at the speed of 10 meters (36 feet) per second, making the whole ascent in 9 minutes. Each cabin of the cableway carries 45 passengers. This is a big time-saver and it provides a succession of superlative views, but the comfort of the railway still appeals to many even though most of the trip is through a tunnel. As you ascend in the tunnel you see markers showing when you reach and pass levels of the Rigi (Lake Lucerne's famous mountain); St. Moritz; Arosa; and the Simplon Hospiz. Still in the tunnel, up aloft, you see the casual sign—*Nach Tirol* (To the Tyrol)—indicating the pedestrian tunnel to Austria.

But let's recapitulate and hold a thought for the cogwheel railway, which is truly a spectacular marvel. Above Eibsee it enters a 3-mile tunnel, the longest, at any level, in Germany, and all the creeping minutes you are in the mountain the trail toils up and ever up. A little English boy seated behind me on one ascent inquired of his mother, "I say, mummy, how did they build this tunnel, with a *shovel?*"

At the Schneefernerhaus there is a delightful sky restaurant finished in a cheerful light wood, a bar and a winter garden—for your siesta. How thrice welcome these three features are. Not far from the restaurant is the entrance to the half-mile pedestrian tunnel (see final section of "Seven Gates to Austria" in Chapter 1) through the Zugspitze to an *Austrian* shoulder of the mountain called the Zugspitzkamm. From the Austrian side you may descend by a swiftly moving aerial cableway to the village of Obermoos, proceed thence by bus to a station on the railway line tying Reutte (in Austria) to Garmisch and so return to your starting point. This up-and-over round trip can be an experience without close parallel elsewhere in Europe.

Mittenwald (Tourist Office: Dammkarstrasse 3), reached from Garmisch-Partenkirchen by a splendid motorway named Karwendel-Panorama-Strasse, is a small market town (population 8600), almost on the German-Austrian frontier. It is a dreamer's picture of what a Bavarian Alpine community ought to look like. Hundreds of its gaily frescoed houses, with their overhanging eaves, are collector's items, and here photography fans click their shutters "like crazy" at every step. In the front yard of the village rises a mountain massif, the Karwendel (reached in 8 minutes by a suspension 35-passenger-cabin cableway) that is overpowering in its effect, and in the back yard rises the Wetterstein, a little less imposing but still marvelous. Mittenwald itself lies in a verdant, forest-girt valley, that of the baby Isar, which is "rolling rapidly" even here; and as a matter of history, the town owes much of its early prosperity to this stream, which made possible the development of an important logging industry. Logs could be felled in the abundant forests and floated down the Isar clear to Munich. But for all its special enchantment to the eye, Mittenwald would be just another Alpine resort were it not for—violins.

On June 11, 1653, Sophie, wife of Urban Klotz, respected tailor of Mittenwald, gave birth to a son. The happy parents named the boy Matthias and when he was ten years old they apprenticed him to a violinmaker. Young Matthias went, in due course, to Cremona, Italy, where he is said to have studied for years with Stradivarius and Nicolò Amati. It is thought that he also had a period of apprenticeship with the celebrated Stainer, near Innsbruck, and in the fullness of his skill he returned to his little mountain village and established the industry that has brought it fame. He lived for 90 years (1653–1743). His statue, with a violin on his knee, now stands in the place of honor before the village church, and some of his lineal descendants still carry on the ancestral business in Mittenwald.

To the lower slopes of both mountains named above cling the white pine and maple forests that made possible the fruition of Matthias Klotz's idea, for these two woods, with a little ebony for the pegs, are the perfect materials for perfect violins. The tops are made of pine, the bottoms and necks of maple.

My first visit to Mittenwald, many years ago, was made about noon of a winter's day, and I shall never forget the first impressions it registered upon me. After having my senses blown to fragments by the scenery, I collected enough of the remains to inquire the location of the Bavarian State School of Violinmaking. I soon found it, and found also a forbidding placard stating that the school was temporarily closed and that the director must not be disturbed except on Tuesday, between 10 and 12. It was then Wednesday, between 12 and 1, and I was only 25 hours late so I rang the bell and the director himself came to the gate. He cheerfully let me in and showed me the entire school.

His manner was resigned, but his story was a sad one. In better days, he said, Mittenwald used to make 15,000 to 20,000 violins a year—every one by hand—and most of them were exported to America. But of late, machine-made fiddles (he tried to keep the sneer out of his tone) had ruined everything. Mittenwald, he said, cannot bring itself to carry on the fight by using mere machines, so it has taken refuge in making limited numbers of only the choicest violins. Whereas factory-made instruments can be mass-produced to sell for $5 to $10 apiece, a master violin, such as the Guarnerius copies that come from the workshop of Herr Johann Reiter, one of the best makers in the village, takes 300 working hours to complete and cannot be sold for less than $600 to $800. The inevitable result is that the output of this mountain village has shrunk almost to nothing—"perhaps two hundred and fifty a year," said the director mournfully.

The violin is among the most personal of instruments. An artist *loves* his violin and looks upon machine-made violins as a breed of unnatural monsters that should be exterminated. "Let the streamlined factories," he says, "turn their attention to saxophones, accordions and drums."

In the storage room of the school the conversation became more cheerful. The director showed me great piles of pine and maple which would some day—God willing—be violins. The pine must be dried for at least 15 years and 30 or 40 years is better. Then it has an extraordinary ring. Tap it sharply with your finger and it gives out a tone as sustained and mellow as a distant bell across some Alpine lake.

He took me, later, to the shop of Johann Reiter himself, who received me as cordially as had the director. He explained to me in detail the three main types of violins which are "built" (the German word is *bauen*). Strads, he said, and Guarneri, have a tone that is *energisch,* like the clarinet; Amatis are soft, like flutes; and Stainers still softer, something like an oboe. He played all three types for me, beautifully, and then, to my no little astonishment and embarrassment, passed them to me to try, assuming, I suppose, that everyone must play a little. I do, as it happens, play a little, or used to, but I will draw a veil over my performance on this occasion, though the kindly old liar said I did very well. To close this rambling report with a more helpful and specific note, let me say that the *Geigenbauschule* (Violin-building School) is at present open to visitors on Tuesday and Friday mornings from 11 to 11:45. The enrollment averages about thirty and at the moment two Americans are among the students. Complementing the school is a Violinmaking Museum showing the evolution of the industry for some three centuries. For one more violin note let me call to your attention that the German 20-mark bill displays a still-life scene in which a violin is prominent, surely in part a tribute to Mittenwald.

THE ALPS—EASTERN PART

Tegernsee; Herrenchiemsee; Bad Reichenhall; Berchtesgaden

The climax of the eastern Bavarian Alps is Berchtesgaden, with the Königssee and Hitler's Eagle's Nest as "feature attractions," and to reach this heart there are many possible routes, all interesting, but for simplicity's sake I will suggest as guideposts Bad Tölz; the circuit of Tegernsee; Schliersee; Miesbach to the Munich-Salzburg autobahn; south shore of the Chiemsee; Reit im Winkl; Bad Reichenhall; and Berchtesgaden.

The *Alpenstrasse* can be used to reach *Bad Tölz,* a big spa known for its iodine springs (*Badhotel Jodquellen,* with iodine water piped into its bedroom baths), and we shall pick it up again later.

From Bad Tölz go due east, starting on Route 472 and then drive clear around the Tegernsee west side, south side, east side, reaching the three lakeside villages of Bad Wiessee, Rottach-Egern and Tegernsee. The first two are of interest chiefly for their hotels (see chapter roundup), but Tegernsee, both village and lake, are special.

Tegernsee, the lake—now hear this, all ecology-conscious youngsters and not-so-youngsters—was the first lake in Germany, and so far as I know, in Europe, to be wholly surrounded by *Kanalismus,* which is to say protective canalization. The job took ten years, was completed in 1966 and cost 20 million DM. Since 1966 not one drop of polluted water or other polluted matter can enter the lake. This was a pioneer achievement to write home about. Other lakes will follow Tegernsee's example and I understand that similar canalizations are even now going forward to surround Starnberger See and Chiemsee.

Tegernsee town is of very ancient vintage and perhaps you remember (from Chapter 13) that monks from Tegernsee were the actual founders of Munich. The Benedictine abbey from which they came was founded in 711 and is still right there, though times have changed and the abbey with them. It is now called a Schloss and it is in three parts. The part adjacent to the lake is a high school; the middle part is a church of the former abbey; and the part farthest in from the lake is the *Brauhaus Tegernsee,* where Tegernsee beer has been made for centuries and is still made. In fact, this part contains a *Bräustüberl* where you and I, tired from driving or walking, may settle down for a good stein of the local product, which I, for one, find a very good beer.

Tegernsee as a lake resort has all that could be desired, including lovely *Seeanlagen* (lake gardens and promenades), a fine Kurhaus, with pleasant reading room, and all facilities for summer and winter sports, music and entertainment. It has, also, something very much its own, namely the Museum of the Works of Olaf Gulbransson, world known in his day, before and after World War I, as Germany's greatest caricaturist. This Norseman, for such he was, cut a most unusual figure, as I know from having had the good fortune to spend an evening in his home above Tegernsee some 35 years ago. He wore sheepskin pants and that's all. He married a relative of the great Norwegian novelist-poet-dramatist Björnstjerne Björnson, whose granddaughter is now the curator of the museum. Two modernistic churches in Rottach-Egern and Schliersee were designed by Olaf Gulbransson, Jr., a gifted young architect who, however, was tragically killed in an auto accident on the Munich-Salzburg autobahn. The museum of the senior Gulbransson will delight you if you have any interest in clever caricatures. In any case it is a cheerful shrine of art worth seeing.

Upon reaching the Munich-Salzburg autobahn from Tegernsee and Schliersee either by the easy way via Miesbach and Route 472, or by a much more complicated but scenically beautiful route via Bayrischzell and the Sudelfeld Pass, you turn east on the autobahn for a short stretch to *Bernau,* from which point a tangent trip may be made to *Prien* for a visit to *Schloss Herrenchiemsee.*

The interlude for Herrenchiemsee seems to me a must. From Stock, a tiny lake port only a little over a mile from Prien, there is a steamer service, frequent in summer, to the *Herreninsel,* on which island Schloss Herrenchiemsee stands. This castle has been described, or briefly sketched, earlier in this chapter, but I did not mention the *candlelight concerts of chamber music,* chiefly Mozart, that are given in the Hall of Mirrors on Saturday evenings in summer. Of all such castle concerts in Germany, and there are many of them, none, I think, can match these in glamour. About 4000 candles are lighted by a corps of some 50 servants. To effect this lighting, huge candelabras suspended on cables are slowly lowered and then raised again. The whole process consumes about 40 minutes and this ceremony is a spectacle in itself. (Special excursion busses leave Munich, from Lenbachplatz, on Saturdays at 2 P.M. and concert tickets may be secured in advance through the American Express Company. Daytime visits to the Schloss, under guidance, take about three quarters of an hour.)

Returning from the island to Prien and then Bernau, you promptly quit the autobahn and head south, through *Marquartstein,* to rejoin the Alpenstrasse and follow that dramatic highway through the picture village of Reit im Winkl (meaning Reit in the

Corner) to *Bad Reichenhall* and Berchtesgaden, as earlier outlined.

Another way to reach the same climactic goal could lead you by the autobahn to the very edge of Austria and then due south to Berchtesgaden by way of Bad Reichenhall. This is an extremely important spa, perhaps Bavaria's greatest (60,000 visitors a year), with a famous spa-hotel, *Grand-Hotel Axelmannstein,* enlarged and renewed in 1970–71, that was once a medieval castle and was metamorphosed in 1848. Two large brine springs, which visitors are shown beneath the *Quellenbau* (Spring House), gush 40,000 gallons a day of water with 24 per cent salt content, and another salty sight is the *Gradierhalle* (Refining Hall), where water drips abundantly down a screen of twigs 50 feet high. Strollers walk back and forth past this screen sniffing its health-giving salinity. It goes without saying that Bad Reichenhall has a lovely Kurpark, a Kurhaus, a Trinkhalle and all the other amenities and pleasures of a big watering place. It also has, in its immediate environs, the spectacular *Predigtstuhl* (Pulpit), a mile-high mountain cliff with viewpoint, reached from the valley in ten minutes by a cableway. The comfortable and fully equipped *Berghotel* on its summit has a big glass view-terrace whose windows are quickly openable at the sun's invitation and from this sheltering inn some marvelously scenic walks may be taken.

Berchtesgaden, as you may see on any map of Germany, lies in a pocket at the extreme southeastern tip of the Bavarian Alps. It is a *district* as well as a market town, for no less than 11 villages work together to cater to the immense tourist traffic, 300,000 visitors annually, on which it chiefly lives. These 11 villages can accommodate 24,000 persons on big summer influxes, 16,000 of them in hotels and pensions, the rest in private homes.

Berchtesgaden is the takeoff point for four very special excursions, which I shall list in the ascending order of their appeal to most visitors, though it is risky to attempt any grading of such wonders.

The *Jennerbahn* is a cableway of fascinating type that lifts you, in 22 minutes, to a 6000-foot mountain shoulder which is a superb belvedere in summer and a skier's paradise in winter. The cableway consists, in summer, of a series of suspended double chairs, roofed against rain, that go up to the mountain and down again on an ever-moving cable, and in winter, of similarly suspended Plexiglas cabins, each built for two.

The *Salzbergwerk,* or Salt Mine of Berchtesgaden, reached by a 20-minute walk, lies about a mile to the northeast of the center. As at Hallstatt (see Chapter 10) guests are conducted into the Salt Mountain in groups for a one-hour tour, each guest being provided with a protective cloak, slacks and a hat against dripping brine, and against the chill, too, for the "inside" temperature is an unvarying 54 degrees. Part of the tour is made on a miniature tram that penetrates deep within a salt tunnel, part of it on a wooden chute by which you are catapulted, toboggan style, to a lower level and part of it on a boat that is rowed around a salt lake within the mountain. This immense mine, which produces two-thirds of all Bavaria's salt, has been worked for nearly five centuries. The salt rock or rock salt is dissolved in water to form brine and is then pumped 64 miles to Bad Reichenhall and Rosenheim, where the refining is done.

The *Königssee* is Bavaria's finest treasure in lake scenery and it would be fair to say that no lake *anywhere* surpasses it in beauty and awesome grandeur. It is 5 miles long, 1¼ miles wide and its greatest depth is just over 600 feet, but statistics reveal nothing of its magnificence. It is like an inland fjord of clear, bottle-green water filling a gash amid mighty mountains.

A tourist village at the northern tip, with its hotels, restaurants, boathouses and bathing beach, is a part of the Berchtesgaden complex. It centers a lively summer-sport and winter-sport area that includes a *Rodelbahn* (bobsled run) that is said to be unique in that it operates on artificial ice. It is nearly a twisting mile long (a shorter run is available for women) and has two roles, being both a bobsled school and a facility, much used, for European and world competitions. For practice runs in summer learners may use a "wheeled bobsled" on the Rodelbahn.

From the tourist village you may set out on the lake in a motor launch that slips quietly through the water with no putt-putt to disturb the silence. Tourist chatter does, however, disturb the silence too much and too loudly, for such majesty as this seems to call for respectful whispers, if one must talk. Perhaps you'll wish to escape the chatter by hiring a rowboat, which can very easily be done on an hourly basis. The boats are usually rowed by two boatmen and they can accommodate up to four passengers. But you'll need at least three hours for a rowboat trip even as far as the historic pilgrim chapel of *St. Bartholomä* and back. The launches do this round trip in half an hour, or the whole lake circuit in less than one hour.

The excursion by launch passes, within a few minutes, a small red cross on the western shore that marks the site of a grim tragedy. Here, on August 24, 1688, a boat containing some 60 Austrian pilgrims was caught by a sudden freak gale and driven against the sheer cliff of the Falkensteinwand. All of the pilgrims were drowned. The August 24 pilgrimage still occurs annually and Austrian pilgrims often include a commemorative halt beside the red cross. As we pass the Falkensteinwand, which juts out into the water, we begin to see the full sweep of the lake. The launch continues to Kessel, on the east bank, and to St. Bartholomä, on the west bank, where passengers usually disembark for a stroll and perhaps for refreshments in the little café back of the chapel, returning by a later launch.

St. Bartholomä lies on a lustrous green delta backed by towering mountains that include the famous *Watzmann*. This looms up to a height of 8901 feet, which is 6025 feet above the lake! Its sheer East Wall, facing toward the lake, is a rock face of staggering magnitude. So formidable a mountain needs a family and Berchtesgadeners assert that the Watzmann is indeed a paterfamilias, having a wife and seven children, namely "sechs Buben und ein Mädl," six boys and a girl. From some points you can see the whole family of peaks.

The fauna of the Königssee and its surroundings are of extraordinary interest, for they include fresh-water salmon weighing up to 115 pounds, wild deer, which come in large numbers to be fed by men at a point on the east bank, and chamois and eagles. Between the two last-named species an intermittent hot war rages, for hunters have actually seen eagles swoop down and try to knock 50 pound chamois off their rocky footholds, hoping that their prey will be killed by the fall and provide luscious repasts. A *successful* attack of this kind has never yet been witnessed, for the chamois are very sure-footed and their rubbery feet can cling to the rock as if bolted there. There are very few eagle families in the whole Berchtesgaden area, but in the past there were many more. One year they became a real pest, swooping down to pick up chickens and even kittens in their talons.

The *Kehlstein,* where Hitler planned to while away happy hours with Eva Braun, but didn't actually manage it more than half a dozen times in all, is commonly dubbed the Führer's Eagle's Nest. It is one of the most-sought tourist goals in the Bavarian Alps, partly for its grand self, as a mountain belvedere, and partly for its grisly associations with Hitler. To reach it most comfortably you drive, or go by bus, from the Berchtesgaden railway station, to a mountainside inn called *Gasthof zum Türken* at *Hintereck* on the Obersalzberg hillside, and continue thence on the climbing Kehlsteinstrasse by a post bus, since private cars are not allowed on this lofty road, to the 5600-foot *Wendeplatte,* a parking place at the very entrance to the Kehlstein, inside which mountain peak an elevator takes you to the summit. I shall presently describe this last stretch, but first a word about the halfway point.

At Hintereck we find not only the *Gasthof zum Türken* (To the Turk), which Hitler often used for his guests, but a big hotel which he completed in 1941 and called the Platterhof, for a fictional character named Judith Platter, and then used as a military hospital. This and everything else in the neighborhood, including Hitler's own residence, was blasted by a terrific air attack on April 25, 1945, but the big hotel was finally rebuilt as the *General Walker Hotel,* for the use of the American Army, and has since then resumed the name Platterhof. It is quite a place for our armed forces, having, in addition to all its physical comforts and good plumbing, a very lovely broad lawn, a terrace café, with a grand view, and even a soldiers' nightclub. Great numbers of American servicemen and their families vacation in the Berchtesgaden area annually. An additional way by which Hintereck and its hotels may be reached from the valley is by taking a cableway, the *Obersalzbergbahn,* from Berchtesgaden to the postwar built *Höhen-*

strasse and hiking for half an hour on this scenic highway, at an average level of 3300 feet, to your goal.

From the Wendeplatte, upper terminus of the post-bus route, one walks into the mountain by a tunnel for about 150 paces to reach the elevator, and *what* an elevator, that Hitler built in 1938. Inside, it is all gleaming brass and mirrors, and its walls are lined with leather seats that accommodate 20 passengers. It hoists us about 400 feet and then we emerge to the pleasant *Kehlsteinhaus,* some parts of which are just as Hitler left them. This summit house, 6000 feet aloft, is a delightful summer café, with tables in the open air and others within the shelter of the building. From here one may look far down to Berchtesgaden and its satellite villages, to the Königssee, and on the Austrian side, to the neighborhood of Salzburg. Perhaps you'll say, "This is where I came in," but I doubt that you'll walk out on the show. More likely you'll see it all again, at least in treasured retrospect.

HOTELS AND RESTAURANTS OF ALPINE BAVARIA, A PERSONAL REPORT

The Western Alps; Hotels and Restaurants

Lindau, in case that city-in-a-lake serves as your takeoff point for motoring through the Alps, has two first-class hotels directly on the lake promenade, namely *Hotel Bayerischer Hof* and *Hotel Reutemann,* while several others, the *Seegarten,* the *Helvetia* and the *Lindauer Hof,* are also on the front and are lower priced. The only one I've stayed in is the Reutemann, and I liked it. A hotel of rather more luxurious mien is *Hotel Bad Schachen,* but this is 2 or 3 miles distant on the mainland shore.

Oberstdorf has hotels of two types. Of the regular hotels, the *Alpenhof,* a bit out of town, is probably the best, followed by the *Mohren,* centrally located on the Marktplatz, and the big *Wittelsbacher Hof,* with all of 46 private baths, located on the outskirts of the resort. Of Kurhotels, which is to say sanatoria, the clear leader is *Kurhotel Adula,* a place of 130 beds, 80 baths and a garage for 40 cars. Its prices are commensurate with its grandeurs, whose architectual leanings are of the chalet type.

Kleinwalsertal, with a population of 4600, has beds, counting those in private homes, for 8600 visitors! The best hotel is clearly the *Ifen*, in the second village, Hirschegg, and I can testify to its merits both for its comforts and its charm, and also for its excellent meals. The best hotels in the first village, Riezlern, are the *Stern* and the *Erlebach;* the best in the third village, Mittelberg, are the *Alte Krone*, with swimming pool, and the *Alpenrose;* and in Baad, the last hamlet, there is the *Sporthotel Baad*, with a good café-restaurant. Aim first for the Ifen and second for the Alte Krone.

The Central Alps; Hotels and Restaurants

Two hotels of Garmisch-Partenkirchen, this two-part resort town, stand out and both are located in Garmisch, namely the long-established *Parkhotel Alpenhof,*—garnished with a full array of dining rooms (winter and summer terrace dining if desired), dance casino, bars and a Stüberl—whose location on the Kurpark justifies its name, and the relatively new (1966) *Alpina*. The former has a gracious perfectionism that invites the soul, while the latter, built in Bavarian country-house style, has many features that attract young and old. Among its talking points are two pools, an outdoor one heated to 77 degrees, and an indoor one, with adjacent sauna, heated to 83 degrees. *Golfhotel Sonnenbichl,* on the northern outskirts of Garmisch adjacent to the golf course, is an attractive, first-class hotel whose coffee terrace (music) squarely faces the Zugspitze, with nothing to lessen the impact of that peak's splendor. Less expensive, but fairly exuding charm, is the centrally placed *Hotel Marktplatz,* so photogenic, with its multibalconied flower façade, that cameras are always clicking at it. *Clausing's Posthotel,* opposite the Marktplatz, is a veteran restored, having been requisitioned after World War II by the American forces. In its renewed form it is more atmospheric than ever. I once used its "profile," with the well-known Post Horn as symbol, for the jacket of an earlier book. The glassed-in dining porch is my personal favorite lunching spot in Garmisch, and if I should eat too much, there is a 1790 *Apotheke* next door, its façade a picture in 18th-century black and white. In Partenkirchen, I have stayed most pleasurably in *Hotel Partenkirchner Hof,* whose cuisine is highly esteemed by the general public, my tastebuds enthusiastically concurring. A couple of miles out of town is *Riessersee Hotel,* in a very lovely rural setting, and I must refer again to the *Schneefernerhaus* at the upper station of the cogwheel railway, altitude 8700 feet. If you cannot overnight there do, in any case, manage to have a meal in its far-viewing restaurant.

Mittenwald, keying its hotels to its simple mountain charm, doesn't go in for big, palatial hotels, but it has some good ones, led, I should say, by the centrally located 84-bed *Rieger,* with a heated pool (82 degrees) and an outdoor sunbathery. The Rieger's cuisine is considered Mittenwald's best and the wine cellar would do justice to a high-grade metropolitan hotel. Almost in the class with the Rieger are two more good hotels, the *Erdt* and the *Wetterstein,* and among small, family-type places are the *Gästehaus Royal,* with a nice minipool on the lawn, which serves breakfast and dinner only, and *Hotels Lerch* and *Wipfelder.* A delightful *Café-Restaurant Ferchensee* will be found directly on the small lake of the same name at the edge of town. So near the lake is it built that the terrace all but hangs over the water.

The Eastern Alps; Hotels and Restaurants

Tegernsee lake is surrounded by little resorts, the first one encountered, on the east side, being a small spa called Bad Wiessee, ornamented with a strikingly beautiful double row of red maples on a street called Wallbergstrasse. This has all the features, even if in relative miniature, that are expected of such a spa, including a Kurhotel, with iodine and sulphur baths, and a gambling casino. The best hotel in this spa is probably the first-class *Lederer.* At Rottach-Egern is the hotel I've been "whispering about," because I couldn't wait to tell you, namely the lakeside *Hotel Bachmair.* It consists, really, of six hotels in one and you wander from luxury to luxury, everything in good taste, nothing suggesting the nouveau riche. There are two pools, outdoor and indoor, and for those in need of exercise some bowling lanes. In the Bachmair's garden restaurant I recently enjoyed a meal whose main dish was a delicious troutlike fish called Renke, right from the lake, and whose calorific dessert was ice cream drowned in warm raspberry (Himbeere) sauce. Near the Bachmair is another deluxe hostelry, *Seehotel Überfahrt* (Crossing—of the Alps), and the two together are sometimes called "retreats of the snobiety," but the tag must be a misnomer, for the people I saw around me in the Bachmair's garden restaurant were just plain folks, like the one now describing them. I think you will love the place, and if you encounter snobiety you'll cut it down to size. In Tegernsee, to continue this round-a-lake hotel comment, the best hotels are the *Bastenhaus am See;* the *Bahn-Hotel Neue Post;* and *Hotel "Der Eybhof."* And for a down-to-beer hour, don't forget the Bräustüberl in the Brauhaus of the former Benedictine abbey. (On the shores of neighboring Schliersee there are good resort hotels along the lake's northern crescent, where Schliersee village is located, and also at Neuhaus, on the lake's southern shore.)

Bad Reichenhall, famous spa, and Berchtesgaden, famous holiday haunt, are the chief magnets at the far-eastern end of the Alpenstrasse, and between them they have interesting hotels of the most varied types and appeals. Bad Reichenhall's deluxe spa hotel *Axenmannstein,* now a unit of the fast-expanding Steigenberger hotel chain and known officially as *Steigenberger Hotel Axelmannstein*—(take it easy on the ten syllables)—has been mentioned in covering the salt story, but I should add here that in 1970 a big new annex was built, with 30 new "Bavaria-look" rooms and a most prideful new "party room, with swimming pool," 81 feet by 46 and with 81 feet of windows looking out on the adjacent park and the majesty of the mile-high Predigtstuhl. It has become one of the ultraspa hotels of Germany.

Berchtesgaden's number one hotel is clearly the *Geiger,* for its comforts, its charm and its outstanding service. Herr Geiger is an art connoisseur and also a clock collector and we see some interesting examples of his hobby. The ceiling and wall woodwork in the main dining room was fashioned by local carpentry talent from a 14th-century farmhouse, and charm is added to charm by a 200-year-old faïence stove. In the main lounge a fireplace crackles every evening of the year, but if this overwarms you, just transfer to another lounge, this one in Biedermeier style. I think you'll like the Geiger, but if that's full you will find the *Vierjahreszeiten* (Four Seasons) and the new *Frauenbühlerhof* very satisfactory. Among places of Gästehaus or pension type I think the *Gästehaus Herkommer* comes out best, followed by *Hotel-Pension Fischer* and *Hotel Bavaria*.

At the "tourist village" at the northern tip of the Königssee two hotels dominate the scene, the big 300-bed *Hotel Königssee* and the 50-bed *Hotel Schiffmeister,* the smaller one, to my mind, being the better. It has an indoor swimming pool, about a third of its rooms have private baths, and its dining room and Stube have a splendid outlook on the lake. This whole section of wide-ranging Berchtesgaden is a major center of sport, especially, but not exclusively, in the winter sports area. There is, in fact, a *Sports Zentrum* here, with about 40 beds, an indoor pool, a shower section and a small dining room. From mid-November winter takes over.

Lots of things are happening in Berchtesgaden's center, including a new (1972) Kurhaus and "Congress Zentrum." Various restaurants and cafés are in evidence, such as the *Café Rotenhöfer;* a *Milchkurgarten,* offering only dairy items (milk, ice cream) and vegetarian dishes, along with a grand view of the Kehlstein from its garden terrace; and a café 400 feet above the town called *Café Lockstein.* And speaking of heights, don't forget to save time for an ascent to the *Kehlsteinhaus,* the Eagle's Nest. There, if the immense view doesn't distract you too much, you may take a seat at an indoor or outdoor table and enjoy a drink-and-a-snack or even a full restaurant meal. What better climax could there be to an Alpenstrasse trek across upland Bavaria?

INDEX

Abersee, *see* Wolfgangsee
Absam, 230
Achensee, 128, 228–229
Admont, 5, 7, 54–55
  hotels, 61–62
  restaurants, 62
Adriach, 141
Agents, travel, 20
Air travel, 27–28, 122–123
Airmail, 26–27
Alpbach, 35
Alpenstrasse, *see* Deutsche Alpenstrasse
Alps, 178, 180, 182, 229
  Bavarian, 9, 307–337
Altaussee, 7, 52, 208, 209
  hotels, 61
Ambras, Schloss, 241–242
Amstetten, 55
Annenheim, 129, 162
Arlberg Express, 12
Arlberg Mountain, 254–256, 258
Arlberg Tunnel, 256
Attersee (Kammersee), 129, 208, 209, 211, 217
Au, 259
  hotels, 270
  restaurants, 270
Augsburg, Germany, 191, 309

Baad, 317
  hotels, 334
Bad Aussee, 51–52, 53, 208
  hotels, 61
Bad Gleichenberg, 146
Bad Hall, 131
Bad Hofgastein, 173, 176
Bad Ischl, 7, 131, 207, 208, 212–213
  hotels, 221
  restaurants, 221–222
  shops and shopping, 222

Bad Kleinkirchheim, 163
  hotels, 170–171
Bad Reichenhall, Germany, 308, 310, 326, 329
  hotels, 310, 336
Bad Reuthe, 260
Bad Tatzmannsdorf, 152
Bad Tolz, Germany, 309, 326–327
Bad Wiessee, 327, 335
  hotels, 335
Baden bei Wien, 138–139
  hotels, 139
Badgastein, 131, 132, 172–176, 226
  hotels, 173, 191–193
  night life, 194
  restaurants, 194
  shops and shopping, 194
Bavaria, 284–285, 307–337
Bavarian Alps, 9, 307–337
Bayrischzell, 328
Berchtesgaden, Germany, 308, 310, 326, 329–330
  hotels, 310, 336–337
  restaurants, 337
Bergsteigerfriedhof, 55
Bernau, Germany, 328
Bernstein, 152
Bernstein Jade, 137
Bezau, 13, 259, 260
  hotels, 270
Bielerhöhe, 260
Bizau, 259
Bled, Yugoslavia, 8
Bludenz, 257, 260
Blumenegg, 13
Bockstein, 173
Bodensdorf, 162
Bodensee, *see* Constance, Lake
Bolzano, Italy, 11
Brand, 261–262
Brandnertal, 261–262

Brawling, The, 7, 54, 55
Bregenz, 4, 8, 13, 15, 128, 257, 266, 267–268, 317
  fairs, festivals and folk pageants, 32–33, 267–268
  hotels, 272
  restaurants, 13, 272
  transportation to, 29
Bregenzer Ache, 259
Bregenzerwald (Bergenz Forest), 257, 258, 259–260
  hotels, 270
Brenner Pass, 8, 10–11
Brennero, Italy, 11
Bressanone, Italy, 10
Bruck an der Grossglocknerstrasse, 181
Bruck an der Mus, 138, 139
Bruneck, Italy, 11
Buchs, Switzerland, 12
Burg Forchtenstein, 134–136
Burgenland, 4, 7, 132–138
  hotels, 152
Buschenschank, 147

Car rentals, 31, 289, 308
Carinthia, 4, 5, 7–8, 21, 149, 153–171, 179
  hotels, 167–171
  restaurants, 168–171
  shops and shopping, 168–171
Chiemsee, 309, 310, 326
Climate, 21–22
Clothing, 22
Cobenzl, 78
Constance, Germany, 13
Constance, Lake, 4, 13, 128, 257, 267, 268
Customs regulations, 22–23

Dachstein Ice Caves, 216
Danube River, 7, 10, 12, 56–61
Dellach, 169
Deutsche Alpenstrasse, 308, 326, 328
Donnerkögel, 215
Dorfgastein, 173, 176
Dornbirn, 266–267
  hotels, 272
Douglasshütte, 262
Drobollach, 170
Dürnstein, 58, 60

East Tyrol, 4, 8, 176–177
Ebensee, 219
Edelbernstein, 137
Edelweiss Spitze (Peak), 180–181

Egg, 13, 14, 260
  hotels, 170, 260
Eggenberg, Schloss, 145
Egger-Lienz, Albin, 42
Ehrenfeld, 147
Ehrenhausen, 146
Eibsee, Germany, 323
Eisenerz, 55
Eisenstadt, 7, 133, 137–138
  hotels, 152
Eisriesenwelt, 216
Erfurterhütte, 229
Europabus, 29–30, 126–127

Faak am See, 170
Faakersee, 161
  hotels, 170
Fairs, 31–33
Falkensteinwand, 331
Felber Tauern Road, 172, 181
  hotels, 195
Feldkirch, 12, 13, 257, 262–263, 266
  hotels, 271
Fernleiten, 195
Festivals, 31–33, 163
Flexen Pass, 258
Flexenstrasse, 257, 258
Folk pageants, 31–33
Food, 67–69
Forchtenau, 134
Franz-Josefs-Höhe, 180, 195
Frauenberg, 54
Frohnleiten, 140, 141
Frojach-Katschtal, 149
Fürstenstand-on-the-Plabutsch, 145
Fusch, 195
Füssen, Germany, 309, 317–318

Gaflei, Leichtenstein, 266
Gaislacher Kogel, 254
Gallspach, 131
Galzip Peak, 254
Gamlitz, 147
Gams, 55
Gargellen, 261
  hotels, 271
Garmisch, Germany, 9, 308, 309, 321–322, 323
  hotels, 334
  restaurants, 334
Gaschurn
  hotels, 270–271
  restaurants, 271
Gastein Valley, 172, 173
Geroldseck, Fortress, 228

Glanz, 146
Gmunden, 129, 209, 217–218
  hotels, 222–223
  restaurants, 222–223
Gosau, 222
Gosau Lakes, 5, 208, 209, 215
Gosaumühle, 215
Grainau, Germany, 9, 322
Graz, 7, 33, 138, 141–145
  hotels, 150
  restaurants, 150–151
  shops and shopping, 151
Gröbming, 148
Grossglockner, 178, 180
Grossglockner Skyroad, 8, 178–181
  hotels, 194–195
  restaurants, 194–195
Gross-Venediger, 178
Grundlsee, 52, 208, 209
Gstatterboden, 55
  hotels, 62
Gurk, 158–159

Hafelekar, 249
Hallein, 33
Hallstatt, 5, 7, 129, 213–215
  hotels, 222
  restaurants, 222
Hallstattersee, 5, 129, 208, 209, 213–216
Health certificates, 19
Heiligenblut, 6, 8, 179–180
  hotels, 180, 195
Hellbrunn, Schloss, 187–188
Herrenchiemsee, Schloss, 309, 311, 314, 328
Herreninsel, Germany, 310, 328
Hieflau, 55
Hilmteich, 145
Hintereck, Germany, 332
Hirschegg, 317
  hotels, 334
Hirschenkogel, 139
Hoch-Osterwitz, 156–157
Hochsölden, 254
Hochstrasse bei Stainz, 147
Hochtannberg Pass, 257, 259
Hochtor Tunnel, 178, 180
Hochwolkersdorf, 134
Hohenschwangau Castle, 311, 318
Hoher Dachstein, 148
Holidays, Austrian, 34
Höllengebirge, 219
Honigkogel (Honey Peak), 182
Horses, Lippizaner, 147–148

Hotels, 10
  laundry and, 72
  service charges, 70
  See also under names of places
Huben, 253
Hungerburg, 249

Igls, 213
  hotels, 248
Immenstadt, Germany, 309
Innsbruck, 8, 11, 12, 16, 231–243
  folk pageants, 32–33
  hotels, 10, 245–250
  night life, 251
  restaurants, 250–251
  roads to, 9, 11, 13
  shops and shopping, 251–252
  sightseeing, 236–243
  steamship service to, 28
  summer study courses, 35
Iselsberg, 179
  hotels, 195
Itter, Schloss, 227–228

Jenbach, 228
Jennerbahn, 329–330
Jochenstein, The, 59
Johnsbach, 55
Jungholz, 307

Kahlenberg, 78
Kammer, 217
Kammersee, *see* Attersee
Kanisfluh, 259
Kaprun
  hotels, 195
Kehlstein, 332–333, 337
Kessel, Germany, 331
Kitzbuhel, 6, 181, 224, 225–227
  hotels, 243–244
  night life, 226
  restaurants, 226, 243–244
Klagenfurt, 8, 149, 153–156
  hotels, 167–168
  restaurants, 168
  shops and shopping, 168
Kleinwalsertal, 15, 259, 307, 309, 316–317
  hotels, 334
Klopeinersee, 162
Klosterneuburg, 10
Klostertal, 257, 260
Königssee, 310, 326, 327, 330–331
Kramerspitze, 309
Krems, 58, 61

Krimml, 181
  hotels, 195
Krimml Glacier, 181
Krippenstein, 216
Krottensee, 211
Kufstein, 9, 12, 228
  hotels, 245
Kurhotel Bad Heilbrunn, 53–54

Lainbach, 55
Landeck, 11, 12, 254, 260
Landsberg, Germany, 309
Landskron Castle, 162
Langbath lakes, 219
Langegg, 146
Langen, 254
Längenfeld, 253
Language, 73–74
Laundry, 72
Lech, 226, 257, 258
  hotels, 269–270
Leoben, 55
Leopoldskron, Schloss, 186
Leutschach, 146
Liechtenstein, 12–13, 262–266
  hotels, 269
Lienz, 8, 11, 153, 176–178, 179
  hotels, 195
Lindau, Germany, 13, 268
  hotels, 333
Linderhof, Schloss, 312–314, 321
Linz, 6, 10, 55, 57, 58–59
  hotels, 62
  restaurants, 62–63
  shops and shopping, 63
Lofer, 224
Loiben, 60
Ludwig I, 284–285
Ludwig II, 285, 308, 309, 310–315, 321
  castles of, 310–315
Luggage, 22
Lünersee, 262

Mail, 25–27
Malbun, Liechtenstein, 266
Mallnitz, 172–173
Maria-Saal, 155
Mariatrost, 145
Maria-Wörth, 5, 129, 160
  hotels, 169
Mariazell, 6, 7, 32, 51, 56
  hotels, 62
Marquartstein, Germany, 310, 328
Matrei-in-Ost-Tirol, 195
Mayerling, 219

Mayrhofen, 33, 35
  hotels, 245
Melk, 10, 57, 58, 60
  hotels, 63
Mellau, 259
  hotels, 270
Merano, Italy, 11, 225, 231
Metric system, 74–75
Miesbach, Germany, 326, 328
Millstatt, 129, 163–166
  hotels, 171
  restaurants, 171
Millstättersee, 129, 163, 164
  hotels, 171
Mirabell, Schloss, 183, 184
Mittelberg, 317
  hotels, 334
Mittenwald, Germany, 9, 225, 308, 309, 324–326
  hotels, 335
  restaurants, 335
Mitterndorf, 53, 132, 316
  hotels, 61
Mittersill, 181, 224
  hotels, 195
Mölltal, 179
Mondsee (lake), 129, 208, 209
Mondsee (town), 129, 209
  hotels, 220
  restaurants, 220
Money, 24–25
Montafonertal, 257, 260–261
  hotels, 270–271
Mörbisch-am-See, 136–137, 138
Mösern, 253
Mozart, Wolfgang Amadeus, 45, 188–191, 210
Munich, Germany, 273–306
  car rental firms, 289, 308
  festivals, 274–275, 281
  history, 284–285
  hotels, 273, 292–298
  museums, 274, 278, 280, 283–284
  night life, 302–304
  Olympics (1972), 274, 289–292
  orientation, 285–288
  restaurants, 298–302
  Schloss Nymphenburg, 282
  shops and shopping, 273, 304–306
  sightseeing, 275–289
  transportation within, 288–289
  travel agencies, 308
Mur River, 141, 142, 148, 149
Murau, 149
  hotels, 152

Nendeln, Liechtenstein, 266
Neuhas, Germany, 336
Neusach
  hotels, 171
Neuschwanstein, Schloss, 309, 311–312, 315, 318
Neusiedlersee, 5, 7, 130, 132–133
Neustift an der Rosalia, 134
Niggenkopf, 262
Nymphenburg, Schloss, 282

Oberammergau, Germany, 308, 319–321
  hotels, 309
Obergurgl, 5, 225, 253
  hotels, 254
Oberlech, 258
Obermoos, 323
Oberndorf, 33
Oberstdorf, Germany, 308, 309, 316
  hotels, 316, 333–334
Obertraun, 216
Oggau, 136
Olympics (Munich, 1972), 274, 289–292
Ort, Schloss, 218–219
Ossiach, 129, 162
  hotels, 170
Ossiachersee, 129, 162–163
  hotels, 170
Ötz, 253
Ötztal, 253–254
  hotels, 253–254

Packing, suggestions concerning, 23–24
Pageants, folk, 31–33
Partenen, 260, 261
Partenkirchen, Germany, 9, 308, 309, 321–322
  hotels, 335
  restaurants, 335
Passau, Germany, 10, 12, 56, 57
  hotels, 62
  restaurants, 62
Passion Play, 319–321
Passports, 19
Pasterzenkees, 180
Patscherkofel, 250
Patznauntal, 260
Pertisau, 229
  hotels, 245
Pferdeschlitten, 317
Photographic supplies, 73
Piber, 147–148
  hotels, 152

Pinzgau, 181
Planspitze, 55
Porcia, Schloss, 164
Pörtschach, 129, 160
  hotels, 168–169
Postage, 26
Predigtstuhl (Pulpit), 329
Predlitz, 149
Prien, Germany, 310, 328
Pürgg, 54
Puszta, 133

Rabenstein, Schloss, 140
Radkersburg, 146
Railroads, 8–12, 29, 123
Ramsau, 148
Reifnitz, 169
Reit im Winkl, Germany, 310, 326, 328
Restaurants
  service charges, 70
  See also under names of places
Reuthe, 260
Reutte, 323
Riegersburg, 146
Rieseneishöhle, 216
Riezlern, 317
  hotels, 334
Romanshorn, Switzerland, 13
Romantische Strasse, 309
Rosaliengebirge, 134
Rosenegg, 13
Rosenheim, Germany, 9
Rosental, 161
Rottach-Egern, Germany, 308, 327, 328
  hotels, 335–336
  restaurants, 335–336
Rottenbuch, Germany, 318
Rüfikopf, 258
Ruhpolding, Germany, 310
Rust, 136, 138

St. Andrä, 162
  hotels, 170
St. Anton am Arlberg, 226, 254–255
St. Anton on the Tyrol, 258
St. Bartholomä, Germany, 331
St. Christoph am Arlberg, 254, 255
St. Florian, Abbey of, 58
St. Gallenkirch, 261
St. Gilgen, 208, 209
  hotels, 220
  restaurants, 220
St. Johann in Tirol, 6, 224
  hotels, 244

St. Wolfgang, 5, 7, 129, 208, 210–211
  hotels, 63, 221
  restaurants, 221
Salzach River, 181, 182, 183
Salzbergwerk (Berchtesgaden), 330
Salzburg (city), 4, 5, 16, 17, 182–191
  architecture, 183–184
  fairs, festivals and folk pageants, 31–33, 182, 190
  history, 183
  hotels and other lodgings, 10, 196–201
  Mozart's influence on, 188–191
  museums, 186
  night life, 203–204
  railway station, 9
  restaurants, 201–203
  roads to, 9–10
  shops and shopping, 204–206
  sightseeing, 184–188
  summer study courses, 34–35, 186
  tourist office, 182
Salzburg (province), 4, 6, 172–206, 207, 208
Salzkammergut, 5, 6, 7, 51–53, 207–223
  hotels, 220–223
  restaurants, 220–223
  shops and shopping, 220–223
Scesaplana (Schesaplana), 262
Schaan, Liechtenstein, 12, 263
Schafberg, 211, 218
Scharnitz, 9
Schattenburg Castle, 262, 263
Schattenlagant Refuge, 262
Schladming, 148
Schliersee, 310, 326, 328, 336
Schlossberg, 141–142
Schmittenhöhe, 182
Schneefernerhaus, 322, 323, 335
Scholastika, 229
Schoppernau, 259
Schorfling, 217
Schröcken, 259
Schruns, 131, 260, 261
  hotels, 261, 270
Schwarzsee, 227, 244
Schwarzenberg, 260
Schwaz, 230–231
Seeboden
  hotels, 171
Seefeld, 225
  hotels, 252
Seegrube, 249
Seewalchen, 217
Semmering, 139

Service charges, 70
Shops and shopping, 18, 72–73
  See also under names of places
Skiing, 53, 54, 148, 226, 254, 258, 316, 317, 322–323
Solbad Hall, 207, 230
Sölden, 253–254
Sölker Pass, 148
Sonnwendstein, 139
Sopron, Hungary, 7, 132
Spas, 131–132, 138, 162
  See also names of spas
Spielfeld, 147
Spittal an der Drau, 163, 164
Spitz, 60
Sports, 4, 161
  winter, 132, 167, 226, 316, 321–323, 337
Staussee, 53
Steamships, 10, 13, 28–29, 56–61, 128, 160, 218
Stein, 60
Steingaden, Germany, 309, 318
Sterzing, Italy, 11
Stock, Germany, 310, 328
Strobl, 34, 210
Stuben, 257, 260
Study courses, summer, 34–35, 186, 210
Styria, 4, 7, 21, 51–56, 138–152, 207, 208, 316
Styrian High Way, 51–56
Sudelfeld Pass, 328

Tauern Tunnel, 172
Tauplitz, 54
Taxes, 70
Techendorf, 166
Tegernsee (lake), 308, 309, 326, 327, 335
Tegernsee, Germany, 229, 308, 309, 327–328
Three Sisters, The, 266
Thurn Pass, 224
Timmelsjoch Pass, 225
Tips, 70, 72
Toplitzsee, 52, 208, 209
Tourist Offices, Austrian, 20–21
Traunkirchen, 129, 219
  hotels, 223
Traunsee, 129, 208, 209, 217, 218, 219
Travel agents, 20
Triesen, Liechtenstein, 266
Tschagguns, 270
Turracher Pass, 149
Turracher See, 149

Tyrol, 4, 8, 11, 21, 176, 224–256
  history, 232–236

Umhausen, 253
Und, 60–61
Upper Austria, 4, 6–7, 58, 207, 208, 210

Vaduz, Liechtenstein, 12, 13, 263, 264
  hotels, 264
  restaurants, 264–265
  tourist office, 265
Velden, 6, 8, 129, 159–160, 161
  hotels, 169–170
Venedigerwarte, 177
Vienna, 16, 64–121
  airlines and, 27
  airport, 9
  architecture, 84–85
  art, 85–87
  Austrian State Archives Office, 97–99
  fairs, festivals and ·folk pageants, 31–33
  history, 3, 39, 88–91
  hotels and other lodgings, 10, 66–67, 103–109
  Mozart and, 188–191
  museums, 85–87
  music and, 3–4, 17–18, 65, 80–84
  night life, 65, 66, 114–117
  orientation, 76–78
  palaces, 99–103
  population, 3
  restaurants, 109–114
  roads to, 51–63
  shops and shopping, 72, 73, 117–121
  sightseeing, 77–78, 79–121
  steamship service to, 10, 56–61
  streets and squares, 91–97
  summer study courses, 34–35, 210
  tourist office, 21, 79–80
  transportation in, 77–78
Vienna (province), 4, 7, 64–121

Villach, 160, 162
Villacher Alpe, 166
Virgen, 178
Visas, 19–20
Voitsberg, 152
Vorarlberg, 4, 8, 13, 14, 21, 225, 257–272
  hotels, 269–272

Walchensee, 309
Warmbad Villach, 162
Warth, 257, 259
Weights and measures, system of, 74–75
Weinstrasse, 146–147
Weissensee, 166–167
  hotels, 171
Widderstein, 317
Wiener Neustadt, 139
Wieskirche, 309, 318–319
Wildegg, 13
Wildpark Rosegg, 161
Winklern, 179
Wolfgangsee, 129, 208, 209, 210, 218
Wolkersdorf, 134
Wörgl, 224, 227
Wörthersee, 5, 128, 159–162
  hotels, 168–170
Würzburg, Germany, 309

Ybbs an der Donau, 63

Zell am See, 6, 128, 181–182, 224
  hotels, 195
Zell am Ziller, 32
Zellersee, 128, 181
Zettersfeld, 177
Zirl, 225
Zugspitze, 14, 308, 309, 322–323
Zugspitzkamm, 323
Zürs, 226, 257, 258
  hotels, 269

WEST GERMANY

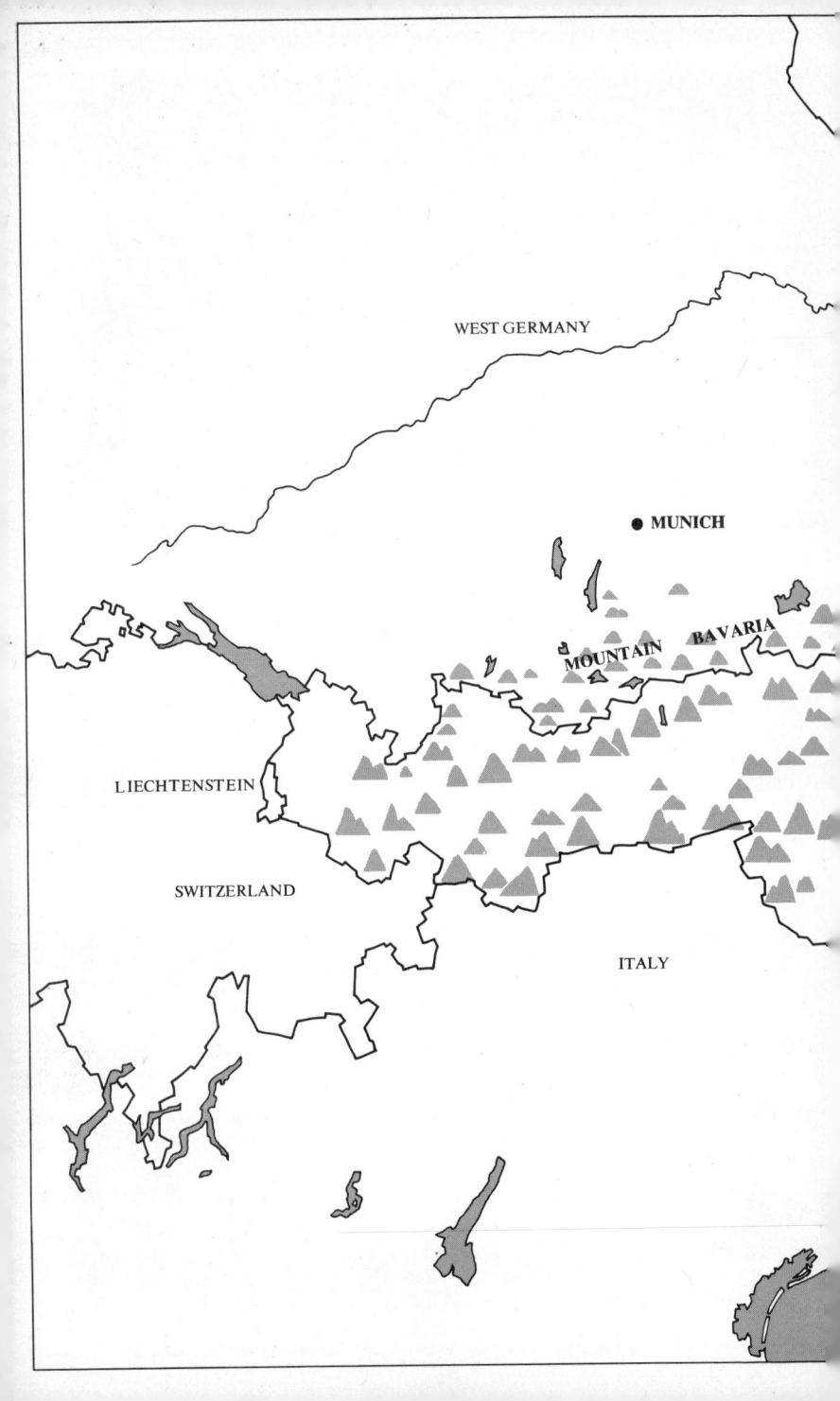

● MUNICH

MOUNTAIN BAVARIA

LIECHTENSTEIN

SWITZERLAND

ITALY